The Final
PROPHECIES
OF NOSTRADAMUS

ERIKA CHEETHAM

Futura

A Futura Book

First published in Great Britain in 1990 by Futura Publications
a Division of Macdonald & Co (Publishers) Ltd, London & Sydney
Reprinted 1991

ISBN 0 7088 4333 6

Typeset by ☎ Tek Art Ltd, Croydon, Surrey
Reproduced, printed and bound in Great Britain by
BPCC Hazell Books
Aylesbury, Bucks, England
Member of BPCC Ltd.

Futura Publications
A Division of
Macdonald & Co (Publishers) Ltd
Orbit House
1 New Fetter Lane
London EC4A 1AR

A member of Maxwell Macmillan Pergamon Publishing Corporation

CONTENTS

Note to Reader

The French text of the quatrains reproduces as closely as possible that of the original edition of 1568 (Benoist Rigaud, Lyon). Any printing faults and errors of that edition are therefore also reproduced here.

ABBREVIATIONS USED IN FOOTNOTES

A.Pr.—Ancien Provençal
L.—Latin
O.F.—Old French
Mod F.—Modern French
Gk.—Greek

★ — This symbol throughout indicates prophecies which
seem to refer to events still in the future.

To Alexander

I wish to thank the readers of my previous books for their many interpretations of the *Prophecies*, some of which I have used in this book. There are far too many to thank individually.

INTRODUCTION

Before writing about the life, times and predictions of Nostradamus, I feel I must write about the extraordinary effect he and his works have had upon my personal life. Some are almost beyond belief.

Certainly it was Nostradamus who turned my ideas toward making writing my career. I first came across a book of the Prophecies at Oxford, when I was about nineteen. At that time I was reading medieval Romance Languages, of which Ancien Provençal was one of the most important. I had ordered some set book in the Taylorian—the linguist's equivalent of the Bodleian Library—and in its stead I received the 1568 edition of *Les Prophéties de M. Michel Nostradamus*. While waiting for the correct book to arrive, I idled through the *Prophéties*. It was fascinating. Names such as Hitler, Napoleon, Franco, Pasteur sprang to the eye. There were many dates too, but the only one that stuck in my mind was 1666, "when the city of London would be destroyed by fire." Not easy to forget, even for someone who is not an historian.

One night a great friend, who was then an editor on *Nova* magazine, sadly now long defunct, came to dinner with some friends. At some point I mentioned Nostradamus, this extraordinary prophet, to her. She was interested and I wrote a long article for the magazine, to which they added an amazing collage of pictures of the people I had mentioned.

The article was an enormous success, voted by *Nova* readers as tying with one other as the best in the magazine that year. From that, and thanks to a clever publisher brother-in-law, Putnam's of New York commissioned a book upon Nostradamus. I do not know to this day how I managed to complete it.

I was working in the day, lecturing two evenings a week for extramural students at London University, running a house and family. Then one of my brothers had the sense to marry a marvelous girl who took away pages of my rather illegible writing, in which I had attempted to produce an original text, a translation and an explanation of the quatrain when I could. These were returned looking so professional I would gaze at them with amazement. Did I really write this?

The first idea I had that it was not just going to be "a book" occurred on the first day of publication. Foyles, the very reputable bookseller, had taken a journalist on for a week to write about the experience. Whether they knew he was a journalist I don't know, but his article stated that he had sold out all the copies of Nostradamus at Foyles in less than a day. I should have been warned.

During the early 1970s I went down to Nostradamus' home towns of Salon and St. Rémy-de-Provence, and did a lot of work in the local archives. I traced Nostradamus' house off the Place de la Poissonerie. At that time the house was partly unsafe and inhabited by various Arab families and in a state of great decay. This has since been rectified. It has been almost totally restored with a *gardien* to show tourists around. But Nostradamus' study at the top of the house is still out of bounds. Why?

Two years ago an Australian TV company came to France and wanted me to go down to Salon and Saint Rémy to do a piece on Nostradamus. It was then I experienced one of the strangest events in my life.

Nostradamus was buried (for the second time, his body having been disinterred during the French Revolution by drunken soldiers) in a side chapel of Notre Dame Church in the Church of Saint Laurent at Salon. Sadly when we arrived it appeared that the portrait of him, one of only three known likenesses, had been stolen, but the engraving in the wall by his second wife, Anne Ponsart Gemelle, was still there.

We went to the church on a Friday evening, so that the crew could work out technicalities of lighting and sound. There was to be a burial early the next morning, so we could not start before ten o'clock. The cart used for carrying the coffin doubled up very well for carrying the heavy lighting equipment. I stood under the engraving on the wall commissioned by Nostradamus' wife, dressed all in black, as it appeared that I was too tall in shoes, my frozen feet on the stone flags.

At last we were ready—lighting, sound boom, everything. I launched into my small introductory speech. I spoke these words: "*Ici, dans cette église restent les os de Michel Nostradamus . . .* " At that very moment there was an enormous crack of thunder which reverberated down the church, followed by a huge fireball which traveled from the altar to the great doors. That was the end of the TV program. Every machine was blown. To compound the injury, such heavy rain fell that everyone in Salon with a basement was calling the *pompiers*, the fire brigade. It was like a mini-flood, but everything happened at enormous speed. I have never experienced anything like it—and the superstitious took note that it happened the moment I mentioned the word Nostradamus. The storm flickered around the Alpilles for the rest of the day. It was very spectacular. Having despaired of getting further material from me for the schedule—although we did get some footage in Nostradamus' house the next day—the Australian crew flew off to Rome to interview the Pope!

As to what this book will bring I do not know, except that it is the last book I shall ever write about Nostradamus. This is the reason for giving the reader the original text as published in 1568, instead of bowdlerizing it to make it easier to read. It will be seen that I have changed some of my interpretatations. Some are obvious from historical facts that have occurred since my last book, such as Gorbachev— "the man with the mark of blood." Until he appeared I had no idea what man from the East Nostradamus had in mind, but the port-wine stain on his head and forehead gives a convincing touch to quatrains I could not definitely ascribe before he came to office.

Another interpretation is that of "glasnost" which has suddenly arrived upon Gorbachev's heels in Russia. But Nostradamus warns us that the treaty between the US and USSR may last for only three years and some months. The instigator of the Third World War, as we might designate it, will come from the East. We have the option of the Middle East or the Far East. At the moment the former is the volatile powder keg, but world politics now change so quickly that neither interpretation can be ruled out. I am writing this piece some time after the Americans had shot down the Iran airbus with nearly 300 passengers on board, all dead, and the Iranians have gone to the United Nations to demand peace. Over two hundred and fifty people have been shot down over Scotland by a terrorist bomb. The Americans and the Israelis are bargaining for hostages. There are so many external influences to bear and understand with all the aids of the modern media to hand, newspapers, radio, television, that we get confused. No wonder Nostradamus may have made mistakes from time to time, although at others, his sense of timing and occasion seem perfect. Maybe the fault lies in the interpreter, as with the Delphic Oracle, whose predictions could always be taken two ways. The resulting success or failure was blamed on the recipient, who was the final judge of his own fate. We can but watch world events and decide for ourselves whether Nostradamus has anything to offer to the present-day world.

We must also remember that the function of the prophet is to warn, and that any event predicted may be averted if we listen with open minds. I think that this may well have happened with the *Prophéties*. There are some very specifc ones that have, quite simply, not happened. This leads to the dual aspect of prediction—if the prophet is heeded his writings are a failure; he is, in an ironic sense, successful only when people fail to recognize the predicted events. He is verified, and the world suffers as a consequence. Job satisfaction is obviously not a concomitant feature of prediction.

Recently, there was a lot of fuss about the White House, in particular of Mrs. Reagan's using astrologers to help the President's timetable. It is the public, not they, who are the fools. Throughout history great rulers have let themselves be guided by them. Elizabeth I relied on John Dee, Catherine de' Medicis on Nostradamus and Luc Gauric. But how many people realize that Stalin had a personal astrologer, Yury Yammakin? One would not have thought him capable of accepting that sort of influence during his bloody years of rule of Russia. But he did. Eventually, Yammakin fell into disgrace and was sent to a concentration camp. From this he was rescued and reinstated by Khrushchev. I think the next question to be asked is whether Mikhail Gorbachev has an astrologer?

THE LIFE AND TIMES OF NOSTRADAMUS

Most people have heard of Nostradamus, usually in his capacity as a prophet. But he was far more interesting than that. A qualified doctor from the Universities of Avignon and Montpellier, renowned through France as a "plague" doctor, adviser to the queen of France, writer of philosophical treaties and a fascinating book on food and cosmetics, he was indeed a great man of his time. He influenced world events before and after his death and his book of *Prophéties* is probably the only book, apart from the Bible, that has been continuously in print since its first complete publication in 1568, two years after his death. Earlier handwritten versions of books were commonly circulated before publication and this seems to be the case where the *Prophéties* were concerned; the first part was published in 1555.

There are two stories about Nostradamus' lineage and background; the second is the true one, but such an over-whelming figure was inevitably bound to be given glamorous antecedents. The legend is as follows, and it is important to know of it because many of his contemporaries believed it, and this must, of necessity, have altered their attitude towards him.

Michel de Nostradame, usually known as Nostradamus after the quarter in St. Rémy-de-Provence where his family were living, was born on December 14, 1503. (This date becomes December 23 by the present Gregorian calendar.) His family were of Jewish ancestry and some of his commentators say from the tribe of Issachar, the tribe that could read the moon and the stars and interpret the heavens. His father, Pierre de Nostradame, had settled in Provence because by the mid-fifteenth century, under the rule of King René of Anjou

(1434–80), a comparatively lenient king, many Jews had come to settle in his kingdom, which apart from Anjou included Lorraine and Provence.

It is stated that René's physician was a Jewish doctor and astrologer, Jean de Saint-Rémy, and René's son, the duke of Calabria and Lorraine, had a physician called Pierre de Nostradame. He is reputed to have worked in Arles until his fellow doctors hounded him out of town, possibly on the charge of "falsifying his drugs." Therefore the two physicians followed their masters through Europe and presumably learned much on their travels.

Jean, duke of Calabria, was poisoned and died in Barcelona in 1478. It is said he recommended his physician, Pierre de Nostradame, to his father. René, after the death of his son, left his glittering court at Anjou and settled in Tarascon en Provence. The two physicians became friends and on René's death in 1480 Jean and Pierre teamed up and settled in Saint Rémy. Pierre had a son, a notary called Jacques, and it was arranged that he should marry Jean's daughter, Renée. Nostradamus gave credence to this story during his lifetime as does Chavigny, the biographer who probably coped with Nostradamus' papers after the prophet's death in 1566.

Six years after René of Anjou's death his heir, Charles de Maine, also died, and so not only Anjou, but now Provence and Maine reverted to the king of France. French royalty were not overanxious to create a Jewish ghetto in these *comtés* and in 1488 Charles VIII of France issued a decree à la Pontius Pilate. All Jews had to be baptized. Not much was done to enforce the order but when the throne reverted to Louis XII he decreed, on September 26, 1501, that all Jews were to renounce their religion within three months, or leave Provence. It is clear that Jean de Saint-Rémy and Pierre de Nostradame decided to submit and on the tax list for Aix, December 12, 1502, both their names appear as being taxpayers in the new Christian Community.

The truth was somewhat different. Many great researchers, including Reynard-Plense in 1940 and Buget in 1862, found that there was no one of the name of Pierre de Nostradamus in the court of King René. But there was a Jewish doctor called Abraham Salomon, who was baptized and then ennobled by King René. It remained to Dr. Edgar Le Roy, a fanatic anti-Nostradamus researcher, to find out the whole truth, in his *Mémoires de l'Institut Historique de Provence*.

The father of Nostradamus was Jaume (Jacques), the son of a certain Peyrot (Pierre) de Nostradame, who came of a long family of Avignon grain dealers. The grandfather, Pierre, was converted when he married a Christian woman, Blanche. His son, Jaume, also dealing in grain, gave it up on his marriage to Reynière de Saint-Rémy. She was the granddaughter of a failed doctor, Jean de Saint-Rémy, who had become a tax collector. All of his family were also converted Jews.

We don't know the date of Jaume de Nostradamus' marriage to Reynière de Saint-Rémy, but Michel de Nostradamus was born in 1503 and he was the eldest son. This helps support the idea that the couple were married before September 26, 1501, when all Jews had to become Christians or leave Provence. Nostradamus had one definite brother, César, who became Procureur du Parliament de Provence. Later it was his son César who wrote the famous *Histoire de Provence*, which sustains the myth of the Nostradamus royal line. He is also credited with three other brothers, Bertrand, Hector and Antoine, but almost nothing is known of them apart from their names.

Nostradamus showed his extraordinarily free thinking and intelligent mind early on. He was educated by his two grandfathers. First Peyrot, who had been a great traveler, brought him up in his home. We are told that he taught his grandson the basics of mathematics, Greek, Latin, and interestingly, Hebrew, and also the rudiments of "Celestial Science," now known as astrology.

After Peyrot de Nostradamus' death—again the exact date is missing in the archives—Michel de Nostradamus returned to his parents' house in the rue de Barri. It appears that his other grandfather then took over his education for a while, but the family decided to send the boy to Avignon, which was at that period the center of Renaissance learning. A century earlier Avignon had been the capital of French Christendom. Imagine the effect it must have had on the brilliant and youthful mind of Nostradamus. It is related that although good in grammar, philosophy and rhetoric, his greatest passion was the study of the stars. Because of this interest and the dialogues Nostradamus had with fellow pupils he became known as "*le petit astrologue*."

It was here, at Avignon, that Nostradamus is reported to have spent many hours in the University libraries, and it is likely that this was the source of his interest in magic and the occult which was to remain with him until his death. Probably on these ancient shelves he first read Ficino's translation of *De Mysteriis Aegyptorium*. This book was used as the source of his method of prediction. He quotes from it in Century I, quatrains I and II.

This interest in astrology, the Celestial Sciences, began to worry his parents and on the advice of his old grandfather he was sent off to study medicine at the University of Montpellier, a university regarded as second only to that of Paris in the whole of France. Indeed, in 1376, Louis I of Anjou bequeathed upon it the dubious right in perpetuity of the body a year for dissection, that of an executed criminal.

Nostradamus arrived there in 1522, aged nineteen, and settled down well. For the first three years he read all those subjects needed for his baccalauréat, tutored by some of the most celebrated doctors in Europe. The process of getting a degree was far more arduous than in the present day, and lasted much longer. The examinations consisted of the following routine. From 8:00 A.M. until noon the pupil was given an oral examination, in Latin, during which he was asked questions demanding complicated answers, having to avoid traps and prove his own learning in return. Once successful, the newly fledged doctor changed his black robes for the red ones of the learned doctor.

But, in the sixteenth century, to get one's degree did not qualify a candidate to practice. Far from it, Nostradamus now had to give five lectures chosen by the Dean of the University over three months. Again in Latin. One must always remember that none of the teaching or work was done in the pupils' mother tongue. Medieval Latin was the *lingua franca* of doctors and other professions. The lectures approved, Nostradamus had to pass the "*per intentionem*" examinations, which consisted of four different questions, each presented one day in advance and each of which had to be discussed for an hour and the format varied. If you were unlucky all four subjects had to be discussed on the same day, or otherwise two on two consecutive days.

That ordeal passed, the candidate was given a further subject eight days later and this was discussed extemporaneously in front of the Chancellor of the University himself. The subject was usually one that had not been discussed earlier. To crown all this, Nostradamus would then be given an aphorism of Hippocrates on which he had to produce a thesis the next day. These last two tests were rightly known as *les points rigoreux*, which they really were. A successful candidate was then given his license to practice by the Bishop of Montpellier. Nostradamus achieved this in 1525.

During this period there was yet another outbreak of the plague then endemic in southern France, and Nostradamus left the University in order to help the victims. He would return later to get his doctorate, our equivalent of a D.Phil., Doctor of Philosophy. It appears that his remarkable reputation as a healer—often the other aspect of prophecy—started there. He was already known to use his own formulas and prescriptions, and to refuse to wear the magic coat of seven colors known as such by contemporaries, worn by all medieval doctors for protection. He is recorded as being very successful. From Montpellier he went to Narbonne where it is rumored he attended courses held by Jewish alchemists. He then moved on to Carcassonne in the service of the Archbishop of Fays. In his book *Moultes Opuscules* of 1555 he prescribes an elixir of life, a love potion for the bishop of interesting content for any jaded man. There is some confusion here. The Bishop of Carcassonne during this period was a certain Martin de Saint-André. Either Nostradamus got the name wrong when he wrote about it or he was thinking of Amaníeu de Foix (Fayes), who was Bishop of Mâcon from 1557. Nostradamus was a shrewd psychologist. The richer the patient, the more expensive the ingredients, so this recipe contains such delicacies as ground pearls. Perhaps the expense justified the means to both patient and doctor. Bishops were not notorious for their celibacy in the sixteenth century.

The next reference we have of him is living in Toulouse in the rue de la Triperie; then on to Bordeaux where the plague was raging particularly virulently. He seems to have been successful in his cures, which included running instead of well water, fresh air, and a refusal to bleed the patient. This inevitably earned him the enmity of the local doctors, a reputation which preceded him on his return to the University of Montpellier.

It was four years since he had left and he decided now to return to take his doctorate. He must have felt that he had gained much by his experience in the field, so to speak. His name is recorded as rejoining on October 23, 1529. He now had to submit to a further series of examinations, known as "*les triduanes*." For this the candidate had to present a list of twelve subjects for questioning; six were chosen. He would be questioned on three chosen by lottery, and on the other three by the dean. He had to argue and discuss his views with the University professors. It is reported that Nostradamus was mainly questioned about his unorthodox remedies. He must have convinced them, at least partially, for he was awarded his doctorate in 1530 together with the distinctive doctor's cap (seen in the two portraits still remaining of him), a gold ring and a book of Hippocrates' works.

Surprisingly, Nostradamus was offered a job in the faculty at Montpellier and he accepted. Perhaps he wished to solidify his position as doctor and physician with the more conservative element? But he was unable to prescribe or teach his own more unorthodox remedies and had to be led by the prescribed texts. So, inevitably, he decided to travel again. It was in his blood; except during the brief period of his first marriage, he was the epitome of the Wandering Jew. It was not until much later that he settled and married his second wife Anne Ponsarde Gemelle at Salon, whose name is also recorded elsewhere as Anne Pons Gemelle and Anne Ponsart Gemelle.

He left the University in 1532 and according to his biographer Bareste he was received in great triumph by all those towns he had earlier visited. We know he went to Bordeaux again, to La Rochelle and Toulouse. It was during his stay here that one of the turning points in his life occurred. Jules César Scaliger, who was considered the second most learned man in Europe to Erasmus, wrote to him saying that he had heard so much of Nostradamus, he wished to see if the man lived up to his reputation. According to Chavigny, writing in 1594, Nostradamus replied with a letter that was "ingenious, learned and spirited." As a result, he was invited by Scaliger to come and stay with him at Agen.

Scaliger and Nostradamus were well pleased with each

other's companionship and friendship. The former was considered a master of mathematics, biology, medicine, poetry and philosophy. This must have added to Nostradamus' breadth of thought, and he decided to take a house nearby at Agen. Finally he decided to marry a young girl "of high estate, both beautiful and amiable." Her name has been given by some as Adrièta de Loubéjac, but this is almost certainly a mixup with Scalinger's wife, Andiethe de Roques-Lobejac. Soon his family was complete with the births of a son and a daughter. We still do not know her name. Nostradamus' only surviving children came of his second marriage, to Anne Ponsarde Gemelle.

The next three years were those of great happiness. His practice was lucrative, he had a beautiful family and the friendship of Scaliger, together with the many important people who visited him. But, the fates then struck, as they do all who have so much. His wife and both children were killed by the outbreak of some type of infectious disease, probably the plague.

It was both tragic and ironic that he could not save his own family, having saved the lives of so many others. Naturally, after this, his patrons deserted him. Who wants a doctor who cannot save his own family? Upon this followed a severe and final quarrel with Scaliger. We don't know the cause, but Scaliger's quarrelsome character is well documented. Sadly, they ceased their friendship and Scaliger was very abusive of him in later years. Interestingly enough, Nostradamus did not retaliate. In 1552 he writes of Scaliger in his *Traité des Fardemens* as one "who seems to have inherited Cicero's soul in the subject of eloquence, Virgil's in poetry, and Galen's twice over in medicine. I owe him more than to anyone else in the world." To crown all those troubles, Nostradamus' dead wife's family sued him to recover his dowry. It is not known whether it was returned.

But the final blow fell when Nostradamus was officially summoned in 1538 to attend the Inquisition at Toulouse—just as much to be feared as its Spanish equivalent. It was reported that when, in 1534, Nostradamus, seeing some workman making a bronze cast of a statue of the Virgin, remarked to the man that he was only "making devils." Whatever he did in fact say, it was extremely unwise of him to say anything

derogatory at that period. His defense, which appears somewhat weak, was that he was only referring to the lack of artistic
form of the statue. It was time, in every sense, for Nostradamus to move on.

The next period of his life, 1538–1544, is little documented.
We glean odd bits of information from his later books *Moultes
Opuscules* and *Le Traité des Fardemens*. We learn that he visited
Lorraine, Venice and traveled even as far as Sicily.

Certainly, he was well known and much thought of despite
his personal tragedy. He seems to have been intent on building
up his medical knowledge and presumably visited many
important astrologers, cabalists, alchemists and physicians.
Many oral legends come down to us about this period of his
life. While in Ancona in Italy we learn that he met a young
swineherd called Felix Peretti. Nostradamus knelt in the road
as the boy passed. Replying to questions as to why he had done
this, Nostradamus replied that he must kneel before His
Holiness. Felix Peretti became Pope Sixtus V in 1585, twenty-
odd years after Nostradamus' death.

Another widely circulated story was related in print in 1656
by Etienne Jaubert. He says, "In this same place when visiting
Monsieur and Madame de Florinville, I learned that Nostradamus had stayed there and treated Madame de Florinville, the
grandmother of the present Seigneur de Florinville, who is still
alive . . . Monsieur de Florinville, walking in the courtyard of
his château in the company of Nostradamus, noticed two
suckling pigs, one black and one white. Determined to have
some sport, he asked Nostradamus what would happen to the
two animals, to which the reply was that 'the wolf will eat the
white one and we will eat the black one.'

"So, Monsieur de Florinville, wishing to disprove Nostradamus' powers, secretly commanded his cook to kill the white
one for that night's supper. This was done, and the pig was
dressed and placed on the spit in the kitchen. But while the
cook was out on an errand, a tame wolf cub belonging to the
household, gnawed at the prepared pig. When the cook
returned and saw what had happened, he took the black pig
and prepared it, serving it up at dinner.

"Monsieur de Florinville, knowing nothing of this because
the cook was afraid to tell him, said to Nostradamus that they
were eating the white pig. The prophet disagreed and insisted

that the black pig had been served up at table. The cook was then asked to come in and eventually confessed what had happened. This gave the company another more agreeable dish to discuss." He goes on to say that "All France recounts diverse events predicted by the author, but I omit them, because I have not been personally assured about them . . . ."

We next come across Nostradamus in Marseilles in 1544, where he apparently thought of settling down. But there was a fresh outburst of the plague in the city during that year, and together with the doctor Louis Serres, Nostradamus worked unceasingly. Then, in November, 1544, Provence suffered one of the worst floods in its history. The plague became even worse, the rivers and springs being polluted with bodies of men and animals. By 1546, the plague was at its height. Aix-en-Provence, the capital town, was in a desperate plight. César de Nostradame, in his *Histoire de Provence*, 1614, says that his father described the situation which faced him when the town sent for him just after May 1, 1546, soon after the plague had broken out.

"People struck by the fever of this illness completely abandon all hopes of recovery, wrap themselves into two white winding sheets and, even while they are still alive say the prayers for the dead—an unheard of thing. The houses are abandoned and empty, men disfigured, women in tears, bewildered children . . . the brave gone and the animals fled. The palace is locked and silent, justice silent and deserted . . . shelter bearers and street porters work on credit as there is no money to be had. The shops are shut, there are no arts, the churches are empty and the priests confused. In short, the streets are foul, wild and full of weeds because of the absence of man and beast during all the 270 days that the plague lasted . . . ."

Nostradamus remained among the sick and dying all that time and ascribed the immunization acquired by his patients to the plague to his rose pills, the recipe for which is given below and appears in his *Moultes Opuscules*, 1555. But one should also remember his insistence on fresh air, running water and his refusal to bleed patients. Unfortunately he does not say anything about hygiene except that the rose pills killed bad breath, bad odors and cleaned teeth, preventing decay, and had to be sucked continuously.

The recipe is not at all unusual for medicine of the time. The ingredients were as follows.

300–400 red roses, picked before dawn.[1]
1 oz. sawdust from green fresh cyprus.
6 oz. Iris of Florence.
3 oz. cloves.
3 drams. sweet smelling calamus, tiger lily.
6 drams. lignaloes.

Pulverize the rose petals, in a mortar, mixed with a powder made from the above. Make the mixture into lozenges, dry and keep enclosed, away from the air. Keep one in the mouth at all times.

Bareste says that the Parliament at Aix voted Nostradamus a pension for life. He is also said to have given many of the rich presents from his wealthy patients to the poor, the widows and orphans of the plague. It is difficult to know how much of this generosity is hearsay, but there must be a foundation for it as this reputation for generosity follows Nostradamus throughout his life.

The plague then afflicted the small, charming town of Salon-de-Provence. Again Nostradamus decided to settle down when it was over, and it became his home until his death.

From a medical point of view, the town was ideally situated for him, between Marseilles, Aix and Avignon. Nostradamus was proved right in his choice because he was settled between the most important cities of Provence and the Midi. He moved there in 1546. In 1547 the town of Lyons sent for him, afflicted by something which may not have been the plague, but possibly whooping cough, still a deadly disease at that period. Nostradamus mentions in his *Traité des Fardemens* a certain chemist, René Hepilievard of Lyons, who produced his prescriptions to a very high quality.

Bareste again recounts Nostradamus' activities at this time, but they are of dubious source. He states that at Lyons Nostradamus quarreled with Antoine Sarrazin, a colleague,

---

[1]As with all recipes using flower petals for medicines or scent it was necessary to pluck them before dawn while the dew was still on them. This is still done with many flower-based perfumes today.

who did not agree with his medical advice. The town is said to have sent a delegation to Nostradamus, begging him not to desert them. He answered that the townspeople must choose between them. They are said to have replied, "We choose Nostradamus, the liberator of Aix." In fact, whoever the doctor was, it was not Sarrazin. He did not get his license, let alone doctorate, until much later, so the story is somewhat suspect. Researches in the various archives have not been able to support this story. Its only source is Bareste plus the indubitable fact that Nostradamus was in Lyons in 1547.

Now comes the final, and it appears the most contented, period of Nostradamus' life, when he obtained international recognition and became adviser to Catherine de' Medicis, queen of France. He was a solid citizen, laden again with honors and gifts, and he married for a second time. Anne Ponsarde Gemelle, a rich and definitely young widow, in view of their numerous future offspring, gave Nostradamus the solid base that had been lacking until then in his life. They were married at Salon on November 11, 1547, before the notary of Salon, Etienne Hozier.

The marriage contract is still in the archives at Salon. They bought a house off the rue de la Poissonnerie, and settled there for the rest of Nostradamus' life.

Salon did not offer much medical competition. Nostradamus appears to have spent most of his time making medicinal and cosmetic preparations for the town notables, by whom he was accepted. But there was an element of distrust and dislike among the ordinary townspeople; presumably his reputation had gone before him. The townspeople abused him as a Jew, his conversion in childhood did not impress them, and he was suspected of being a Huguenot (Protestant) sympathizer. This last was patently untrue as is seen throughout his writings, but it was the age of Calvin and Luther, and the wars of religion which would ravish France for nearly a century were about to begin. The fact that many of the Provençal nobility turned Huguenot did not help. The Catholic peasants banded into groups called Cabans, and became notorious for pillaging the rich Huguenot houses. To the cynical it may well appear that their motive was greed rather than religion. Nostradamus had a low opinion of the Cabans. In the *Traité des Fardemens* he wrote in 1552, "Here where I reside I carry on my work among animals, barbarians, mortal enemies of learning and letters."

It was around this time that he converted the top floor of his house into his study and spent his time reading occult books which were eventually to make him one of the best-known persons in France. He started upon his literary predictive career with a series of *Almanachs*. The first one was published in 1550, which presumably means he wrote it at some period in 1549. It was very successful although it contained only limited information about the weather, crops and the odd supernatural occurrence. Many of these predictions were wrong, but the *Almanachs* were a great success. La Croix du Maine in 1594 wrote that Nostradamus wrote an "infinite number of *Almanachs* and *Prognostications* which were very well received and sold so well that several imitations of them were made in his name."

The so-called *Prophecies of Orval*, by Philip Olivarious, supposedly printed in 1542 and which predicted the coming of Napoleon, were fakes printed around 1820. There is no record of Nostradamus going to Orval although he may have passed through it. However, according to Mlle Le Normand, Napoleon always carried a copy of the Orval prophecies around with him. Le Normand was a great friend of the Empress Josephine: she was a mystic and soothsayer who was very successful and made a great deal of money during and after the Revolution.

It is certain that Nostradamus continued to produce these even while writing the *Prophéties* because in the Salon archives there is a receipt from two Lyons printers for twenty crowns for the *Almanachs* of 1562. One wonders if their success led him to conceive the idea of the *Prophéties*? At the same time however he produced his *Traité des Fardemens* in 1552; in modern terms one might have called him a workaholic.

He also became involved around this period with something quite different. A young man called Adam de Craponne dreamed of building a canal which would connect the Rhône with the Durance, and bring water to the arid land around Salon. Nostradamus became his patron, giving money and doubtless offering advice as well. The canal was started in 1557 and finished in 1559 and is still functioning, bringing water to Salon and the surrounding communities. He was a sound businessman as well as a prophet. We don't have records of his percentage revenue on this venture but I don't doubt it was substantial. There is an impressive statue to Adam de Craponne at Salon, just as grand as that to Nostradamus.

It was approximately in 1554 that a certain Jean Aymes de Chavigny, ex-mayor of Beaune, arrived in Nostradamus' life. Jean Aymes de Chavigny, from now on referred to as Chavigny, was thirty years old in 1554 and held a doctorate in law and theology. He had been elected mayor of the town of Beaune in 1548 and had a brilliant future awaiting him. But he suddenly decided to give all this up, and was advised by Jean Dorat, a court poet and professor of Greek at the Collège de France, to go to Nostradamus as a pupil. He was obviously close to the prophet during his life, but not enough to be mentioned in Nostradamus' will. He is important in that it was he and Anne Ponsarde Gemelle who published together the first final and definitive copy of *Les Prophéties* in 1568, two years after Nostradamus' death. His influence on Nostradamus' widow has long been a matter of question, but one that I think will never be resolved.

How much Chavigny influenced Nostradamus' widow over the publication of the second part of the quatrains is impossible to estimate. Not only did Chavigny claim to be the adopted son of Nostradamus, but of this there is no proof, he was also his scribe and amanuensis. It is unlikely that Anne Ponsarde Gemelle Nostradamus was a very literate woman, and nowhere during Nostradamus' lifetime is she referred to in connection with the *Prophéties*. But it is Chavigny who gives some of the best definite biographical information on Nostradamus. He wrote a book, now lost, the *Receuil des présages prosaïques de M. Nostradamus*. This was followed in 1594 by his major work, *La Première face de Janus François*. Chavigny studied his master's work for a good thirty years. Chavigny used Nostradamus' writings to ally himself with Henri de Navarre, which proved an extremely wise political move. To research Chavigny in depth is a purely academic effort, and I think it is sufficient here to leave him with his second book, *Janus François*, a discussion of various predictions chosen by Chavigny.

The other main source of reference to the prophet was Nostradamus' eldest son, César, who states in his *Histoire de*

Provence that Nostradamus was convinced great historical change would occur in France during the 1550s. He writes of one episode which affected Nostradamus deeply.

"In the year 1554, what tragic and unhappy events occurred . . . fellow creatures born deformed and hideous . . . At the end of January a child was born at Senas, monstrous, with two heads . . . . He was brought to my father and seen by several people." After the birth of a two-headed horse which Nostradamus seems to have been persuaded to see, he diagnosed it as being the forerunner of a great split due in French history. With all the trouble brewing between the Catholics and the Huguenots it would not be a difficult interpretation. A child born in England in 1988 with two heads has been declared by its doctors to be "viable." A dreadful thought. However, in the twentieth century, we do not allot meanings to these tragic freaks. Nostradamus was a shrewd psychologist. He understood the value of symbols in his society and used them accordingly.

During the first part of the 1550s Nostradamus was working at full stretch. He was writing his monthly *Almanachs* and *Prognostications*. He was treating his patients and above all he was writing the first part of the book for which he is most remembered, *Les Prophéties de M. Nostradamus*, which first appeared in 1555. However, as far as this book is concerned I shall take the total edition of the *Prophéties* to which were added the further Centuries VIII–X to give us the first definitive complete version, which was published by Benoît Rigaud in 1568. Since Nostradamus had been dead for two years, it seems fair to contemplate the possibility that Chavigny, the faithful pupil, may have tampered with some of the *Prophéties* with the consent of Nostradamus' wife. But this is still Nostradamus' essential work.

The Prophéties of Nostradamus were intended to contain predictions until the end of the world. The *Almanachs* were a yearly publication. How Nostradamus worked out his date for the end of the world is difficult to decide. In many ways he is a Millennium man, believing that the world will come to an end at A.D. 2000 or maybe, but with far less reason A.D. 3000. Although civilized and cultured, Nostradamus belonged more to the fifteenth century than to the Renaissance. His thoughts went backwards to the First Millennium, A.D. 1000, rather than forward to A.D. 2000. The influence of the Church during the first Millennium had been enormous, preaching that the world was coming to an end and its influence was widespread. Therefore people let their fields lie fallow, neglected their beasts, made no plans for the future. When the year A.D. 1000 was reached and passed without singular incident, it took at least two years for a semblance of normality to return to people's lives. And the Church? It preached that an error had been made and that all would be fulfilled in the next millennium, A.D. 2000. From most of Nostradamus' prophecies it seems that he inclined to A.D. 2000, but was not wholly certain due to the influence of such writings as *The Book of Enoch*, which stated the Millennium would come in 7000 years. Unfortunately this book does not say from when this date should be calculated. Perhaps the wordly side of Nostradamus was hedging his bets.

It is now necessary to say how the *Prophéties* were composed. They were intended to be a series of one thousand predictions, divided into books of a hundred centaines or quatrains. The word "*centaine*" has nothing to do with time, a hundred years, but refers to the fact that it is a set of 100 four-line predictions. These were joined together in a book, for the first time, in 1568: *Les Prophéties de M. Michel Nostradamus. Dont il y en a trois cens qui n'encores iamais este imprimées. A Lyon. Par Benoît Rigaud. Auec permission.* But since this book was published after his death, there is room for some speculation. The seventh Century contains only 42 quatrains and there seems no evidence to prove that the remaining quatrains were used elsewhere. My personal opinion is that possibly Nostradamus had simply not completed the 1000 before his death. The Benoît Rigaud edition also contains the Préface, the first seven Centuries (as seen in an edition by Antoine du Rosne of Lyons), and also the Epistle to Henri II and Centuries VIII–X inclusive. This definitive publication resulted in an immediate spate of copies and fakes throughout Europe, and gives one some idea of the influence the name of Nostradamus carried in its wake. They all contain material, much of it very crudely faked, of forged quatrains not in the editio princeps of 1568.

The "*Sixaines*", a series of predictions in six lines, first turned up in 1605, at Chantilly. They were presented to Henri IV. They purported to have been in the possession of a certain Henry Nostradamus, a nephew of Nostradamus. This cannot be verified either way. Nostradamus had two other brothers, and we have no record as to whether he had any sisters. But the *Sixaines*, in my opinion, are forgeries, which is why I do not include them in this book. The style is not similar to that of Nostradamus, neither were they mentioned by his great follower and pupil Chavigny.

Another fact that makes them suspect is that many appear to be retrospective, applying to the conspiracy of the duc du Biron which rocked the French court in 1602. Anyway, there seems no reason for Nostradamus to change from his successful convoluted style of the quatrains, which had made him famous; they were his trademark, after all.

To return to the *Prophéties*: Chavigny, in a short biography of Nostradamus in 1594, wrote as follows: "Nostradamus . . . foreseeing the important changes and revolutions which were to occur throughout all Europe, the bloody civil war and the dangerous troubles fatally approaching the French realm . . . set out to write his Centuries, which he kept a long time without wishing to publish them feeling that the novelty of the content could not fail to cause infinite attacks, calumnies . . . as indeed happened. Finally, overcome by a wish to be of service to the public, he produced them, with the result that their fame rang throughout the mouths of both Frenchmen and foreigners, with great wonderment."

The reaction of the ruling class was enthusiastic. They had time to read this tiny book, 6″ × 4″ approximately, a size convenient to carry around in their pockets. Its influence spread downward from the court to other areas often through oral tradition as well as book form.

The *Prophéties* became the rage and greatly influenced the queen, Catherine de' Medicis. But equally Nostradamus was vilified on all sides; doctors, philosophers even astrologers objected to the quatrains. A clever Latin verse was soon repeated all over France.

> *Nostra damus cum falsa damus nam fallere nostrum est*;
> *Et cum falsa damus, nil nisi notra damus.*

Roughly translated this means, "When we give our own we

give false things. And when we give false things, we give but our own."

We don't know exactly when the name of Nostradamus came to the ears of Catherine de' Medicis. She had for some time been interested in astrology and possibly necromancy, particularly during those first ten years of her marriage, when she was barren. We know that the king sent a royal command for Nostradamus to come to Paris.

He set out on July 14, 1556. Because of his mission he was able to make use of the royal post, and the journey took about half the time it would have taken an ordinary traveler. He reached Paris on August 15 and lodged in the Inn of Saint Michel at Nostradame. The following day the Constable of France himself, Anne de Montmorency, ordered Nostradamus to the court, which was based that month at Saint-Germain-en-Laye.

We know little of this visit other than that Nostradamus spent several hours with Catherine. What they discussed is impossible to guess but it is generally agreed that the quatrain I.XXXV particularly occupied the queen, as she had also been warned by her Italian astrologer, Luc Gauric, that her husband would die in a duel. The letter Gauric sent to Henri is dated February, 1556, and warns the king "to avoid all single combat in an enclosed place, especially near his 41st year." Henri is said to have told Montgomery, the captain of his Scottish guard, who, ironically, was the person to be involved in his death, "I care not if my death be in that manner more than in any other. I would even prefer it, to die by the hand of whoever he might be, so long as he was brave and valiant and that I kept my honor."

Returning to Paris, rather dissatisfied with the payments he had received, which totaled one hundred and thirty crowns, Nostradamus was lodged at the palace of the Archbishop de Sens. Since his journey had cost him a hundred crowns he was soon short of money and borrowed money from a stranger, Jean Morel. Nostradamus later acknowledges a loan of two rose nobles and twelve crowns in the only authenticated letter that has remained signed by himself, underneath the name of a secretary. All other communications relating to Nostradamus that have survived have been written by scribes.

However, once comfortably settled in Paris, Nostradamus resolved to make good use of his reputation and gain something from it. We learn that he had an attack of gout and was confined to his rooms for ten days. But that did not stop the rich and the credulous from seeking him out. There is a pleasant legend about this period. Nostradamus was in bed when he was woken by a loud knocking at his door. The intruder was a page of the Beauveau family, who had lost one of their dogs. Before he could state the reason for his interruption, Nostradamus is said to have cried out, "You are making a lot of noise over a lost dog. Go and look on the road to Orléans. You will find it there on a leash." According to the page's story he found a servant on the road leading the dog back. This story spread mightily around the court and increased the Nostradamus legend.

Eventually the other reason for his journey was made clear. Catherine wanted to know the fates of her children. Nostradamus was summoned to Blois to draw up their horoscopes. It must have been a difficult task as all the Valois children would die, leaving France no direct heir. Her first son, François II, would be king for a year and leave his child bride, Mary Queen of Scots, to her tragic destiny.

Eleven-year-old Elisabeth would be married off to old Philip II of Spain, as his third wife, and die in childbirth. The next daughter, Claude, who became the duchesse de Lorraine, was also to die in her twenties. Then came Charles IX, who would celebrate his coronation banquet wearing a woman's dress and in whom lurked the tragedy of St. Bartholomew, the massacre of the Huguenots, noble and otherwise, which took place in Paris on St. Bartholomew's Day, August 24, 1572. The Huguenots had flocked to the city to celebrate the marriage of the Huguenot king Henri of Navarre to Marguerite de Valois. It was an attempt to quash the influence of the Huguenot Admiral Coligny, who was attempting to draw Charles IX into a war with Spain, which Catherine, his mother, greatly opposed. She persuaded the king that the massacre was a measure of public safety. The king himself arranged the manner of the execution of the massacre. It began on Sunday, August 24, at daybreak and lasted until September 17. It is reported that Charles himself fired upon Huguenots from a window of the Louvre. The Catholic powers rejoiced greatly at this slaughter and Pope Gregory XIII commanded bonfires to be lit and a medal struck to commemorate the event.

Charles IX was followed by Henri III, king of Poland and France, twice times king, killed by the assassin Clément. Then there was the duc d'Alençon, Elizabeth I of England's perpetual suitor, her "little frog," titular ruler of the Netherlands. Finally, la belle Marguerite, who married the Huguenot king of Navarre, and because she became bored with his provincial court and sought solace in various love affairs, was imprisoned by her husband in a grim convent for the rest of her life. A tragic life for two reasons. She would outlive all her siblings and also see her former husband take over France as Henri IV.

It is difficult to imagine what Nostradamus did tell Catherine, but obviously it sufficed, because she retained her faith in him until her death. As we know, she visited Salon with Charles IX in 1564 and conferred upon Nostradamus the title of Physician in Ordinary and a present of 200 crowns. How he explained away the predictions he had already written one cannot guess.

It was soon after this that Nostradamus began to see the danger signs in Paris. He was burned in effigy in one of the city squares. The Justice of Paris wished to question him. So he returned, triumphantly, to Salon. Here, it appears, he received many important visitors. The canal was at the point of completion, and his second son, André, was born. Presumably, he was also finishing off the *Prophéties*. There is another typical Nostradamus story at this period.

The prophet was seated in front of his house one evening, and a young girl passed him on her way to the woods. She greeted him: *"Bonjour, Monsieur de Nostradame."* He replied, *"Bonjour fillette."* On her return she again greeted him, to which his reply was, *"Bonjour petite femme."* He knew what she was doing in the woods. A charming tale.

In the summer of 1559 the court celebrated the double marriage of Elisabeth, Henri's eldest daughter, aged fourteen, to Philip II of Spain, and of his sister, Marguerite, to the duc de Savoie. To celebrate these events a grand tourney was planned. It started on June 28 and was to be held for three days in the rue Saint-Antoine. The king joined in the jousting and was very successful for the first two days. But on the third, the mood changed. Catherine sent him a note begging him not to proceed as she felt a great unease.

An unknown boy among the spectators is said to have cried out, "The king will die." But Henri disregarded these warnings and towards evening rode against the Captain of his Scottish guard, Montgomery. They jousted twice, neither succeeding in unseating the other. Then Montgomery, too, became afraid and begged the king to ride no more. But Henri insisted. They clashed lances, but unfortunately Montgomery did not raise his in time, and he struck the king in the head, through his gilded helmet. Some record a second wound in the head, thus fulfilling Nostradamus' prediction: I.XXXV, *deux claffes un*. He died ten days later in great agony, pleading with Catherine and the court not to take action against the wretched Montgomery. The latter, however, had the sense to flee the court immediately, but ultimately Catherine caught up with him and wreaked her revenge. Montgomery is said to have exclaimed of Nostradamus, "Cursed be the magician who predicted so evilly and so well."

The immature François II, already married to Mary Stuart, Mary Queen of Scots, from childhood, succeeded his father. Like all his family he had a passion for hunting and probably initially caught a chill in his ear in November, 1560. It is interesting to note that the various court ambassadors were extremely worried about the young king, each remembering quatrains X.XXXIX and X.LV. The remaining centuries had been circulated in handwritten form, a common practice. The Venetian ambassador, Michele Suriano, wrote on November 20, 1560, to the doge at Venice, "Each courtier now remembers the XXXIX quatrain of Century X of Nostradamus and comments upon it under his breath." The Tuscan ambassador, Niccolò Tornabuoni, wrote to Duke Cosimo of Florence on December 3, "The health of the king is very unsure and Nostradamus in his predictions for this month says that the royal house will lose two young members from unexpected illness." I cannot find the quatrain which predicts the death of two young men of the royal house, but François II died two days later on December 5 and a young cousin, the son of the duc de Roche-sur-Yon, died in the same month.

It is probable that sitting quietly down in Salon, Nostradamus was not aware of the political impact of his predictions throughout Europe.

In January of the following year, 1561, the Spanish ambassador, Chantonnay, wrote to his master, Philip II: "It has been noticed that in the period of one month both the first and least members of the royal house have died. These troubles have stupefied the court, together with the predictions of Nostradamus: it would be better to chastise him than allow him to sell such prophecies which lead to ignorant and superstitious beliefs."

In 1561, Nostradamus was asked by Marguerite of Savoie and her husband to predict the future of the child she was bearing. He went to Nice to draw up the horoscope of the future Charles-Emmanuel. Nostradamus claimed he would be the greatest captain of his age. He was known as Charles-Emmanuel the Great; but apart from disagreeing totally about the rights of Henri IV to the French throne, his main claim to fame was as the ruler of Savoie. In May, 1561, Suriano again voiced his suspicions to the doge: "There is another prediction very widely spoken in France, coming from the famous astrologer Nostradamus, which threatens the three sons, in claiming that the Queen Mother will see them all as kings." Which indeed she did.

Nostradamus' reputation was again increased by the prediction X.XXXIX, which was now openly quoted at the court: "The eldest son; a widow, an unfortunate marriage without any children; two islands in discord, before eighteen still a minor. For the other one, the betrothal will be even younger."

This was widely believed to apply to François II, eldest son of Henri II. He died six weeks before reaching the age of eighteen, leaving a widow, Mary Queen of Scots, whose return to her own country as a rightful queen was to put two realms in discord. To compound the interest, François' younger brother Charles, later to become Charles IX, had been betrothed at the earlier age of eleven to Elizabeth of Austria.

It was in 1564 that Catherine de' Medicis decided to make a grand progress throughout France, partly to try to help to quell the religious troubles and also to meet her daughter Elisabeth, whom she had not seen for five years. Perhaps she had memories of her own unhappy arrival in France aged fourteen, exactly the same age as Elisabeth had been when she set off to marry the dour king of Spain. All her family came with her, but because of the length of the trip—it was to last nearly two years—she took with her a reduced court of eight hundred.

During this progress, which included Provence, Catherine decided that she would visit Nostradamus and Salon. César Nostradamus, his son, gives us a vivid but lengthy description of the visit. The royal family arrived at Salon on October 17 at 3.00 p.m. But a few days before, the plague had reappeared and five people died, so the town was almost empty. King Charles IX ordered that people return to welcome the royal party under threat of penalty.

It is worth noting Charles's attire. "He was seated on an African horse, with a harness of black velvet with large trimmings and fringes of gold. His person was robed in a cloak of Tyrian purple, adorned with silver ribbons. He wore an amethyst in one ear and a sapphire in the other . . . ."

The two consuls of Salon received their king and "at once begged Michel de Nostradamus . . . to speak to Her Majesty at the reception, guessing quite correctly that she would especially desire to see him." Nostradamus, with unusual modesty told his friends "he wanted to move about independently and greet Her Majesty away from the vulgar people and this crowd of men, being aware that he would be asked for and sent for when she arrived." Apparently Nostradamus was pointed out to the king by the consuls and greeted him suitably in Latin. According to César, who never left his father's side during this occasion. Nostradamus, with his velvet hat in one hand and a Malacca cane with a silver handle in the other, which he used because he suffered from gout, went up to the château where the royal family were staying and spent a long time talking with the king and queen regent.

Here is an interesting anecdote omitted by César but quoted by many other commentators. The queen, Catherine, asked Nostradamus to cast the horoscope of her youngest son, the duc d'Anjou, which Nostradamus did, saying he would become king.

This, as at their first meeting at Blois four years earlier, seemed to satisfy Catherine. But Nostradamus was far more interested in a ten-year-old page in the king's suite. He tried to see the boy, who was frightened and ran away. He therefore arranged to see him at his levée the following morning. Henri

IV often told this story in later years, saying that his servants delayed in giving him his shirt so that Nostradamus could see him at his leisure, while he feared that a whipping was awaiting him. As the boy stood naked, waiting to be ceremonially dressed as usual, Nostradamus remarked the moles upon his body. This was a common method of prediction akin to chiromancy or reading the hand. Nostradamus was convinced this was the boy who would be the future king of France. He said to the servants at the levée, "You will have as a master the king of France and Navarre." The boy was a cousin of the king, of the family of Navarre, and thus united France and Navarre on his accession to the French throne after his defeat of Henri III in 1589 as Henri IV of France.

There is a painting of this episode by Valverane which is in the Old Museum at Salon. It happened on October 18, 1564, shortly before Nostradamus' death in 1566.

After the court's leaving Provence Nostradamus sank back into obscurity—but that was only technically, as it were. The corridors of the royal court were still humming. The new ambassador to Spain was Don Francisco de Alava. He reports upon one of the quatrains concerning the duc d'Anjou, the permanent courtier, and Elizabeth I of England. "Tomorrow, there leaves secretly a gentleman sent to visit the queen of England. The first day that the King and Queen saw Nostradamus [at Salon] he declared to them that the king would marry the aforesaid Queen." Another dispatch, sent some months later, shows de Alava's low opinion of the prophet, and his certainty that Nostradamus was acting for personal motives of greed, which I believe to be probably untrue. "To the king of Spain: In order that Your Majesty may see how duped people are here in France, I report that the Queen, when she passed through the place where Nostradamus lives, summoned him and presented him with two hundred crowns. She ordered him to draw up the horoscope of the King and the Queen." (It is uncertain whether the Queen here is Charles IX's fiancée, Elizabeth of Austria, or Catherine herself.) "Since he is the most diplomatic and never wishes to displease anyone, he drew up two horoscopes which flattered them, and they ordered him to follow their court as far as Arles . . . The Queen spoke with me today. 'Do you know,' she said, 'Nostradamus has assured me that in 1566 a general peace should reign all over the world' . . . and when saying this she had as confident an air as if she were quoting the gospels of St. John or St. Luke."

But by the end of 1565, Nostradamus was seriously ill. Suffering from arthritis and gout, he was confined to his house at Salon. Joseph Roche, his notary, was summoned on June 17, 1566, to draw up his will. His detailed estate included coins to the value of 3,444 crowns. (For contemporary evaluation, Leoni states that a room in a good house in Paris could be rented for four crowns a year.) His daughter Madeleine received the largest legacy of 600 crowns, while her two sisters Diana and Anne received 500 each. Anne Ponsarde Gemelle Nostradamus received 400 crowns and most of the contents of the house. His sons, unnamed, received 100 crowns each, but not until they were twenty-five. There were several minor bequests to charities and beggars of the parish—six sous each! He also gave instructions for his burial. His body was to be placed between the great door and the altar of Saint Martha in the local Franciscan monastery.

This was changed on June 30, when a codicil was drawn up, giving his eldest son, César, his astrolobe and his large gold ring, and Madeleine, obviously his favorite daughter, two walnut chests with their contents, without having to wait for her marriage.

Chavigny states that dropsy set in around June 25. On July 1, the superior of the Franciscan monastery, Father Vidal, was sent for to give the last rites. Nostradamus knew he was dying. Despite being a doctor he had predicted it, stating that Chavigny would find him the next morning, *trouvé tout mort entre le lit et le banc*. The *banc* had been set by Nostradamus' bed to enable him to climb into it in his weakened state. He also told Chavigny he would not find him alive at sunrise. He died sometime during the early morning, after eight days of severe pain.

Nostradamus was buried as he asked, upright in the monastery "so that the feet of the vulgar should not walk over him." His headstone, written in Latin, composed by his wife, reads as follows: "Here lie the bones of the illustrious Michel Nostradamus, alone of all mortals judged worthy to record events of the entire world with his almost divine pen, under the influence of the stars. He lived 62 years, 6 months and 7 days. He died at Salon in the year 1566. Let not prosperity disturb his rest. Anne Pons Gemelle wishes her husband true happiness."

Of Nostradamus' wife, Anne Ponsarde or Pons Gemelle, we have no further information. César, his eldest son and author of the *Histoires de Provence*, died in 1631. He was described by Pitton as "a good poet, painter and good historian." He was twice consul of Salon.

He married, but had no children. It seems that any descendants of Nostradamus came from the female line. The second son, André, who went to Paris soon after his father's death, killed an adversary in a duel and was arrested. He vowed to take Orders if freed, and it is said that he became a Capuchin monk and was buried at a monastery near Toulon. The third son, Charles, tried, unsuccessfully, to make his name as a Provençal poet.

An interesting story of a charlatan can be introduced here. He normally called himself Michel le Jeune. He made a glorious exit at the siege of Poussin, 1574, as related by Théodora-Agrippa d'Aubigné, the mother of the wife of Louis XIV, Madame de Maintenon. It appears that Poussin was under siege and the "young Michel" was asked by the commander, Saint-Luc, what would happen to the town. Michel le Jeune gave the deliberated reply that the town would be burned down by fire. Sadly, he was caught setting fire to sites all over the town. He was killed by the troops. Already Nostradamus' name was one to conjure with.

All that remains to add is that Nostradamus' tomb soon became a place of pilgrimage. During the Revolution it was sacked, despite the solemn warning on the headstone. The soldiers scattered his bones, and there is a rumor that they drank wine out of his skull. However, his bones were collected under the order of the then mayor, a M. David, and reinterred in the Church of Saint-Laurent at Salon. The town put up a new epitaph in 1792: "In this year 3 of Liberty, the tomb of Nostradamus, who honored Salon, his native land, and whose memory will always be cherished by French patriots, was opened because of his predictions of the rule of Liberty. The citizens divided his bones amongst one another. The municipality has recovered part of them, which are contained in this tomb."

But, once the fervor of the Revolution had passed, the old epitaph of his wife, Anne Ponsarde Gemelle, was replaced in marble over Nostradamus' new resting place. One other small touch. The locals of Salon were so convinced that Nostradamus did not die in 1566 that a legend ran that he was shut up in his tomb with pen and ink and would continue to write the *Prophéties*.

Perhaps this is time to give a physical description of Nostradamus. Chavigny describes him thus: "He was a little under medium height, robust, nimble and vigorous. He had a large and open forehead, a straight nose and gray eyes which were usually pleasant but which blazed when he was angry. His face was both severe and smiling, but along with this severity there was a great kindness. His cheeks were red, even in his old age, and his beard long and thick. Except in his old age his health was good and his senses acute. He had a lively and inquiring mind and a remarkable memory. He spoke little, but thought a great deal. He slept only four or five hours a night. He praised freedom of speech and approved of the Catholic Church, outside of which he believed there was no salvation. He hated vice. I can remember his charity to the poor towards whom he was very generous."

JEWISH SOURCES WHICH INDICATE THE COMING OF THE MILLENNIUM

As I have mentioned, Nostradamus' family had declared themselves converts to the Christian religion by 1502, two years before he was born. But they never entirely left their Judaism behind. We learn that among the first things Nostradamus was taught by his grandfather was Hebrew, so the ancient creed must have been a strong tradition among the family.

The Old Testament predicts that seven great events will happen at roughly the same time, all of which shall be indicators that mankind is approaching Armageddon, Nostradamus' Millennium. Horrifyingly enough, these events appear to have already started and mankind will have to act quickly if the predictions are not to be fulfilled.

The first is religious deception, false religions. The movement away from major Christian, Islamic and Hindu beliefs is increasing daily. Particularly we see the basic tenets of the Church being changed or ignored. Women deacons, and already some women priests, married priests, and the schism in early 1988 by Archbishop Lefèbvre and his followers plus the intransigence of Muslim fundamentalists.

We have a spate of newly founded mystic religions, quite apart from television evangelists and Bible Thumpers. One of the most dangerous and prolific of these religions is that of Sun Myung Moon, a Korean, who has houses all over the world. Induction into this cult is so severe that parents have been known to kidnap their children to get them away from this pernicious sect and actually have them deprogrammed. He claims among other things to be the second coming of the Messiah.

Maharaj Ji of India also claims to be the Messiah and has a large following. He sometimes calls himself "The Lord from Heaven in a 747." All these sects accrue immense sums of money from their followers and most are impenetrable due to their claiming charity status where taxes are concerned and are therefore difficult to prosecute under the law.

David Moses is another. His cult are known as The Children of God. He has a strong following among young people and sends messages to his followers, apparently known as the "Mo Letters" to his "families" of adoring disciples. He too claims to be the Messiah.

The most dreadful of these cult leaders was the Reverend Jim Jones. He led some nine hundred people into the jungles of Guyana in the 1970s, only to serve them a cocktail of death; men, women and children together.

Another aspect of these "false gods" is the current revival of the occult. It was not taken too seriously in the early sixties but now one can read about it regularly in even the more serious newspapers. Whether these so-called covens actually do much harm is improbable, but they worship Satan as their God.

Under this heading may also come the amazing advance of astrology. Not only is it found in its most basic form in every daily newspaper and magazine that is published, but there is a wide network of people who today use personal astrologers to conduct their daily lives. Some astrologers are serious in their work, but many are charlatans. The average person accepts occult and psychic phenomena as normal. This is not to be confused with the few scientific experiments in laboratories working upon ESP and telepathy. They are attempting to sound out the extent of man's unconscious brain power.

It must be realized that not all supernatural or psychic phenomena are essentially good. There is a malevolent side to all these happenings, very often desired by those who dabble in it. Timothy 4.1 says, "The spirit clearly says that in later times some will abandon the faith and follow deceiving things." This is the demonic aspect of psychic phenomena, which although fortunately very rare, is desperately dangerous. Exorcisms are hard and sobering events to go through. The spate of films such as *The Exorcist* have made people more aware of the possibility of this happening, but not of the savage truths behind it.

The second Biblical warning Nostradamus would have us heed is one of internal revolution. The end of the eighth decade of this century makes it appear worldwide. In Russia we have the revolt of the Armenians trying to regain control over the Azerbaijan. Burma, Korea, Kampuchea, Ethiopia, Sudan, Latin America, South Africa, let alone the Gulf War, the tragic position of the Kurds, and the position of the Christian Lebanese against their terrorist-backed countrymen. The list can go on forever. I don't believe the world has ever been in such a state of insurrection. Most of these wars and uprisings are upheld in the name of liberation, and are financed mainly by the USSR or the USA. Not even embassies are safe places anymore. They are shelled or burned. It appears that not a year goes by without at least one national government being overthrown.

The third event that should warn us is war: "You will hear of wars and rumours of war," Matthew 24.6. No century has witnessed such an escalation of war as we have since the Second World War. Some are front-page news. Others, such as that in Burundi, are hardly heard of, but there is practically no country in the world today that is not fighting some kind of war. Even Britain has the problem of the indiscriminate terrorism of the IRA, although at the time of writing this, Europe does seem to be the most stable area.

When General MacArthur signed the peace treaty after the Second World War in 1945 he gave his warning, unfortunately unheeded: "We have had our last chance. If we do not devise some greater and more equitable system, Armageddon will be at our door."

Since then we have had wars in the Middle East, the Israel/Palestine problem, the Cold War (now hopefully coming to an end with "Glasnost"), the Korean War, the Vietnam War, the war in Afghanistan and the Gulf War. These have all been full-fledged wars, killing as many civilians as soldiers. Many countries now appear to have the capacity both to make atomic bombs and to utilize chemical weapons. There is always a chance that there may be a nuclear war by the end of the 1990s. That is the Holocaust, the Armaggedon, the Millennium.

As Nostradamus says, our chances of survival are slim. They

depend upon the intelligence of our world leaders. At least, in this, Reagan and Gorbachev have started down this path of defusing world pressures. A small start, but a definite one.

The fourth warning is famine. Of course, famine is partly caused by the enormous population explosion, particularly in the Third World. However, despite many dying in disasters such as local wars, floods and famine, the world population is growing at an alarming rate. This is even despite the many sophisticated forms of contraception we now have. This decade has never been more conscious of the widespread famine throughout the Third World. First there was Ethiopia, and it still remains. Now we have the Sudan, Bangladesh, the great exodus of the boat people from Vietnam and Cambodia, the Iraqi Kurds in inadequate camps in Turkey and even the dreadful drought that has ruined so many farmers in the United States. Famine now appears to be ever present. Dr. William Paddock, a noted environmentalist, wrote a book in 1975 called *Famines*, and in it he predicted an age of famine which would begin in the 1970s and escalate beyond all our control. He appears to have been right. Dr. Borlaug, one of the world's greatest nutritionists, states, "The. hunger and misery of millions would provoke a great global holocaust." We seem to be at this point now. Creations such as the European food and wine "mountains" now in storage should immediately be given as famine relief.

The fifth problem we are warned to face is the poisoning of the earth, pollution. The overwhelming impact of industrial pollution now affects every area of our lives. The earth is troubled by the "greenhouse effect" due to our constant use of fluorocarbons. The seas are so contaminated with over a thousand different chemicals being pumped into them in enormous quantities that we are now losing our sea mammal population. Seals, dolphins, porpoises, all at the top of the food chain, die of dreadful disfigurements, and the present epidemic of seal distemper is certainly partly due to the fact that the seals' immune systems have been lessened by the effluent. What should worry us more is that the fish we eat often contain dangerous levels of these same pollutants. Add to this the problems of acid rain and the deforestation of the globe, it makes one wonder where mankind will be in fifty years' time. Many of us now will drink only bottled water and with reason. Nitrites and nitrates used by farmers to increase their crops are leached into the rivers and reservoirs, the source of all our tap water.

The changing weather pattern, extreme heat (such as in the USA in 1988) and the appalling summers we have been having in Europe are another variable which affects food production. Dr. John Gribbin, scientist and co-author of *The Jupiter Effect*, says that these problems are aggravated by shifting planet orbits: "The unusual planetary alignment due to occur in the early 1980's will affect the sun. This in turn shakes up the planet earth. But we realized while studying the repercussions in the area of earthquakes that the link works through the atmosphere. What we are really talking about is an effect of the sun on the circulation of the atmosphere. This determines weather pattern shifts."

The sixth warning given is the Earthquake. "In various places there will be great earthquakes." These are something Nostradamus worries about, an interesting fact in that his France was not an "earthquake zone." Earthquakes are dreadful, sudden and devastating. The one that occurred recently on the Nepal/India border at about 6.7 degrees on the Richter scale has still left that part of the world greatly isolated. No communications, no railways, no roads, and—worst of all—no shelter for those fortunate enough to survive. Since then there has been the dreadful earthquake in Armenia with a total of over 70,000 dead and 100,000 injured.

It is a fact that there has been an unprecedented increase in earthquake activity in the twentieth century. The number of earthquakes has roughly doubled in each of the ten-year periods since 1950. Nostradamus may well therefore not be so far off when he predicts an enormous earthquake on the west coast of America in the near future, which will occur in May. One of the unpleasant side effects of earthquakes is great floods, should dams built over faults be destroyed. This would also apply to nuclear plants built near them. It has been stated by contemporary astrologers that May 1989 would be an extremely dangerous period because on the 8th of that month the three planets Mars, Uranus and Saturn would turn into retrograde action, which is malevolent and associated with earthquakes.

The final seventh sign of the Millennium will be plagues and disease. Plagues such as the Black Death, polio and smallpox seem to have been eliminated through medical development in most parts of the world. But a new and far more dreadful one has appeared, AIDS, for which as yet we have no cure, only means to retard its inevitable progress. Nostradamus certainly was aware of this new mutation in disease. He says unfortunately that "although relief will be found, the remedy will be far off." Let us hope that, in this prediction at least, he is partially wrong. The number of AIDS victims is multiplying at an appalling rate, and hospitals say that within a few years the majority of their beds will be occupied by people suffering from this disease.

It is a dreadful decade we have to look forward to.

THE MODERN MILLENNIUM

Apart from the Jewish influence on Nostradamus' opinions concerning the Millennium, as well as the Christian aspect, it appears to me that we could do much by simply sitting down, as it were, and analyzing the state in which the world finds itself at the end of the ninth decade of the twentieth century.

Never have there been so many continual disasters, both natural and manmade. Never have there been so many wars, so many available instruments of global destruction, so much wealth in the Western World and so much unimaginable poverty in the Third World, let alone those natural phenomena such as earthquakes and enigmatic plagues such as AIDS which threaten to decimate the human race.

There are many disaster areas worldwide. Bangladesh admits to hundreds of thousands drowned, millions homeless and 80 percent of the whole country underwater during the floods in 1988. That tragedy came a month after the catastrophic flooding in Sudan. The problem was caused just as it was in the Sudan according to scientists by "the thin end of the deforestation wedge." That is, the effect upon the climate by our relentless policy of destroying the great forests of the world, which causes changes in the weather. It is now much more generally understood that deforestation could cause the destruction of the world's entire ecological balance, changing everything from the air we breathe to the food we eat.

The human race is destroying areas of rain forest about the size of two hundred football pitches every minute. In this century alone we have removed about 50 per cent of the forests. If we continue at this rate, another 20 percent will be destroyed by the year 2000.

Deforestation has four definite and tragic side effects. The first is flooding. When the soil is eroded by wind and rain, water from the melting snow caps of Tibet (in the case of Bangladesh) is not absorbed into the earth. Were there trees, the roots would absorb the water and bond the topsoil. Later, the water would be drawn up through the branches and released into the atmosphere, forming rain clouds. Where the land is subject to deforestation, the rain simply washes away the topsoil.

Secondly, there is what is now known as the greenhouse effect. This happens when gases created by the burning of timber form a layer of carbon dioxide around the planet, trapping heat and raising the atmospheric temperature. The earth's average temperature has already been raised by 0.5°C in the past ninety years. If the current destruction rate continues, the earth's temperature will rise by a further 0.5°C, thus raising the world sea level by anything up to sixty meters due to the melting of the polar ice cap. This would obliterate many cities, including London and New York.

Environmentalists have claimed that another side effect of deforestation is the extinction of many plant and animal species, and that at least one plant or animal species becomes extinct every half hour, an enormous environmental disaster. Another school of thought says that of the five to ten million species of organisms now inhabiting the earth, one million could die within the next ten years. Tropical forests have also been the main dispensary of raw materials for medicines, in particular those containing anticancer properties.

Plant and animal destruction in turns leads to the destruction of our few remaining primitive tribes. In the Carajas region of the Amazon, an area of rain forest the size of England and France combined was cleared in 1982 for a $600-million iron-ore project. The removal of essential sources of food and shelter forced the last nomadic tribe in South America, the Guajas, to near extinction, and two neighbouring tribes, the Parakana and the Xikrin, now exist only in photographs or the slums of Rio de Janeiro.

What has happened to man's sense of proportion, his value of nature, his ultimate source of survival, his sense of decency? We have become, however unwittingly, the victims of those people selfish and greedy enough to attain their aims at whatever cost to others. The age of individual protest is past. It is pointless. Very often it is circumvented by those same exploiters who change the names of sources of food and other requirements on a ship's manifest, and usually succeed, as has happened recently in Britain. An individual is hard put to boycott the products of an individual country. Man must unite. Ten more years is a very short time indeed. Whether one gives credence to what Nostradamus writes or not, it must appear obvious to any right-minded, thinking person that the cooperation between nations is rapidly becoming impossible and that only global intervention will be of any use. The Millennium will arrive for the disbelievers as well. The Apocalypse (whatever one wishes to call it) which is already wiping out human, plant and animal life, has its roots in the acts of mankind as well as the will of God.

Michael Robinson of Washington's Smithsonian Institution said recently, "We are facing the first human-created extinction style cycle that is on the same scale as major geological events of the past, but condensed into an incomparably smaller span of time. This is not hyperbole, not even hypothesis, BUT IMMINENT ACTUALITY."

An example of this is Sir Edmund Hillary's first ascent of Everest in 1953. The steep sides of the Khumbu Valley were covered with juniper bushes. Now 75 percent of these are destroyed, by climbers and environmental changes.

In the Third World Pakistan, India, Nepal, and Tibet—in addition to Bangladesh—have all suffered deforestation. This has eroded the fertile topsoil from the hills, caused landslides, and clogged rivers and reservoirs with so much silt that they cannot cope with the waters from the mountains so that they overflow, well before they reach their natural outlet, the Ganges.

It is estimated that at the present rate of cutting, the Himalayas will be treeless in twenty-five years and the climatic effects will probably turn the now fertile plain into a new Sahel, a severely drought-stricken region of Central Africa.

In Nepal, where the population is expected to double to 38 million by A.D. 2000, they clear an average of 120,000 acres of forest annually. Most of the wood is used for firewood. The rest is cleared to make room for crops and livestock.

Three decades ago, floods afflicted 62 million acres on India each year. Now it is well over 100 million acres. Appallingly, the highwater mark on the river Brahmaputra at Dibrugarh in East Assam has *never once* been below danger level since 1960.

Still in the Third World, but on the other side of the globe, the Brazilians will celebrate the onset of the next dry season by torching the rain forests. Before the next rainy season it is estimated that they will have burned down approximately 100 million acres of forest. This will compound the world's problems and is an area over which governments seem to have little control.

One may continue in this vein indefinitely. Blame cannot be placed on the Third World alone. The West German Danzer Group are ripping out vast areas of jungle to give us teak coffins and mahogany kitchen units. But there are a few tiny grounds for optimism.

Perhaps the last word, however, lies with an environmentalist quoted in the London *Sunday Times* September 11, 1988. "Peasants don't listen to biology lectures." They don't. They live off the land and fulfill their immediate needs. What they cannot understand is that this fulfillment may well not only drown or starve their families but also affect the rest of humankind.

Deforestation leads to famine, drought and flooding. Add to this disease, chemical pollution, warfare; you have the perfect ingredients for Nostradamus' Millennium.

PARIS 1989

Century I

I.I

Estant assis de nuict secret estude
Seul reposé sur la selle
d'aerain:
Flambe exigue sortant de solitude
Fait psperer q n'est à croire
vain.

Sitting alone at night in secret study, it rests solitary on the brass tripod. A slight flame comes out of the emptiness, making successful that which would have been in vain.

This and the following quatrain I.II are an attempt to describe Nostradamus' methods of divination, a prelude to his predictions. The method he uses is that of the fourth century neo-Platonist, Iamblichus, a reprint of whose book was published at Lyons in 1547. It was almost certainly read by Nostradamus, and may even have been the source of his experiments once he realized he had a gift for prediction or second sight. It was soon after its publication in France that Nostradamus' first attempt at written prediction appeared— the *Almanachs*. Admittedly they were not up to much—a bucolic *Moore's Almanach*—but they were read seriously in the region. As to when he first decided to write the Centuries is not known, but my impression is sometime during the early 1550s.

All the ingredients necessary for magic practices are in this quatrain. It is night—solitude. Nostradamus is alone in his study. The brass tripod which held a bowl of water is identical to the method used by Iamblichus. The seer gazed into the water until it became cloudy and pictures of the future were revealed. Interestingly enough, Nostradamus was not only a clairvoyant but an audiovoyant as well, which will become clear in the second quatrain. He heard as well as saw his visions. The *flambe exiguë* is the tenuous light of inspiration which takes over Nostradamus as he begins to prophesy.

Century I

I.II

La verge en main mife au milieu de BRANCHES,[1]	The wand in the hand is placed in the middle of the legs of the
De l'onde il moulle [2] & le limbe[3] & le pied:	tripod. He sprinkles with water both the hem of the garment and
Vn peur & voix fremiffent par les manches:	its (his) foot. Fear, a voice runs trembling through the sleeves (of
Splendeur diuine. Le diuin pres s'afsied.	his robe). Divine spendor; the God sits nearby.

[1]*BRANCHES*. Capitals in the original text. Refers to the three limbs or branches of the brass tripod. It could also be an indirect reference to the prophetess at Branchus.

[2]*moulle*. Mod. F. *mouille*, to moisten.

[3]*limbe*. L. *limbus*, the hem of a garment.

Nostradamus here reveals more of his method. He touches
the water on the tripod with his wand and then moistens his
robe and his feet with it. The Apollonian prophetesses[1] used
the same method at the oracles of Branchus in Classical times.
Nostradamus appears to be afraid of the power thus evoked.
He both hears and sees the visions as they appear to him, and
writes them down while still possessed. But once the God—the
gift—sits down beside him, he feels unafraid. This dual aspect
of prophecy is rare enough to be worth noting when trying to
interpret the Prophéties.

Century I

I.III

Quand la lictiere du tourbillon verſee,	*When the litter is overturned by the whirlwind and faces are*
Et feront faces de leurs manteaux couuers:	*covered by their cloaks, the republic will be troubled by its*
La republique par gens nouueaux vexée,	*new people. At the time, both reds and whites will rule badly.*
Lors blancs & rouges iugeront à l'enuers.	

The key word to this quatrain is "republic". Nostradamus
always calls France a kingdom until the time of the Revolution
of 1789. The aristocracy were always carried in litters and this,
their symbol, is overturned by the violent whirlwind of the
Revolution. The line about faces covered with cloaks is
interesting. It could possibly refer to the many exiles who fled
from France at that time, or possibly to the many heads which
fell from the guillotine and were thence hidden from sight in
quicklime. Nostradamus feels that the republic will be greatly
troubled by its new rulers.

White was the color of the Bourbon kings and red that of
the revolutionaires. Both committed excesses during their
terms of power, *à l'enuers.*

Century I

I.IIII

Par l'vniuers fera faict vn monarque,	An universal monarch shall be created, who both in life and peace will last for a short time. At this point the ship of the Papacy will founder, governed to its greatest detriment.
Qu'en paix & vie ne fera longuement,	
Lors fe perdra la pifcature barque[1],	
Sera regie en plus grand detriment.	

Napoleon crowned himself (*fera faict*) King and Emperor of France on May 18, 1804, and reigned for ten years, abdicating in April, 1814—not a long reign. Peace was certainly not a characteristic of his era—the Napoleonic Wars are still remembered. Under General Miollis, the French army captured Rome, the *pifcature barque*, in 1809.

Pius VII (1800–1823) first came to France to crown Napoleon, but on his second visit he was held prisoner and only released by Napoleon's abdication at Fontainebleau on January 23, 1814. The last line probably refers to the religious anarchy that held sway in France after the dissolution of the clergy in 1792.

Century I

I.V

Chaffés feront pour faire long combat,	They will be driven away for a long drawn out fight, those in the countryside will be the most troubled. Town and city will have the greater struggle; Carcassonne and Narbonne will have their hearts tried.
Par le pays feront plus fort greués:	
Bourg & cité auront plus grand debat,	
Carcaf[2]. Narbonne auront coeur efprouuez.	

---

[1]*pifcature barque.* L. *pifcature*, to fish, and the barque of Saint Peter. The fish has been a common symbol of Christianity since the early centuries, and its significance has remained.

[2]*Carcaf.* simply an apocope of Carcassonne to fit the scansion.

This almost certainly refers to the Huguenot troubles in Provence, officially dated as starting in 1502. However, sporadic trouble had been breaking out long before that and Nostradamus would have been aware of it. Technically the wars broke out between Huguenots and Catholics before the succession to the French throne of Henri de Navarre. But since Nostradamus had seen the young boy, when aged ten, and declared him to be the future king of France, he would have been in little doubt. Carcassonne declared itself for the Catholic League, but the Huguenots seized part of the town, and Narbonne also suffered a great deal from the fighting. Henri IV was a Huguenot but on taking Paris became a Catholic with the cynical statement, "Paris is worth a Mass."

Century I

I.VI

L'oeil de Rauenne ſera deſtitué,
Quand à ſes pieds les aelles
*   failliront:*
Les deux de Breſſe auront
*   conſtitué,*
Turin, Derſeil que Gaulois
*   fouleront.*

The eye of Ravenna will be desti-tute, when his wings will fall at his feet. The two of Bresse will have made a constitution for Turin and Vercelli, which the French will trample (underfoot).

The clues to this quatrain are in the place names: Ravenna has been part of the Papal States since 1509 and Bresse, 1601, Turin, 1640 and Vecelli, 1904, were all occupied by the French. All that is certain is that all these States, except for Varenne, were occupied after the death of Nostradamus.

Century I

I.VII

Tard arriué l'execution faicte,
Le vent contraire lettres au
*   chemin prinſes:*
Les coniurez xiiii d'vne ſecte:
Par le Rouſſeau ſenez les
*   entreprinſes.*

Arrived too late, the act has been done. The wind was against them, letters intercepted on the way. The party of conspirators numbered fourteen. By Rous-seau will these enterprises be undertaken.

The minister who was called upon to review the case of Alfred Dreyfus in 1899 was a Monsieur Waldeck-Rousseau. It is on this name that I base my interpretation. Dreyfus, a Jewish man and French soldier, was condemned for the treasonable act of selling military secrets (*lettres*) to the Germans in 1894. He was publicly degraded and transported to a penal colony, l'Ile du Diable, in 1895. But in 1899 he was brought back for a retrial. Due to the strong anti-Semitic bias of the period he was again found guilty, but with extenuating circumstances. Ten days later he was publicly pardoned by President Loubet and a further investigation of the case was ordered. The letters were declared to be forgeries and Dreyfus to be innocent. The case troubled the French social conscience for some years.

There was much debate as to where to put up a statue in his honor. It has been decided to place it in the Tuileries. The original plan was to place it on the playground of the Ecole Militaire, where Dreyfus was degraded before being sent to l'Ile du Diable. This was refused by the Socialist former French minister Charles Hernu, who did not think it was "suitable that the military college should be constantly reminded of the injustice."

Nostradamus describes the proof of Dreyfus' innocence as arriving too late, because his sentence had been passed and he had been sent to l'Ile du Diable. The *vent contraire* is the anti-Dreyfus element of public opinion. Monsieur Waldeck-Rousseau, who sentenced Dreyfus the second time, was a known anti-Semite. This sentence was overturned by a public pardon. The number of conspirators may well have been fourteen—this subject has never been cleared up.

Century I

I.VIII

Combien de fois prinſe cité ſolaire	How often will you be captured, O city of the sun?
Seras changeant les loys barbares & vaines:	You will change laws that are barbaric and strange:
Ton mal s'approche. Plus ſera tributaire,	Bad times approach you. No longer will you be enslaved.
La grand Hadrie recourira tes veines.	The great Hadrie will revive your veins.

Paris has often been known as the City of the Sun, after
Louis XIV, the Sun King. This quatrain possibly refers to the
siege in 1590 by Henri IV of Navarre (Hadrie) who stormed
Paris for six months (from April to September) before the city
capitulated. The barbarous and strange laws then refer to the
innovations of the *Seize*, the first truly revolutionary parlia-
mentary faction to govern Paris. The siege occurred less than
twenty years after Nostradamus' death, *ton mal s'approche*. The
last line could mean that there is a new bloodline (Navarre) on
the French Valois throne, and it could also refer to the fact
that during the siege Henri allowed food to be passed through
the lines to the starving people of Paris.

Century I

I.IX

De L'Orient viendra le coeur
  Punique
Faſcher Hadrie & les hoirs[1]
  Romulides
Accompagné de la claſſe[2] Libyque
Temples Mellites & proches iſles
  vuides.

*From the Orient will come the
African heart to trouble Hadrie
and the heirs of Romulus.
Accompanied by the Libyan fleet
the temples of Malta and nearby
islands shall be deserted.*

I think this is a dual quatrain, the first two lines referring to
Henri IV and the Duke of Parma, the second two to the siege
of Malta in 1565. If that is the case, Henri IV was troubled
from the East by the duke of Parma, who in 1590 compelled
Henri to raise his siege of Paris to confront the Spanish army
marching from Flanders. This annoyed the Pope, *les hoirs
Romulides*, who favored the Navarre claim and was hostile to
Spanish policy at this point. The siege of Malta took place in
1565, just before Nostradamus' death. The Libyan fleet would
represent the Turkish navy, then roaming the Mediterranean.

---

[1]*hoirs*. O.F. heirs. The heirs of Romulus are the Italians and, by
extension, the Vatican.
[2]*claſſe*. L. *classus*, a fleet. A word commonly used in Nostradamus'
Centuries.

Century I

I.X

Serpens¹ tranſmis dans la caige de fer,	*A shroud is put into the iron vault, where the seven children of the king are held. The ancestors and forefathers will come forth from the depths of hell, lamenting to see thus dead the fruit of their line.*
Où les enfans ſeptains² du Roy ſont pris:	
Les vieux & peres ſortiront bas de l'enfer,	
Ains mourir voir de fruic̨ mort & crys.	

This quatrain must refer to the fall of the House of Valois, and in particular to the removal in 1610 of the remains of the last Valois king, Henri III, to the family sepulcher at Saint Denis.

The seven children, referred to several times during the quatrains, are those of Henri II and Catherine de' Medicis, who, as is related earlier, was a great follower of Nostradamus. The prophet seems quite certain the Valois line will die out; he predicted it earlier when he saw the then ten-year-old Henri of Navarre as a page in the royal suite, but it must be said that Henri III was not the last to die. Marguerite de Navarre, the sixth Valois child, lived until 1615, but she had been discarded by the king for adultery and spent a good thirty years shut up in a convent. So perhaps Nostradamus felt that Henri III was the last Valois of any political importance.

---

¹*Serpens.* Gk. *serpos*, shroud.
²*enfans ſeptaines.* 1) François II, 1549–60; 2) Elisabeth, 1545–1568; 3) Claude, 1547–1575; 4) Charles IX, 1550–1574; 5) Henri III, 1551–1589; 6) Marguerite (de Navarre), 1552–1615; 7) François, duc d'Alençon, 1554–1584.

Century I

I.XI

Le mouument de ſens, coeur,
    pieds, & mains,
Seront d'accord Naples, Lyon,
    Sicille:
Glaiues, feux, eaux puis aux
    nobles Romains,
Plongez tuez mors par cerueau
    debile.

The movement of senses, heart, feet and hands will be in agreement between Naples, Lyon and Sicily. Swords, fire, floods; the noble Romans drowned, killed or dead, because of a degenerate brain.

The only comment I can make on this is that if one reads *Leon* for *Lyon*, these cities were part of the Spanish Hapsburg empire. This may be a prediction that was avoided. It seems to have no relevance to the present day.

Century I

I.XII

Dans peu dira faulce brute
    fragile,
De bas en hault eſleué
    promptement:
Puis en instant desloyale &
    labile,
Qui de Veronne aura
    gouuernement.

Soon they will talk of a treacherous man, quickly raised from low to high estate. Suddenly he will become disloyal and volatile, and will become the governing power in Verona.

Verona was governed by a podestà between 1405 and 1562, who was meant to be replaced yearly. It was the equivalent in rank to the office of captain. The last podestà was Jacobo Sansabastiani, 1539–62, but there is no proof he was ever a traitor.

Century I

I.XIII

Les exilez par ire, haine intestine,	Through anger and internal hatreds, the exiles will hatch a
Feront au Roy grand coniuration:	great conspiracy against the king. Secretly they will place ene-
Secret mettront ennemis par la mine,	mies to threaten him, and his own old party against them:
Et ses vieux siens contre eux sedition.	there will be sedition.

This quatrain describes the Conspiracy of Amboise, which occurred in 1560, during Nostradamus' lifetime. The power of the Guise family in France—Mary Stuart was the bride of François II for a year until his death, and her mother was a Guise—caused other parties, in particular the Montmorencys and the Bourbons, to conspire to kill the duc de Guise and to kidnap the king, François II. But the plot was leaked out in advance and suppressed.

Century I

I.XIIII

De gent esclaue chansons, chants & requestes,	From the enslaved populace come songs, chants and
Captifs par Princes & Seigneur[1] aux prisons:	demands, while Princes and the Ruler are captive in prison. In
A l'aduenir par idiotz sans testes,	the future they will be seen as headless, through idiots by holy
Seront reçeus par diuines oraisons.	prayers to heaven.

Most commentators believe this quatrain refers to the songs and demands of the French populace while Louis XVI was imprisoned with his family in the Temple. The headless idiots therefore become the early ringleaders of the terror. At first these people are regarded as inspired leaders; then all changes and they follow the aristocracy to the guillotine.

[1] *Seigneur.* Used in the singular may indicate King Louis XVI himself.

Century I

I.XV

*Mars nous menaſſe par la force
    bellique,
Septante foys fera le ſang
    eſpandre:
Auge[1] et ruyne de
    l'Eccleſiaſtique,
Et plus ceux qui d'eux rien
    voudront entendre.*

*Mars threatens us with warlike
strength and will cause blood to
be shed seventy times. Moreover,
the clergy will be both exalted
and reviled, even more by those
who wish to know nothing of
them.*

Serious commentators of the nineteenth century, such as
Nicollaud, take the first two lines as referring to Napoleon
(Mars) and the many wars of his Empire. The clergy suffered
much during this period. It was disbanded in 1792 and
religion had almost disappeared from France during the early
days of the Directoire (the government of the Revolutionaries). But by 1804, Napoleon had to recognize the Pope, and
therefore the clergy, to legitimize his coronation. General talk
of trouble facing the Catholic Church is a common theme
throughout the Centuries, and religious practice is certainly
on the decline almost everywhere. However, there is no use of
the key word "empire" which normally, but not always,
indicates Napoleon.

Could a possibility be modern Iran, where the clergy, led by
the Ayatollah Khomeini, are both at their height and decline,
and certainly not welcome in the West? They have now ended
their eight-year-long war with Iraq and, due to the intervention of the United Nations, initiated by the failing Iran, the
fighting has ceased.

---

[1]*Auge.* L. *augere,* to increase.

Century I

I.XVI

Faulx[1] à l'eftang[2] ioinct vers le Sagitaire,
En fon hault AUGE[3] de l'exaltation.
Pefte, famine, mort de main militaire,
Le fiecle approche de renouation.

A scythe joined with a pond in Sagittarius at its highest ascendant. Plague, famine, death from the military hand, the century approaches its renewal.

According to this quatrain when Saturn (scythe) and Aquarius (pond) are in the ascendant towards the end of a century, a great war should be expected, with the usual concomitants of disease and famine. This description is so general it could fit the twentieth century as well as any other. Nostradamus refers later in the Centuries to a possible war toward the end of our present century.

Century I

I.XVII

Par quarante ans l'Iris n'apparoiftra.
Par quarante ans tous les iours fera veu:
La terre aride en ficcité croiftra,
Et grans deluges quand fera aperceu.

For forty years the rainbow will not be seen. Then for forty years it will be seen every day. The dry earth will grow even more parched, and there will be great floods when it is seen.

A general quatrain of doom and gloom. Even in Africa there is no record of a forty-year drought followed by forty years of rain and flooding, nor has there been so anywhere else, to my knowledge.

---

[1] *Faulx*. O.F. scythe, the zodiac sign of Saturn.
[2] *l'eftang*. O.F. pond, a water sign designating Aquarius.
[3] *AUGE*. L. *augere*, to increase. No reason to be seen for capitals.

Century I

I.XVIII

Par la difcorde negligence
  Gauloife,
Sera paſſaige à Mahommet
  ouuert:
De ſang trempé la terre & mer
  Senoiſe,
Le port Phocen[1] de voilles &
  nefz couuert.
	Because of French discord and negligence, a passage will be opened to the Mohammedans. Both the land and sea of Sienna will be soaked in blood and the port of Marseilles covered with ships and sails.

One tentative opinion is that this quatrain relates to the chaos in France and its colonies in 1940, which allowed the Italian armies into North Africa. The blood spilled would refer to the various battles. The harbor of Marseilles was constantly operative during the war, although it was in German hands.

Century I

I.XIX

Lors que ſerpens viendront
  circuir l'are,[2]
Le ſang Troyen vexé par les
  Eſpaignes:
Par eulx grand nombre en ſera
  faicte tare.
Chef fruict,[3] caché aux mares[4]
  dans les ſaignes.[5]
	When the serpents will surround the altar, the Trojan blood is troubled by the Spanish. A great number will be decimated by them. The leader flees, hidden in the marshy swamps.

After the death of her husband Henri II, Catherine de' Medicis, Regent of France, changed her personal emblem to a serpent curled around a star, biting its tail. Nostradamus usually calls French royal blood Trojan, a derivation from the

[1] *Phocen.* Marseilles; founded by the people of Phocaea, its mother city is in west Asia Minor.
[2] *are.* L. *are*, altar.
[3] *fruict.* here equals L. *fuit*, fled.
[4] *mares.* O.F. swamp, marsh.
[5] *ſaignes.* O.F. swamp, marsh.

medieval legend that the French royal family were descended from Francus, a mythical son of Priam. French troubles with Spain did not really come to a head until the interregnum of 1589–94 and the later Wars of the Spanish Succession. The last line is unclear.

Century I

I.XX

Tours, Orleans, Blois, Angiers, Reims, & Nätes, *Cités vexées par subit changement:* *Par langues estranges feront tendues tentes,[1]* *Fleuues, dards Renes, terre & mer tremblement.*	*The cities of Tours, Orléans, Blois, Angers, Reims and Nantes are troubled by a sudden change. People of foreign tongues will pitch their tents. Rivers, darts at Rennes, the earth will quake by land and sea.*

Another fruitless quatrain. All the cities mentioned, except for Reims, are situated on the Loire and have suffered various foreign invasions, mainly the Prussian and Russian armies in 1815, the Prussians again in 1870 and 1940, and the Americans in 1917–1919 and 1944–1945. There has been no notable earthquake at Reims since publication in 1568.

Century I

I.XXI

Profonde argille blanche nourrit rochier, *Qui d'vn abisme istra[2] lacticineuse[3]:* *En vain troublez ne l'oseront toucher,* *Ignorans estre au fond terre argilleuse.*	*The depths of the rock contain white clay which will come out milk white from a cleft. People, needlessly troubled, will not dare to touch it, not realizing that the foundation of the earth is of clay.*

[1] *tentes*. L. *tentere*, to attack, i.e., a position taken by attackers.
[2] *istra*. O.F. *aller*, to go (*ira*).
[3] *lacticineuse*. L. *lac*, milk or *lacticineum*, milky food.

I have no explanation for this quatrain. Perhaps the language has alchemistic undertones?

Century I

I.XXII

Ce que viura & n'ayant aucun fens,
Viendra leſer à mort ſon artifice:
Auſtun, Chalon, Langres & les deux Sens,
La greſle & glace fera grand malefice.

A thing living without any senses will cause its own death through artifice. At Autun, Chalon, Langres and the two Sens there will be great damage through hail and ice.

Garencières gives a highly improbable solution to this quatrain. He states that in 1613 a petrified embryo was removed by an operation (*artifice*) from a woman named Colomba Chantry who lived in Sens. A woman in her sixties had been discovered seven years earlier in Italy carrying a petrified embryo. But these medical facts—which would be of interest to Nostradamus, who was a well-qualified doctor—do not seem to me to merit a quatrain. Also, a petrified embryo could not be called live (*viura*). So I can offer no explanation.

On the factual side, all the towns mentioned belonged to the Duchy of Burgundy. There is a second town of Sens near Louhans. The comments about the weather are equally imprecise.

Century I

I.XXIII

Au moys troiſieſme ſe leuant le Soleil,
Sanglier, Liepard, au champs Mars pour côbatre:
Liepard laiſſé, au ciel extend ſon oeil,
Vn Aigle autour du Soleil voit s'esbatre.

In the third month, at sunrise, the Boar and the Leopard meet on the battlefield. The fatigued Leopard looks heavenwards and sees an Eagle battling around the sun.

This is one of Nostradamus' more impressive quatrains, with some of the visual qualities we seldom get from his predictions. The background is the battle of Waterloo, June 18, 1815. Blücher, the Prussian boar (*Sanglier*), had been beaten back at Ligny. The British forces, with Wellington at their head, had not been able to make a coordinated stand with the Prussians at Waterloo.

The French troops battered the English (*Liepard*) from sunrise to evening. Wellington waited for his ally Blücher to arrive and turn the French flank. Wellington's position faced south, so he would have seen the Imperial standards, the French eagle, flying against the sun. As the day drew to a close, the British were exhausted. Then a cloud of dust was seen. Napoleon thought it was Grouchy, but it was Blücher. The end had come.

The Imperial Eagle, symbol of Revolutionary France, is often used in the Centuries to describe Napoleon himself. On this occasion it applies both to the standards and the man. Napoleon used to call the English heraldic lion "the Leopard of England."

The battle took place in June, just over three months after Napoleon's return from Elba (*au moys troisiesme*). This cryptic comment may also contain references to Napoleon's reign of one hundred days, which ended with this battle. Equally, dating the year from the March solstice, as Nostradamus would have done by the then current Julian calendar, June would be the third month. This is Nostradamus at his most convoluted and is typical of his style.

Century I

I.XXIIII

A cité neufue penſif pour
  condemner,
L'oiſel de proye au ciel ſe vient
  offrir:
Apres victoire à captifs
  pardonner,
Cremone & Mâtoue grâs maulx
  aura ſouffert.

At the New City he thinks to condemn. The bird of prey offers itself to the heavens. After victory he pardons his captives. At Cremona and Mantua great hardships will be suffered.

This appears to continue the Napoleonic theme. During his campaigns in Italy, 1795–97, when Napoleon arrived at Villa Nova (*cité neufue*) he was uncertain what to do, having received no instructions from the Directoire. By June 1796, Napoleon had laid siege to Mantua, a city which, despite horrendous bombardments, held out until February, 1797. Napoleon is reputed to have treated his prisoners generously in their defeat, *à capitfs pardonner*. Since Cremona is situated near Mantua, it must have suffered from the French siege.

Peace with Mantua, however, was of short duration. In 1799 it was retaken by the Austrians, and although restored to the French in 1801 (as Lunéville), it once again reverted to the Austrians from 1814 to 1836. The whole of Lombardy suffered severe political persecution between 1849 and 1859, after the peace of Villafranca. Note again the bird of prey as a symbol of Napoleon.

Century I

I.XXV

Perdu trouué, caché de ſi long ſiecle,	*The lost thing is discovered, hidden for long centuries. Pasteur*
Sera Paſteur demy Dieu honoré:	*will be celebrated almost as a*
Ains que la Lune acheue ſon grand ſiecle,	*god. This is when the moon completes her great cycle, but he will*
Par autres vents sera deshonoré.	*be dishonoured by other rumors.*

This quatrain contains not only a proper name, Pasteur, but also a specific dating, towards the end of the cycle of the moon, *acheue son grand ſiecle*. This cycle ran, in astrological terms, from 1535 to 1889.

Pasteur founded the Institut Pasteur on November 14, 1889. His discovery that germs polluted the atmosphere was vital to medical history and led to Lister's theory and practice of sterilization. The *Encyclopaedia Britannica* says that Pasteur, the *demy Dieu*, was the acknowledged head of the greatest chemical movement of the time. The reference to rumors that dishonored him may well refer to the violent opposition that his methods aroused among powerful members of the French Academy, particularly against the new practices of the Institut with vaccines, such as those against hydrophobia.

Century I

I.XXVI

*Le grand du fouldre tumbe[1]
d'heure diurne,
Mal & predict par porteur
poſtulaire:
Suiuant preſage tumbe d'heure
nocturne,
Conflit Reims, Londres, Etruſque
peſtifere.*

*The great man will be struck
down in daytime by a thunderbolt. An evil deed, foretold by a
bearer of a petition. According to
the prediction another is struck
at night. Conflict in Reims, London, pestilence in Tuscany.*

The first three lines of this quatrain could apply to the
assassinations of the two Kennedy brothers. John F. Kennedy
was struck down (*fouldre*) in broad daylight in Dallas, Texas,
November 22, 1963, by the presumed assassin Lee Harvey
Oswald. Linked with him is another killed at night, in fact early
dawn, Robert F. Kennedy, shot down on June 5, 1968, during
the celebrations for his presidential primary elections at an
hotel by Sirhan Sirhan. Line 2 may refer to the fact that both
men received death threats and warnings during their terms
of office. Then, presumably, line 4 refers to the world
repercussions to the assassinations.

Century I

I.XXVII

*Deſſouz de chaine[2] Guien du ciel
frappé,
Non loing de la eſt caché le
treſor:
Qui par longs ſiecles auoit eſté
grappé,
Trouué mourra, l'oeil creué de
reſſort.*

*Beneath the oak tree of Guienne,
struck by lightning, not far from
there is the treasure hidden. That
which for long centuries had
been kept, when found, he will
die, his eye pierced by a spring.*

---

[1]*tumbe*. O.F. *tumber*, to fall.
[2]*chaine*. O.F. *chene*, oak tree, but could possibly mean *chaine*, chain
of mountains, etc.

This is one of several puzzling quatrains linking the finding of a tomb, a man dead for many centuries, and a treasure (see quatrain IX.VII for another example). None of these quatrains, unfortunately, make much sense. Guienne was an ancient province of southwest France, therefore this quatrain does not refer to the violation of Nostradamus' tomb, which took place during the Revolution, after which his remains were transferred to a side chapel of Nôtre Dame in the Church of Saint Laurent at Salon. Alternatively, *Guien* could stand for *gui*, meaning mistletoe, but that meaning gets one no further in deciphering the quatrain.

Century I

I.XXVIII

La tour de Boucq craindra fuſte[1] Barbare, Vn temps, long temps apres barque heſperique: Beſtail, gês, meubles tous deux feront grant tare[2] Taurus & Libra quelle morelle pique?[3]	Tobruk will fear the barbarian fleet for a long time, then much later the western fleet. Cattle, people, possessions for both will be quite lost. What a great struggle in Taurus and Libra.

If one accepts *tour de Boucq* as Nostradamus' version of Tobruk, then the quatrain is placed definitely in North Africa. The first line would apply to Tobruk's checkered history as a trading port between the Greeks and Libyans, until, for strategic reasons, it fell under the interest of the Italians.

In modern times, Tobruk suffered invasion by the British in 1941 during the Second World War. The word "*heſperique*" in line 2 is ambiguous. It can mean either "western" or "Spanish," but in view of the word "fleet," I take the first meaning. The British Army was fighting the Italians in Tobruk in 1941, but the attack on Pearl Harbor occurred in December, the same month as Tobruk was liberated, so

---

[1] *fuſte*. low draught galley with both sails and oars.
[2] *tare*. O.F. loss
[3] ? presumably printer's error for full stop (period).

heſperique may well refer to the American (Western) fleet. Rommel reached Tobruk on April 8th (the time of Taurus) and besieged it until December, 1941, when it was relieved by British reinforcements. As Libra is October, not December, Nostradamus was two months off in his calculations, but that's not so bad over five centuries.

Century I

I.XXIX

Quand le poiſſon tereſtre &
  aquatique,
Par forte vague au grauier ſera
  mis:
Sa forme eſtrange ſuaue &
  horrifique,
Par mer aux murs bien toſt les
  ennemis.

When the fish that travels over land and sea is cast up on the shore by a great wave; its shape foreign, smooth and frightful. From the sea the enemies soon reach the walls.

This quatrain could possibly describe a missile fired from a submerged submarine, which causes a great upheaval of the water. Equally well it may describe the American equivalent, SUBROC which, although fired under water, flies through the air to its target.

Century I

I.XXX

La nef eſtrange par le tourment
  marin,
Abourdera pres de port
  incongneu:
Nonobſtant ſignes de rameau
  palmerin,[1]
Apres mort pille bon auis tard
  venu.

Because of the storm at sea the foreign ship will approach an unknown port. Notwithstanding the signs of the palm branches, afterwards, death and pillage. The good advice comes too late.

---

[1]*palmerin.* L. *palmarins,* of a palm tree.

An unspecific quatrain. The *rameau palmerin*, palm branches, usually indicate peaceful intent, which seems in this case to be trickery on the part of the inhabitants of unknown harbor.

Century I

I.XXXI

Tant d'ans les guerres en Gaule dureront, *Oultre la courſe du Caſtulon[1] monarque:* *Victoire incerte trois grands couronneront,* *Aigle, coq, lune, lyon, ſoleil en marque.*	The wars in France will last for so many years beyond the reign of the Castulon kings. An uncertain victory will crown the great ones, the Eagle, Cock, Lion, Sun in its house.

Despite many ingenious interpretations of this quatrain concerning the French Revolution, it seems to be dated by means of a great war in France after the downfall of the Spanish monarchy, and therefore from the founding of the Spanish Republic in 1923. This leads us to the period of the Second World War, 1939–45, from which Spain remained officially detached, neutral, and during which time there were *guerres en Gaule*. The uncertain victory was won by the USA (Eagle), France (Cock), and Britain (Lion). The final capitulation of the Japanese (Sun) was to herald the end of the war. Also the Japanese surrendered on August 12, during the period of a sun sign. The double meaning is typical of Nostradamus.

The sheer immensity of all these ideas by a medieval mind is astonishing. Spain was one of Europe's greatest contemporary monarchies, but Nostradamus envisages a war on a global scale!

---

[1]Caſtulon: an old Iberian city, standing for Spain.

Century I

I.XXXII

Le grand empire sera tost
translaté
En lieu petit qui bien tost
viendra croistre:
Lieu bien infime d'exigue comté,
Ou au milieu viendra poser son
sceptre.

The great empire will soon be exchanged for a small place, which will soon begin to grow. A very small place of tiny area in the middle of which he will come to lay down his scepter.

The key word in this quatrain is "empire"; Nostradamus practically never calls France a kingdom after the Revolution. The great Empire of the Imperial Napoleon soon dwindles to the island of Elba. It begins to grow again on Napoleon's escape, but only for the Hundred Days. Then he is sent to an even smaller place, St. Helena, where he finally relinquishes all claim to power, putting down his scepter for good.

Century I

I.XXXIII

Prés d'vn grand pont de plaine
spatieuse,
Le grand lyon par forces
Cesarées:
Fera abbattre hors cité
rigoureuse,
Par effroy portes luy seront
reserées.

Near a great bridge a spacious plain. The great lion with the Imperial forces will cause ruin outside the austere city. For fear the gates will be reinforced against him.

If one takes the "austere city" to be Geneva, home to the rigorous doctrine of Calvinism, then the plain may be Lombardy and the Lion an imperial troop. The bridge is probably a mountain pass.

But if Nostradamus hoped for the fall of Geneva through the pressures of the Holy Roman Empire he was completely wrong. It is necessary to remember Nostradamus' strong anti-Protestant feelings, which sometimes surface almost in spite of himself. He may well have seen and comprehended this quatrain quite wrongly. See, however, I.XLV.

Century I

I.XXXIIII

L'oy*feau de proye volant à la fene*ftre,[1] Auant conflict faict aux François pareure:[2] L'vn bon prendra l'vn ambigue finistre, La partie foyole tiendra par bon augure.	*The bird of prey flying to the left makes preparations before joining with the French. Some will regard him as good, others bad or wrong. The weaker party will regard him as a good omen.*

Although Nostradamus often applies the bird of prey to Napoleon, here Hitler seems more appropriate. The "left" would have meant little to Nostradamus other than in a geographical sense, that is the low countries. Hitler invaded France through Holland and Belgium, having made his preparations, *pareure*, well in advance. Corruption and uncertainty among French (and other) politicians follows in the early days of the war, finding its culmination in the Pétainists who colluded with Hitler, and the Vichy cabinet (*partie foyole*).

Century I

I.XXXV

Le lyon ieune le vieux furmontera, En champ bellique par fingulier duelle: Dans caige d'or les yeux luy creuera, Deux cla*ffes[3] vne, puis mourir, mort cruelle.	*The young lion will overcome the old, in a field of combat in a single fight. He will pierce his eyes in a golden cage, two wounds in one, he then dies a cruel death.*

This is the quatrain that made Nostradamus' reputation in contemporary France. Although the Centuries had not yet

---

[1] *fene*ftre. L., *sinistre*, left, F. *sinister*.
[2] *pareure*. O.F. preparation.
[3] *cla*ffes. Gk. *klasis*, a fracture. The Latin *classus*, fleets, makes no sense here, since there was no union of fleets anywhere in the world at this time.

been published at the time of its fulfillment, it was known and understood by the queen, Catherine de' Medicis and referred to in letters by several important foreign diplomats. Presumably, therefore, Nostradamus circulated the first part of his still-unpublished book in handwritten or pamphlet form. In 1555 he published the first 353 quatrains of the Centuries.

The queen was greatly perturbed by this quatrain, which she understood to predict the death of her husband in a duel. It so troubled her that in July, 1556, she sent for Nostradamus to come to Paris and explain the prediction to her. Nostradamus was not the only person to predict this event. The Italian astrologer Luc Gauric had warned Henri that both the beginning and the end of his reign would be marked by duels.

The first duel took place soon after his accession—an extraordinary event when one realizes that under French court etiquette, the king could not technically be challenged to a duel. But Henri, who had little time for prophets, took no notice of this early warning.

The second duel was fought in 1559, on the occasion of the marriage of his daughter Elisabeth to old King Philip of Spain—the same one who had married Mary Tudor of England so long before—and that of his sister Marguerite to the duc de Savoie. The latter couple would visit Nostradamus several times in his house at Salon. During the festivities, which lasted three days, the king joined in the jousting at St. Antoine. He was victorious for the first two days but on the third he insisted on riding against the Captain of his Scottish guard, Montgomery.

The reference to *lyon* is interesting in that both the king and Montgomery had a lion in their coat of arms. In the first bout, Henri failed to unseat his opponent; it was only on the third bout that they splintered lances successfully. But Montgomery's lance pierced the king's gilt helmet and entered his face and brain just above the eye. Some report he received a second wound in the throat, which turned into a severe ulcer before he died in agony ten days later.

Century I

I.XXXVI

Tard le monarque ſe viendra repentir,	Too late the king will repent that he has not put his adversary to death. But he will soon come to agree to far greater things which will cause the death of all his line.
De n'auoir mis à mort ſon aduerſaire:	
Mais viendra bien à plus hault confentir,	
Que tout ſon ſang par mort fera deffaire.	

This is another of Nostradamus' famous double quatrains. It can equally possibly refer to the death of the Guise brothers in 1588 through the influence of Henri III, or possibly to Louis XVI.

Henri III caused both the duc de Guise and his brother to be murdered at Blois on Christmas Day, 1558, in an effort to quash the increasing influence of the Guise family in French politics. However, he did not kill the real ringleader, the duc de Mayenne, and he was forced to take further action to eliminate their powers, *à plus hault confentir.*

Other commentators interpret this quatrain as describing Louis XVI and his brother and adversary, the duc d'Orléans. It is certain that Orléans intrigued against the king, was a sworn enemy of the queen, Marie Antoinette, and even debated joining up the revolutionaries at one point. If one accepts this interpretation, then line 3 refers to the constitutional monarchy that Louis was forced to accept, and to the later imprisonment of himself and his family which led to their deaths by the guillotine. But Orléans did not die (*tout son sang*), he returned to France in 1814 as Louis XVIII, so I regard this as a less satisfactory interpretation.

Century I

I.XXXVII

Vn peu deuant que le soleil s'esconse,
Conflict donné grand peuple dubiteux:
Profligés, port marin ne faict responce,
Pont & sepulchre en deux estranges lieux.

Shortly before the sun sets battle is engaged, a great nation uncertain. Overcome, the port does not reply, both bridge and grave in foreign places.

I cannot make any sense of this quatrain except that its subject is probably a sea battle. *Pont* in line 4 often stands for Pope (*Pontifex*) in Nostradamus' writings. There might then be a tenuous link with Pius V, who died at Valence in 1799, captured by the French. His death occurred in August, so the first line might refer to the summer. The French people were certainly *dubiteux* in 1799, as the Directoire had suffered defeats in both Italy and Germany and the success of Napoleon's Egyptian campaign was not yet assured. Line 3 cannot refer to the English fleet, who were scouring the seas for Napoleon, not resting in port.

Century I

I.XXXVIII

Le Sol & l'aigle au victeur paroistront,
Responce vaine au vaincu l'on asseure:
Par cor ne crys harnois n'arresteront,
Vindicte paix par mors si acheue à l'heure.

The sun and the eagle will appear to the victor. An empty answer is given to the defeated. Neither bugle nor shouts will stop the soldiers. Peace will be vindicated by death, if achieved in time.

This quatrain probably followed upon I.XXIII in Nostradamus' original writings, before he deliberately confused the order of the verses. It continues the description of the Battle of Waterloo—the Imperial Eagle, Napoleon, coming out of the mist to attack Wellington. Both generals were aware that it was

a fight to the finish, but for Napoleon it was even more
desperate, as it was his final stand after the frantic Hundred
Days. No reasonable terms awaited if he lost (*responce vaine*)
nothing but permanent exile on St. Helena. Once the men
engaged in battle they could not be stopped, *par cor ne crys
harnois n'arresteront*. Napoleon's Grenadiers fought until the last
man dropped, refusing to retreat. Nostradamus saw that
liberty and peace would return eventually to Europe, but only
through Napoleon's end, whether political or through his
death.

Century I

I.XXXIX

*De nuict dans lict le suprefme
    eftrangle,
Pour trop auoir feiourné, blond
    efleu:
Par troys l'empire fubroge
    exancle,[1]
A mort mettra carte, et pacquet
    ne leu.*

*At night the final (claimant?)
will be strangled in his bed
because he became too involved
with the blond heir-elect. The
Empire is enslaved by three and
substituted. Dead, neither letter
or packet are read.*

The last of the Condé line, supporter of the Royalist claim,
was found dead in his bedroom, but he had been hanged, not
strangled. But both of these methods of death involve
squeezing by the throat. Perhaps the duc was hanged after his
death to cover the signs of strangulation? It has been
suggested that he was murdered because he supported the
cause of the duc de Bordeaux, the comte de Clambord, whom
Nostradamus rightly describes as *efleu*, as he was the grandson
of Charles X and the legitimate heir to the French throne.

As to the three who usurped power, there are two possible
explanations: the three are either the régimes which followed
Charles X; Louis Philippe, who became king in 1830, the
Republic, and then the Buonapartes; or more specifically, the
three who intrigued against the Condé family—Charles X, the
duc d'Angoulême and the duc de Bourgogne. According to
the nineteenth century commentator Le Pelletier, Condé was

[1]*exancle*. L. *exancilatus*, enslaved.

fair-haired and had written a will (*carte et paquet*) in favour of Bordeaux. This was said to have been destroyed and replaced by an earlier will in favor of the duc d'Aumale, son of Louis Philippe.

Century I

I.XL

La trombe fauſſe diſsimulant folie,
Fera Biſance vn changement de
  loix:
Hyſtra d'Egypte qui veut que
  l'on deſlie,
Edict changeant monnoyes &
  aloys.[1]
	The false trumpet pretending madness will cause Byzantium to change its laws. From Egypt will come forth a person who wants the edict withdrawn, changing money and values.

This is another difficult quatrain. It seems to refer to a political situation between the Ottoman Empire (*Biſance*) and Egypt. The debasement of coinage was an old practice of various Christian monarchies, and may have been copied by Byzantium. But Egypt only revolted under Napoleon, so this may therefore refer to the new values established in France under the Directoire.

Century I

I.XLI

Siege en cité eſt de nuict aſſaillie,
Peu eſchapé: non loin de mer
  conflict:
Femme de ioye, retours fils
  defaillie,
Poiſon & lettres cachees dans le
  plic.
	The besieged city is assaulted by night, few escape; a battle not far from the sea. A prostitute faints with joy at the return of her son, poison in the fold of the hidden letters.

Some commentators believe this quatrain refers to the French invasion of Italy, 1556–57, others to Dunkirk, 1940,

---

[1] *aloys. alloy*, a standard of metal.

when the French Revolution came to be regarded as a *prostitute*, and the poison would be the Nazi doctrines, *lettres dans le plic*. I find neither explanation at all convincing.

Century I

I.XLII

Le dix Kalende d'Auril de faict Gotique,	The tenth day of the April Calends, calculated in Gothic
Refufcité encor par gens malins:	fashion, is revived again by evil
Le feu eftainct affemblee diabolique,	people. The fire put out, the diabolic gathering seek the bones
Cherchant les os du d'Amant & Pfelin.	of Amant and Pselin.

A fascinating quatrain. Nostradamus seems clearly to understand the change in 1582 from the Julian calendar of his day to the Gregorian calendar, which is still used today. This, of course, leads to another complication. Most of his futuristic dates appear, because of affirming circumstances, to be by the modern calendar, but I feel there are other predictions in which he may be using the Julian, for confusion's sake. He was, after all, a past master where confusion is concerned.

The tenth day of the Kalends of April is the 10th, as the Kalends were the first day of the Roman month. When the Gregorian calendar was introduced, ten days were removed — much to the annoyance of most of the populace of Europe, who demanded their ten days back! Possibly here Nostradamus means the April 1, Gregorian-style, a Good Friday, which is regarded as the best day for magical evocations. Possibly Nostradamus is indicating that this was the first day on which he started writing the Centuries. (He is believed to have started them circa the end of March, 1554.)

It is believed that the last line should read "*Cherchant les os du Demon & Psellus*," but Nostradamus suppressed it, remembering his earlier troubles with the Catholic authorities. Psellus mentions that he used a bowl of water in order to predict, "which seems to bubble and a faint voice murmurs words which contain the revelation of future events."

Century I

I.XLIII

Auant qu'aduienne le changement d'empire,	Before the coming of the end of the empire a miraculous event will take place. A field moved, the pillar of porphyry put in place on the gnarled rock.
Il aduiendra vn cas bien merueilleux:	
Le champ mué, le pillier de porphire,	
Mis tranflaté fus le rocher noilleux.	

Line 1 probably places this quatrain before 1789. There are several other references to pillars of porphyry in the Centuries. I cannot decipher them.

Century I

I.XLIIII

En bref feront de retour facrifices,	Shortly sacrifices will be resumed, those opposed will be martyred. There will no longer be monks, abbots or novices. Honey will be far more expensive than wax.
Contreuenans feront mis à martire:	
Plus ne feront moines, abbez, ne nouices,	
Le miel fera beaucoup plus cher que cire.	

The worship of God was forbidden by the French Revolutionary government in 1793. The sacrifices in line 1 symbolize the restoration of paganism. The Cult of Reason was established in 1794 and this was followed by a Festival of the Supreme Being on June 8. The Constitution of 1790 had declared the dissolution of the clergy, *plus ne feront moines, abbez, ne nouices*, and of all ecclesiastical orders. Many who refused to embrace the new ideology were persecuted, *mis à martire*, and priests who refused to accept the Civil Constitution of the Clergy were expelled as citizens. The last line is interesting. It implies that under the new order, when fewer church candles will be needed, the price of wax will drop to less than that of honey. Guesswork perhaps, but astute all the same.

Century I

I.XLV

Secteur de *sectes* grand peine au
  delateur,
Bette en theatre, dreßé le ieu
  scenique,
Du faict antique ennobly
  l'inuenteur,
Par *sectes* monde confus &
  schismatique.

A founder of sects, much trouble
to the informer. A beast in the
theater prepares the scene and
plot. The author ennobled by acts
of older times: the world is confused by schismatic sects.

I think this is probably a tirade against the schisms and
heresies of the sixteenth century, rather than a prediction, and
probably directed against Calvinism. (See I.XXXIII.)

Century I

I.XLVI

Tout aupres d'Aux, de *Lestore*
  & Mirande,
Grand feu du ciel en trois
  nuicts tumbera:
Cause aduiendra bien *stupende*
  & mirande,
Bien peu apres la terre
  tremblera.

Very near Auch, Lectoure and
Mirande a great fire will fall
from the sky for three nights. The
cause will appear both stupefy-
ing and marvelous; shortly
afterwards there will be an
earthquake.

One of the many earthquake quatrains, but unfortunately
Nostradamus does not say where it will occur. He links it with
amazing events which will occur in Auch, Lectoure, and
Mirande, all towns in the Département of Gers in southwest
France. But the question remains for the reader—is the
earthquake linked to the five geographically or by a time
factor? We have no way of knowing.

Century I

I.XLVII

Du lac Leman[1] les fermons fafcheront,	The speeches at *Lac Leman* will become angry, the days will drag out into weeks, then months, then years; then everything will fail. The authorities will damn their useless powers.
Les iours feront reduicts par les fepmaines:	
Puis moys, puis an, puis tous deffailliront,	
Les magiftrats damneront leurs loix vaines.	

Lac Leman, Lake Geneva, was important as the situation of the League of Nations whose first assembly was held there on November 15, 1920. The quatrain describes vividly the years of fruitless argument and failure until its final disbandment after the war, in August 1947. One must admit it really ceased to be effective after early 1940. This is a clear achieved quatrain. There may also be a somewhat oblique reference to the League of Nations in V.LXXXV.

Century I

I.XLVIII

Vingt ans du regne de la Lune paffez,	When twenty years of the Moon's reign have passed, another will take up his rule for seven thousand years. When the Sun takes up his final cycle then will my prophecy and warnings be accomplished.
Sept mil ans autre tiendra fa monarchie:	
Quand le Soleil prendra fes iours laffez,	
Lors accomplit & mine ma prophetie.	

According to Nostradamus, and quite correctly as early printings show, his predictions, although not the complete version, will be published after twenty cycles of the Moon. According to Roussat this lasted from 1535 to 1889, and 1555,

---

[1] Lac Leman, in Switzerland, Lake Geneva.

twenty cycles after the moon, was the year of the publication of the first part. Nostradamus seems to envisage here that the world, and his predictions, will last for another seven thousand years. This contradicts many of his other predictions which seem to envisage world destruction at the time of the second millennium, A.D. 2000.

However, it is interesting that this quatrain gives the date of publication, although it can hardly be regarded as precognitive, as Nostradamus was alive when the first part was printed.

There was a commonly held view in the Middle Ages that the world would come to an end at the end of the seventh millennium. This theory originated from the Book of Enoch, which was general reading during the first and second centuries A.D., until it was removed from the Church Canon in A.D. 300.

Nostradamus also refers to seven thousand years in X.LXXIIII, but since it seems that no commentator can agree as to the date from which this calculation should begin, this dating remains somewhat abstruse.

Century I

I.XLIX

Beaucoup auant telles menees,
Ceux d'Orient par la vertu
*   lunaire:*
L'an mil sept cens feront
*   grands emmenees,*
Subiugant preſque le coing
*   Aquilonaire.*

Long before these events those in the East, influenced by the Moon, in the year 1700 will cause many to be carried off, and will almost subdue the Northern area.

Several astrologers (Roussat as well as Nostradamus) believed the years 1700–1702 would be the start of great upheavals, but it appears they were all wrong.

There were several invasions in the north, *Aquilonaire*, in 1700, but none of the import described in the quatrain. In February, 1700, August II invaded Livonia. Peter the Great of Russia took Azov and Kouban from the Turks. Charles XII occupied Iceland and Peter the Great then declared war upon Sweden. None of these events subdued (*subiugant*) northern Europe, so this quatrain must be regarded as hit and miss.

Century I

I.L

De l'aquatique triplicité naiſtra,
D'vn qui fera le ieudy pour ſa
  feſte:
Son bruit, loz, regne, ſa puiſſance
  croiſtra,
Par terre & mer aux Oriens
  tempeſte.

From the three water signs will
be born a man who will celebrate
Thursday as his feast day. His
renown, praise, rule and power
will grow by land and sea,
bringing trouble to the East.

All one can say of this quatrain is that it describes a person
with the signs of Aries, Cancer and Aquarius in his birth chart.
He is presumably not Christian or a follower of any of the
great religions of today, *jeudy pour sa feſte*. His power will
become so great it will bring wars to the East. This may be one
of the many quatrains referring obliquely to the third
Antichrist.

Century I

I.LI

Chef d'Aries, Iupiter & Saturne,
Dieu eternel quelles mutations?
Puis par long ſiecle ſon maling[1]
  temps retourne,
Gaule, & Italie quelles
  eſmotions?[2]

At the height of Aries, Jupiter
and Saturn, eternal God what
changes! Then after a long century the bad times will return;
great upheavals in France and
Italy.

The conjunction of Jupiter, Saturn and Aries took place on
December 13, 1702, during the War of the Spanish Succession
waged by Louis XIV. Presumably therefore, the bad times
which return after a century, give a take a few years, refer to
the French Revolution. By 1802, France was embroiled in the
Italian campaign and it was in January of that year that
Napoleon was declared President of the Italian Republic. The
next time this inauspicious conjunction will occur is December
2, 1995; possibly an indicator of the Third World War?

[1] *maling.* O.F. *malin*, evil.
[2] I think the question marks in lines 2 and 4 are simply printer's
errors.

Century I

I.LII

*Les deux malins de Scorpion
    conioinct,
Le grand feigneur meurtry
    dedans fa falle:
Pefte à l'Eglife par le nouueau
    Roy ioinct,
L'Europe baffe & Septentrionale.*

*Two evil influences are in con-
junction with Scorpio. The great
lord is murdered in his hall. A
newly anointed king persecutes
the Church, in lower Europe
and in the north.*

The two evil influences in Scorpio are Mars and Saturn;
unfortunately, this conjunction has occurred fourteen times
since 1555. A particular example occurred in 1807, when the
Sultan of Turkey, whose title was *seigneur*, was deposed,
although he was not murdered until the following year. The
newly anointed king who persecutes the Church is, of course,
Napoleon, who restored the Catholic hierarchy in France but
at the same time held Pope Pius VII prisoner. By this time
Napoleon had also defeated Austria and Prussia (*l'Europe basse*)
and Russia (*Septentrionale*).

Century I

I.LIII

*Las qu'on verra grand peuple
    tourmenté,
Et la Loy faincte en totale
    ruine:
Par autres loix toute la
    Chreftienté,
Quand d'or, d'argent trouue
    nouuelle mine.*

*Alas, we shall see a great nation
sorely troubled and the holy law
in utter ruin. All Christianity
taken over by other laws, when a
new source of gold and money is
discovered.*

I believe this quatrain refers to the discovery of oil,
particularly in the Middle East, where the laws of Islam
prevail, *autres loix tout la Chreftienité*. The great nation that is
tormented may well refer to Iran, subjected to the barbaric
laws of the Ayatollah Khomeini and his followers. Certainly,
oil is the twentieth century source, *nouuelle mine*, of immense
fortunes.

Century I

I.LIIII

Deux reuolts faicts du maling falcigere,[1]	*Two revolutions caused by the evil scythebearer marks a change*
De regne & ſiecles faict permutation:	*of reign and centuries. The*
Le mobil ſigne à ſon endroict ſi ingere,[2]	*mobile sign moves into its house,*
Aux deux egaux & d'inclination.	*equally favoring both sides.*

The evil scythe-bearer is Saturn, who caused a change of reign in two centuries. The first is the French Revolution and the second the Russian. An interesting double meaning here, when one considers communist Russia's insignia of the hammer and sickle.

The mobile sign is Libra, the Balance, which according to astrologers governs Austria as one of its countries. Nostradamus seems to feel that Libra's influence was not strong enough to tip the balance in favor of Austria, *aux deux egeaux*, and so the malign influence of Saturn is able to cause war in Austria too—the assassination of the Archduke Ferdinand at Sarajevo, with the consequent result of the First World War.

Century I

I.LV

Soubs l'oppoſite climat Babylonique,	*In the land opposite to Babylon*
Grande ſera de ſang effuſion:	*there will be a great shedding of blood. Both on land and sea and*
Que terre & mer, air, ciel ſera inique,	*in the air the heavens will seem unjust. Sects, famine, kingdoms,*
Sectes, faim, regnes, peſtes, confuſion.	*plagues, confusions.*

---

[1]*falcigere.* L. a compound word, *falcams geruns,* bearing a scythe.
[2]*ingere.* L. *ingerere (se),* to penetrate, enter. The *"ſi"* may be a misprint for *se.*

This is a totally obscure quatrain, the only point of interest being the use of the word *air* in line 3. As in further quatrains it will be seen that Nostradamus envisages that man will move in this dimension, both personally and with the use of rocket-type weapons, in the future.

Century I

I.LVI

Vous verrez tost & tard faire grand change,	Sooner or later you will see great changes made, dreadful horrors and vengeances. For as the moon is led by its angel, the heavens draw nearer to the Balance.
Horreurs extremes, & vindications;	
Que si la lune conduicte par son ange,	
Le ciel s'approche des inclinations.	

Another astrological quatrain promising disaster in Libra, either the sign itself or one of the countries under its aegis. If it means the domination of Libra in astrological terms, that ended in 1879 (See I.LIIII.)

Century I

I.LVII

Par grand discord la trombe tremblera	The trumpet will shake with great discord. An agreement broken, lifting the face to heaven. The bloody mouth will swim with blood; the face anointed with milk and honey lies on the ground.
Accord rompu dressant la teste au ciel:	
Bouche sanglante dans le sang nagera,	
Au sol la face ointe de laict & miel.	

In 1793, amidst the horrors of the French Revolution, Louis XVI accepted the new decrees of the National Assembly which negated his position as absolute monarch, *accord rompu.* As Louis went to his execution on the tumbril he is recorded as reciting the Third Psalm, which he had sung at his coronation, *exultus caput meum*, "*dreſſant la teſte*." When a victim is guillotined blood rushes out of his mouth, *bouche sanglante*. One of Nostradamus' grisly details: the head of Louis, anointed with milk and honey at his Coronation, *ointe de laict & miel*, lay on the ground after his execution before being placed in a basket. A tragic yet successful quatrain.

Century I

I.LVIII

Tranché le ventre, naiſtra auec deux teſtes, *Et quatre bras: quelques ans entiers viura:* *Iour qui Alquiloye[1] celebrera ſes feſtes,* *Foſſen, Turin, chef Ferrare ſuyura.*	Through a slit in the belly a creature will be born with two heads and four arms. It will survive for some years. The day that Aquiloye celebrates its holidays, Fossana, Turin and the ruler of Ferra will follow.

This is an involved political quatrain dealing with both Napoleon and the Bourbon family, but in which Nostradamus has reversed the time sequence.

One could possibly refer to the first line literally, as a Cesarian section. But elsewhere Nostradamus uses the word *tranche* quite specifically to mean the blow of the guillotine. Therefore, if Louis XVI, the guillotined, is the belly, *ventre*, from him came forth two heirs, Louis XVIII and Charles X, *deux teſtes*. The four arms may then be understood as the dukes of Angoulême, Normandy, Berry and Bordeaux. The family was deposed by *Aquiloye*—the rule of the Eagle, Napoleon. The ruler of Farrare (Fossana) was the Pope, who "followed" Napoleon back to France as a prisoner. Alternatively, one may interpret Fossana and Turin as standing metaphorically for the rest of Italy, captured by the French.

[1] *Aquiloye*. L. *Aquila lex*, the rule of the Eagle.

Century I

I.LIX

Les exilez deportez dans les iſles,
Au changement d'vn plus cruel
    monarque
Seront meurtris: & mis deux les
    ſcintiles,[1]
Qui de parler ne feront eſtez
    parques.[2]

The exiles deported to the
islands, at the advent of an even
crueller king will be murdered.
Two will be burned to death,
who were not sparing in their
speech.

Nicollaud ascribes this quatrain to the events of the Coup
d'Etat of 1857, when many members of French secret societies
were deported to the Cayenne Islands. The even more cruel
king was Napoleon III, who imprisoned and deported people
who spoke against his régime, *ne feront eftez parques.*

The lines fit this reading, but I am not wholly convinced.
Some commentators, like Henry C. Roberts, believe this refers
to the cremation of the Jews, but if he can believe that a man
of Jewish blood, as Nostradamus was, could reduce six million
deaths to two, *mis deux les ſcintilles,* he is completely mistaken to
say the least.

Century I

I.LX

Vn Empereur naiſtra pres
    d'Italie,
Qui à l'Empire ſera vendu bien
    cher:
Diront auec quels gens il ſe
    ralie,
Qu'on trouuera moins prince
    que boucher.

An Emperor will be born near
Italy who will cost the Empire
very dear. When they see the people who ally with him they will
say he is less a prince than a
butcher.

Another Emperor quatrain. Napoleon was born in Corsica,
near Italy. He cost his Empire dearly in both manpower and
strength. The last two lines may refer either to the Créole

---

[1]*ſcintiles.* L. *scintilla*, sparks, flames.
[2]*parques.* L. *parcus*, sparing, economic.

blood of his wife, the Empress Josephine, or to the fact that his non-royal brothers were made kings of Naples, Spain, Holland and Westphalia. The butchery of line 4 must refer to the enormous number of troops killed in the Napoleonic campaigns. A good quatrain.

Century I

I.LXI

La republique miſerable infelice,[1]
Sera vaſtee[2] du nouueau
   magiſtrat:
Leur grand amas de l'exil
   malefice,
Fera Sueue[3] rauir leur grand
   contract.

The wretched, unfortunate republic will again be ruined by a new authority. The great amount of ill will accumulated in exile will make the Swiss break their important agreement.

The republic, created by Napoleon, will be in trouble again with the German Swiss. This may apply to the French Prince-President Napoléon III, 1852–70. If the German Swiss are the Prussians, this may refer to the Franco-Prussian war of 1870. However, I feel this is a poor interpretation.

Century I

I.LXII

La grande perte las que feront
   les lettres,
Auant le cicle de Latona
   parfaict:
Feu, grand deluge plus par
   ignares ſceptres,
Que de long ſiecle ne ſe verra
   refaict.

Alas! what a great loss there will be to learning before the cycle of the moon is completed. By fire, great floods, ignorant rulers; how long the century until it is seen to be restored.

Scholarship is seen to be suffering a great loss before the end of the Moon's cycle (in 1889). This quatrain appears to be

[1]infelice. L. infelix, unhappy.
[2]vaſtee. L. vastus, ruined, devastated.
[3]Sueue. L. Suevi, German Swiss tribe.

open to two possible interpretations. One, that a piece of scholarship is lost through a series of disasters, *Feu, grand deluge*. The alternative is that true scholarship becomes vulgarized by lower standards and general availability to the public. Like all scholars of his day—and one must remember, even without taking into account the Centuries, Nostradamus was definitely a scholar—he regarded himself as a member of the intellectual elite.

Century I

I.LXIII   ★

Les fleurs[1] paſſés diminue le monde,	Pestilences passed, the world becomes smaller, for a long time lands will be inhabited peacefully. People will cross through the skies, safely, over land and seas; then wars will start up again.
Long temps la paix terres inhabitées:	
Seur marchera par ciel, terre mer, & onde:	
Puis de nouueau les guerres ſuſcitées.	

The most remarkable thing about this quatrain is that Nostradamus predicts the world will become a smaller place, *diminue le monde*. This must refer especially to the air travel mentioned in line three, as well as to the then-known methods of travel over land and sea.

As to the placing of the age of pestilence (*fleurs*), there is no indication as to when this, war or pestilence, will pass—but after the two great wars of this century followed by a time of peace, he envisages that wars, note the plural, will start up again. Certainly, from 1945 until the present there has been no global war, but Korea, Algeria, Cambodia, Vietnam, Afghanistan, Pakistan, Iran and Iraq have been or are still at war. But since Nostradamus always considers France above all, the *paix terres inhabitées* should certainly be included in this line, possibly its influence in the Middle East and Africa?

There are several other vague and not so vague references to this state of affairs in the Centuries. The last line may simply

---

[1] *fleurs.* misprint for *fleaux,* scourge, pestilence.

apply to a Third World War but the plural *guerres* makes it unlikely.

Century I

I.LXIIII

De nuict foleil penferont auoir veu,	At night they will think they have seen the sun, when they see the
Quand le pourceau demy homme on verra:	half pig man. Noise, screams, battle fought in the skies. The
Bruict, chant, bataille, au ciel battre aperceu:	dumb beasts will be heard to speak.
Et beftes brutes à parler lon orra.	

Despite the apparently nonsensical aspect of this quatrain on first sight, it is, to the modern eye, a vivid picture of an air battle. The sun appearing at night is a searchlight piercing the sky, or possibly the glare of exploding bombs. The piglike man, which no one to date has interpreted, seems a clear picture in silhouette of the pilot in an oxygen mask, helmet and goggles. The breathing apparatus would certainly look like a pig's snout to Nostradamus, gazing into the water on the tripod, trying to decipher what the picture meant.

This interpretation is supported by the noises that Nostradamus also hears: screams, and battles in the skies. He hears these creatures speaking to each other, *Et beftes brutes à parler lon orra*. The *beftes brutes* could of course be the sounds of the battling planes, or the whine of the bombs as they fall to earth and explode, or possibly even radio instructions. The word *aperceu*, seen, watched, indicates that the battle was also seen from the ground.

This quatrain is an excellent prediction that is both aural and visual. I think it is very successful, when one considers that Nostradamus is trying to describe something completely beyond his ken.

Century I

I.LXV

Enfant *ſans* mains iamais veu *ſi*
   grand foudre,
L'enfant royal au ieu d'oeſteuf
   bleſsé:
Au puy briſes[1] fulgures[2] allant
   mouldre,
Trois ſouz les chaines par le
   milieu trouſſés.

A child without hands, never so
great a thunderbolt seen, the
royal child wounded at a game
of tennis. At the well lightning
strikes, chaining together three
by the middle.

An unsuccessful quatrain. There have been several royal
children born with various defects, mostly mental, as for
example in the Hanover/Windsor line, but none with such a
specific deformity, which sounds something like a Thalido-
mide victim.

Century I

I.LXVI

Celuy qui lors portera les
   nouuelles,
Apres vn peu il viendra reſpirer
Viuiers, Tournon, Montferrant
   & Pradelles,
Greſle & tempeſtes les fera
   ſouſpirer.

He who then brings the news
after a short while will (stop) for
breath. Vivers, Tournon, Montferrant and Pradelles; hail and
storms will make them suffer.

I cannot decipher this quatrain. Viviers and Tournon are in
the Ardèche and Pradelles is across the border in east central
France. Montferrant was in the Puy-de-Dôme until it joined
Clermont (Clermont-Ferrand) in 1731. However, this gets me
nowhere.

---

[1]*briſes*. O.F. briser, to fracture, break.
[2]*fulgures*. L. *fulgur*, flash of lightning.

Century I

I.LXVII

La grand famine que ie fens
   approcher,
Souuent tourner, puis eftre
   vniuerfelle:
Si grande & longue qu'on
   viendra arracher,
Du bois racine, & l'enfant de
   mammelle.

The great famine that I sense
approaching will often appear
in different areas, then become
worldwide. It will be on such an
enormous scale and last such a
long time that roots will be grub-
bed from trees and children from
the breast.

Famine is now global and we are far more aware of it these
days than people would have been in Nostradamus' time.
However, he seems to see it traveling from one country to
another, *souuent tourner*. At the moment, many parts of Africa
are in a dreadful state, and the corn belt of America has been
reduced to about 30 percent of its normal production.

Considering that millions of tons of grain and other help
have been pouring into Africa over the past few years, it seems
tragic that the present state of that continent is worse than
before. This quatrain should be regarded as a warning.

Century I

I.LXVIII

O quel horrible & malheureux
   tourment,
Trois innocens qu'on viendra à
   liurer;
Poyfon fufpecte, mal gardé
   tradiment,[1]
Mis en horreur par bourreaux
   enyurez.

O to what a dreadful and
wretched torment three innocent
people will be delivered. Poison
suspected, badly guarded, betrayal. Delivered up to horror by
drunken executioners.

A quatrain too vague to be of use. One is tempted to place
it in the French Revolution when Louis XVI, Marie Antoinette
and their son, technically *innocens*, were delivered up to the

[1] *tradiment*. O.F. betrayal.

guard of the mob. The *poyſon ſuſpect* has no meaning here, but
they were certainly *mis en horreur* by drunken executioners,
and their son did not go to the guillotine. He was most
probably walled up in his own excrement until his early death.

Century I

I.LXIX

La grand montaigne ronde de
  ſept ſtades,[1]
Apres paix, guerre, faim,
  inondation:
Roulera loin abiſmant grans
  contrades,
Meſmes antiques, & grand
  fondation.

The great mountain will measure seven stadia around, after
peace, war, famine, flooding. It
will spread far drowning great
countries, even antiquities and
their mighty foundations.

This probably describes an enormous flood after a time of
peace, war, and famine. The flood will apparently inundate
many areas including antiquities which happened in Lyons at
the end of 1988. It could possibly arise as the result of an
earthquake, either on land or sea.

Century I

I.LXX

Pluie, faim, guerre en Perſe
  non ceſſée,
La foy trop grand trahira le
  monarque:
Par la finie en Gaule
  commencee,
Secret augure pour à vn eſtre
  parque.

Nonstop rain, famine and war
in Persia; too great a trust will
betray the monarch. The result,
started in France, will end there,
a secret treaty for someone to be
lenient.

The linking of the two place names, Persia and France,
makes it likely that this quatrain refers to the Ayatollah

[1] *ſtades*. L. *status*, a measure roughly a furlong in length; seven stadia
would be just under a mile in circumference.

Khomeini, who toppled the monarch, the Shah of Iran, because the Shah placed too much trust in him, or held him in too little suspicion.

The Ayatollah spent years of exile in Paris plotting the Shah's downfall. Since these events will also end in France, the secret treaty, *secret augure*, may well refer to France's methods in modern years of paying Iran with both large sums of money and arms for the release of their hostages. However, at the time of writing the Ayatollah was reported to be dying of terminal cancer, and so the last line may contain a reference to things to come.

Century I

I.LXXI

La tour marine trois fois prife & reprife, *Par Hefpagnols, Barbares, Ligurins:[1]* *Marfeille & Aix, Arles par ceux de Pife,* *Vaft,[2] feu, fer, pillé Auignon des Thurins.*	The marine tower will be captured and retaken three times by Spaniards, Barbarians and Ligurians. Marseilles, Aix and Arles by men of Pisa, devastation, fire, sword. Pillage at Avignon by the Turinese.

This is an irritating quatrain, which I cannot decipher despite the plethora of proper names. The keystone is probably the meaning of *la tour marine*, which could be related to the conflict between the Spaniards, French and Italians. Could it possibly refer to the Tour de Boucq in I.XXVIII?

[1]*Ligurins.* L. people of Liguria in Italy.
[2]*Vaft.* L. *vastus*, laid waste, devastated.

Century I

I.LXXII

Du tout Marſeille des habitans
  changee,
Courſe & pourſuitte iuſqu'au pres
  de Lyon,
Narbon. Tholoze par Bourdeaux
  outragee,
Tuez captifs preſque d'vn
  million.

The inhabitants of Marseilles
are completely changed, fleeing
and pursued as far as Lyons.
Narbonne and Toulouse are
angered by Bordeaux. The killed
and capitve amount to almost a
million.

The enormous number of dead must place this quatrain in
modern times *(Tuez captifs preſque d'vn million)*. For the last war,
the official casualty list for soldiers in France gives a total of
675,000 dead or wounded. Since this sum does not include
any Allies who fought beside the French, Nostradamus' total
may be nearer the mark.

Century I

I.LXXIII

France à cinq pars par neglect
  aſſaillie,[1]
Tunys, Argel eſmeuz par
  Perſiens:
Leon, Seuille, Barcelonne faillie
N'aura la claſſe par les
  Venitiens.

France will be accused of neglect
by her five partners. Tunis,
Algiers stirred up by the Persians. Leon, Seville and Barcelona having failed, they will not
have the fleet because of the
Venetians.

Towards the end of de Gaulle's presidency, France was
under pressure from her Common Market partners (at that
time, five of them) over various policies. This would agree in
time with the trouble in North Africa, *Tunys*, in 1969, when
Gadaffi's revolution toppled King Idris. The reference to
Persia is interesting. In Nostradamus' day, Persia was part of
the Ottoman Empire, part of which now belongs to the USSR.

[1] *aſſaillie.* F. *assaillir*, to assault. France has only once been attacked on
five sides—in 1813–14, and then it was by European allies, so this
cannot apply here.

Are the Soviets, by implication, involved in the Middle Eastern troubles? This is obviously the case, even though they are now withdrawing from Afghanistan.

Century I

I.LXXIIII

Apres feiourné vogueront en Epire,	After a rest they will travel to Epirus, great help coming from around Antioch. The dark curly-headed one (king?) will strive greatly for the Empire. The bronze (brazen) beard will be roasted on a spit.
Le grand fecours viendra vers Antioche:	
Le noir poil crefpe tendra fort à l'Empire,	
Barbe d'aerain fe rouftira en broche.	

Sometimes in the Centuries Nostradamus uses the anagram *noir* for king, *roi*. It seems impossible here to indicate whether he had a single meaning or both in mind. The dark-haired king recurs in other quatrains, as does the red-headed man. I am tempted by the explanation that it refers to the family of Algerian pirates called Barbarossa, but their plunderings were contemporary with Nostradamus, so that this quatrain, in this sense, is not predictive.

Century I

I.LXXV

Le tyran Sienne occupera Sauone,	The tyrant of Siena will occupy Savona, having won the fort he will restrain the marine fleet. Two armies under the standard of Ancona; the leader will look upon them with fear.
Le fort gaigné tiendra claffe marine:	
Les deux armees par la marque d'Anconne,	
Par effrayeur le chef s'en examine.	

Until April, 1535, roughly at the time of the publication of the first part of the predictions, of which this quatrain was one, Siena was a free town, and held out with French help against the Florentines. Otherwise, all that is of note is that Savona was a protectorate of the Genoese republic and Ancona part of the Papal States. It is impossible to get much information out of this quatrain.

Century I

I.LXXVI

*D'vn nom farouche tel proferé
    sera,
Que les trois seurs auront fato[1]
    le nom:
Puis grand peuple par langue
    & faict dira,
Plus que nul autre aura bruit
    & renom.*

This man will be called by a barbaric name that the three sisters will receive from destiny. He will speak then to a great people in words and deeds, more than any other he will have fame and renown.

This quatrain almost certainly refers to Napoleon, as Le Pelletier, another commentator, believed. This is due to the Greek derivation of his name *(nom farouche) NEAPOLLUON*, meaning destroyer. That his name was spelled this way, with the extra *e*, is evident from the inscription on the Column in the Place Vendôme: NEAPOLIO. IMP. AUG.

Napoleon was also barbaric in a more general sense, being the younger son of a Corsican family whose language and manners were not those of polite Parisian society. He was also renowned for his great speeches to his troops *(par langue dira)* before battle, a characteristic he shared with Hitler.

Century I

I.LXXVII

*Entre deux mers dressera
    promontoire,
Que puis mourra pars le mords
    du cheual:
Le sien Neptune pliera voille
    noire,
Par Calpre & classe aupres de
    Rocheual.*

Between two seas there stands a promontory; a man will die from the bite of a horse. Neptune unfurls a black sail for his man; the fleet is between Gibraltar, near Rocheval.

[1]*fato.* L. *fatum*, destiny.

This is a excellent quatrain describing the Battle of Trafalgar, October 21, 1805. Gibraltar is the promontory separating the two seas, the Atlantic and the Mediterranean. The French and English fleets fought the battle of Trafalgar between Gibraltar and Cape Roche *(Rocheual)*, Trafalgar itself being a point between two bays.

The Admiral of the French fleet, Admiral Villeneuve, was reputedly strangled by one of Napoleon's Mamelukes with the bridle of a horse, when at an inn in Rennes in 1806. He had returned to France after being captured by the English. When the English Admiral, Nelson, was mortally wounded, his ship raised a black sail on its return voyage to England.

Rocheual may just be Nostradamus' word for "*roche*," rock, which is the name often given to Gibraltar itself, The Rock.

Century I

I.LXXVIII

D'vn chef vieillard naiſtra ſens hebeté
Degenerant par ſauoir & par armes:
Le chef de France par ſa ſoeur redouté,
Champs diuiſez, concedez aux gendarmes.

To an old leader will be born an idiot heir, weak both in knowledge and in warfare. The head of France is feared by his sister, battlefields divided, conceded to the military.

Several commentators believe the weak leader is Marshal Pétain, who took over the government from Reynaud in 1940. If the sister stands for France itself, she had reason to fear the duplicity of her leaders and the horrors of the Second World War. However, I find this too general a quatrain to be satisfactory.

Century I

I.LXXIX

*Bazaz, Leſtore, Condon, Auſch,
  Agine,
Eſmeus par loix querelle &
  monopole:
Car[1] Bourd. Toulouze Bay[2].
  mettra en ruine.
Renouueller voulant leur
  tauropole.[3]*

From the sixth bright celestial

*Basas, Lectoure, Condom, Auch
and Agen are troubled by laws,
disputes and monopolies. Carcassonne, Bordeaux, Toulouse
and Bayonne will be ruined
when they wish to renew the
slaughter.*

All of these towns are in southwest France. The quatrain
may contain a reference to a trading dispute and the granting
of monopolies in the locality. But the massacre is unclear.

Century I

I.LXXX

*De la ſixieſme claire ſplendeur
  celeſte,
Viendra tonner ſi fort en la
  Bourgongne:
Puis naiſtra monſtre de
  treshideuſe beſte,
Mars, Auril, May, Iuin grand
  charpin[4] & rongne.*

*From the sixth bright celestial
planet, there will be great storms
in Burgundy. Then a monster
will be born of a very hideous
beast; in March, April, May and
June, great wounding and trouble.*

This general quatrain is believed by many commentators to
refer to spring, 1918. Saturn being the sixth planet, the
portents of war will occur during the period governed by him.
But why the great storms in Burgundy? There is no record of
anything outstanding occurring there during this time. The
monster born *de treshideuſe beſte* must presumably refer to the
war, but it is an exceptionally muddled quatrain, even for
Nostradamus.

[1]*Car*. F. because, or apocope of Carcassonne.
[2]*Bay*. F. apocope of Bayonne.
[3]*Tauropole*. L. *Taurobolium*, the sacrifice of a bull, metaphorically
massacre, slaughter.
[4]*charpin*. O.F. wound, or rags to dress wounds.

Century I

I.LXXXI

D'humain troupeau neuf feront mis à part,
De iugement & confeil feparez:
Leur fort fera diuifé en depart,
Kappa, Thita, Lambda, mors bannis efgarez.

Nine will be set apart from the human race, separated from judgment and advice. Their fate is to be divided as they depart. Kappa, Theta, Lambda dead, banished and scattered.

This quatrain certainly has no reference to the past that one can see. Leoni believes that it suggests pioneer astronauts. But the implication is that the expedition will be unsuccessful (*mors bannis efgarez*) and those hurt will have names beginning with the letters K, T (Th), and L, here produced as letters of the Greek alphabet.

Century I

I.LXXXII

Quand les colomnes de bois grande tremblee,
D'Aufter conduicte couuerte de rubriche:
Tant vuidera dehors grande affemblee:
Trembler Vienne & le Pays d'Auftriche.

When the columns of wood tremble greatly in the south wind, covered with blood, then such a great multitude pours forth that Vienna and the land of Austria will tremble.

It was in the autumn of 1918, when the leaves trembled in the wind, that Austria was overturned and the new revolutionary rule, *rubriche*, represents the autocratic reign of the Hapsburgs. The great assembly represents the World Powers, whose Triple Entente annoyed Austria. Austria's problems first arose in the south (*Aufter*), in Turkey and Balkan States. The last line speaks for itself.

Century I

I.LXXXIII

La gent eftrange diuifera butins,
Saturne en Mars fon regard
   furieux:
Horrible eftrange aux Tofquans
   & Latins,
Grecs qui feront à frapper
   curieux.

A foreign nation will divide the
spoils; Saturn in a dreadful
aspect with Mars. Terrible and
strange to the Tuscans and
Latins; Greeks who will wish to
strike.

The last two lines seem to place this quatrain in the midst
of the struggles with Mussolini's Italian forces who occupied
Greece in 1940. The booty *(butins)* taken by the Germans was
proverbial. It is still appearing sometimes in the various sale
rooms of the world, *diuifera*. Mars is the God of War with
Saturn, in a bad aspect, which indeed did turn out so for the
Italians who allied themselves to the losing Nazi side.

Century I

I.LXXXIIII

Lune obfcurcie aux profondes
   tenebres,
Son frere paffe de couleur
   ferrugine:[1]
Le grand caché long temps foubs
   les tenebres,
Tiedera fer dans la plaie fanguine.

The moon eclipsed in great
gloom, his brother becomes the
color of blood. The great one,
hidden for a long time in the
shadows, will hold a blade in the
bloody wound.

The comte d'Artois is the man in eclipse, for he was in exile
when his brother died bloodily *(paffe ferrugine)* on the guillotine.
D'Artois remained away for a long time before he returned to
France with his family, as Charles X.

The reference to blades and blood applies very neatly to his
son, the duc de Berry, who was attacked and fatally stabbed,
fer dans la plaie fanguine, at the Opéra on the night of February
13, 1820. As he died clutching the hilt of the knife he said, "I
am murdered, I am holding the hilt of the dagger." His

[1]*ferrugine*. L. *ferruginus*, blood colored.

attacker was Louvel, keeper of the royal greyhounds, a fanatic Republican, who actually accompanied Napoleon to Elba.

Century I

I.LXXXV

Par la reſponce de dame Roy troublé,	The king is troubled by the queen's reply. Ambassadors will fear for their lives. The greater of his brothers will doubly disguise his action. Because of the two, they will die of anger, hatred and envy.
Ambaſſadeurs meſpriſeront leur vie:	
Le grand ſes freres contrefera doublé,	
Par deux mourront ire, haine, enuie.	

The king who is troubled by the queen's reply is Henri III of France, because Catherine de' Medicis, the queen mother, was furious at Henri's action in killing not only the powerful duc de Guise but also his equally powerful brother, the Cardinal de Guise, on December 23, 1588.

Catherine quite rightly saw the political troubles these murders would bring in their wake. The ambassadors who fear for their lives are almost certainly the Estates General, whom the king assembled to meet him at Blois. They protested against the murders as strongly as they could.

The greater brother who survived was the duc de Mayenne, who at that time led the Catholic League, and became an important figure at the French court as Lieutenant General of France (*contrefera doublé*), although these words could also apply to the king himself.

Century I

I.LXXXVI

La grande royne quand ſe verra vaincue,	When the great queen sees that she is conquered, she will show an excess of masculine courage. Naked, on horseback she will cross the river pursued by the sword: she will be an outrage to her faith.
Fera excés de maſculin courage:	
Sus cheual, fleuue passera toute nue,	
Suite par fer: à foy fera outrage.	

Mary, Queen of Scots, is almost certainly the subject of this quatrain. In May, 1568, having been defeated for the second time by Murray, her half-brother, she escaped from her prison and fled to England to the hoped-for mercy of Elizabeth I, taking with her only the clothes she was wearing, *toute nue*. She fled on horseback, but crossed the border by ferry. Both Catherine and Protestants believed she had outraged her faith, *à foi fera outrage*, because of her affair and subsequent marriage to Bothwell.

Century I

I.LXXXVII

Ennofigee[1] feu du centre de terre,	*Earthshaking fire from the center of the earth will cause tremors*
Fera trembler au tour de cité neufue:	*around the New City. Two great immovable powers will war for a*
Deux grands rochiers long têps ferôt la guerre	*long time, then Arethusa will redden a new river.*
Puis Arethufe rougira nouueau fleuue.	

This quatrain talks of a "great explosion" near a new city, which normally in Nostradamus' writings refers to New York. But this particular verse seems to give a clear indication of a volcanic explosion. Lava forms red rivers, and pours from the earth's center.

I think therefore that we have here a possible description of the eruption at Mount St. Helens on May 12, 1980. Later Nostradamus links this eruption with a city at 45° parallel. The town of Newberg in Oregon is also on this standard. At the time of its explosion, Mount St. Helens literally became a hollow mountain. The volcano's ash-type debris could be seen as far away as New York. The destruction this explosion wrought upon miles of forests and farmland will take generations to renew. (See X.XLIX.)

---

[1]*Ennofigee.* Gk. *ennosigaeus*, earthshaking. A name often given to Neptune.

Century I

I.LXXXVIII

*Le diuin mal surprendra le
  grand prince,
Vn peu deuant aura femme
  espousee.
Son apuy & credit à vn coup
  viendra mince,
Conseil mourra pour la teste
  rasee.*

*Divine wrath overtakes the great
prince a short time before he will
marry. Both his supporters and
his credit will suddenly diminish.
Advised, he will die because of
the shaven heads.*

The key phrase here is *la teste rasee*. This was a common term for the Roundheads in England who wore their hair short, as opposed to the curled wigs of the Royalist following of Charles I of England. It appears several times in the *Prophéties*. Divine retribution overtook Charles I when he was sentenced by Parliament, but the real trouble arose originally around the time of his marriage in 1625 to Henrietta of France. On his wedding day Charles proclaimed an edict that the persecution of Catholics should cease. Parliament refused this and demanded instead subsidies for the war against Spain. This lead to his death, demanded by the Roundheads, in 1649. (See IX.XLIX.)

Century I

I.LXXXIX

*Tous ceux de Ilerde[1] seront dans
  la Moselle,
Mettant à mort tous ceux de
  Loire & Seine:
Le cours marin viendra pres
  d'haute velle,
Quant Hespagnols ouurira toute
  veine.*

*Everyone from Lerida will be in
the Moselle, killing all those
from the Loire and the Seine.
The sea route will come through
a high valley, when the Spanish
open up every way.*

This seems to be a general quatrain about the Peninsular War, 1808–1814, when Wellington pushed up through Spain and Portugal across the Pyrenees to Bordeaux. The killing of

[1] *Ilerde*. Lerida, a city in Spain.

the people in the Loire and further north towards Paris, *Seine*, does not occur until later. James Laver suggests that *haulte velle* may be Nostradamus' groping towards the unfamiliar name of Wellington.

Century I

I.XC

Bourdeaux, Poitiers au son de la campane, *A grand classe ira iusques à l'Angon:* *Contre Gauloys sera leur tramontane,* *Quand monstre hydeux naistra pres de Orgon.*	At the sound of the bell Bordeaux and Poitiers will go with a fast fleet as far as Langon. A great anger will surge up against the French, when an hideous monster is born near Orgon.

This quatrain does nothing but describe an invasion by the French which is countered with strong resistance.

As for hideous monsters, Nostradamus was very interested in them. During the Protestant troubles, a calf with two heads was born near Salon. Nostradamus predicted that it would mean the separation of France through the two religions, Catholicism and Calvinism. He was right, of course, but any thinking politician of the day would have said the same thing. For what it is worth, a two-headed child was born in England in May, 1988, so these strange abnormalities still go on. The doctors have declared that the child will live, a truly tragic situation.

Century I

I.XCI

Les dieux feront aux humains apparence, *Ce qu'ilz seront auteurs de grand conflict:* *Auant ciel veu serein espee & lance,* *Que vers main gauche fera plus grand afflict.*	The gods will make it seem to mankind that they are the authors of a great war. Before the sky was seen to be free of weapons and rockets: the greatest damage will be afflicted towards the left side.

There have been many great wars, but my inclination is to say that this one has yet to happen. Here Nostradamus states that we will not know which side starts the war, although he contradicts in later quatrains when he places the responsibility on the East, China. He says that after a peaceful interlude (I.LXIII) the air will be full of weapons of combat, rockets pointing like lances to the skies. Visually, the left-hand side of a map or globe is America, and he states that this country will face great losses. However, the redeeming factor is that in IV.XCV he states that the war's victor will be born in America. It is to be hoped that the factors in this quatrain remain allied to the Western cause. With Nostradamus, there is no guarantee.

Century I

I.XCII

Souz vn la paix par tout sera clamee *Mais non long temps pillé & rebellion:* *Par refus ville, terre, & mer entamee,* *Mors & captifs le tiers d'vn million.*	*Under one man peace will be proclaimed everywhere, but not long afterwards will be looting and rebellion. Because of a refual, both town, land and sea will be broached. A third of a million will be captured or dead.*

If the universal peace, *la paix partout*, refers to the French Empire, one might bear in mind Napoleon's statement, "*L'Empire, c'est la paix.*" The Franco-Prussian war, which started when the king of Prussia refused to give in to humiliating French demands, is depicted in the remainder of the quatrain. The *Encyclopaedia Britannica* gives the number of dead and wounded in the war as approximately 300,000, which is close enough to Nostradamus' estimate.

Century I

I.XCIII

Terre Italique pres des monts tremblera,
Lyon & coq non trop confederez:
En lieu de peur l'vn l'autre s'aidera,
Seul Catulon[1] & Celtes moderez.

The Italian land near the mountains will tremble. The Cock and the Lion are not strongly united. Instead of fear they will help each other. Freedom alone moderates the French.

The Italians certainly trembled when Napoleon mounted his Italian campaign in 1795. Having captured Toulon, he set out upon the Italian wars and France *(coq)* saw the start of the enmity which grew up between her and England *(Lyon)*. This situation is followed by one of mutual alliance, *l'vn l'autre s'aidera*. After the accession of Louis XVIII, the French, *Celtes*, regain their freedom from tyranny.

Century I

I.XCIIII

Au port Selin le tyran mis à mort,
La liberté non pourtant recouuree:
Le nouueau Mars par vindicte & remort,
Dame par force de frayeur honnoree.

The tyrant Selim will be put to death at the harbor, but Liberty will not be regained. The new war arises from vengeance and remorse. A lady is honored through force of terror.

At the Battle of Lepanto, fought on October 7, 1571, Ali Pasha, the Admiral of Selim II's fleet, was killed onboard ship. Selim's aggression in the Mediterranean was finally quashed by the defeat at Lepanto. However, the crusade by Christian countries to put down Turkish influence did not succeed for some centuries. Line 4 may refer to the fact that the Pope

---

[1]*Catulon*. A.Pr. Liberty.

declared that the victory of Lepanto was due to the direct intercession of Our Lady, *Dame*.

Century I

I.XCV

Deuant mouſtier trouué enfant beſſon,
D'heroic ſang de moine &
* veſtutiſque:*
Son bruit par ſecte langue &
* puiſſance ſon,*
Qu'on dira fort eſleué le
* vopiſique.*

In front of a monastery the twin son of a monk of illustrious line will be found. His fame, renown and power through sects and speech is such that they will say the living twin is deservedly chosen.

This states that the twin son of a monk will become an important leader. He is unknown. Many commentators refer this quatrain to the Man in the Iron Mask, the possible son of Queen Anne and Cardinal Mazarin. But where is his twin? The whole quatrain is probably erroneous.

Century I

I.XCVI

Celuy qu'aura la charge de
* deſtruire*
Temples, & ſectes, changez par
* fantaſie:*
Plus aux rochiers qu'aux viuans
* viendra nuire,*
Par langue ornee d'oreilles
* reſſaſie.*

A man will be charged with the destruction of temples and sects, he will be changed by visions. He will harm the rocks rather than the living; ears satiated by ornate speeches.

This may indicate some form of religious revival, whose destiny is concerned with people rather than with the bricks and mortar of the temples of accepted religions. Otherwise it is totally vague.

Century I

I.XCVII

Ce que fer, flamme n'a fceu
  paracheuer,
La douce langue au conseil
  viendra faire:
Par repos, fonge, le Roy fera
  refuer,
Plus l'ennemy en feu, fang
  militaire.

That which neither weapon nor
flame could accomplish will be
achieved by a sweet speaking
tongue in council. Sleeping, in a
dream, the king will see the
enemy, not in war or of military
blood.

Henri III of France was killed, not in battle, but while in
council in 1589. A monk, Jacques Clément, came to the king
while he was staying at Saint Cloud, saying that he had a secret
letter for His Majesty. When granted an audience, Clément
leaned towards Henri as though to speak to him confidentially,
and stabbed him in the stomach. The king died the next day.
It is possible that *douce langue* is a typical Nostradamus
deviation on the name of Clément.

What is extremely interesting is that this is a rare example
of double precognition. It is well authenticated that Henri had
dreamed of his death. Three days earlier the king said that he
dreamed that his royal regalia—his blue cloak, two crowns, the
scepter, and his sword and spurs, were all trodden underfoot
by monks and the populace.

Century I

I.XCVIII

Le chef qu'aura conduit peuple
  infiny,
Loing de fon ciel, de meurs &
  langue eftrange:
Cinq mil en Crete & Theffalie
  finy,
Le chef fuyant fauué en marine
  grange.[1]

The leader will lead great numbers of people far from their
skies, to foreign customs and
language. Five thousand will
die in Crete and Thessaly, the
leader fleeing in a seagoing supply ship.

[1] *grange.* O.F. literally, wooden barn.

During Napleon's flight from Egypt, 1798–99, he successfully avoided the British Navy to land in France, *le chef fuyant.* He left behind an army of approximately 5,000 men to cope with the Turks. It was they who ruled Thessaly and Crete, and Napoleon did flee in a wooden ship, *marine grange.* This fact alone precludes the prediction from applying to the British Expeditionary Forces in Crete and Thessaly in 1940; ships at that time were made of metal and the numbers of combatants involved were much greater.

Century I

I.XCIX

Le grand monarque que fera
  compagnie,
Auec deux Roys vnis par
  amitié:
O quel fouspir fera la grand
  mefgnie,[1]
Enfans Narbon à l'entour quel
  pitié.

The great king will join with two kings, united in friendship. How the great household will sigh; around Narbonne, what pity for the children.

I cannot interpret this quatrain.

Century I

I.C

Long temps au ciel fera veu gris
  oifeau,
Aupres de Dole & de Toufcane
  terre:
Tenant au bec vn verdoyant
  rameau,
Mourra toft grand & finera la
  guerre.

For a long time a gray bird will be seen in the sky near Dôle and the lands of Tuscany. He holds a flowering branch in his beak, but dies too soon and the war will end.

The comte de Chambord, son of the duchess de Berry and last legitimate heir to the French throne, was known at his birth as the dove of peace. Unfortunately, the throne was

[1] *mefgnie.* O.F. household, court.

unsurped by the Orléans family and the comte was exiled to
Venice, near Dôle and to Modena, near Tuscany, where he
married the daughter of the duke of Tuscany in 1846. He died
without regaining the French throne, but he and the duc
d'Orléans, the pretender, were reconciled when the latter was
also sent into exile by the new Republic. It was the death of
the comte de Chambord, the dove of peace, which averted the
possibility of another war between the monarchists and the
Republicans.

Century II

II.I

*Vers Aquitaine pars infuls
  Britãniques
De pars eux meſmes grâdes
  incursiõs
Pluyes gelées ferõt terroirs
  iniques,
Port Selyn fortes fera inuaſions.*

*Towards Aquitaine there are
assaults by the British, and also
great invasions. Rain and frost
make the terrain unsafe, against
Turkey they make mighty incur-
sions.*

This is an important quatrain. When France (Aquitaine) and
Britain were deadlocked, *grâdes incursiõs*, on the Western
Front during 1915, Winston Churchill persuaded the Allies to
open a new front against Turkey *(Port Selyn)*. The general plan
was to attack the Dardanelles to reach Constantinople. The
weather was dreadful, *pluyes gelées*, and the troops suffered
appallingly from it throughout much of the First World War.

Century II

II.II

*La teſte blue fera la teſte blanche
Autant de mal que France a
  faict leur bien,
Mort à l'anthene grand pendu
  ſus la branche,
Quand prins des ſiens le Roy
  dira combien.*

*The blue leader will inflict upon
the white leader as much damage
as France had done them good.
Death from the great antenna
hung from the branch, when the
king will ask how many of his
men have been captured.*

The blue and white leaders occur several times in the quatrains and appear to apply specifically to the Ayatollah *(la tefte blanche)* who is often referred to as being followed by the Perse *(tefte bleu)*. *Perse* has two meanings in French, blue and Persian. Nostradamus is so ambiguous about this man that he almost certainly envisages both meanings. France's links with the Ayatollah are well known, from the time he was granted freedom there when exiled by the then Shah of Persia, to the French government's general dealings with Iran in both money and arms.

If this is a prophetic quatrain, the Ayatollah's successor is going to deal with France in a far less sympathetic manner. Perhaps he will refuse to allow French prisoners to be redeemed by ransom? Predictive thinking too may be contained in the reference to *l'anthene*; could this refer to an aerial or broadcasting of some kind, which gives or receives messages of death? The information demanded in line 4 may refer to the slaughter of the current Iran-Iraq war, of which then death would indicate that Iraq will be the eventual winner. Since 1989 Iran has broken diplomatic relations due to the fundamentalist stand of its government against the West; it is possible the quatrain may refer to this.

Century II

II.III

Pour la chaleur folaire fus la mer,	Because of heat like that of the sun on the sea, the fish around Negrepont will be half-cooked. The local people will eat them when in Rhodes and Genoa there is lack of food.
De Negrepont les poiffons demis cuits:	
Les habitans les viendront entamer,	
Quand Rhod, & Gennes leur faudra le biscuit.	

Such heat exploding upon the sea so that all the fish are dead implies something of far greater strength than a freak heat wave. Possibly an atomic explosion, somewhere over the Aegean sea, as Negrepont is the Dalian name for the island of Ruboea? The second statement, that people are starving in Italy and other parts of Greece, indicates conditions of famine and possibly war. Nostradamus talks of an explosion over the sea in France in V.XCVIII, where again he describes the fish as being boiled by the heat.

Century II

II.IIII

Depuis Monach iuſque aupres de Sicile,
Toute la plage demourra deſolée:
Il n'y aura fauxbourg, cité, ne ville,
Que par Barbares pillée ſoit & vollée.

The coast will remain deserted all along the coast from Monaco as far as Sicily. There will be no suburbs, cities or towns which will not have been pillaged and robbed by Barbarians.

This seems to be continuation of the last quatrain, II.III, unusual in Nostradamus as he states that he deliberately confused the time sequence of the quatrains in order to avoid further trouble with the Inquisition.

This therefore foresees the disaster extending through most of southern Europe, from Monaco to Sicily. As to the barbarians who will pillage rich cities and towns, this word contains some difficulty in translation, as it comes from the Greek, *barbar*, meaning anyone not speaking the Greek tongue. So the identity of the enemies is uncertain.

Century II

II.V

Qu'en dans poiſſon, fer & lettre enfermée,
Hors ſortira qui puis fera la guerre:
Aura par mer ſa claſſe bien ramée,
Apparoiſſant pres de Latine terre.

When the weapons and documents are enclosed in a fish, out of it will come a man who will then make war. His fleet will have voyaged far across the ocean to appear near the Italian shore.

The fish in this quatrain must presumably mean a submarine, since it contains not only documents and weapons as well as carrying a man, one who appears to be responsible for inciting a war. He is described as actually coming out, *hors fortira*, of the machine, exactly as Nostradamus describes the hostile soldiers in I.XXIX. The fleet of the unknown man has apparently traveled a great distance to reach the Italian shores, whether Adriatic or Mediterranean.

It is tempting to link this man with Nostradamus' Third Antichrist, whom he believes will start a Third World War in this present century. Line 1 may contain an astrological meaning, although somewhat tortuous, "When Mars and Mercury are in conjuration in Pisces." According to Norab, the next time this will occur is March 23, 1996. In I.LI, Nostradamus states it may start in 1995, and in II.XLI, 1993, which are close enough to be consistent and disconcerting since they were written over four hundred years ago.

Century II

II.VI

*Aupres des portes & dedans
    deux cités,
Seront deux fleaux & oncques
    n'apperçeu vn tel:
Faim, dedans peſte, de fers hors
    gens boutés,
Crier ſecours au grand Dieu
    immortel.*

*Near the harbor and in two cities
will occur two scourges the like
of which have never been seen.
Hunger, plague within, people
thrown out by the sword will cry
for help from the immortal God.*

Both Nagasaki and Hiroshima are upon the sea, *portes*, and in 1945 experienced a plague, *fleaux*, such as had never before been seen on earth, that of radiation from the two atomic bombs that were dropped upon both cities. The immediate survivors would have looked similar in many ways to victims of the plague, and remember that Nostradamus was probably the best plague doctor of his time in Europe. Plague turned its victims' bodies black, hence its contemporary name, *le charbon*. Radiation turns victims black too, and there was famine among the miserable survivors who left the cities because of the war, *de fers hors gens bouté*. The last line implies an immutable, implacable God who does nothing but listen to the victims' helpless cries for mercy.

Century II

II.VII

Entre plusieurs aux isles deportés,
L'vn estre nay à deux dents en
*   la gorge:*
Mourrant de faim les arbres
*   esbrotés,*
Pour eux neuf Roy, nouuel
*   edict leur forge.*

Among many people deported to
the islands will be a man born
with two teeth in his mouth. They
will die of hunger, having stripped the trees. A new king will
pass new laws for them.

Apart from assuming that the islands referred to are part
of the French penal colonies, I cannot decipher this quatrain.
The new king who passes new laws may predict the closing of
the penal settlements. Most of the tropical ones are already no
longer in use.

Many children are born with several teeth already formed.
The destiny of the man described here is not made clear,
except that he lives during a time of famine when many die.

Century II

II.VIII

Temples sacrez prime façon
*   Romaine,*
Reiecteront les goffres
*   fondements*
Prenant leur loix premieres &
*   humaines,*
Chassant, non tout des saincts les
*   cultements.*

Temples consecrated in the early
Roman fashion, they will reject
the broken foundations; taking
their early human laws, expell-
ing almost all the cults of the
saints.

This general quatrain may have been intended for the
Huguenots of Nostradamus' time. It predicts a return to
simpler religious precepts and practices, and a rejection of the
elaborate cult of saints in the Roman Catholic Church.

In this latter prediction he was greatly wrong. During May,
1988, Pope John Paul II consecrated approximately a
thousand Vietnamese who had died during the Vietnamese
War, and it appears that there is a record number of names
waiting for beatification. But it does seem that the influence

of the saints upon Roman Catholics is less intense, and worship of individual saints less freqeunt. However, this ties in with the twentieth century attitude to religion generally among the masses. The division between Church and people has never been stronger.

Century II

II.IX

Neuf ans le regne le maigre en paix tiendra,
Puis il cherra en foif si fanguinaire:
Pour luy grand peuple fans foy & loy mourra,
Tué par vn beaucoup plus debonnaire.

For nine years the reign of the slim thing will continue, then it will fall into so bloody a thirst that a great lawless nation will die because of it; killed by a better natured man.

This quatrain seems best to apply to the disease of AIDS, known in Africa, where it originated, as the "slim," or "thin," disease "*maigre*". It is unclear whether there are nine years before its specific discovery as a disease, or whether the victim can last for as long as nine years.

A 1988 research project in the USA predicted that although the disease may take a long time to emerge, within a decade "99% of those infected will eventually die of AIDS if they do not die from other causes as a result of it."

"A great nation will die of it" seems somewhat overstated, but neither Africa nor America can be ruled out since many in those countries are severely affected by it. Presumably the final cure is found by the better natured man (*debonnaire*), but no date is given as to when that might happen.

Century II

II.X

Auant long temps le tout ſera rangé,
Nous eſperons vn ſiecle bien ſeneſtre:
L'eſtat des maſques & des ſeuls bien changé,
Peu trouueront qu'à ſon rang vueille eſtre.

Before long everything will be controlled; we await a very evil century. The state of the masked and the solitary people greatly changed, few will find that they wish to retain their rank.

Some apply this to the French Revolution, 1789, during which the state of the social orders became dangerous and were changed. The two orders most affected were the court, *masques*, and the clergy, *les ſeuls*—so called because of their traditional celibacy. Both these classes were abolished in 1790. They obviously suffered financial loss and many were guillotined because of their social rank and function.

However, I wonder whether the first two lines might refer to Russia, after its Revolution in the twentieth century. *Le tout ſera rangé* seems to me to smack of the intolerance of the Communist régime of the USSR, and Nostradamus always describes the twentieth century as being a particularly evil one.

Century II

II.XI

Le prochain fils de l'aiſnier paruiendra,
Tant esleué iuſque au regne des fors:[1]
Son aſpre gloire vn chacun la craindra,
Mais ſes enfans du regne gettez hors.

The following son will succeed the elder, very greatly raised to a kingdom of privilege. His bitter renown will be feared by all, but his children will be thrown out of the kingdom.

This almost certainly is a quatrain about Napoleon, but it is very convoluted because of the several meanings of *prochain*

[1]*fors.* O.F. privileges, dues.

and *aiſnier*. *Prochain* may mean next, nearest, younger, or favorite; and *aiſnier* either elder or a falcon, conveying the metaphor of a bird of prey similar to Napoleon's eagle. If one accepts that it does refer to Napoleon, the rest of the quatrain falls very neatly into place. He was a second son, elected to an Empire and privilege. He was greatly feared throughout Europe, but after his exile his children were deprived of any rights to kingship by Louis XVIII. However, Napoleon's nephew, Louis-Napoleon, re-established himself as Emperor in 1852 and ruled until the advent of the Third Republic of 1871. Since then France has had no royalty, not even a token figurehead as in some European countries.

Century II

II.XII

Yeux clos, ouuerts d'antique fantaſie,
L'habit des ſeuls ſeront mis à néant:
Le grand monarque chaſtiera leur frenaiſie,
Rauir des temples le treſor par deuant.

Eyes unseeing, open to the great myth, the habits of priests will be abolished. The great monarch will punish their frenzy, stealing the treasure from the front of the temples.

Nostradamus was always more concerned with France than any other country in his quatrains, and, whether he was a Crypto-Jew or not, he worried a great deal about the Church because it appeared to him as essential to the basic fabric of society.

From 1789 the wearing of any ecclesiastical costume was banned. The clergy were suppressed during the French Revolution in 1790, and the Cult of Reason was established in 1793. The king can be interpreted either as Louis XVI, who had already helped despoil the monasteries, or Napoleon who continued to do so until the time of his Coronation, when he needed the Pope and found it necessary to restore Roman Catholicism to France. If this is the correct interpretation, it is another example of Nostradamus' failing to confuse the quatrains and it follows straight on from II.XI.

Century II

II.XIII

Le corps ſans ame plus n'eſtre en ſacrifice.	The body without a soul is no longer at the sacrifice. At the day of death it comes to rebirth. The divine spirit will make the soul rejoice seeing the eternity of the world.
Iour de la mort mis en natiuité:	
L'esprit diuin fera l'ame felice,	
Voyant le verbe en ſon eternité.	

This seems to be a religious statement in which Nostradamus states he believes in the transmigration of souls, "At death it is brought to rebirth."

Since this doctrine is not Christian or Jewish, he may have been influenced by his predictive faculties. He uses the phrase *esprit diuin* in I.II to describe the spirit which enlightens him. An interesting sidelight on Nostradamus the man.

Century II

II.XIIII

A Tours, Gien, gardé ſeront yeux penetrans,	At Tours and Gienne the watchful eyes will be guarded. They will spy from far off the serene Highness. She and her followers will enter the harbor, combat joined, sovereign power.
Deſcouuiront de loing la grand ſereine:	
Elle & sa ſuitte au port ſeront entrans,	
Combat, pouſſez, puiſſance ſouueraine.	

Since both Tours and Gien are situated on the Loire, this quatrain is placed firmly in France. It may refer to the Regency of Catherine de' Medicis 1559–89, *la grand ſerine*, for she traveled the country continually in an effort to subdue the wars of religion which troubled France from 1542 to 1598. The queen died, lonely and weakened by constant illness, in 1599, having seen all three of her sons predecease her, as predicted.

Century II

II.XV

Vn peu deuant monarque
    trucidé?[1]
Caſtor, Pollux en nef, aſtre
    crinite[2]:
L'erain[3] public par terre & mer
    vuidé,
Piſe, Aſt, Ferrare, Turin, terre
    interdicte.

A short while before a king is
murdered, Castor and Pollux in
the ship, a bearded star. Public
treasure plundered on land and
sea; Pisa, Asti, Terrara and
Turin are forbidden territories.

One can only approach this quatrain through the astrological dating. Castor and Pollux, the twins, stand for Gemini, the
ship for Argo and the bearded star, as elsewhere in Nostradamus, is a comet. Linked with this is an assassinated king, a war
effort with money being raised on land and sea plus the Italian
States being placed "*interdict.*" This last event has never
occurred and it seems unlikely that it will. A failed quatrain
perhaps?

Century II

II.XVI

Naples, Palerme, Sicille,
    Syracuſes,
Nouueaux tyrans, fulgures[4]
    feux celeſtes:
Force de Londres, Gand,
    Bruxelles, & Suſes,
Grand hecatombe, triomphe
    faire feſtes.

There are new tyrants in Naples,
Sicily, Palermo and Syracuse,
thunder and lightning in the
skies. An army from London,
Ghent, Brussels and Susa; a
great massacre, then triumph
and festivities.

The new tyrants in the Italian towns were probably
Mussolini's *Fascisti.* By extension, the thunder and lightning
may stand for the sound of war. London declared war against

[1]*trucidé.* L. *trucidare,* to slaughter.
[2]*crinite.* L. *crinitus,* bearded.
[3]*erain.* L. *eranus,* public fund or treasury.
[4]*fulgures.* L. *fulgur,* lightning.

Italy, allied with Brussels, and after the use of a great force (*grand hecatombe*), eventually wins the war.

Century II

II.XVII

Le camp du temple de la vierge vestale,	The field of the vestal virgin's temple is not far from Ethne and the Pyrenees. They lead the great one, hidden in a trunk; in the north, the rivers overflow and the vines are destroyed.
Non esloingé d'Ethne & monts Pyrenées:	
Le grand conduict est caché dans la male,[1]	
North[2] getez fleuues & vignes mastinées.[3]	

The key to this quatrain probably lies in the word "*Ethne*", the Greek anagram for Elne, since *the* is one letter in the Greek alphabet. Elne is in the Pyrenees between the rivers Tech and Réart, both of which flow into the Mediterranean. I cannot decipher this quatrain further.

Century II

II.XVIII

Nouuelle & pluie subite impetueuse,	New, unexpected and heavy rain will suddenly hinder two armies. Stones from the skies will form a stony sea. The death of the seven suddenly by land and sea.
Empeschera subit deux exercites[4]:	
Pierre ciel, feux faire la mer pierreuse,	
La mort de sept terre & marin subites.	

The resolution of this quatrain lies in the word *sept*. It refers to the death of the last of the seven Valois children of Catherine de' Medicis. When Henri III left Paris in 1587, the city was invaded by two armies, *deux excercites*, 35,000 German

---

[1] *male*. F. 1) *malle*, a trunk, or possibly 2) *mal*, evil.
[2] *North*. one of the rare uses of English in Nostradamus.
[3] *mastiner*. O.F. to bruise, destroy.
[4] *exercites*. L. *armies*.

and Swiss troops. The duc de Guise rushed with his troops of the Huguenot League to Montargis, but the decisive battle was prevented by a violent rainstorm, *pluie subite*. Henri, the last of the Valois kings, was assassinated in 1589, a direct result of his clash with the Leaguers and the assassination of the two Guise brothers (see I.LXXXV).

Century II

II.XIX

Nouueaux venus lieu basty sans defence.	Newcomers will occupy an unde- fended place; occupying a place
Occuper la place par lors inhabitable:	uninhabitable until then. Meadows, houses, fields, towns
Prez, maisons, châps, villes prêdre à plaisance,	will be taken at their pleasure. Famine, plague, war (over)
Faim, Peste, guerre arpen long labourable.	much arable land.

I cannot interpret this quatrain.

Century II

II.XX

Freres & seurs en diuers lieux captifs,	Brothers and sisters captive, in varying places, will find them-
Se trouueront passer pres du monarque:	selves passing near the monarch. His attentive offspring will look
Les contempler ses rameaux[1] ententifz,	at them, displeased to see the signs on their chins, foreheads
Desplaisant voir méton, front, nez, les marques.	and noses.

Jaubert applies this to an event which occurred soon after publication. In September, 1557, some Huguenots were captured during a raid and Henri II went to see them, taking his children. The king was reportedly angry at seeing so many of the captives wounded and bruised. However, the quatrain is so general that it may apply to many similar events.

[1]*rameaux*. F. literally branches, by extension offspring, children.

Century II

II.XXI

L'ambaſſadeur enuoyé par biremes, *A my chemin d'incogneus repoulsez:* *De ſel renfort viendront quatre triremes,* *Cordes & chaines au Negre pont trouſſez.*	*The ambassador sent by the trir-emes is repulsed halfway by an unknown man. Four triremes come reinforced with salt. He is bound with cords and chains to the Negroponte.*

Biremes are oared galleys with two bridges and triremes larger ones with three. Salt in the *Prophéties* often stands for taxation because of the French salt tax, the infamous *gabelle.* It may also contain the Biblical sense of wisdom. Negroponte is the Italian name for Euboea which belonged to the Turks until 1831, when it became part of Greece:

Century II

II.XXII

Le camp Ascop[1] d'Europe partira, *S'adioignant proche de l'isle ſubmergée:* *D'Arton[2] claſſe phalange pliera,* *Nombril du monde plus grand voix ſubrogée.[3]*	*The aimless army will depart from Europe and join up close to the submerged island. The NATO (or bread-giving) fleet will fold up its standard in the navel of the world, giving in to a greater voice.*

The clue to this quatrain probably lies in the submerged island, *l'isle submergée,* which also occurs in IX.XXXI, where it is ascribed to Britain, the island of St. George. The army is described as aimless—possibly on an exercise, and therefore not acting with warlike intent? The fleet of bread, *Arton* (or possibly an anagram of NATO), folds up its standard for the same reason. The navel of the world is normally applied to

---

[1] *Ascop.* Gk. *askpops,* incredible, aimless.
[2] *Arton.* Either anagram for NATO or Gk. artos, bread.
[3] *ſubrogée.* L. *subrogatus,* substitute.

Italy, but could be applied here, I think, to the Middle East, the Gulf, near the Garden of Eden where man was metaphorically born.

At the moment, the USA is acting as a protective shield in the Gulf, covering the many tankers (U.S. and foreign) which fly the American flag. But Nostradamus says that this too will be overcome, *plus grand voix ſubrogée*. Maybe a NATO naval force will take over, particularly since the tragic shooting down of the Iran Airbus July 4, 1988, as the American and other national forces are becoming too intensive a presence in the area.

Century II

II.XXIII

*Palais, oyſeaux, par oyſeau
   dechaſſé,
Bien toſt apres le prince
   paruenu:
Combien qu'hors fleuue ennemi
   repoulſé,
Dehors ſaiſi trait d'oyſeau
   ſouſtenu.*

The palace, birds, chased out by a bird, very soon after the arrival of the prince. So many of the enemy repulsed beyond the river, the bird in place seized from without by a trick.

The story of a prince, perhaps one who wears highly colorful clothing like a bird, who is captured in his palace through trickery by an upstart. Some commentators translate line 4 as "captured outside, a shaft held by a bird," i.e., an arrow.

Century II

II.XXIIII

*Beſtes farouches de faim fleuues
   tranner,[1]
Plus part du champ encontre
   Hiſter ſera.
En caige de fer le grand fera
   treiſner,
Quand rien enfant de Germain
   obſeruera.*

Beasts wild with hunger will cross the rivers, the greater part of the battlefield will be against Hitler. He will drag the great one in a cage of iron, when the child of Germany observes no law.

[1] *tranner*. L. *tranare*, to cross.

One of the remarkable series of quatrains which mentions a German called Hister. There can be little doubt that Hitler is referred to. Until 1936 approximately, all commentators on the Centuries thought that the word referred to the river Danube, the Ister. But there is no doubt in this and later verses that Nostradamus had a person in mind. Ironically by the mid-1930's, Hitler believed these applied to himself and Goebbels made great use of them for propaganda purposes, as did the Allies, especially the British. Evidence of this may be found in Ellic Howe's book *Nostradamus and the Nazis.* During the first years of the Second World War Germany's development depended to a great extent on its armies crossing the major rivers of Europe in a never-ending stream of manpower and weapons during the early years of the war. This child of Germany obeyed no law except his own, and his armies pillaged and looted as they went, *farouches de faim.* (See I.XXXIIII, III.XXXVI, III.LIII, III.LXI, IIII.LXVIII, V.XXIX, V.XCIIII, VI.LI, IX.XC.)

Century II

II.XXV

La garde eſtrange trahira fortereſſe,	The foreign guard will betray the fortress, the shadowy hope of
Eſpoir & vmbre de plus hault mariage:	an important marriage. The guard deceived, the fort cap-
Garde deçeue,[1] fort prinſe dans la preſſe,	tured in the crowd. Loire, Saône, Rhône, Garonne outraged unto
Loyre, Son Roſne Gar. à mort oultrage.	death.

The defender of a fortress who betrays his trust while chasing the illusion of a higher post, *plus hault mariage,* may be Bazaine, who in 1870 handed over the fortress of Metz and his troops to the Germans. This gave the Germans access to the French interior during the Franco-Prussian war. Much has been written about Bazaine's motives for such an act of treachery, but eventually it seems to boil down to money and the illusory promise of power when the Prussians won the war.

[1]*deçeue.* L. *decisus,* cut down, or F. deceived.

Century II

II.XXVI

Pour la faueur que la cité fera,
Au grand qui toſt perdra camp
*   de bataille.*
Fuis le rang Pau Theſin verſera.
De ſang, feux mors noyés de
*   coup de taille.*

Because of the favor that a city
will show towards a great man
who later loses on the battlefield,
the ranks will flee, rushing into
the (rivers) Po and Tessin;
blood, shooting, dead men
drowned and slashed.

Century II

II.XXVII

Le diuin verbe ſera du ciel
*   frappé,*
Qui ne pourra proceder plus
*   auant:*
Du referant[1] le ſecret eſtoupé,[2]
Qu'on marchera par deſſus &
*   deuant.*

The divine voice will be struck
from heaven and he will not be
able to continue further. The secret hidden until the revelation,
so that people will walk both
above and overhead.

People walking above indicates that this quatrain may be
referring to the grave of a religious man or someone similar
(*le diuin verbe*). To walk *par deſſus et deuant* in French means to
be confined in an underground cell or to be buried at the foot
of a wall. Nostradamus may well be referring to himself. After
his death in 1556 his wife buried him, according to his wishes,
in the Franciscan monastery at Salon between the great door
and the altar of St. Martha. He had requested that he should
be buried upright, so that the people of Salon should not walk
upon his grave.

During the early part of the French Revolution, however,
his body was disinterred by drunken soldiers. Eventually his
bones were reburied in the Chapel of Virgin in the Church of
Saint-Laurent, where they remain, together with his burial
plaque, to this day. An oil painting of him, one of three extant,
used to hang above the plaque, but was stolen in the early
1980s.

[1]*referant*. L. *reserare*, to lock.
[2]*eſtoupé*. O.F. to shut up, imprison.

Century II

II.XXVIII

*Le penultiefme du furnom du
    prophete,
Prendra Diane pour fon iour &
    repos:
Loing vaguera par frenetique
    tefte,
Et deliurant vn grand peuple
    d'impos.*[1]

The last but one of the prophet's
name will take Monday for his
day of rest. He will wander far
in his frenzy, delivering a great
nation from subjection.

Several ingenious readers have suggested that this quatrain
could refer to the Moonies, the cult of Sun Myung Moon, in
that Monday was the day of Diana, goddess of the Moon. But
I feel that far from rescuing a nation from subjection, this
subversive cult does exactly the opposite. Sun Myung Moon is
Korean. This may relate to the following quatrain.
      Possibly Nostradamus is referring to Mohammed or Maho-
met?

Century II

II.XXIX   ★

*L'Oriental fortira de fon fiege,
Paffer les monts Apennins voir
    la Gaule:
Tranfpercera le ciel les eaux &
    neige,
Et vn chafcun frappera de fa
    gaule.*

The Eastern man will come forth
from his seat and cross the Apennines to France. He will cross
through the sky, the seas and the
snows and he will strike everyone
with his rod.

This is a curious verse. The millenniumists of the year A.D.
1000 fully believed that the devil would bring forth his legions
from the East at the time of the end of the world. Nostradamus
certainly had a strong belief in the second millennium, as is
seen in many of the Predictions. The use of the word *fortira*
rather than *ira* indicates that this man of the East is leaving his

---

[1]*impos.* O.F. *impost*, taxation.

country with deliberate intent, presumably to go to France. France, *La Gaule*, is one of the few countries which still maintains a diplomatic relationship with Iran. The third line clearly indicates Nostradamus' understanding of air travel. The last line is very ambiguous. The word *gaule* also means a stick or rod, it may even be a weapon, and also an indirect reference to de Gaulle, with whom postwar France is linked, just as Churchill is with Great Britain.

Note the curiously threatening tone underlying line 4. Possibly this man from the East is the Third Antichrist, who, elsewhere, Nostradamus states will appear before the second millennium?

Century II

II.XXX

Vn qui les dieux d'Annibal infernaux,	A man who is reborn from the infernal Gods of Hannibal, the
Fera renaiftre, effrayeur des humains:	terror of mankind. Never more horror nor papers tell of worse
Oncq' plus d'horreur ne plus dire iournaulx,	things than will come to the Romans through Babel.
Qu'auint viendra par Babel aux Romains.	

Taking the eternal gods of Hannibal as the key to this quatrain, meaning North Africa, or the Middle East, there comes forth a man who will bring trouble to the whole world (*Babel*). The word *iourneaulx* for the source of information is interesting. In Nostradamus' time this could only have been understood as pamphlets—newspapers did not exist. There is a possibility that the last line may refer to a general worldwide collapse of religions and that the Catholic Church will suffer from it, particularly the *Romains*.

Century II

II.XXXI

*En Campanie le Caſſilin[1] ſera
   tant,
Qu'on ne verra que d'aux les
   champs couuers:
Deuant apres la pluye de long
   temps,
Hors mis les arbres rien l'on
   verra de vert.*

In Campanie the (river) Cassilin
will grow so much that one will
only see fields covered with
water. Before and after the long
lasting rain, nothing green will
be seen except for the trees.

This seems to predict a flood on the Volturno River,
perhaps the flooding Capua itself, as the town was built on the
ruins of the Roman town of Casilinum. One of a series of
quatrains which predict alternating times of flood and
drought.

Century II

II.XXXII

*Laict, ſang grenoilles eſcoudre[2]
   en Dalmatie,
Conflict donné, peſte pres de
   Balennes
Cry sera grand par toute
   Eſclauonie,
Lors naiſtra monſtre pres &
   dedans Rauenne.*

Milk, blood, frogs will be prepared in Dalmatia; battle
engaged, plague near Balennes.
A great cry will go up throughout Slavonia; then a monster
will be born near Ravenna.

The only clues to this quatrain, apart from the rains of milk,
blood, fish and frogs, which are well documented, are the
place names. The prediction appears to cover both sides of the
Adriatic—Dalmatia is on the eastern Adriatic, Balennes was
Trebula Balliensis near Capua, and Ravenna is in central Italy.
Slavonia is now part of northern Yugoslavia.

In Birmingham, England, on June 12, 1954, hundreds of
frogs were reported falling from the skies, bouncing off

---

[1] *Caſſilin*. town on the Volturno River.
[2] *eſcoudre*. L. *excudore*, to prepare.

witnesses' umbrellas and scaring everyone. On January 2, 1973, the same thing was repeated at Arkansas, Texas, where a shower of frogs was reported "the size of tiny nickels" during a thunderstorm. In Singapore, 1851, an area of approximately fifty acres was found covered by a local species of catfish. In late 1988 in the Australian state of Queensland, Brisbane residents were showered with hundreds of sardines. Scientists said that updrafts probably took the fish from shallow water into the atmosphere. When it rained, they fell.

Century II

II.XXXIII

Par le torrent qui deſcent de Veronne,
Par lors qu'au Pau guidera ſon entrée:
Vn grand naufrage, & non moins en Garonne,
Quant ceux de Gênes marcheront leur contree.

Through the torrent which pours down from Verona, where the entrance is guided to the Po; a great wreck, and not less so in Garonne, when the people of Genoa will march against their country.

This quatrain, which may be linked with quatrain II.XXXII, describes three sixteenth-century states—France, Verona and Genoa. Verona is situated on the river Adige, which enters the Adriatic parallel to the Po about ten miles distant. Nothing really specific.

Century II

II.XXXIIII

L'ire inſenſee du combat furieux,
Fera à table par freres le fer luire:
Les, deſpartir, bleſſé, curieux,
Le fier duelle viendra en France nuire.

In the senseless rage of a furious struggle, the brothers will draw their weapons at table. They are separated, wounded and curious. The proud duel will bring harm to France.

The duel described here, which occurs between brothers or cousins who were formerly friends (eating at the same table), in some way causes trouble to France. I am unable to pin down any specific incident, but see II.LV for a possible link and explanation.

Century II

II.XXXV

Dans deux logis de nuict le feu prendra,
Plusieurs dedans estouffez & rostis:
Pres de deux fleuues pour seul il auiendra:
Sol, l'Arq, & Caper tous seront amortis.

Fire will take hold in two houses at night, several people inside suffocated or burnt. It will definitely happen near two rivers, when the sun, Sagittarius and Capricorn are all diminished.

The astrological dating in line 4 occurs every year on December 22nd (Gregorian calendar), for this is the day that the sun moves out of Sagittarius into Capricorn. All the commentators who wrote from about 1600 onwards seem to relate the quatrain to a great fire at Lyons which happened in December, 1582. Lyons is situated at the mouth of two rivers.

Century II

II.XXXVI

Du grand Prophete les lettres seront prinses,
Entre les mains du tyran deuiendront:
Frauder son Roy seront ses entreprinses,
Mais ses rapines bien tost le troubleront.

The letters of the great Prophet will be intercepted and fall into the hands of the tyrant. He will make efforts to deceive his king, but soon his thefts will give him trouble.

Abbé Torné, the expansive nineteenth century commentator on Nostradamus, believed this quatrain applied to himself, but gives us no specific reason why it should do so. Nostradamus may be talking of some event in his own life, when he was in Paris advising Catherine de' Medicis and a letter of credit to some friends was stolen (see "The Life and Times of Nostradamus," p. 11).

Century II
II.XXXVII

De ce grand nombre que lon enuoyera
Pour ſecourir dans le fort aſſiegez,
Peſte & famine tous les deuorera,
Hors mis ſeptante qui ſeront profligez.[1]

Out of the great number that are sent to relieve the besieged fort, disease and hunger will destroy them all, except seventy who will be killed.

I have no explanation for this quatrain.

Century II
II.XXXVIII

Des condamnez ſera fait vn grand nombre,
Quand les monarques ſeront conciliez:
Mais l'vn deux viendra ſi malencombre,
Que guere enſemble ne ſeront raliez.

There will be a great number of condemned people when the monarchs are reconciled. But one of them will be so unfortunate that they will hardly remain allies.

This may be interpreted as a general quatrain describing the alliance between Hitler and Stalin from the years 1939 to 1941. Others, who apply it to the breakdown of the Yalta conference of 1945, interpret line 1 as referring to the Nuremberg Trials and the "misfortune" as the beginning of the Cold War with Russia.

---

[1]*profligez*. L. *profligare*, to destroy, kill, ruin.

Century II

II.XXXIX

*Vn an deuant le conflict
    Italique,
Germains, Gaulois, Heſpaignols
    pour le fort:
Cherra l'eſcolle maiſon de
    republicque,
Où, hors mis peu, ſeront ſuffoqué
    mors.*

*A year before the war in Italy,
Germans, French and Spanish
will be for the strong one; the
schoolhouse of the republic will
crash, where, except for a few,
they will be suffocated to death.*

The quatrain appears to apply best to Europe in general
during 1939, the year before Italy became involved in the
Second World War, declared on June 10, 1940. The Spanish,
although technically neutral, backed the German cause, and
there was definitely a pro-German element in France, as was
proved by the Vichy régime. The strong man at this period
must certainly be Hitler. The schoolhouse republic which
crushes so many people could refer to either Italy or France,
but the adjective "*eſcolle*" is difficult to interpret.

This seems to lead on to the following quatrain (II.XL),
which claims that after the alliances between Germany, Spain
and France, there will be world battles on land and sea—the
Second World War.

Century II

II.XL

*Vn peu apres non point longue
    interualle,
Par mer & terre ſera faict
    grand tumulte:
Beaucoup plus grande ſera
    pugne[1] naualle,
Feux, animaux, qui plus feront
    d'inſulte.[2]*

*Shortly afterwards, not a very
long interval, a great tumult
will be raised by land and sea.
The naval battles will be greater
than ever. Fires, creatures which
will make more tumult.*

[1]*pugne.* L. *pugna*, battle.
[2]*inſulte.* A.Pr. insult or turmoil.

If, as I stated, this is linked with the previous quatrain, the theme of the Second World War continues. The importance of sea domination was obvious; possibly the creatures represent the submarines which came into prominence at this time—Nostradamus has described submarines as fish on various occasions. *Feux* may be translated as firing, or weaponry, which would make the creatures armed ships.

Century II

II.XLI

La grand' eſtoille par ſept iours bruſlera,
Nuée fera deux ſoleils apparoir:
Le gros maſtin toute nuict hurlera,
Quand grand pontife changera de terroir.

The great star will burn for seven days and the cloud will make the sun appear double. The large mastiff will howl all night when the great pontiff changes his abode.

Several popes have changed their abodes—this means surely something more permanent than the summer trips to Castel Gandolfo, or even the present Pope John Paul II's world tours. The most notable examples of this were Pius VI, who died in Valence in France, and Pius VII, who was forcibly detained by Napoleon before returning to Rome.

The reference to the comet may place this quatrain in 1986, the time of Halley's comet and of Pope John Paul II to whom the Irish prophet Malachy allotted the motto "*de laboris solis,*" of the toil of the sun. Perhaps it implies a war towards the end of this century, when the Pope may well have to leave the Vatican, and possibly even Europe. If the seven days stand for seven years, dated from the time of Halley's Comet, we arrive at 1993, near to the date Nostradamus gives elsewhere in the *Prophéties* for the start of a Third World War.

Century II

II.XLII

Coq, chiens & chats de fang
  feront repeus,
Et de la playe du tyran trouué
  mort.
Au lict d'vn autre iambes &
  bras rompus,
Qui n'auoit peur mourir de
  cruelle mort.

The Cock, cats and dogs will be
replete with blood when a tyrant
is found wounded in the bed of
another. Both arms and legs broken, he, who was not afraid, dies
a cruel death.

The Cock is the symbol of France, and by extension, the cats
and dogs replete with blood might describe the rabble during
the Reign of Terror, under the Committee led by Robespierre.
Revolutionary fervor grew so out of hand that in sixteen days,
July 12–28, 1794, 1,285 victims died on the guillotine.
Robespierre was certainly a tyrant but even he took fright at
the horrors that were being perpetrated. On July 26 he
renewed the Committee of Public Safety. Too late: Robespierre was arrested, but freed by the troops of the Commune
who took him to a strange bed in the Hôtel de Ville. The
National Guard recaptured him and he was shot in the jaw,
not limbs. After a long night of agony he was executed without
further trial on July 29 at the Place de la Révolution, now
known as the Place de la Concorde.

Century II

II.XLIII

Durant l'eftoille cheuelue
  apparente,
Les trois grans princes feront
  faits ennemis:
Frappés du ciel paix terre
  tremulente,
Pau, Timbre vndans, ferpent fus
  le bort mis.

During the appearance of the
bearded star, the three great
princes will be made enemies.
The tremulous peace on earth
will be struck from the skies; the
Po, the winding Tiber, a serpent
on the shore.

The comet, a hairy star with a tail, was the emblem of Pope
Leo XIII and Malachy gave him the motto "*Lumen in Caelo.*"

The motto seems to be the key to this quatrain because it was during his Papacy that the Triple Alliance, *trois grans princes*, was formed in 1881, with Germany, Austria and Italy allying against France. The tremulous nature of the peace probably refers to the Triple Entente which ultimately led to the First World War. The snake in line 4 is unclear.

Century II

II.XLIIII

L'aigle pousée entour de pauillons,	The eagle driven back from circling the tents will be harried by
Par autres oyseaux d'entour sera chassée:	the other birds around him. Then when the cymbals, trum-
Quand bruit des cymbres tube & sonnaillons	pets and bells sound, sense will be restored to a senseless woman.
Rendront le sens de la dame insensée.	

The eagle, as always, stands for nineteenth century France and here seems to apply to Napoleon, driven back from Moscow and harried by the other birds of prey, Russia, Austria and Prussia.

The last two lines have two possible interpretations: they may refer to the martial music of the Royalist party, which brings France back to her senses, in that it restores the monarchy of Louis XVIII—Nostradamus was a fervent Royalist. Alternatively, they may refer to Napoleon's second marriage, to Marie Louise of Austria, and the grief and distress of the Empress Josephine, *"dame insensée."* It was a common popular belief that Napoleon's luck deserted him when he discarded Josephine de Beauharnais.

Century II

II.XLV

Trop le ciel pleure l'Androgyn¹
   procrée,
Pres de ciel fang humain
   refpandu:
Par mort trop tard grand
   peuple recrée,
Tard & toft vient le fecours
   attendu.

The heavens weep too much at
the birth of Androgyn; human
blood is spilt near to heaven. It is
too late for the great nation to be
revived because of the death; the
awaited help comes soon, yet too
late.

Androgyn implies either an hermaphrodite or, more likely,
a victorious king who causes some form of aerial warfare (line
2). The rest is very general.

Century II

II.XLVI

Apres grãt troche² humain plus
   grãd s'apprefte,
Le grand moteur les fiecles
   renouuelle:
Pluye, fang, laict, famine, fer &
   pefte,
Au ciel veu feu, courant longue
   eftincelle.

After great misery for mankind
an even greater one approaches,
when the great cycle of the centuries is renewed. It will rain
blood, milk, famine, war and
disease. In the sky will be seen a
fire, dragging a tail of sparks.

Again the great catastrophe of war and plagues which so
occupied the millenniumists is linked with a comet appearing
towards the end of a century. Comets were believed to have
magical properties and to predict events of great import. The
last important comet of this decade was Halley's Comet, which
appeared in 1986, so presumably we are to understand that
this great war shall occur between that time and the end of the
century—in keeping with the various dates Nostradamus
predicts for the war in the 1990s. Line 1 probably refers to the

---

¹Androgyn. Androgens, the son of Minos of Crete, killed at Athens
because he won all the prizes in a contest at the Pantheon.
²troche. Gk. trikos, misery.

Second World War, *grāt troche humain*, as the earlier appearance of Halley's Comet in this century was 1910, before the Great War.

Century II
II.XLVII

L'ennemy grand vieil dueil meurt de poiſon,
Les ſouuerains par infiniz ſubiuguez:
Pierres plouuoir, cachez ſoubz la toiſon,
Par mort articles en vain ſont alleguez.

The great enemy watches with grief the man dying of poison; the kings are completely overcome. It rains stones, hidden under the fleece, in vain articles asserted by the dead.

I cannot interpret this quatrain.

Century II
II.XLVIII

La grand copie[1] qui paſſera les monts,
Saturne en l'Arq tournant du poiſſon Mars:
Venins cachés ſoubz teſtes de ſaulmons,
Leur chief pendu à fil de polemars.[2]

The great army will pass over mountains when Saturn is in Sagittarius and Mars moving into Pisces. Poison hidden under the heads of donkeys. Their chief hung with a cord, during war.

The conjunction mentioned in line 2 is very rare. It last occurred on July 17, 1951, and will next happen July 13, 2193. The only clue in the 3rd line is that *saulmon* in Ancien Provençal means a donkey head, but this gets one little further. Line 4 talks about the hanging of a leader during wartime.

---

[1]*copie. copia,* troops.
[2]*polemars.* Gk. *polemardes,* one who leads in war; or A.Pr. twine or thick string.

Century II

II.XLIX

Les conſeilliers du premier
   monupole,[1]
Les conquerans ſeduits par la
   Melite:
Rodes, Biſance pour leurs
   expoſant pole,[2]
Terre faudra les pourſuiuans de
   fuite.

The counselors of the first conspiracy, victors won over the part
of the Maltese. Rhodes and
Byzantium open their towns to
them, the fleeing pursuers will
need land.

This probably refers to an obscure incident during the reign
of the Ottoman Empire, given the connection between
Istanbul (Byzantium), Rhodes and Malta. The quatrain may
well be retrospective.

Century II

II.L

Quand ceux d'Hainault, de
   Gād & de Bruxelles,
Verront à Langres le ſiege
   deuant mis:
Derrier leurs flancz ſeront
   guerres cruelles
La plaie antique ſera pis
   qu'ennemis.

When the people of Hainault,
Ghent and Brussels see siege laid
before Langres. Behind their
flanks will be dreadful wars, the
older wound being worse than
the enemies.

Hainault, Flanders (Ghent), and Brabant (Brussels) were the
richest provinces of the sixteenth century Netherlands. Nostradamus envisages them in a state of war, besieging Langres,
which was an important frontier city during the Hapsburg
wars. Thus, line 3 could refer to the uprising of the
Netherlands in 1568, two years after Nostradamus' death. But
la plaie antique? Possibly this refers to some internal dissension?

---

[1]monopole. Gk. monopulum, conspiracy.
[2]pole. Gk. polis, town.

Century II

II.LI

Le ſang du iuſte à Londres fera
  faulte,
Bruſlés par fouldres de vint trois
  les ſix:
La dame antique cherra de
  place haute,
De meſme secte pluſieurs ſeront
  occis.

The blood of the just will be
demanded of London, burnt by
fire in three times twenty and six.
The ancient lady falls from her
high position, and many of
the same denomination will be
killed.

The only great fire occurring in London in a year '66 (three
times twenty plus six) is the Great Fire of London 1666.
Neither before nor since has there been anything to equal it.
This is an interesting quatrain because the date is definite
enough to be checked historically. It was quite common in the
16/17 centuries to leave off the figures denoting the century
from a date, i.e., 1666 is written '66. This can be seen on many
gravestones in France and England of the period. It may also
be a result of Nostradamus' natural caution.

The *dame antique* is usually interpreted as St. Paul's Cathedral, in the City of London, inside whose porch was a large
statue of the Virgin Mary. According to the contemporary
sources, this fell on people seeking refuge from the fire. Many
people rushed to St. Paul's and other stone buildings in an
effort to escape the fire. Sadly the heat and smoke were so
intense that they did not escape, nor were the buildings
unscathed. The *iuſte ſang* is understood as meaning that the
victims of the fire did not deserve their fate. This quatrain is
linked with II.LIII by the key words *iuſte ſang* and *grand dame*.

Century II

II.LII

Dans pluſieurs nuits la terre
    tremblera:
Sur le printemps deux effors
    ſuite:
Corinthe, Epheſe aux deux mers
    nagera,
Guerre s'eſmeut par deux
    vaillans de luite.[1]

For several nights the earth will
shake; in the spring, two great
upheavals in succession. Corinth
and Ephesus will swim in the
two seas. War will be aroused by
two men, valiant in combat.

It has been suggested that Corinth and Ephesus represent
the United Provinces which were engaged in a naval war with
England in 1665–67. However, it takes some stretch of
imagination to link them with Greece.

Century II

II.LIII

La grande peſte de cité
    maritime,
Ne ceſſera que mort ne ſoit
    vengée
Du iuſte ſang par pris damné
    ſans crime,
De la grand dame par feincte
    n'outraigée.

The great plague in the maritime
city will not be stopped until
death is avenged by the blood of
a just man, taken and condemned for no crime. The great
lady is outraged by the pretense.

If, as is commonly believed, the death of the just man refers
to Charles I's execution in London, the maritime city, this links
this quatrain with II.LI, the Great Fire following a year later
upon the Great Plague, 1665. The outraged lady, whether the
Church itself as designated by St. Paul's Cathedral, or the
statue of the virgin, is outraged because soon afterwards
Protestantism was re-established in England under William
III.
    Nostradamus is always hostile to any Protestant beliefs, not,
I think, because he was that fervent a Catholic, but because

---

[1]*luite*. Romance. fight, combat.

trials and tribulations brought to Europe by Calvin were unforgivable to him. He wanted a secure niche in his society, being of Jewish origin, not the religious wars which persecuted his generation.

Century II

II.LIIII

Par gent eftrange, & Romains loingtaine,
Leur grand cité apres eaue fort troublee:
Fille fans trop different domaine,
Prins chef, ferreure[1] n'auoir efté riblée.[2]

Far from the Romans, by a foreign people, their great city will be damaged by water. A girl of not greatly different estate, taken by the leader; the lock has not been removed.

During a time of flooding, Rome will be attacked by a distant enemy. Whether this quatrain is to be understood literally or metaphorically is unclear.

Century II

II.LV

Dans le conflict le grand qui peu valloit,
A son dernier fera cas merueilleux:
Pendant qu'Hadrie verra ce qu'il falloit,
Dans le banquet pongnale l'orgueilleux.

In the conflict the great man who is of little worth will perform an astonishing deed at his end. While Hadrie sees what is needed, during the banquet he stabs the proud one.

By 1594 the revolutionary ideas of the Paris Seize (People's Parliament) were becoming too strong for the League to cope with, and the Duc de Mayenne, claimant to the throne through the House of Guise, carried out a "coup d'état". He invited all

[1] *ferreure*. Almost certainly a misprint for *serreure*, lock.
[2] *riblée*. O.F. *ribler*, to pillage, rob.

the leaders of the Seize to a banquet in order to lull their suspicions, and had them all killed on the following night. Mayenne hoped that he would be able to hold Paris for the Catholic League, but Henri IV of Navarre (*Hadrie*) realized the situation and realized that he would have to become a Catholic and thus unite France. "Paris is worth a Mass".

Century II

II.LVI

Que pefte & glaiue n'a fceu definer,[1]	One whom neither plague nor sword could kill, will die on a
Mort dans le puys fommet du ciel frappé:	hilltop, struck from the sky. The abbot will die when he sees the
L'abbé mourra quand verra ruiner,	people, ruined in the shipwreck, trying to hold on to the reef.
Ceux du naufrage l'efcueil voulant grapper.	

Someone killed by lightning, having lived a charmed life for many years, together with a shipwreck. I cannot interpret this quatrain.

Century II

II.LVII

Auant conflict le grand tombera,	Before the battle the great man will fall, the great one killed,
Le grand à mort, mort, trop fubite & plainte,	death too sudden and lamented. Born imperfect, he will go the
Nay miparfaict: la plus part nagera,	greater part of the way: near the river the ground is stained with
Aupres du fleuue de fang la terre tainte.	blood.

Mort, trop fubite implies a death before it is due, a murder or assassination. *Nay miparfaict* implies someone suffering from some type of deformity. I believe this verse applies to John F.

[1] *definer*. O.F. die, finish, decide.

Kennedy's stand against Khrushchev over the Cuban missiles. The Russian fleet certainly came "the greater part of the way," before turning back. It was after this confrontation that Kennedy was killed in Dallas *trop subite et plainte*. The infirmity (*nay miparfaict*) may refer to the back trouble he suffered during his Presidency, which was so severe that he normally had to wear a brace all the time for relief. Equally, it might refer to his morals, as Kennedy was a great womanizer.

Century II

II.LVIII

Sans pied ne main dend ayguë & forte,
Par globe[1] au fort de port & lainé nay:
Pres du portail defloyal tranfporte,
Silene[2] luit, petit grand emmené.

Without either foot or hand, strong and sharp teeth, through the crowds to the fortified harbor, with the eldest born. He crosses over near the gates, treacherous. The moon shines little, great pillage.

Some commentators interpret the last line as "the moon shines, the great little man carried off," to mean Napoleon. They apply the same interpretation to *petit grand* in II.LXXXV. But I am not wholly convinced by either quatrain.

Century II

II.LIX

Claffe Gauloife par appuy de grande garde,
Du grand Neptune, & fes tridens fouldars:
Rongée Prouence pour fouftenir grand bande,
Plus Mars Narbon par iauelotz & dards.

The French fleet through the support of the main guard of great Neptune and his trident warriors; Provence ravaged to sustain this great band. Moreover, fighting at Narbonne, with javelins and arrows.

[1] *globe*. L. *globus*, crowd or throng.
[2] *Silene*. Gk. *selene*, moon.

Turkey was the dominant naval power in the Mediterranean during Nostradamus' lifetime, so the "trident troops" are probably the Turks. There does not appear to have been any trouble in Narbonne at this time, so I think this is a failed, or retroactive quatrain, referring to events before Nostradamus' birth.

Century II

II.LX

La foy Punicque en Orient
 rompue,
Grand Iud[1]. & Rofne, Loyre &
 Tag[2]. changeront:
Quand du mulet la faim fera
 repue,
Claffe efpargie,[3] fang & corps
 nageront.

Faith with Africa is broken in the East. Great Jordan, Rosne, Loire and Tagus will change. When the hunger of the mule is slaked, the fleet is scattered and bodies swim in blood.

This probably refers to the many troubles in Africa—several countries there have strong links with China, the Middle East, *Grand Iud*, and France. Spain and Portugal are less influential there now, but I am still tempted to place this unresolved quatrain in the twentieth century.

Century II

II.LXI

Euge,[4] Tamins,[5] Gironde & la
 Rochele,
O fang Troyen Mort au port de
 la flefche:
Derrier le fleuue au fort mife
 l'efchele,
Pointes feu grand meurtre fus la
 brefche.

Bravo, men of the Thames, Gironde and La Rochelle, O Trojan blood, killed by an arrow at the harbor. Beyond the river the ladder is put up against the port. Flashes of fire, great slaughter in the breach.

[1] *Iud.* abb. for Jordan.
[2] *Tag.* abb. for Tagus.
[3] *efpargie.* O.F. *efpargier*, to sprinkle.
[4] *Euge.* L. bravo, congratulations.
[5] *Tamins.* syncope of *Tamisiens*, people of the Thames.

Nostradamus refers in I.XIX to the legend of the French royal family descending from the Trojans *(fang Troyen)*, but this bloodline had finished by the time the English and French fought together on the same side. So it is probably being used to indicate French royalty in a general sense. There is not, however any record of a prince of the blood being killed or wounded at a harbor.

Century II

II.LXII

Mabus puis toſt alors mourra, viendra,	*Mabus will soon die and there will happen a dreadful destruction of*
De gens & beſtes vne horrible defaite:	*people and animals. Suddenly, vengeance will appear, a hundred*
Puis tout à coup la vengeance on verra,	*hands, thirst and hunger, when the comet passes.*
Cent, main, ſoif, faim, quand courra la comete.	

After Nostradamus mentions a comet together with destruction and war, *la vengeance*. The "hundred hands" is very evocative of the many refugee camps all over the world where people are suffering from famine, "thirst and hunger." When Halley's Comet passed in 1986 there were famines in Africa, the Far East and South America. Is Mabus the name, possibly an anagram, of the Third Antichrist to come? I think it is more likely that he is envisaged as a forerunner, *purs tost alors mourra*, so the time of the Antichrist is still awaited. (See I.LXIII, VIII.LIX, VIII.LXXVII, X.LXXII, X.LXXIIII, X.LXXV.)

Century II

II.LXIII

Gaulois, Aufone[1] bien peu subiuguera, *Pan, Marne & Seine fera Perme l'vrie:* *Qui le grand mur contre eux dreffera,* *Du moindre au mur le grand perdra la vie.*	*The French will soon subdue Ansonia, while the world, Marne and Seine will make Perme drunk. He who raises the great wall against them, the great one, will lose his life from the least on the wall.*

Perme l'vrie offers a most interesting possibility. In 1590 the duc de Parme was ordered to France from the Netherlands to help the Catholic Leaguers against Henri de Navarre. Parme was defeated by Henri at the Battle of Ivry, 1590. But he did not die until 1592, from wounds received from an unknown soldier in battle. Quite a close quatrain nonetheless.

Century II

II.LXIIII

Seicher de faim, de foif, gent Geneuoife, *Efpoir prochain viendra au defaillir:* *Sur point tremblant fera loy Gebenoife.[2]* *Claffe au grand port ne fe peut acuillir.*	*The people of Geneva will dry up from thirst and hunger, nearby hope will fail. The law of the Cévennes will be at breaking point; the fleet cannot be received at the great harbor.*

After the revocation of the Edict of Nantes 1685 by Louis XIV, the Calvinist people of Cévennes rose in revolt. The fleet may possibly be trying to take supplies to Lake Geneva and is foiled.

[1] *Aufone*, Ausonia in southern Italy.
[2] *Gebenoife*, Cévennes in Switzerland.

Century II

II.LXV

Le parc enclin grande calamité, *Par l'Hefperie & Infubre fera:* *Le feu en nef pefte & captiuité,* *Mercure en l'Arc Saturne* *fenera.*	*In the feeble lists, great calamity* *throughout the West and Lom-* *bardy. Fire in the ship, plague* *and captivity. Mercury in Sagit-* *tarius, Saturn threatening.*

This is an astrological dating, sadly not of much use. The commentator Wöllner gives the next date for this configuration as December, 2044. The last was in 1839, when there were no specific dangers to the West and Italy. Things are no clearer if one takes *Hefperie*, the West, to mean America.

Century II

II.LXVI

Par grans dangiers le captif *eschapé,* *Peu de temps grand a fortune* *changée:* *Dans le palais le peuple eft* *attrapé,* *Par bon augure la cité affiegée.*	*The captive having escaped* *great dangers, his fortune is* *greatly changed in a short time.* *The people are trapped in the* *palace; by good omen, the* *besieged city.*

The captive who escapes great dangers and whose fortunes change so dramatically in a short time is Napoleon when he escapes from Elba on March 1, 1815. But this line can also be read inversely, meaning that the good fortune will soon change back again, as happened at the defeat of Waterloo, 1815. The third line is interesting. When Napoleon returned victorious to Paris after his escape, the Parisian mob invaded the palace and court of Louis XVIII, and physically carried their hero Napoleon on their shoulders up the stairs to the king's private chamber. The crowd was so enormous that no one could get in or out of the palace for some hours. The final line probably refers to Paris, the city besieged by the Allies, whose monarch will be restored *par bon augure*, which happened to Louis XVIII on July 8, 1815.

Century II

II.LXVII

Le blonde au nez forche viendra commettre,	The blond man will come into conflict with the hook-nosed one
Par le duelle chassera dehors:	in a duel and will drive him out.
Les exilés dedans fera remettre,	He will restore the exiles, placing
Aux lieux marins commettant les plus fors.	the strongest in the marine places.

The blond man was understood by authors of contemporary pamphlets to stand for the fair-haired William of Orange, who drove out James II in 1688. The Stuart party, *les exilés*, decided to reinstate James and put all their efforts into a sea battle. James based himself in Ireland and the French fleet came to his aid. In 1690, William and the Allies were badly beaten in a naval battle off Beachy Head, but on the same day William won the Battle of the Boyne. James II was forced to flee to France, from which he never returned. It took another two years for the British to subdue the French and assure maritime supremacy at Cap de la Hague in 1692.

Century II

II.LXVIII

De l'aquilon[1] les effors feront grands.	In the North the efforts will be great. The harbor will be open
Sus l'Occean fera la porte ouuerte:	across the ocean. The rule on the island will be re-established.
Le regne en l'isle fera reintegrand,	London will be afraid of the fleet when it is sighted.
Tremblera Londres par voille descouuerte.	

I believe this quatrain continues the action of II.LXVII, despite Nostradamus' claim that he mixed up all the quatrains. If this is the case, the great efforts, *effors feront grands*, in the North, are those of England's invader, William III of Orange.

[1]*aquilon.* North Wind, North.

The English fleet, badly commanded at the time by the Earl of Torrington, lost several battles to the French and Stuart fleets, particularly those of Beachy Head and Bounty Bay. It was William III's strength on land, not sea, that kept him on the throne. Line 2 could hold a second interpretation, that the seas were open and undefended, which allowed William III to cross uncontested to England. In line 3, the fact that island, *isle*, is in the singular, rather than the plural, which Nostradamus always used for Britain, indicates that it means Ireland, where James II took refuge.

Century II

II.LXIX

Le Roy Gaulois par la Celtique dextre,	A Gallic king from the Celtic right, seeing the discord of the great Monarchy will flourish his scepter over the three leopards, against the king of the great Hierarchy.
Voiant discorde de la grand Monarchie:	
Sus les trois pars fera florir son sceptre,	
Contre la cappe[1] de la grand Hierarchie.	

The key word to this quatrain is in line 3, *pars*. In another of his books, the *Horapollo*, Nostradamus describes three leopards of England in the same manner as the English heraldic lions. So this quatrain too, seems to follow on its two predecessors and continues the theme of the expulsion of James II of England by William III of Orange. William may be understood as the Celtic king from northern Gaul (Holland) who sees England in trouble under James II. It is interesting to note that Nostradamus makes no mention of war. William's was not a bloody invasion, but one of invitation. *Cappe*, as in other quatrains is the usual Nostradamus spelling of Capet, the then French royal line. The French were bitterly opposed to the establishment of the House of Orange in England, and allied themselves with the deposed James II and supplied him with troops and naval aid.

[1]*Cappe.* Capet, one of the names of the French royal line until the last of the Bourbon kings.

Century II

II.LXX

Le dard du ciel fera fon
eſtendue,
Mors en parlant: grande
execution:
La pierre en l'arbre la fiere
gent rendue,
Bruit humain monſtre purge
expiation.

The arrow from heaven will
make its journey. Dead while
speaking; a great execution. The
stone in the tree, the pond nation
brought down. The rumor of a
human monster, purge and
expiation.

Most commentators relate this quatrain to Napoleon, but I
think it is too general and lacking in key words to be
satisfactory. In theory, the theme is the Battle of Waterloo,
1815, and the arrow from the skies is understood as vengeance
from heaven. The *grande execution* refers to the carnage of the
battle, and the stone, possibly, to an axe which will cut down
the Bonaparte line, *l'arbre*. France surrenders, expiates its guilt
and the monster Napoleon is removed to St. Helena. Ingenious, if one can accept it.

Century II

II.LXXI

Les exilés en Sicile viendront,
Pour deliurer de faim la gent
eſtrange:
Au point du iour les Celtes luy
faudront
La vie demeure à raiſon: Roy ſe
range.

The exiles will come to Sicily to
deliver the foreign nations from
hunger. The Celts will fail them
at daybreak. Life is governed by
reason: the king joins as an ally.

Reason in line 3 suggests the Age of Reason during the
French Revolution. The rest appears incomprehensible.

Century II

II.LXXII

*Armée Celtique en Italie vexée,
De toutes pars conflict &
grande perte:
Romains fuis, ô Gaule repoulſée,
Pres du Theſin,[1] Rubicon
pugne[2] incerte.*

*The Celtic Army will be troubled
in Italy, great conflict and loss
on both sides. O France repelled,
flee the Romans. The battle of
the Rubicon (the river); Thessin
is uncertain.*

This quatrain sounds so specific, yet nothing it contains has happened since it was published in 1566. Probably a retroactive prophecy. Lines 1–2 could well describe the Battle of Pavia in 1525, line 3 the strategy of the Imperial forces. Even so, Pavia was a definite victory for the Italians, not uncertain.

Century II

II.LXXIII

*Au lac Fucin[3] de Benac[4] le
riuaige,
Prins du Leman[5] au port de
l'Orguion:[6]
Nay de trois bras predict
bellique image,
Par trois couronnes au grand
Endymion.[7]*

*From the shore of Lake Garda to
Fucino, taken from Lake
Geneva to the harbor of
Orguion. Born with three arms
it predicts a warlike semblance,
through three kingdoms for the
great Endymion.*

Many wild interpretations have been suggested for this quatrain, including Allen's in 1948, that Endymion (the youth with the gift of eternal sleep) is a metaphor for the USA. I cannot understand this interpretation. Three arms and three kingdoms may refer to the triple tiara of the Pope, thus linking

[1] *Theſin*. River Ticino, which flows into the Pau near Pavia.
[2] *Pugne*. L. *pugna*, battle.
[3] *Fucin*. Lake Fucino in Italy, drained in 1876.
[4] *Benac*. Lake Garda, Italy.
[5] *Leman*. Lake Geneva, Switzerland.
[6] *Orguion*. possibly Organ in the south of France or Origano in Italy?
[7] *Endymion*. Gk. The youth loved by Selene, the Moon, who had the gift of eternal sleep.

the USA with the Vatican States or an alliance of three Italian States.

Century II

II.LXXIIII

De Sens, d'Autun viendront
  iusques au Rosne,
Pour passer outre vers les monts
  Pyrenées:
La gent sortir de la Marque
  d'Anconne,
Par terre & mer suiura à grans
  trainées.

From Sens, from Autun they will come as far as the Rhône, to cross over the Pyrenees. The people leaving the Marches of Ancona will follow in great trailing (hordes) over land and sea.

Yet another confused quatrain. Leoni, 1961, suggests that the Pyrenees are a mistake for the Alps, which would help the geography, as Sens and Autun are in northeastern France, but the Rhône does not fit as it was not on the route to the Alps. If one accepts the mountains as the Alps, the quatrain describes an invasion of Italy; the Marches of Ancona stretch from Rimini to the north of Giulianova. However, even by Nostradamus' standards, to mistake the Alps for the Pyrenees seems rather farfetched. Probably a failed quatrain, as it does not fit into twentieth century geopolitical thought.

Century II

II.LXXV

La voix ouye de l'insolit oyseau,
Sur le canon du respiral estage:[1]
Si hault viendra du froment le
  boisseau,
Que l'homme d'homme sera
  Antropophage.[2]

The call of the unwelcome bird is heard on the chimney stack. Bushels of wheat will rise so high. As a result man will devour his fellow man.

[1] *Sur le canon du respiral estage:* literally translated, on the pipe of the breathing floor. Some kind of machinery? Probably metaphor for chimney.
[2] *Antropophage.* Gk. *anthro-phagus,* man-eating.

The unwelcome bird on the chimney stack is usually interpreted as an owl, which is meant to bring warning of famine. The amassed bushels of wheat, *froment le boiſſeau*, which are stacked in storage and not given to the starving bring the famines in Ethiopia and the Sudan in this century to mind. World famine is always Nostradamus' Millennium warning as a presage to the Third World War.

Century II

II.LXXVI

Foudre en Bourgongne fera cas portenteux,	Lightning in Burgundy will reveal portentous events.
Que par engin[1] oncques ne pourroit faire,	Through trickery, a thing (achieved) that could never have
De leur ſenat ſacriſte fait boiteux.	been done. The lame priest will
Fera ſçauoir aux ennemis l'affaire.	reveal affairs of the enemy to the Senate.

Charles Maurice de Talleyrand-Périgord is a suitable candidate for this quatrain. The lame priest, *ſacriſte fait boiteux*, fits him admirably. He became lame just before his fourth birthday when a chest of drawers fell on his foot, injuring him permanently. Destined by his family for the Church, he took orders in 1778, and the following year was made Bishop of Antin. By 1790 he totally identified with the revolutionaries and he was banned by the Pope in the following year. By 1807, he resigned his position as grand chamberlain to Napoleon because he disapproved of the Emperor's policies.

He secretly advised the Emperor Alexander I of Russia not to pressure Austria, despite Napoleon's wishes to the contrary. When Alexander I stayed at the Hôtel Talleyrand, he was advised by Talleyrand that the only solution for the French was the restoration of the Bourbon kings. On April 1, 1814 Talleyrand convened the Senate, to "reveal affairs of the enemy to the Senat." They pronounced Napoleon to have forfeited his crown.

---

[1] *engin*. L. *ingenium*, genius, trickery, ruse.

Century II

II.LXXVII

Par arcs feux poix & par feux
   repouſſés,
Cris hurlements ſur la minuit
   ouys:
Dedans ſont mis par les rampars
   caſſez,
Par cunicules[1] les traditeurs[2]
   fuys.

Repulsed by bows, burning pitch
and fire, cries and shouts will be
heard in the middle of the night.
They will get in through the broken defenses. The traitors escape
through underground passages.

Too general to be of much interest.

Century II

II.LXXVIII

★

Le grand Neptune du profond
   de la mer,
De gent Punique[3] & ſang
   Gaulois meſlé:
Les Iſles à ſang pour le tardif
   ramer,[4]
Plus luy nuira que l'occult mal
   celé.

Great Neptune from the depths
of the sea; of mixed African race
and French blood, the islands
remain bloody because of the
slow one. It will harm him more
than the badly concealed secret.

This quatrain may refer in part to modern Africa. It is, I
think, a split quatrain. Neptune, as used by Nostradamus in
II.LIX, refers to the Turkish fleet, a Moslem fleet, and to the
Franco-Turkish agreements of Nostradamus' day. The Barbary pirates were based in northern Africa. However, it is
possible that the "slow one" affecting the Africans and the
French à ſang may refer to AIDS, which has brought so much
harm to Europe from Africa and is still regarded as a plague
disease. It has been a "badly concealed secret" for its victims
for a long time and with no actual cure to date.

[1]*cunicules*. L. rabbit, by extension burrow, passage.
[2]*traditeurs*. L. *traditor*, traitor.
[3]*Punique*. Carthage in North Africa.
[4]*ramer*. Romance. to remain, stay.

Century II

II.LXXIX

La barbe crespe & noire par engin, *Subiuguera la gent cruelle & fiere:* *Le grand CHIREN ostera du longin[1]* *Tous les captifs par Seline[2] baniere.*	*The man with the curly black beard through his skill will subdue the cruel and proud nation. The great Chiren will take from afar everyone captured under the Turkish banner.*

The clue to this quatrain lies in the interpretation of *CHIREN*. All commentators have taken it as an anagram for HENRIC, an alternative spelling of HENRI. If that is so, this verse may be attributed to the Battle of Lepanto, 1571, which forced over 1,500 Christian slaves into the Turkish fleet, *captifs par Seline baniere*. The snag to this is that Charles X was King of France at this time; Henri III did not accede until 1574. Perhaps the word *CHIREN* is used as a symbol for France? It was at Lepanto that the Christians raised their last crusade against the Turks, of the crescent banner, *seline*. Don John of Austria who commanded them was dark and bearded, *barbe crespe & noir*.

Century II

II.LXXX

Apres conflict du lesé l'eloquence, *Par peu de temps se trame faint repos:* *Point l'on n'admet les grands à deliurance,* *Des ennemis sont remis à propos.*	*After the battle, the eloquence of the man left behind, brings a short respite for a short time. None of the great will be allowed to go free. They are delivered to their enemies at the proper time.*

A quatrain that could apply to many situations.

---

[1]*longin.* A.Pr. *longinc*, far off, distant.
[2]*Seline.* Gk. *Selene*, moon, crescent.

Century II

II.LXXXI

Par feu du ciel la cité presque
   aduste,
L'vrne¹ menace encor
   Ceucalion,²
Vexée Sardaigne par la
   Punique fuste,³
Apres que Libra lairra son
   Phaëton.

The city is almost burned to ashes
by fire from the sky. Water again
threatens Deucalion. Sardinia is
vexed by the African fleet after
Libra has left Leo.

This quatrain, with its description of a city destroyed by fire
which comes from the air (bombing or something similar),
appears to be set in the twentieth century. The devastation is
followed by a flood; Deucalion was the equivalent of Noah in
Greek mythology. In astrological geography, Libra normally
stands for Austria.

Century II

II.LXXXII

Par faim la proye fera loup
   prisonnier,
L'assaillant lors en extreme
   detresse,
Le nay⁴ ayant au deuant le
   dernier,
Le grand n'eschappe au milieu
   de la presse.

Through hunger the wolf will
make the prey prisoner. Then the
attacker is in great distress, the
elder holding the younger in
front. The great man cannot
escape in the middle of the
crowd.

It is possible to invert the meaning of line 1, but this does
not help to interpret the quatrain.

---

¹*vrne.* Metaphor for water, flooding.
²*Ceucalion. Deucalion* in all other editions. Probably a misprint.
³*fuste.* L. *fustus.* low oared galley.
⁴*Le nay.* Probable corruption of *l'aisné,* elder.

Century II

II.LXXXIII

Le gros traffic d'vn grand Lyon
  changé,
La plus part tourne en priſtine
  ruine.
Proye aux ſoldats par pille
  vendengé:[1]
Par Iura mont & Sueue[2]
  bruine.

The great trade of great Lyons
changed, the main part falls into
early rain. A prey to the soliders
pillaging a harvest. Fogs
through the mountains of Jura
and Switzerland.

Nicollaud interprets this quatrain through the memories of
the marquis de Beauregard, who writes that during October,
1795, when the Revolutionary troops were putting down an
uprising at Lyons, "we saw large crowds of peasants . . . who
with great empty sacks rushed to Lyons to pillage the town."
This was the end of a two-month siege and many of the town's
inhabitants had been massacred. Fog or mist would have been
normal over the mountain areas at that time of year.

Century II

II.LXXXIIII

Entre Campaigne; Sienne,
  Flora, Tuſtie,
Six mois neuf iours ne ploura
  vne goutte:
L'eſtrange langue en terre
  Dalmatie,
Courira ſus: vaſtant la terre
  toute.

Between Campania, Sienna,
Florence and Italy there will be
not a drop of rain for six months
and nine days. A foreign language will be spoken in Dalmatia. It will overrun the country
devastating all the land.

This must be a failed quatrain. Such a specific drought has
never been recorded in Dalmatia, which in Nostradamus' time
belonged to the Venetians and was surrounded by the
Ottoman Empire. Did Nostradamus think it would be taken
by the Turks, *eſtrange langue?*

[1]*vendengé*. O.F. harvest, vendage.
[2]*Sueue*. L. *Suevi*, Swiss.

Century II

II.LXXXV

Le vieux plain barbe ſoubs le
ſtatut ſeuere,
A Lyon faict deſſus l'Aigle
Celtique:
Le petit grant trop outre
perſeuere,
Bruit d'arme au ciel: mer rouge
Lyguſtique.[1]

Beneath the severe authority of
the old man with the flowing
beard, he is put above the Celtic
Eagle at Lyons. The small great
one presses on too far; noise of
weapons in the sky; the Ligurian
sea is red.

The small great one, *petit grant*, was possibly used to describe
Napoleon in II.LVIII, and the theme may be continued here.
The Celtic Eagle is certainly the eagle of the French; the
Hapsburg Imperial Eagle cannot be described as Celtic. But
who is the bearded man who is more important than Napoleon
at Lyons?

Century II

II.LXXXVI

Naufrage à claſſe pres d'onde
Hadriatique,
La terre tremble eſmeuë ſus l'air
en terre mis:
Egypte tremble augment
Mahometique,
L'Herault ſoy rendre à crier eſt
commis.

The fleet is wrecked near the
Adriatic sea, the earth trembles,
rises into the air and falls again.
Egypt trembles; Mahometan
increase. The herald is sent for to
ask for surrender.

The key words in this interesting quatrain are Adriatic,
Egypt and herald. In 1799, during Napoleon's expedition to
Egypt, the British and French fleets met on the Nile. The
French were roundly defeated by Sir Richard Abercromby.
From this victory, Napoleon led his troops against the Turks
at Acre, but during the siege his men were struck by the plague
and so Napoleon decided that he would withdraw back to
Egypt if he could not break down the Turkish resistance. A

[1] *Lyguſtique,* Ligurian, N.E. Mediterranean.

herald was sent to demand the surrender of Acre, but when the Turks refused, Napoleon had to lift the siege.

Century II
II.LXXXVII

Apres viendra des extremes contrees,
Prince Germain, deffus le throfne doré:
La feruitude & eaux rencontrees,
La dame ferue, fon temps plus n'adoré.

Later a German prince will come from a distant country, to a golden throne. Servitude is accepted from over the seas. The lady subordinated, in her time no longer adored.

This quatrain is a perfect description of the accession of George of Hanover to the English throne as George I, in 1714. He came from Germany, a distant country, and was a German Prince. The word *germain* also means "cousin." George was a cousin, a German one, of Queen Anne, so this may well be one of Nostradamus' famous double meanings. The English throne was regarded in Europe as a great prize, *doré*. The great lady, Anne, or Britain, was subordinate in that George was offered the English throne, it was not won in battle. The *dame ferue* may also refer to the old religion, Catholicism, which ceased finally to be the major religion in Britain.

Century II
II.LXXXVIII

Le circuit du grand faict ruineux,
Le nom septiefme du cinquiefme fera:
D'vn tiers plus grand l'eftrange belliqueux,
Mouton, Lutece,[1] Aix ne garantira.

The completion of a great, disastrous action, the name of the seventh will be that of the fifth. Of the third (name) a greater, foreign warmonger. Paris and Aix will not remain in Aries.

---

[1] *Lutece.* L. *Lutetia*, Paris.

This is an interesting quatrain and may be one of those that
influenced Catherine de' Medicis in her long conversations
with Nostradamus concerning the fates of her husband and
children. Catherine had seven Valois children, of whom the
fifth will be the seventh and last king, Henri III *(tiers)*, whose
younger brother, the duc d'Alençon, had died earlier and
whose sister Marguerite had married a foreigner with the
same name as his, Henri de Navarre, *l'eftrange belliqueux*. Henri
de Navarre became Henri IV of France through war; he
besieged Paris before France capitulated. He started the siege
in the sign of Aries (March-April), after the battle of Ivry,
1590. It is therefore reasonable to suppose that line 1 refers
to the Massacre of St. Bartholomew, as it was this action that
finally sowed the destruction, *circuit ruineux*, of the Valois and
one of the reasons, it is claimed, behind the assassination of
Henri III by Jacques Clément, which left the throne open for
Henri de Navarre.

Century II

II.LXXXIX   ★

*Vn iour feront demis les deux
    grands maiftres,
Leur grand pouuoir fe verra
    augmenté:
La terre neufue fera en fes hauts
    eftres,
Au fanguinaire le nombre
    racompté.*

One day the two great leaders
will be friends; their great power
will be seen to grow. The new
land will be at the height of its
powers. To the man of blood the
numbers are reported.

Most editions of this quatrain have the word *demis* written
as *d'âmis*. I have accepted this version because to understand
the word *demis* as meaning "halved" would make nonsense of
line 2. The two *grands maiftres* I understand as being the great
powers, and line 3, the *terre neufue* of America links these
things together. It could possibly mean the New World, but
that also implies the USA. The quatrain seems to state that
when America is at the height of its powers, it allies with the
other great power, Russia. Then, the man of blood, the Third
Antichrist, will start to assess his position.

When I translated this quatrain in 1978 I put Russia in inverted commas with a question mark. But now is the age of glasnost and Gorbachev and this seems quite acceptable, but not so good in prediction VI.XXI. Nostradamus also states that the alliance will last only three years and seven months. Will Gorbachev be removed by the other leaders of the Communist party for being too ambitious? We shall see.

Century II

II.XC

Par vie & mort changé regne
  d'Ongrie,[1]
La loy sera plus aspre que
  seruice:
Leur grand cité d'vrlemens
  plaincts & crie,
Castor & Pollux[2] ennemis dans
  la lice.

Through life and death the rule of Hungary will be changed, the law becoming more bitter than obedience. Their great city calls out with howls and lamentations. Castor and Pollux are enemies in the field.

The life-and-death change in Hungary certainly occurred during the Revolution of 1957 when Premier Nagy renounced the Warsaw Pact on November 1. The Russians advanced into his country on November 4. The violence of the street fighting, the strictness of the new imported régime which followed, from which many thousands escaped to the West, is well documented. The great city of Budapest was occupied and badly damaged. The heavenly twins of the last line, Castor and Pollux, probably stand for the relationship between Russia and its satellite state of Hungary, *ennemis dans la lice*. I do not think that it is an astrological dating.

[1]*Ongrie*. Hungary
[2]*Castor & Pollux*. Gemini, the heavenly twins.

Century II

II.XCI   ★

Soleil leuant vn grand feu l'on verra,
Bruit & clarté vers Aquilon tendants:
Dedans le rond mort & cris l'on orra,
Par glaiue, feu, faim, mort las attendants.

At sunrise a great fire will be seen, noise and light extending towards the North. In the globe death and cries are heard. Death awaits, through weapons, fire and famine.

If one applies this quatrain to the future, it is a very frightening one. It implies that a northern country—either Russia or America—will be bombed at sunrise. In a modern context, this can only mean an atomic explosion of some kind, which will be followed by a period of great devastation.

In I.II and V.LXXV Nostradamus states the destruction will be greater in America, but the victor will be born "on American soil," and therefore, hopefully, sympathetic to the West. (See also II.LXXXIX, VII.XXI, VIII.LXXVII, VIII.LIX, X.LXXVII.)

Century II

II.XCII

Feu couleur d'or du ciel en terre veu,
Frappé du haut nay, faict cas merueilleux:
Grand meurtre humain: prinſe du grãd nepueu,
Morts d'eſpectacles eſchappé l'orgueilleux.

From the sky, fire, the color of gold is seen on earth, struck by the high born, a marvelous event. Great slaughter of humanity. A nephew taken from the high born one. Death to the spectator, the proud one escapes.

The probable clue to this quatrain is the word nephew, *nepueu*, in line 3. Nostradamus describes Napoleon III, the nephew of Napoleon, several times in this way. The second line refers to an incident in August 2, 1870, when, during an assassination attempt, a bullet hit the ground by the prince imperial's feet, an event much publicized in the newspapers. The spectator, the prince imperial, was captured during the French capitulation of 1870, but escaped death. He was the last of the French kings and emperors as Louis XVIII.

Century II

II.XCIII

Bien pres du Tymbre preſſe la Lybitine;[1]	*Very near the Tiber death hurries, a short while before a great flood. The captain of the ship taken, put into the bilges; the castle and the palace burned down.*
Vn peu deuant grand' inondation:	
Le chef du nef prins, mis à la ſentine,[2]	
Chaſteau, palais en conflagration.	

Tiber normally stands for Rome, linked here with the captain of the ship (the Barque of St. Peter)? This implies that a pope will come to a dreadful end before a flood. The castle and palace would be Sant' Angelo and the Vatican.

Century II

II.XCIIII

GRAND Pau grand mal pour Gaulois receura,	*Great Po will suffer great harm from a Frenchman, a vain terror to the maritime Lion. An infinite number of people will cross the sea and a quarter of a million will not escape.*
Vaine terreur au maritin Lyon:	
Peuple infiny par la mer paſſera.	
Sans eſchapper vn quart d'vn milion.	

Italy, the Po, suffered greatly under Napoleonic rule, and Napoleon also terrified the maritime British Lion, but in vain, *vaine terreur*, as he did not manage to invade Britain. Napoleon led a great army across the seas to Europe, and at least a quarter of a million men died either during campaigns or from the plague.

[1] *Lybitine.* L. *Libitina*, goddess of Death.
[2] *ſentine.* L. *sentina*, bilges, dregs.

Century II

II.XCV

Les lieux peuplez feront
  inhabitables:
Pour champs auoir grande
  diuifion:
Regnes liurez à prudents
  incapables,
Lors les grands freres mort &
  diffention.

The unpopulated lands will
become uninhabitable; great disagreement in order to obtain
lands. Kingdoms given to a man
incapable of prudence. Then for
the great brothers, death and dissension.

Some commentators apply this to the present or near future
on the strength of line 1. The last line could refer to the three
Kennedy brothers, as there has been no other set of important
brothers to whom one can relate this line during the last half
of this century. (See VIII.LXVII, and VII.LXXVII, also
II.XCI.)

Century II

II.XCVI

Flambeau ardent au ciel foir fera
  veu,
Pres de la fin & principe du
  Rofne:
Famine, glaiue: tard le fecours
  pourueu,
La Perfe tourne enuahir
  Macedoine.

A burning torch will be seen in
the sky at night, near the foundation and source of the Rhône.
Famine, weapon; help provided
too late, Persia will turn and
invade Macedonia.

The most specific part of this quatrain is line 4. Nostradamus predicts that the Persians, never part of the Ottoman
Empire, would inflict great defeat upon the Turks, Macedonia, in order to open up the Balkans. If the rest is to be
accepted, he states that a light in the sky will be seen from the
source of the Rhône, at the Furka Pass, as far as the mouth of
the river west of Marseilles.

Century II

II.XCVII

Romain Pontife garde de
  t'approcher,
De la cité que deux fleuues
  arrouse,
Ton sang viendras aupres de là
  cracher,
Toy & les tiens quand fleurira
  la rose.

Roman pontiff, beware of
approaching a city watered by
two rivers. You will spit blood in
that place, both you and yours,
when the roses bloom.

The only pope who suffered in a city between two rivers was
Pius VI, who was imprisoned at Valence by the French after
they had taken Rome in 1799. The two rivers are the Rhône
and the Saône at Lyons. Pius VI died spitting blood, from an
attack of acute gastro-enteritis in the summer, *quand fleurira la
rose,* on August 29, 1799. His people *(les tiens)* were the thirty-
two priests imprisoned with him. The word *rose* (red) may have
the typical Nostradamus double meaning of the color of the
Revolutionaries and of the blood they shed. A convincing
quatrain.

Century II

II.XCVIII

Celuy du sang reperse[1] le visage,
De la victime proche sacrifiée,
Tonant[2] en Leo augure par
  presage,
Mis estre à mort lors pour la
  fiancée.[3]

His face is spattered with the
blood of a newly sacrificed victim. Jupiter and Leo warn
through prophecy. He will be put
to death for the promised one.

I can find no explanation for this quatrain.

[1]*reperse.* L. *respergere,* to sprinkle, splash.
[2]*Tonant.* L. *Tonans,* Jupiter, the Murderer.
[3]*fiancée.* R. promise or assurance; L. bride.

Century II

II.XCIX

Terroir[1] Romain qu'interpretoit augure,
Par agent Gauloyse par trop sera vexée:
Mais nation Celtique craindra l'heure,
Boreas,[2] claffe[3] trop loing avoir pouffée.

Roman land that the augur interprets will be greatly molested by the French nation. But the French will come to dread the time of the North wind, having driven their fleet too far.

The Papal States were enveloped into the French Empire in 1810. But by 1812 Napoleon is suffering from the defeat of his Russian campaign due mainly to the cold weather *(Boreas)* and the folly of his overdeployment of troops. The fleet, *claffe*, may refer to the earlier defeat at Trafalgar.

Century II

II.C

Dedans les isles fi horrible tumulte,
Bien on n'orra qu'vne bellique brigue
Tant grand sera des predateurs l'insulte,
Qu'on se viendra ranger à la grand ligue.

Within the islands will be so dreadful a tumult although only the warlike party is heard. So great will be the threat of the plunderers that they will come to join in the great alliance.

Line 4 gives the clue. It refers to the *Grand Succurso* raised by all the Christian powers sent to Malta in 1565 in order to save Europe. The great alliance is probably the supranational order of Malta's Grand Knights, *les isles*, allied to the Christian forces.

[1]*Terroir.* L. *terra*, land.
[2]*Boreas.* L. north wind.
[3]*claffe.* L. *classus*, fleet.

Century III

III.I

Apres combat & bataille
nauale,
Le grand Neptune à ſon plus
haut befroy:
Rouge auerſaire de peur viãdra
paſle
Mettant le grand Ocean en
effroy.

After the combat and naval bat-
tle, great Neptune in his highest
belfry. The red adversary will
become pale with fear, putting
the great Ocean into a state of
terror.

This appears to be a failed quatrain. In II.LIX, Nostradamus uses Neptune as a synonym for the Turkish and Algerian
fleets who were ravaging the Mediterranean. The Spanish flag
is red, they were their adversaries, but of course red can also
be understood as "bloodlike." It is here the quatrain fails. The
Spanish, far from *viãdra paſle*, won the battle with the Turks
at Lepanto in 1571. However, the Barbary Corsairs continued
to dominate the Mediterranean for some time to come. This
leads into the following quatrain III.II.

Century III

III.II

Le diuin verbe donrra à la
ſubſtance,
Cãprins ciel terre, or occult au
laict¹ myſtique:
Corps, ame, eſprit ayant toute
puiſſance,
Tant ſoubz ſes pieds comme au
ſiege Celique.²

The divine word will give to the
substance (that which) contains
heaven and earth, occult gold in
the mystic act. Body, soul and
spirit are all powerful. Every-
thing is beneath his feet, as at the
seat of heaven.

I believe this verse to be an important description of
Nostradamus' experiences with the occult, *diuin verbe*, when he
is prophesying. The substance is, in this case, the bowl of water
on a brass tripod, mentioned in I.I, in which is portrayed the

---

¹*laict.* certainly misprint for *faict*, deed, found in other editions.
²*Celique.* O.F. celestial, heavenly.

various revelations of the *Prophéties*. The *diuin verbe* may be the incantation used by Nostradamus—his mantra—which makes him all-powerful in body and spirit. The last line could mean that during these sessions Nostradamus felt disembodied, a common enough mystic experience, with everything at his feet and he looking down, "as at the seat of heaven."

Century III

III.III

Mars & Mercure & l'argent[1] ioint enfemble, *Vers le midy extreme ficcité:* *Au fond d'Afie on dira terre tremble,* *Corinthe, Ephefe lors en perplexité.*	With Mars, Mercury and the Moon in conjunction towards the South, there will be a great drought. An earthquake will be reported from the depths of Asia; both Corinth and Ephesus then in a troubled state.

This is the second and only other reference to a linking of Corinth and Ephesus. The first can be found in II.LII, where I interpret them allegorically as standing for England and Holland. When there is a great drought in the south, could Nostradamus mean Africa rather than the conventional interpretation of *midi*, southern France. There will be earthquakes in Asia, and England and Holland will have problems. Possibly the IRA terrorists, and those of many other outlawed organizations, who find a safe house among the Dutch? But if Corinth and Ephesus mean Africa Minor, perhaps this quatrain has not been fulfilled. I cannot interpret line 1, although it must be an astrological dating.

[1] *argent.* an alchemistic term for the moon, because of its silvery color.

Century III

III.IIII

Quand feront proches le defaut
　des lunaires,
De l'vn à l'autre ne diftant
　grandement,
Froid, siccité, danger vers les
　frontieres,
Mefme où l'oracle a prins
　commencement.

When the downfall of the lunar
ones is very close, they will not be
very distant from one another.
Cold, drought, danger around
the frontiers, even where the oracle had its source.

The people of the moon, *lunaires*, are normally described as people of Islam, of the crescent flag. Two Islamic countries who are very close to each other and near a state of collapse are obviously Iran and Iraq, who were at war for close on nine years, and who, certainly more so in the case of Iran, exhausted most of their manpower, and even that of their twelve-year-old boys, who were sent in waves in advance of the more experienced troops, to search out mines, etc., rather in the manner of World War I. As they share a common frontier where there is cold and danger, this seems to strengthen the interpretation. If the oracle has his source here, it may refer to the mysterious Perse, who elsewhere in the quatrains is reputed to be born in the Middle East and will be involved with the coming of the Third Antichrist in some way or another.

Century III

III.V

Pres loing defaut de deux
　grands luminaires,
Qui furuiendra entre l'Auril &
　Mars:
O quel cherté mais deux grans
　debonnaires,
Par terre & mer fecourront
　toutes pars.

Not long after the eclipse of two
great moon signs which will
occur between March and April,
what a great loss. But two great
good influences will help on all
sides, by land and sea.

This may follow on the last quatrain. If so, we can expect a
cessation of hostilities between Iran and Iraq between March
and April, or in the sign of Aries. The two great good
influences for peace are presumably America and any of the
three European powers trying to keep peace in the Gulf—
England, France, and Italy *(par terre & mer)*. A state of cease-
fire has been declared by the United Nations in August, 1988,
so perhaps peace will be finalized in March/April of 1989?

Century III

III.VI

Dans temple clos le foudre y entrera, *Les citadins dedans leur fort greuez:* *Cheuaux, boeufs hommes, l'ōde mur touchera,* *Par faim, foif, foubs les plus foibles armez.*	*Lightning will strike inside the closed temple and harm the citizens in their stronghold. Horses, cattle, men, the flood will reach the walls; through hunger and thirst, those armed beneath the weakest.*

If the temple stands for a church, nineteenth century
commentators accept that this quatrain refers to a famous
incident in 1819 at Châteauneuf, when a church was struck by
lightning. Nine people were killed and eighty-two injured
among the congregation. But this seems rather flimsy to me,
and the last line does not fit. I think this is probably a failed
quatrain.

Century III

III.VII

Les fugitifs, feu du ciel fus les piques. *Conflict prochain des corbeaux s'esbatans,* *De terre on crie aide fecours celiques,* *Quand pres des murs feront les combatans.*	*The fugitives, the weapons with fire from heaven. The next conflict will be that of the flying crows. They call upon earth and heaven for help, when the aggressors draw near the walls.*

This almost certainly describes the fall of France in 1940, when both the French army and multitudes of refugees were driven back in confusion along the roads to Paris. They were strafed and gunned down by German planes, *corbeaux s'esbatans*. The crows could also be a literal meaning in that they picked at the bodies of the dead lying on the roadsides. The aggressors are the German forces about to march upon Paris.

Century III

III.VIII

Les Cimbres ioints auecques leurs voiſins, *Depopuler viendront preſque l'Eſpaigne:* *Gens amaſſez, Guienne & Limoſins,* *Seront en ligue, & leur feront compaigne.*	The Cimbrians, allied with their neighbors, will come to ravage almost all of Spain. People gathered in Guienne and Limousin will join in alliance with their company.

The Cimbrians were a north German tribe who intermixed with the Teutones and vanished around 100 B.C. Therefore this quatrain may describe Germany and her neighbors Prussia and Italy, who supported the Fascist cause of Franco during the Spanish Civil War of 1936–39. The last two lines may refer to the wide support for Nazi policies in France during this period, or to the many French who went to fight for the insurgent armies in Spain. It must also be remembered that after the Spanish Republican army's defeat at Teruel in 1938, its soldiers actually took refuge in France. This was followed by a mass exodus of Spanish refugees into France in 1938 and early 1939. (See IX.XVI.)

Century III

III.IX

*Bourdeaux, Rouan, & la
  Rochelle ioints,
Tiendront autour la grand mer
  Occeane,
Anglois, Bretons, & les
  Flamans conioints,
Les chasseront iusque au pres de
  Rouane.*

*Bordeaux, Rouen and La
Rochelle allied will hold all
around the open seas. The
English, Bretons and Flemish
together will drive them as far as
Roanne.*

Despite the detailed place names and peoples, this quatrain
remains completely obscure. Bordeaux and La Rochelle are
close to each other, but Rouen is to the north. Roanne is on
the upper Loire.

Century III

III.X

*De sang & faim plus grande
  calamité,
Sept fois s'appreste à la marine
  plage:
Monech[1] de faim, lieu pris,
  captiuité,
Le grand mené croc[2] en ferree
  caige.*

*Even greater calamity with blood
and famine. Seven times it
approaches the seashore.
Monaco captured, in captivity
from hunger. The great golden
one crushed in an iron cage.*

Monaco was already a semi-independent state under the
House of Grimaldi in Nostradamus' time, but it has never been
captured or besieged. Many readers have written to me saying
that they believe line 4 to refer to Princess Grace of Monaco,
she of the golden hair and film star fame, dying in a car
accident with her daughter Princess Stephanie, *croc en ferree
caige*.

[1]*Monech.* L. *Moneceus*, Monaco.
[2]*croc.* L. *crocens*, yellow; O.F. *croquer*, to crunch; *croc.* Prov. a hook.

Century III

III.XI

Les armes battre au ciel longue
 ſaiſon,
L'arbre au milieu de la cité tombé:
Verbine,[1] rongne, glaiue en face
 tyſon,
Lors le monarque d'Hadrie
 ſuccombé.

The weapons fight in the sky for
a long time. The tree fallen in
the midst of the city. The sacred
branch broken, a sword opposite
Tison, then the King of Hadrie
is fallen.

The first line of this quatrain appears to put it into the
twentieth century, with wars in the air, *armes battre au ciel*. But
a far more interesting legend may relate this quatrain to the
assassination of Henri IV in 1610, a seventeenth century
version of the story of the Angels of Mons of the First World
War. Apparently when Henri IV was assassinated by Ravaillac
on May 14 of that year, there appeared in the *Mercure Français*
a story of a ghastly army seen marching in the skies. Henri is
the tree, the fount of his line, chopped down in the center of
Paris. He was the last of the direct Valois line, as he was
descended from Louis XIII, by his second wife, Marie de'
Medicis. Henri is sacred because he was an anointed king. He
was actually stabbed with a knife in the rue Ferroniers, not far
from the corner which branches off the rue Tison. It is this
small detail which convinces me of the veracity of the quatrain.

Century III

III.XII ★

Par la tumeur de Heb, Po,
 Tag, Timbre, & Rome[2]
Et par l'eſtang Leman[3] & Aretin:[4]
Les deux grands chefs & citez de
 Garonne,
Prins mors noyez. Partir humain
 butin.

Because of the overflow of the
Ebro, Po, Tagus, Tiber and
Rhône; by the lakes of Geneva and
Arezzo the two great, chief cities of
the Garonne taken, dead, drowned.
The human booty is shared out.

[1] *Verbine*. L. *verbene*, sacred branch.
[2] *Rome*. misprint for Rhône in most editions.
[3] *Leman*. L. *Lemannus*, Lake Leman, Lake Geneva.
[4] *Aretin*. L. *Arentuis*, Arezzo.

This is one of the many quatrains describing a flooding so vast it covers most of Europe, Spain and Portugal, Italy and France. Probably another general warning of the Millennium, possibly the end result of the ozone gaps over the Arctic pole and the resultant greenhouse effect.

Century III

III.XIII

Par fouldre en l'arche[1] or &
    argent fondu,
De deux captifs l'vn l'autre
    mangera:
De la cité le plus grand eſtendu,
Quand ſubmergee la claſſe[2]
    nagera.
	Through lightning in the ship gold and silver are melted, the two captives will devour each other. The greatest one of the city is stretched when the fleet travels under water.

Line 4 certainly refers to a submarine fleet, and I imagine the lightning in the ship which dissolves metals is probably some form of undersea missile. It is possessed by both sides in the battle and creates mutual destruction, *l'vn l'autre mangera.* However, the quatrain is vague as to actual time, place, etc.

Century III

III.XIIII

Par le rameau[3] du vaillant
    perſonnage,
De France infime, par le pere
    infelice:
Honneurs richeſſes, trauail en ſon
    vieil aage,
Pour auoir creu le conſeil
    d'homme nice.[4]
	Through the offspring of a valiant personality, of weakened France due to an unfortunate father. Honors, riches and war in his old age because he believed the counsel of an inexperienced man.

[1] *l'arche.* L. *arx,* ship, barque, box.
[2] *claſſe.* L. *classus,* fleet.
[3] *rameau.* literally branch, offshoot.
[4] *nice.* Rom. simple, inexperience.

It was Louis XV, son of the glorious but unfortunate Sun King, who weakened France. He came to the throne when aged five, and his Regency was totally governed by the duc d'Orléans. France deteriorated into such a poor financial state that it was declared bankrupt under the banker John Law in 1712. The inexperienced man who counseled the king badly was Fleury, his tutor and priest, who did not come to Louis XV's aid until 1726, when he was already seventy-two. Fleury's inexperience in politics helped towards the general unrest which led to the attempted assassination of the king by Damiens in 1757. See the following quatrain.

Century III

III.XV

Coeur, vigueur, gloire le regne changera,	The heart of the kingdom will change in vigor and glory. On all sides its adversary will be opposed. Then through death a child will rule over France, the great Regent will be much to its detriment.
De tous points contre ayant son aduersaire,	
Lors France enfance par mort subiuguera,	
Vn grand regent sera lors plus contraire.	

Yet another of Nostradamus' double quatrains. It continues with the subject of Louis XV. The kingdom under his uncle, Louis XIV, one of vigor and glory, will change when a child rules over France. The great regent, Philippe, duc d'Orléans was the complete opposite both in private and public life to his late brother, *aduersaire*. There has been no other underaged king and male regent of France since the quatrains were published. The line "then through death a child will rule over France" may refer to the popular rumor of the time that both the duc de Burgundy and the duc de Bretagne, Louis XV's grandfather and father, had been poisoned by the regent.

Century III

III.XVI

*Vn prince Anglois Mars à ſon
  coeur de ciel,
Voudra pourſuiure ſa fortune
  proſpere:
Des deux duelles l'vn percera le
  fiel,
Hay de luy, bien aymé de ſa
  mere.*

*An English prince, Mars to his
heart in the heavens, will wish to
follow his prospering fortune. In
two duels in one he will be
pierced in the gallbladder.
Hated by him, but well loved by
his mother.*

Almost certainly an unfulfilled quatrain. No English, nor
even Scottish princes satisfy this prediction, and it seems
unlikely that duels will take place in the future.

Century III

III.XVII

*Mont Auentine bruſler nuict ſera
  veu,
Le ciel obſcur tout à vn coup en
  Flandres:
Quand le monarque chaſſera ſon
  nepueu,
Leurs gês d Egliſe commettront
  les eſclãdres.*

*Mount Aventine will be seen
burning at night, when suddenly
the sky at Flanders will be darken-
ed. When the king drives out his
nephew, their churchmen will
act scandalously.*

Since Mount Aventine is one of the hills of Rome it probably
stands for Rome itself. The *ciel obſcur* at Flanders may mean an
eclipse of the sun, but I am unable to link it with a king.
Napoleon however did commit great atrocities against the
Roman Catholic Church: he abolished it and later imprisoned
the Pope in France. He did not personally drive out his
nephew, Napoleon III, but the latter was driven out from
Holland as a child when his father King Louis abdicated. Line
1 may then refer to Napoleon's sack of Rome.

Century III

III.XVIII

Apres la pluye laict aſſés
    longuette,
En pluſieurs lieux de Reims le
    ciel touché:
O quel conflict de ſang pres
    d'eux s'appreſte,
Peres & fils Roys n'oſeront
    approcher.

After the rather long milky rain several places in Reims will be touched by lightning. O, what a bloody battle approaches them, fathers and sons, kings will not dare approach.

The rain of milk also occurs in the following quatrain.

Century III

III.XIX ★

En Luques ſang & laict viendra
    pluuoir,
Vn peu deuant changement de
    preteur:[1]
Grand peſte & guerre, faim &
    ſoif fera voir
Loing où mourra leur Prince
    recteur.[2]

In Lucca it will come to rain blood and milk, shortly before a change of governor. Great plague and war, famine and drought will appear far from where the Prince and ruler lies.

Lucca was a duchy between Tuscany and Modena. Together with the rain of milk, we now have a rain of blood, a favorite of Roman historians. This also occurs in modern times, usually when red dust clouds from the Sahara or similar deserts are sucked up into rain clouds, and the raindrops are red. Black rain fell after the atomic bombs were dropped on Japan in 1945. The governor and the prince cannot be identified, so the whole quatrain remains an enigma. Some commentators now identify the blood and milk (semen) as indicating AIDS since they are the major source of infection by this disease.

[1]*preteur.* L. *praetor,* governor.
[2]*recteur.* L. leader, ruler.

Century III

III.XX

Par les contrees du grand
  fleuue Bethique,[1]
Loing d'Ibere[2] au royaume de
  Grenade:[3]
Croix repouſſees par gens
  Mahometiques,
Vn de Cordube trahira la
  contrade.[4]

Through the lands of the great
Guadalquivir River far from
Spain, to the kingdom of Gra-
nada. The cross spurned by the
Mohammedans, a man from
Córdova will betray his country.

This quatrain is preoccupied with Spain. Granada, south of
the Guadalquivir River, was the last Moorish outpost of Iberia,
conquered in 1492. After its conquest by the Christians, Jews
were allowed to remain provided they accepted Christianity.
In 1610, the remainder of the Jewish colony were accused by
Philip II of a lack of sincerity in their religious practices and
turned out of Spain. This was despite the contract drawn up
by Ferdinand and Isabella of Spain with Gonsalvo Fernández
de Córdova, who had helped to negotiate the treaty. So
Nostradamus was wrong in saying that he betrayed his
country; his treaty was betrayed. *Cordube* is the key word in this
quatrain.

Century III

III.XXI

Au Cruſtamin[5] par mer
  Hadriatique,
Apparoiſtra vn horrible poiſſon:
De face humaine & la fin
  aquatique,
Qui ſe prendra dehors de
  l'ameçon.

Near the Conca by the Adriatic
sea will appear a horrible fish
with human features and of
aquatic purpose; it will be
caught without a hook.

[1] *Bethique*. L. Baetis, Guadalquivir River.
[2] *Ibere*. Gk. Spaniards, particularly around the Ebro.
[3] *Grenade*. Southern Spain.
[4] *contrade*. Pr. country.
[5] *Cruſtamin*. L. Crustumius, River Conca.

Commentators disagree about this obscure quatrain. Garen-cières (1672) says that a mermaid-type creature, perhaps a manatee or a dugon, was seen near Rome in 1523, and Rondeletius records a similar happening in 1531. Edgar Leoni (1961) states in his commentary that the records of Cattolica, where the Conca flows into the Adriatic, show no such event. This quatrain is one that lends itself to wishful thinking.

Century III

III.XXII

Six iours l'affaut deuant cité donné:
Liuree fera forte & afpre bataille:
Trois la rendront & à eux pardonné,
Le refte à feu & fang tranche traille.

For six days the assault is made in front of the city. It will be freed in a strong and bitter fight. Three will hand it over, and they will be pardoned: the rest will go to the fire, bloody slaughter and slashing.

Another quatrain which is too specific to be of any value.

Century III

III.XXIII

Si France paffes outre mer lyguftique,[1]
Tu te verras en ifles & mers enclos:
Mahommet contraire, plus mer Hadriatique,
Cheuaux & d'Afnes tu rongeras les os.

France, if you cross the Ligurian sea, you will find yourself besieged among islands and seas. With Mahomet against you, more so the Adriatic, you will gnaw the bones of horses and asses.

France will get into difficulties if it marches against Yugoslavia (across the Ligurian sea). This is probably a prediction of general disaster for contemporary France and the Ottoman Empire. Nostradamus speaks of France in the singular, affectionate "*tu*" because it was the country he loved above all.

[1] *lyguftique*. L. *ligusticus*, Ligurian.

Century III

III.XXIIII

De l'entreprinſe grande confuſion,	Great confusion results from the expedition, immense loss of men
Perte de gens, threſor innumerable:	and treasure. You must never attempt to expand there again.
Tu n'y dois faire encore tenſion[1]	France, take note of my predic-
France à mon dire fais que ſois recordable.[2]	tion.

This seems to continue on from the previous quatrain and is not a real prediction but a general warning against the Ottoman Empire. Note again the use of the familiar tense of the verb "*(tu) ſois recordable.*"

Century III

III.XXV

Qui au Royaume Nauarrois paruiendra,	He who attains the kingdom of Navarre when Sicily and Naples
Quand de Sicile & Naples feront ioints:	are allies will hold Bigorre and Landes through Foix and
Bigore & Landes par Foyx loron tiendra,	Oloran, from one who will be too strongly allied with Spain.
D'vn qui d'Eſpaigne ſera par trop conioint.	

The inheritor of Navarre is Henri IV. Sicily and Naples were joined together sporadically for centuries but this alliance was formalized only twice: first by Philip II of Spain on his marriage to Mary Tudor in 1554 and again by Joseph Buonaparte in the nineteenth century. Henri became king of Navarre in 1562 and king of France in 1594. All of the places in line 3 are situated in Navarre; Bigorre has a double meaning because *Bigorre* was also the rallying cry of his Huguenot armies. Possibly the person who is too strongly allied with Spain, *par trop conoint,* may be Henri's cousin

[1]*tenſion.* L. *tensio,* extension.
[2]*recordable.* O.F. memorable.

Elisabeth, daughter of Henri II of France, who married Philip of Spain in 1559. All the same, it is a rather unsatisfactory quatrain.

Century III

III.XXVI

*Des Roys & Princes dreſſeront
 ſimulacres,
Augures, creuz eſleuez aruſpices:[1]
Corne, victime doree, & d'azur,
 d'acre,
Interpretez ſeront les extipices.[2]*

They will raise up idols of kings and princes, augurers and hollow priests elevated. A victim, its horn gilded with gold and azure, dazzling, the entrails will be read.

I leave the interpretation to the reader.

Century III

III.XXVII

*Prince libinique puiſſant en
 Occident,
François d'Arabe viendra tant
 enflammer,
Sçauans aux lettres fera
 condeſcendent,
La langue Arabe en François
 tranſlater.*

The Libyan prince will be powerful in the West, the French will be so enamored of Arabia. Learned in letters he will condescend to translate the Arab language into French.

The Libyan Prince who will become powerful in the West is surely President Gadaffi. His terrorist organization, the P.L.O., have strong connections with the French, who have pursued a less severe course with them, despite their being an avowed terrorist organization, than most European countries. The French have also had strong links with North Africa over many centuries. The last line is unclear. The first French-Arabic dictionary came out in 1505, just after Nostradamus was born. I cannot think of any other great works of literary

[1]*aruſpices*. O.F. auspices.
[2]*extipices*. L. *extispicus*, soothsayer.

merit translated in the present time which may link line 4 with
Gadaffi.

Century III

III.XXVIII

*De terre foible & pauure
  parentele,[1]
Par bout & paix paruiendra
  dans l'empire:
Long temps regner vne ieune
  femelle,
Qu'oncques en regne n'en
  ſuruint vn ſi pire.*

A person possessing few lands
and of poor parentage through
intent and peace will attain to
the Empire. For a long time a
young woman shall reign; never
has so bad an influence been
exerted on the kingdom.

This is regarded by most commentators as a split quatrain,
referring to two different people and circumstances. I am not
certain. The first two lines are related as describing Henri de
Navarre, whose court was renowned for its poverty and
simplicity.

The second part is described as relating to Elizabeth I of
England. However, Henri and Elizabeth only reigned contem-
poraneously between the years of 1594 and 1601. Henri
achieved the kingship of the French empire. Elizabeth's
Protestantism would rate the epithet *n'en ſuruint vn ſi pire*,
because of Nostradamus' fervent anti-Protestantism. She was
a young girl when she acceded to the English throne and
reigned for a very long time, nearly half a century. But there
is always the possibility that the person of lowly origin, *pauure
parentele*, could refer to the comparatively low estate of Anne
Boleyn, Elizabeth's mother, and the poverty to which Elizabeth
was subjected as a child.

---

[1]*parentele*. O.F. parentage, family line.

Century III

III.XXIX

Les deux nepueux en diuers
    lieux nourris:
Nauale pugne,[1] terre peres
    tombez:
Viendront si haut esleuez
    enguerris,[2]
Venger l'iniure ennemis
    succombez.

Two nephews will be brought up in different places. A naval battle, fathers fallen to the ground. They will be greatly elevated by making war to avenge their injury; the enemies are overcome.

The nephews may possibly be those of the Constable of France, Anne de Montmorency, but they were three, not two—Coligny, Châtillon, and d'Andelot. The question of war and avenging their honor fits them but partly. This may well be a failed quatrain.

Century III

III.XXX

Celuy qu'en luitte & fer au
    faict bellique,
Aura porté plus grand que luy
    le pris:
De nuict au lict six luy feront la
    pique,
Nud sans harnois subit sera
    surprins.

He who in a struggle with a weapon in a warlike deed, will carry off the prize from one greater than he. At night, six will bring harm to his bed; naked, without his armor, he will suddenly be surprised.

This refers to the sad story of the comte de Montgomery, who was captain of the Scottish Guard under Henri II. He inadvertently wounded the king in a festive tournament for the marriage of his sister and daughter Elisabeth in 1559. Tragically, the king died ten days later. Henri had given orders that he should be pardoned, but Catherine demanded his life, determined to avenge her husband's death. Montgomery fled to England as a Huguenot, and returned later to Normandy to lead the rebellious Protestants.

[1] *pugne*. L. *pugna*. battle.
[2] *enguerroir*. O.F. to fight, make war.

After various successes in battle, he was surrounded by the Marshal at Domfront and forced to surrender. Under the terms of the surrender, his life was to be spared, but Catherine would have none of that. Secretly, she sent six men of the royal guard to arrest him. He was captured in his bed, *de nuict au lict*, on May 27, 1574, and sent under Catherine's orders to the Conciergerie. It is not known what happened after this nor the manner of his dying. Nostradamus leaves that out, too.

Century III
III.XXXI

Aux champs de Mede, d'Arabe
& d'Armenie,
Deux grans copies trois fois
  s'aſſembleront:
Pres du riuage d'Araxes la
  meſgnie,
Du grand Soliman en terre
tomberont.

On the battlefields of Media, Arabia and America, the two great armies will gather three times. Near the border of Araxum, the establishment of great Soliman will fall to the ground.

Many commentators attribute this quatrain to events which occurred during Nostradamus' lifetime, particularly the Battle of Araxes, 1514. But James Laver's opinion seems more likely to be correct. He ascribes it to the Battle of Lepanto, 1571, in which Don John of Austria beat Selim II, the son of Soliman. The Battle of Lepanto was fought off Cape Papa, then known as Cape Araxum, in the Mediterranean.

Century III
III.XXXII

Le grand ſepulchre du peuple
  Aquitanique,
S'approchera aupres de la
  Toſcane:
Quand Mars ſera pres du coing
  Germanique,
Et au terroir de la gent
  Mantuane.

The huge sepulcher for the French nation, approaches from the direction of Italy. When war is near the German corner and in the hands of the Italian people.

A very good general quatrain on the Second World War, because of Nostradamus' vision of a war killing many Frenchmen, involving both Italy and Germany. Aquitaine stands for France, and Tuscany and Mantua for Italy. The war in the *coing Germanique* is obvious in that the Second World War was started by the Germans' marching into Poland.

Century III

III.XXXIII

En la cité où le loup entrera,
Bien pres de là les ennemis
feront:
Copie eftrange grand pays
gaftera,
Aux murs & Alpes les amis
pafferont.

In the city which the wolf will enter, the enemies will be very close by. A foreign army will devastate the great country; friends will pass by the walls and the Alps.

Unfortunately this quatrain has no link word other than the Alps. If we knew whose foreign army had devastated the unknown country, we might get somewhere. The wolf is presumably a traitor on the side of the enemy.

Century III

III.XXXIIII

Quand le deffaut du Soleil lors
fera.
Sur le plain iour le monftre fera
veu:
Tout autrement on
l'interpretera,
Cherté n'a garde nul n'y aura
pourueu.

When there is an eclipse of the sun in broad daylight, the monster will be seen. Many will interpret it in different ways. They will not care about money or make any provision for it.

Another quatrain impossible to interpret, as we are given no dating for the sun's eclipse. Since this is a comparatively common event the quatrain is even harder to decipher. Line 4 indicates an unexpected famine or drought for which no provision will have been made.

Century III

III.XXXV

Du plus profond de l'Occident
  d'Europe,
De pauures gens vn ieune
  enfant naiſtra:
Qui par ſa langue ſeduira
  grande troupe,
Son bruit au regne d'Orient
  plus croiſtra.

From the deepest part of Western
Europe a child will be born of a
poor family, who will entice
many people with his oratory.
His reputation will grow even
greater in the kingdom of the
East.

This is an excellent example of Nostradamus' ambiguous
quatrains, those which seem to fit various peoples at varying
times. The truism that history repeats itself is made easier by
the facts being so general in scope.

Most commentators ascribe the quatrain to either Hitler or
Napoleon. I believe it to refer to Hitler, as Austria is better
described as in deepest Western Europe l'Occident d'Europe,
than Corsica, which is nearer the shores of Africa. If Corsica
is preferred, profond must be translated as lowest.

Both Hitler and Napoleon came from comparatively humble origins. Both were famous for their personal magnetism
and powers of oratory. This can be confirmed in Hitler's case
by many films of events such as the Nuremberg rallies. But it
is line 4 which convinces me most. The Kingdom of the East,
Japan, allied with Hitler. The nearest Napoleon got to the East
was Egypt. (See II.XXXIX.)

Century III

III.XXXVI

Enſeuely non mort apopletique,
Sera trouué auoir les mains
  mangees:
Quand la cité damnera
  l'heretique,
Qu'auoit leurs loix ſe leur
  ſembloit changees.

Burned, apopletic but not dead,
he will be found to have gnawed
his hands. When the city con-
demns the heretic, who, it seemed
to them, had changed their laws.

The burned person who is *apopletique* presumably suffered from a stroke, and is buried, presumed dead. This is not an uncommon occurrence, even in the twentieth century with its vast amount of medical knowledge. His hands are hurt, banging against the lid of the coffin when he regains consciousness. Sadly, we are not told if he is rescued. The fact that this occurs when a city revolts against its leader is not specific enough to help identify either event.

Century III

III.XXXVII

Auant l'affaut l'oraison[1] prononcee,	A speech is proclaimed before the assault: Milan, deceived by the ambush, is captured by the eagle.
Milan prins d'aigle par embufches deceuz:	The ancient walls are breached by cannon fire. In the fire and the blood, few receive quarter.
Muraille antique par canons enfoncee,	
Par feu & fang à mercy peu receus.	

This quatrain can be understood well through the linking of the Eagle, Napoleon, with Milan. Napoleon took the city twice; on May 15, 1796, and on June 2, 1800. It appears to be the first assault that is referred to here. Napoleon made a famous speech which was printed in most of the newspapers of Europe: "Soldiers, you are ill-fed and half-naked. The government owes you much but can do nothing for you . . ." It is said that the speech so rallied his men that the defending Austrians retired without making any further attempts to defend Milan.

It is possible that lines 3 and 4 could apply to the battle of Pavia, soon after the Milan assault, but at Pavia the inhabitants rose up against the French. The city walls were bombarded and breached and the city totally sacked. For *oraifon* see II.XXXV.

---

[1] *oraifon*. O.F. prayer, speech.

Century III

III.XXXVIII

La gent Gauloiſe & nation eſtrange,
Outre les monts, morts prins & profligez:
Au mois contraire & proche de vendange,
Par les Seigneurs en accord redigez.

The French people and a foreign nation beyond the mountains will be captured, killed and overcome. In a different month, near harvest time, by the Lords they will be put back into order.

Traditionally this quatrain is accepted as describing the peace declared by the Pope and the Spanish in September, 1557, at the time of the grape harvest. Jaubert states that in this treaty the interests of the troops of the duc de Guise, mainly French and Swiss, were totally ignored.

However, it could possibly refer to the Second World War, with the nation over the mountains being either Austria or Italy, both of which suffered as much as France from the Germans, although in Italy's case in rather a different way. The Lords who put things back in order, *en accord redigez*, might be the Lords of Justice at Nuremberg, but the trials lasted through harvest time, from November, 1945, to October, 1946.

Century III

III.XXXIX

Les ſept en trois mois en concorde,
Pour ſubiuguer des Alpes Apennines:
Mais la tempeſte & Ligure couarde,
Les profligent en ſubites ruines.

The seven are in agreement for three months to subjugate the Apennines. But the storm and the cowardly Ligurian destroy them in sudden ruin.

This quatrain seems to refer to one of the leagues of sixteenth century Italy, probably the Holy League of 1576. It implies that the agreement is upset by Genoa (Liguria).

Century III

III.XL

*Le grand theatre ſe viendra
    redreſſer,
Les dez iettez & les rets ia
    tendus:
Trop le premier en glaz viendra
    laſſer,
Par arcs proſtrais de long temps
    ia fendus.*

The great theater will be raised
up again, the dice thrown and
the nets already cast. The leader
who tolls the death bell, will
become too tired, destroyed by
bows split a long time ago.

Ancient Rome is conjured up in the first two lines, but the quatrain remains totally obscure.

Century III

III.XLI

*Boſſu ſera eſleu par le conſeil,
Plus hideux monſtre en terre
    n'apperceu,
Le coup voulant[1] creuera l'oeil,
Le traiſtre au Roy pour fidelle
    reçeu.*

The hunchback will be selected
by the council, a more hideous
creature never seen on earth.
The deliberate shot will pierce his
eye; the traitor whom the king
received as loyal.

Many commentators have remarked upon the success of his quatrain. It concerns Prince Louis de Condé, a hunchback, and his death on March 13, 1569. Louis de Condé was proclaimed chief of the Huguenot Assembly in 1560. But he was reconciled to the king and Catholicism several times. He even made a public confession of his loyalty to Charles IX in 1560 and again in 1562 but all the while continued to plot against him. He was finally captured at the Battle of Jarnac, March 13, 1569, and, although a prisoner, was deliberately shot through the head, *le coup voulant creuera l'oeil*, and killed.

[1]*voulant.* misspelling of *volant*, flying.

Century III

III.XLII

L'enfant naiſtra à deux dents en
    la gorge,
Pierres en Tuſcie par pluye
    tomberont:
Peu d'ans apres ne ſera bled ni
    orge,
Pour ſaouler ceux qui de faim
    failliront.

A child will be born with two
teeth in his mouth, stones will
fall like rain in Tuscany. A few
years later there will be neither
wheat nor barley, to satisfy those
weakened from hunger.

Another general reference to famine together with other
phenomena, this time stones falling from the sky in Tuscany.
A person born with two teeth is referred to in II.VII. Louis
XIV was reputedly born with some teeth fully grown, but this
is not uncommon.

Century III

III.XLIII

Gens d'alentour de Tarn Loth,
    & Garonne,
Gardez les monts Apennines
    paſſer:
Voſtre tombeau pres de Rome &
    d'Anconne,
Le noir poil creſpe fera trophee
    dreſſer.

People from around the Tarn,
the Lot and Garonne, beware of
crossing the Apennine mountains. Your tomb is near Rome
and Ancona. The man with dark
curly hair will set up a trophy.

The man with the dark curly hair, noir creſpe, is also referred
to in I.LXXIIII and II.LXXIX. He has not been identifed, so
it is possible these quatrains are still to be fulfilled. The idea
of a trophy (trophee dreſſer) implies a warlike intent. Perhaps he
should be linked with the Aenobarbe quatrains? The Tarn and
the Lot are tributaries of the river Garonne in France, and
Ancona is situated on the eastern coast of Italy.

Century III

III.XLIIII

Quand l'animal à l'homme
  domeſtique,
Apres grands peines & ſauts
  viendra parler,
De fouldre à vierge[1] ſera ſi
  malefique,
De terre prinſe & ſuſpendue en
  l'air.

When the animal tamed by man
begins to speak after great efforts
and difficulty; the lightning so
harmful to the rod, will be taken
from the earth and suspended in
the air.

I wonder if Nostradamus is trying to describe wireless
communication and electricity, the animal force *(l'animal)*? He
often uses the word "animal" to describe machines that have
lifelike qualities—that move, make a noise or emit light.
Perhaps the tamed animal is the discovery of sound waves and
the wireless a form of communication, *viendra parler*. The
lightning hostile to the rod could imply that it is a radio mast
or some form of aerial sending out electrical charges. It might
describe a lightning conductor, the principle of which was
discovered in 1752.

Century III

III.XLV

Les cinq eſtranges entrez dedans
  le temple
Leur ſang viendra la terre
  prophaner:
Aux Tholouſains ſera bien dur
  exemple,
D'vn qui viendra ses loix
  exterminer.

The five foreigners having
entered the temple, their blood
will desecrate the land. The
example made of the people of
Toulouse will be very hard,
made by the man who comes to
wipe out their laws.

The five foreigners are understood to be the five great
powers who allied against Napoleonic France *(le temple)*:
England, Austria, Russia, Spain and Prussia. France is deso-

[1]*vierge*. O.F. rod or wand.

lated by their invasion, much blood is spilled in battle. The
Battle of Toulouse fought by Wellington in 1814 was regarded
as brutal, even by the standards of the time. It is the Allied
Powers who wipe out the laws because they are the cause of
Napoleon's downfall.

Century III

III.XLVI

Le ciel (de Plancus la cité)
    nous presage,
Par clers insignes & par estoilles
    fixes:
Que de son change subit
    s'aproche l'aage,
Ne pour son bien ne pour ses
    malefices.

*The heavens foretell (concerning
the city of Plancus), through
clear skies and fixed stars. Suddenly the time of change
approaches, neither for its good
nor evil future.*

Plancus is the city of Lyons, named after its founder Lucius
Munatius Plancus in 43 B.C. The general gloom presaged by
the stars, astrology, is similar to II.LXXXIII, which also
mentions Lyons.

Century III

III.XLVII

Le vieux monarque dechassé de
    son regne
Aux Orients son secours ira
    querre:
Pour peur des croix ploiera son
    enseigne,
En Mitylene ira par port &
    par terre.

*The old king chased out of his
kingdom will go to seek help
from the people of the East. For
fear of the crosses he will fold his
banner. He will travel to Mitylene by land and sea.*

I thought initially that the old king chased out of his realm
might be the Shah of Persia, someone who is not a Christian
pour peur des croix. But there is no evidence that he ever sought
help in the East; he initially fled to Egypt. But equally he did
not go to Mitylene, Lesbos, which became part of Greece in

1913. Could the crosses refer to the swastika, and the help from the East to that of the Japanese? But again, where does Lesbos fit in except as part of the general theater of war between 1940 and 1945?

Century III

III.XLVIII

Sept cens captifs eſtachez rudement,
Pour la moitié meurtrir, donné le ſort:
Le proche eſpoir viendra ſi promptement,
Mais non ſi toſt qu'vne quinzieſme mort.

Seven hundred captives, roughly tied up. Lots are drawn for half to be murdered. Sudden hope will come very quickly, but not fast enough for about fifteen dead.

No definite information has come to light about this very general quatrain, despite the specific number of prisoners and dead.

Century III

III.XLIX

Regne Gaulois tu ſeras bien changé,
En lieu eſtrange eſt tranſlaté l'empire:
En autres moeurs & loix ſeras rangé,
Roan, & Chartres te feront bien du pire.

Kingdom of France, you will be greatly changed, the Empire expands to foreign places. You will be set up with other laws and customs. Rouen and Chartres will do their worst towards you.

The key words here are very explicit. France ceases to be a kingdom but becomes an Empire, which occurred under Napoleon. The Code Napoléon gave France *autres moeurs & loix*. It is possible that the last part of this prediction has yet to be fulfilled.

Century III

III.L

La republique de la grande cité,	*The republic's government of the*
A grand rigueur ne voudra	*great city will not consent to*
consentir:	*rigorous suppression. The king,*
Roy sortir hors par trompette cité.	*summoned by trumpets to leave*
L'eschelle au mur, la cité	*the city, a ladder at the wall; the*
repentir.	*city will repent.*

The people's government of a city refers surely to the famous *Journée des Barricades*—May 12, 1588. The Leaguers took Paris the following day and they and the people drove out King Henri III and his followers. Henri retaliated by joining up with Henri de Navarre at St. Cloud, and together they resolved to besiege Paris. But Henri III was assassinated by Jacques Clément in 1589 before this was accomplished. (See I.XCVII.)

Century III

III.LI

Paris coniure vn grand meurtre	*Paris conspires to commit a great*
commettre,	*murder. Blois will ensure that it*
Blois le fera sortir en plain	*is fully carried out. The people of*
effect:	*Orléans will want to replace*
Ceux d'Orleans voudront leur	*their leaders. Angers, Troyes*
chef remettre,	*and Langres will do them a dis-*
Angiers, Troye, Langres, leur	*service.*
feront vn meffait.	

Henri III murdered the two Guise brothers at Blois on December 23, 1588. He had planned the murder in Paris but the duc de Guise had fled to Blois. The duc was killed by the king's bodyguard outside the royal appartments, and the cardinal, his brother, was killed the next day. At this period, the town of Orléans rose up against the governor, Balsac d'Entragues. Charles de Lorraine, a prominent Leaguer and supporter of the Guise cause, took over the rule. The last line is only partially correct. Angers and Langres allied with the Leaguers, but Troyes remained neutral.

Century III

III.LII

En la campaigne *ſera ſi* longue
    pluye,
Et en la Pouille *ſi* grande
    ficcité:
Coq verra l'Aigle, *l'aeſle* mal
    accomplie,
Par Lyon *miſe ſera* en extremité.

In Campania there will be rain
for so long and a very great
drought in Apulia. The Cock
will see the Eagle, its wing badly
damaged, put into difficulties by
the Lion.

The Cock stands for France, whether as a kingdom or a
republic. The Eagle probably refers to Napoleon. In this case,
Nostradamus uses the Lion to symbolize England, rather than
his usual use of Léopard, as in I.XXIII. England causes
Napoleon's defeat. Rain and drought are not found in
contemporary records, but it is possible that the troubles in
Italy, Apulia, could refer to the devastation wrought by the
Napoleonic campaigns.

Century III

III.LIII

Quand le plus grand emportera
    le pris,
De Nuremberg, *d'Auſpourg &*
    ceux de *Baſle*
Par Agrippine[1] chef Frankfort
    repris:
Trauerſeront par Flamant
    iuſqu'en Gale.

When the greatest man carries
off the prize of Nuremberg,
Ausburg and those of Basle.
Frankfurt is retaken by the
leader from Cologne. They will
go through Flanders as far as
France.

All the place names mentioned have one thing in common,
they were part of the Holy Roman Empire. But it might be
that this quatrain connects with Hitler through Nuremberg. It
was while he held his famous rallies there that he became
leader of Germany and his troops did invade France from the
north

---

[1]*Agrippine.* ∟ Colonia Agrippina, and Cologne.

Century III

III.LIIII

L'vn des plus grans fuira aux
    Eſpaignes
Qu'en longue playe apres
    viendra ſaigner:
Paſſant copies par les hautes
    montaignes,
Deuaſtant tout & puis en paix
    regner.

One of the greatest men will flee
to Spain which will bleed with a
great wound thereafter. Troops
will pass over the high mountains devastating everything.
Then he will reign in peace.

This quatrain fits General Franco and the Spanish Civil War
(1936–39) very aptly. Franco was exiled from Spain in 1936
and sent to the Canary Islands as military governor. He then
went (*fuira*) to Morocco and back to Spain to incite the
rebellion which led to the Civil War. The great wound from
which Spain bled, *longue playe*, presumably refers to the
appalling number of casualties sustained in the war; the
approximate number of dead is given at 611,000. The armies
which crossed the Pyrenees, the border, were the 50,000
Italians and 10,000 Germans who fought for Franco's Nationalist party. Also, 20,000 Russian soldiers came to support the
Loyalists, the Republicans. It is ironic that the last line talks of
peace, but Spain, by remaining neutral throughout the Second
World War, did, in a sense, *puis en paix regner*. See **IX.XVI**
where Franco is mentioned by name.

Century III

III.LV

En l'an qu'vn oeil en France
    regnera,
La court ſera à vn bien
    facheux trouble:
Le grand de Bloys ſon amy
    tuera,
Le regne mis en mal & doubte
    double.

In the year that France has a
one-eyed king, the court will be
in very great trouble. The great
man from Blois will kill his
friend, the kingdom put into
difficulty and double trouble.

This quatrain was believed by Catherine de' Medicis and contemporaries to be linked with I.XXXV, the famous quatrain which predicts Henri II's death in a duel, which happened in 1559. Henri is described as the one-eyed king, *vn oeil en France regnera*, when he was wounded in a duel with his Captain of the Scottish Guard, being pierced in the eye by Montgomery's lance. He died in agony after ten days. His second son, Henri III, assassinated the Guise brothers at Blois—one of the most powerful families in France. This act was followed by general unrest throughout the kingdom. *Doubte double* probably refers to the two factions, the Leaguers and the Catholics, and also to the wars of religion which continued throughout the sixteenth century.

Century III

III.LVI

Montauban, Nifmes, Auignon & Befier,
Pefte tonnerre & grefle à fin de Mars:
De Paris pont, Lyon mur, Montpellier,
Depuis fix cens & fept vingts trois pars.

Montauban, Nîmes, Avignon and Béziers plague, lightning and hail at the end of March. Of the bridge at Paris, the wall at Lyons and Montpellier, since then six hundred and seven, three score pairs.

If the last line of this quatrain is used to give a date, it is extremely difficult to unravel, as it can be read several ways. It may be 736 or 2031 (1555, date of publication of this part of the *Prophéties* plus 736), or 607 plus 23 pairs, which adds up to 1853, or 2208 if added to the publication date. It is very obscure and may be a failed quatrain. As for the place names, all those in line 1 are situated in the south of France, but the connection between the bridge of Paris, the walls of Lyons and Montpellier as yet makes no sense, except perhaps in the context of modern travel.

Century III

III.LVII

*Sept fois changer verrez gent
   Britannique,
Taintz en fang en deux cens
   nonante an:
Franche non point par appuy
   Germanique,
Aries doubte fon pole Baftarnan.*

Seven times the British nation
will be seen to change, dyed in
blood for two hundred and
ninety years. Not at all free,
through German support, Aries
fears for the protectorate of
Poland.

Initially this seems a remarkably lucid quatrain. But it is
written by Nostradamus, and in his Centuries little is as it
seems. The reader's problem is to find the date from which
the 290 years affecting Britain starts. If one takes a starting
date of 1603 (by working backwards, as below) the whole verse
is comprehensible, including the last line linking Britain's fate
with that of Poland, *Baftarnan*, and a war, Aries. Nostradamus
is saying that there will be a crisis in Polish affairs, the invasion
by the Nazis, at the same time as Britain is facing a warlike
crisis with Germany. It also implies that the present royal line,
George VI and Queen Elizabeth II, will be the start of the last
royal dynasty of any note.

   1603. New Stuart monarch, James I of England and VI of
          Scotland.
   1649. The execution of Charles I and the declaration of the
          Commonwealth.
   1660. The Restoration of the Stuarts under Charles II.
   1688. The usurpment of the Stuarts by William of Orange.
   1702. The Restoration of the Stuarts under Queen Anne.
   1714. The Hanoverian succession starts under George I.
   1939. The British declare war after the German invasion of
          Poland.

I don't find any other commentators reliable, because their
excuses for the last line make no sense. It is valid only in the
context of 1939.

Century III

III.LVIII

Aupres du Rhin des montaignes
    Noriques,
Naiſtra vn grand de gens trop
    tard venu.
Qui defendra Saurome &
    Pannoniques,
Qu'on ne ſçaura qu'il ſera
    deuenu.

Near the Rhine, from the Norican mountains will be born a
great man of the people, came
too late. He will defend Poland
and Hungary and they will
never know what became of him.

Lech Walesa, the founder of the world-famous Solidarity
movement in Poland, is the hero of this quatrain. Norican was
the Latin term for Austria and Walesa, *vn grand de gens trop
tard venu*, the great leader who comes too late to save his
country, was born in Poland on the other side of the Austrian
mountains. His present battle with the Polish authorities seems
to be losing momentum and credibility, but one must hope
that Solidarity will be accepted by the Polish government.

The Samartians, now southern Russia, was Lithuania in
Nostradamus' day, having united with the Crown of Poland in
1447. Nostradamus implies that either the idea of Solidarity
or of free Trade Unions will move into Hungary as well. The
last two lines seem to indicate the power of *glasnost*, of Lech
Walesa in Poland and of Istovan Horvath of Hungary. I
originally thought this quatrain might apply to Hitler, but this
begs line 2, and uses the word "defend" in the Hitlerian sense
of protect by occupation.

Century III

III.LIX

Barbare empire par le tiers
    vſurpé,
La plus grand part de ſon ſang
    mettra à mort:
Par mort ſenile par luy le quart
    frappé,
Pour peur que ſang par le ſang
    ne ſoit mort.

The barbarian empire is usurped
by a third (party), the greater
part of its people will be put to
death. The fourth man, senile,
struck dead by his country, fears
lest his blood line should be
extinguished.

I think that here *tiers* may be accepted as the *Tiers Etat* of
the French Revolution. The rest of the quatrain then proceeds
very smoothly. The word *empire* places it in the time of
Napoleon, and *barbare* refers to the fact that religion was
abolished until Napoleon had need of the Pope for his
coronation.

There were three Committees of Public Safety during the
Reign of Terror; those of Danton, Robespierre and the
Directoire. The fourth man, *par mort senile frappé*, is Napoleon,
who took over from the Directoire in 1799, and eventually
died, senile, in St. Helena.

Napoleon had always feared that his line might not be
continued, particularly when he realized that his marriage to
Josephine was barren. On May 3, 1804, the Tribunal of France
declared that "the imperial dignity should be declared hereditary in the line of Bonaparte." He divorced Josephine in 1810
because of her barrenness and married Marie Louise of
Austria in the same year, by whom he had an heir, the king
of Rome. When Napoleon abdicated on June 22, 1814, Marie
Louise was given the Duchy of Parma with her son, the king
of Rome. Napoleon abdicated in favor of his son, but realized
it was but a formality. He was succeeded in 1808 by Napoleon
III, the third son of Napoleon's brother, Louis Bonaparte and
Josephine's sister, Hortense de Beauharnais. As a nephew and
adopted grandson of Napoleon, he was not a strong contender
for the throne. There were also many contemporary rumors
that he was illegitimate. Napoleon's fears as to the future of
his line were well founded.

Century III

III.LX

Par toute Asie grande
   proscription,
Mesme en Mysie, Lysie, &
   Pamphylie:
Sang versera par absolution,
D'vn ieune noir remply de
   felonnie.

Throughout Asia there will be
great proscription, also in
Mysia, Lycia and Pamphalia.
Blood will flow because of a
young dark man, filled with evil.

In this quatrain Nostradamus envisages an enormous military call-up in the East, in China. All the countries mentioned in line 2 are in Asia Minor. He foresees China as growing in power and influence, *sang verfera*, through war and conquest. The terrible history of Kampuchea may be a warning of future events to come. After all, Nostradamus predicted a rapport between America and the Soviet Union, and that has already come to pass. Asia Minor covers Turkey, Iran and Iraq in modern terms. These countries have now negotiated a cease-fire. Again, we have the young dark-haired man, *ieune noir*, whom I cannot identify, but who may be the mysterious "Brodde". Due to the dating of the Iran-Iraq war, he may be either the Antichrist but more probably his mysterious predecessor. This quatrain is certainly not fulfilled.

Century III

III.LXI   ★

La grande bande & fecte crucigere,	The great following of the sect of the cross, will arise in Mesopota-
Se dreſſera en Meſopotamie:	mia. The light company (regim-
Du proche fleuue compagnie legiere,	ent?) at the nearby river will regard such a law as inimical.
Que telle loy tiendra pour ennemie.	

The enigmatic solution to this quatrain lies in the words *fecte crucigere*. It could be the swastika—the *croix gammée*, as it was known in France, but I am inclined to place this quatrain in Iraq, as Mesopotamia is now known. The two rivers are the Tigris and the Euphrates. This would then place the quatrain in the war between Iran and Iraq, *tiendra pour ennemie*. Since the Christian cross is straight, we are certainly not dealing with a Christian army. It may even have the convoluted meaning that the followers are totally inimical to the cross.

Century III

III.LXII

Proche del duero par mer
    Cyrrene cloſe,
Viendra perſer les grands monts
    Pyrenées:
La main plus courte & ſa
    percee[1] gloze,[2]
A Carcaſſonne conduira ſes
    menées.

Near the Douro enclosed by the
Cyrenian Sea he will come to
cross the great mountains of the
Pyrenees. The shortest route and
his opening noted, he will take
his followers to Carcassonne.

This apparently talks of a leader who will cross the Pyrenees
from Spain into France. The river Douro rises in the
mountains around Burgos in Spain, and the Cyrenian Sea is
the Mediterranean. But who this man is or what he did is
obscure. Line 3 is difficult to translate.

Century III

III.LXIII

Romain pouuoir ſera du tout
    abas,
Son grand voiſin imiter les
    veſtiges:
Occultes haines ciuiles &
    debats,
Retarderont aux bouffons leurs
    folies.

The power of Rome will be quite
cast down, following the footsteps of its great neighbor. Secret
hatreds and civil disputes will
delay the stupidities of the buffoons.

This is a reasonably accurate description of the state of Italy
under Mussolini and its great neighbor, Hitlerian Germany in
1937, in whose footsteps Mussolini tried to follow. The name
Mussolini literally means muslin-maker, a craft regarded as
the lowest of the low, and yet it is this man who becomes the
dictator of Italy. The histrionics of both Hitler and Mussolini
could certainly qualify them as buffoons *aux bouffons leurs folies*,
and the word *folie* also contains the element of failure. The
great hatreds and civil disputes, *occultes haines ciuiles & debats*,

[1]*percee*. O.F. perce, stake, pole, entry.
[2]*gloze*. A.Pr. gloza, commentary, notes.

may also refer to Hitler's certain insanity in later years, and almost certainly that of his second-hand follower, Mussolini.

Century III
III.LXIIII

Le chef de Perſe remplira grande Olchade, *Claſſe Trireme contre gent Mahometique:* *De Parthe, & Mede, & piller les Cyclades,* *Repos long temps au grand port Ionique.*	*The Persian leader will gather in great Spain. A fleet of tri-remes (will advance) against the Mohammedans for Parthia and Media. He will take the Cycla-des; then a long wait in the great Ionian harbor.*

Some Iranians hope that this indicates the revival of a Persian leader to replace the Ayatollah, a theme which occurs several times in Nostradamus', but he would not use the classical *triremes*. Perhaps Nostradamus fails for once to use a word which might describe large ships? The quatrain implies that this man will have help from within Persia: Media and Parthia are part of Iran. It is unclear why he should sack the Greek islands around Delos in the Aegean. The harbor in which he shelters could be anywhere in the Ionian Sea between Greece and Sicily. Possibly an unfulfilled quatrain to date.

Century III
III.LXV

Quand le ſepulcre du grand Romain trouué, *Le iour apres ſera eſleu Pontife:* *Du Senat gueres il ne ſera prouúe,* *Empoiſonné ſon ſang au ſacré ſcyphe.*	*When the tomb of the Great Roman is found, a pope will be elected the following day. He will not be approved by the Sen-ate, his blood poisonous in the sacred challice.*

The dating of this quatrain is found in line 1. A possibly "true" tomb of St. Peter was discovered in 1979, but some doubts remain. Pope John Paul I was elected in 1978, a very unexpected candidate. His death soon afterwards was surrounded by suspicious circumstances. Approximately one month after his election he was invited to dine with his cardinals. He died, unattended, that night. The ensuing scandal in the European newspapers in particular did great harm to the Vatican's reputation. The most suspicious facts were that the nuns who were supposed to attend him that night had been absent for some hours, and his body was cremated at speed, not buried, which is against the Catholic religion.

John Paul I is reputed to have been unpopular with the Curia. However, in my book of 1972 I was skeptical of Nostradamus' prediction of two assassinations of a twentieth century pope. I think he probably referred to this extraordinary situation and also to the attack on Pope John Paul II in May, 1981, by the Turk Mohamet Ali Agça, when he suffered severe injuries. According to Nostradamus, yet another attempt was to come. This happened in Manila in May, 1983, when a news flash on the World Service stated that a priest had tried to assassinate the Pope with a bayonet cut down. It does seem that this prediction has been recently fulfilled.

Century III

III.LXVI

Le grand Baillif d'Orleans mis à mort,	*The great Bailiff of Orleans is condemned to death by a person*
Sera par vn de fang vindicatif.	*vindictive for his blood. He will*
De mort merite ne mourra, ne par fort,	*not die a deserved death, nor one by jurors. They will keep him*
Des pieds & mains malle faifoit captif.	*captive (bound) inefficiently by his hand and feet.*

The post of the Bailiff of Orléans had been inherited by a member of the Greslot family since 1530, so Nostradamus must have intended this prediction for one of them. A certain Jerôme Greslot was condemned to death for having opened the gates of the town to marauders in 1562, but he was not actually condemned to death for this until 1569. Does Nostradamus mean the gap between his capture and execution was *mal le faifoit captif?*

Century III

III.LXVII

Vne nouuelle fecte de Philofophes,	*A new sect of philosophers despising death, gold, honors*
Mefprifant mort, or, honneurs & richeffes:	*and riches will not be contained by the German mountains. There*
Des monts Germains ne feront limitrophes,	*will be crowds and support among their followers.*
A les ensuyure auront appuy & preffes.	

Try as hard as I can, I do not find an easy solution to this quatrain. I think it is probably retroactive, referring to the sect of the Anabaptists, who had been almost wiped out in 1536. It is just possible Nostradamus foresees a revival of these or other Protestant sects from the direction of Germany, but both Luther and Calvin had made their stand before publication of the Prophecies.

Century III

III.LXVIII

Peuple fans chef d'Efpaigne & d'Italie,	*Leaderless people from Spain and Italy, dead and overcome in*
Morts, profligez[1] dedans le Cherroneffe:[2]	*the Peninsula. Their leader will be betrayed by stupid folly. Blood*
Leur dict[3] trahi par legiere folie,	*will flow everywhere in the area.*
Le fang nager par tout à la trauerfe.	

This is a quatrain certainly set in the twentieth century, a time when Spain and Italy have elected leaders, *dict*, not being of royal blood. The traitor betrayed is Mussolini and it is possible that by *à la trauerfe* Nostradamus is referring to Mussolini's final death by hanging. *La trauerfe* also means a

---

[1]*profligez.* L. *profligatus,* vanquished, overcome.
[2]*Cherroneffe.* Gk. peninsula.
[3]*dict.* alternative *duict,* leader.

crossroads, which was the standard site for a gibbet throughout most of Europe. It is possible that perhaps this quatrain is
not yet fulfilled.

Century III

III.LXIX

Grand exercite conduict par
   iouuenceau,
Se viendra rendre aux mains
   des ennemis:
Mais le vieillart nay au demy
   pourceau,
Fera Chalon & Maſcon eſtre amis.

*A great army led by a young man
will happen to give itself up into
the enemies' hands. But the old
man, born to the half pig, will
make Châlon and Mâcon into
friends.*

The original half man-half pig occurs in I.LXIIII and as a
half man in VIII.XLIIII. Either the man in line 3, *nay au demy
pourceau,* is from a generation such as the 1980s when the flier
in an oxygen mask is now commonplace, who will fall into
enemy hands with the army, through a headstrong young
man, or possibly it is derived from the false etymology of the
city of Milan itself. According to legend it was derived from
the finding of an animal half sheep-half pig at its foundation.
But the relevance to either interpretation of Châlon and
Mâcon, both in Burgundy, escapes me. I lean towards the
more modern interpretation.

Century III

III.LXX

La grand Bretaigne comprinſe
   l'Angleterre,
Viendra par eaux ſi haut à
   inonder
La ligue neufue d'Auſonne[1] fera
   guerre,
Que contre eux ils ſe viendront
   bander.

*The whole of Great Britain,
including England, will be
covered by very deep floods. The
new league in Ausonne will
declare war so that they will ally
against them.*

[1]*Auſonne.* Ausonia; southern Italy, especially Naples, but can stand
for the whole of Italy.

England did not become Great Britain until the unification of the Scottish and English thrones under James I. He assumed the title of King of Great Britain on October 24, 1604. Incidentally, there were great floods covering Bristol and Somerset for an area of thirty miles in 1607, but this is hardly the whole of Great Britain. If we are in the correct period, the last two lines refer to the renewal of the Holy League in 1606, Ausonia standing for Italy. A quatrain that is almost right but leaves one dissatisfied.

Century III

III.LXXI

Ceux dans les iſles de long temps aſſiegez,
Prendront vigueur force contre ennemis:
Ceux par dehors mors de faim profligez,
En plus grand faim que iamais ſeront mis.

Those besieged in the islands for a long time will take strong measures against their enemies. Those who are outside, overcome will die of hunger, by such starvation as has never occurred before.

The blockade of Britain by the German Navy during the Second World War seems clearly described in this quatrain, as are the strong countermeasures taken by the British in opening up Atlantic routes for supplies and troops. It appears that during the siege of Britain there was never more than a six-week supply of food in the country, a fact well hidden from the populace. The final two lines are obvious enough. The British did not starve, but there was appalling famine in occupied Europe. This must refer in particular to the labor camps, so called, of the Nazi régime, where starvation killed off many of the tragic survivors of the gas chambers.

Century III

III.LXXII

Le bon vieillart tout vif
  enfeuely,
Pres du grand fleuue par fauſſe
  ſouſpeçon:
Le nouueau vieux de richeſſe
  ennobly,
Prins à chemin tout l'or de la
  rançon.

The good old man is buried
while still alive through supersti-
tion, near a great river. The
newcomer is old, ennobled by
wealth, having taken all the ran-
somed gold on the way.

This obscure quatrain has a counterpart in III.XXXVI,
where someone is also buried alive, but nothing else leads to
any clue. Probably a failed quatrain.

Century III

III.LXXIII

Quand dans le regne
  paruiendra le boiteux,
Competiteur aura proche
  baſtard:
Luy & le regne viendront ſi fort
  roigneux,
Qu'ains qu'il gueriſſe ſon faict
  ſera bien tard.

When the lame man comes into
the kingdom, a bastard close to
him will compete with him. Both
he and the kingdom will be
greatly diminished before he
recovers; his action will be too
late.

This interesting quatrain is full of facts. The heir to King
Charles X of France was the duc de Bordeaux, who became
lame as the result of a riding accident in 1841. The illegal
contender for the throne was the comte de Paris. The
trimming away of the kingdom, *fi fort roigneux*, then refers to
the Franco-Prussian War. By the time the French came to
terms with the duc de Bordeaux, the French had declared
France's Third Republic, and both he and the comte de Paris
died in exile.

Century III

III.LXXIIII

Naples, Florence, Fauence, &
*   Imole,*
Seront en termes de telle
*   fafcherie:*
Que pour cãplaire aux
*   malheureux de Nolle,*
Plainct d'auoir faict à fon chef
*   moquerie.*

Naples, Florence, Faenza and
Imola will come to terms so dis-
agreeable in order to comply with
the wretches of Nola, that they
complain that their chief had
been mocked.

I can make no sense of this quatrain. Faenza and Imola were in the Papal States. Florence is the capital of Tuscany and Naples of the Two Sicilies. Nola is close to Naples in the East. I think this is definitely a failed quatrain.

Century III

III.LXXV   ★

Pau, Verone, Vicence,
*   Sarragouffe,*
De glaiues loings terroirs de
*   fang humides:*
Pefte fi grande viendra à la
*   grand gouffe,[1]*
Proche fecours, & bien loing les
*   remedes.*

Pau, Verona, Vicenza, Sara-
gossa, swords dripping with
blood from distant lands. A very
great plague will come in the
great shell, relief near, but the
remedies far away.

All the cities here are in Europe and Nostradamus seems to indicate that a devastating plague will afflict them, "within the great shell." This might imply chemical warfare, as used in Iran and Iraq. But I feel the last line is the most important. The *pefte fi grande* may well apply to AIDS. The relief so near for those who suffer it, *proche fecours*, is probably the drug used to contain the HIV-positive condition, which can be main-tained and stabilized for as long as five years. But unfortun-ately the cure for either HIV infection or full-blown AIDS will be a long time arriving, *& bien loing les remedes*. AZT is an example of the drugs used to contain it. Line 2 indicates there

[1] *gouffe*. O.F. shell, husk, scab.

may be a war waged against Europe from a distant country. It
is impossible to say from where. Nostradamus' guess is China.

Century III

III.LXXVI

En Germanie naiſtront diuerſes
    ſectes,
S'approchant fort de l'heureux
    paganiſme,
Le coeur captif & petites
    receptes,
Feront retour à payer le vray
    diſme.

*Various sects will arise in Ger-
many which will come near to a
happy paganism. The heart is
captive, the returns small. They
will return to pay the true title.*

Although this quatrain can be easily applied as yet another
of Nostradamus' obsessions against the many Lutheran,
Anabaptist and Calvinist sects which were springing up
around him in the sixteenth century and which he cordially
disliked, I have the impression that this quatrain actually
applies to modern Germany. Under Hitler, before the war of
1939, religion almost disappeared and the Jews were made to
disappear. Hitler, a monomaniac until the very end at the
Bunker in Berlin, will soon lose his earlier gains in the war,
petites receptes, and it was not only he and his followers who will
have to repay their dreadful acts, but also a large proportion
of the German people.

Century III

III.LXXVII

Le tiers climat ſous Aries
    comprins,
L'an mil ſept cens vingt & ſept
    en Octobre:
Le Roy de Perſe par ceux
    d'Egypte prins:
Conflit, mort, perte à la croix
    grand opprobre.

*The third climate included
under Aries; in the year 1727 in
October, the king of Persia will
be captured by the people of
Egypt. Battle, death, loss, a
great shame to the cross.*

At first glance this appears to be an extremely correct quatrain. It contains not only the year, but also the month and the place! I can only assume that in some way Nostradamus overlooked these details when he set out to confuse the quatrains. It appears correct in every detail. In October, 1727, a peace was concluded between the Turks and the Persians (Egypt belonged to the Ottoman Empire and represents the Turks).

The loss to Christianity may be explained by the fact that the Shah Ashraf, in return for the recognition of his dynasty, gave the lands of Emvan, Tauris and Hamadam to the Turks, and recognized the sultan as the legitimate successor to the caliph. Ottoman power continued in strength until the twentieth century and the Christians raised no more Crusades.

Century III

III.LXXVIII

Le chef d'Escoſſe auec ſix d'Alemaigne,	The leader from Scotland together with six Germans will be captured by Eastern sea warriors. They will go through Gibraltar and Spain and be presented in Persia to the new dreadful king.
Par gens de mer Orientaux captif:	
Trauerſeront le Calpre & Eſpaigne,	
Preſent en Perſè au nouueau Roy craintif.	

From the content, this appears to be a totally failed quatrain. No Scots leader has allied himself with six Germans (although Nazi leader Hess journeyed to Scotland alone to see the duke of Hamilton). But then how does the rest of the quatrain fit?

Century III

III.LXXIX

*L'ordre fatal sempiternel par
   chaisne,
Viendra tourner par ordre
   consequent:
Du port Phocen sera rompue la
   chaisne,
La cité prinse, l'ennemy quant
   & quant.*

*The fatal and eternal order of
the cycle will turn in its normal
course. The chains of Marseilles
will be broken, both the city and
the enemy taken at the same time.*

Chains were used as booms in Marseilles harbor until
recently. Otherwise this is quite obscure.

Century III

III.LXXX

*Du regne Anglois l'indigne
   dechassé,
Le conseiller par ire mis à feu:
Ses adherans iront si bas tracer,
Que le bastard sera demy receu.*

*The unworthy man is chased out
of the English kingdom. The
counselor will be burned through
anger. His followers will stoop to
such depths that the pretender
will almost be received.*

Charles I, 1600–1649, lost his kingdom mainly due to his
own behavior and his irresponsibility towards Parliament. One
of his counselors, Strafford, was beheaded in 1641 and
Archbishop Laud was burned for treachery in 1645. The
followers, *Ses adherans*, who stooped so low were the Scots, who
sold the king back to the English Parliament in 1646. The
Pretender, or bastard *(bastard)*, who is almost received in the
kingdom is Oliver Cromwell, the man who was not born to
rule, but who almost achieves kingship as Lord Protector.

Century III

III.LXXXI

Le grand criar ſans honte audacieux,
Sera eſleu gouuerneur de l'armee:
La hardieſſe de ſon contentieux,
Le pont rompu cité de peur paſmee.

The great speechmaker, shame-less and bold will be elected gov-ernor of the army. The audacity of his contention, the broken bridge, the city faint from fear.

There is a beautiful clue in this quatrain—the broken bridge, *pont rompu*. If this is a typical Nostradamus pun from the Latin *pons*, a bridge, and *fractus*, broken, it stands for Pontefract, the town famous for holding out for Charles I in two great sieges during the Civil War. The great speechmaker is Cromwell, for whom Nostradamus had as little affection as he later shows for the Republican Napoleon.

Century III

III.LXXXII

Freins, Antibor, villes autour de Nice,
Seront vaſtees fort par mer & par terre:
Les ſaturelles terre & mer vent propice,
Prins, morts, trouſſez, pillés, ſans loy de guerre.

Fréjus, Antibes; the towns around Nice will be greatly devastated by land and sea. The locusts over land and sea, the wind being favorable, captured, dead, trussed up, plundered without law of war.

Could an invasion of the coast of southern France by air be implied by the quatrain? Nostradamus normally describes modern machines as types of animals. Locusts, read literally, could not cause the death and destruction of line 4.

Century III

III.LXXXIII

Les longs cheueux de la Gaule Celtique,	*The long-haired person of Celtic Gaul, joined by foreign nations will capture the people of Aquitaine, in order that they should succumb to their plans.*
Accompaignez d'eftranges nations:	
Mettront captif la gent Aquitanique,	
Pour fuccomber à internitions.[1]	

The long-haired person from Celtic Gaul is Louis XVIII of France, known by his contemporaries as *le Chevelu*, his long hair being a great contrast to the short-cropped hair of the Revolutionaries and Bonapartistes. The foreign armies, *Accompaignez d'eftranges nations*, are the Allied armies who helped defeat Napoleon and put Louis on the throne of France. Aquitane may stand for England: it was English for over three hundred years. (See IX.VI.) But its application to the plans in line 4 is unclear.

Century III

III.LXXXIIII

La grand cité fera bien defolee,	*The greaty city will soon be quite deserted, not a single one of the inhabitants will remain. Wall, sex, temple and virgin violated, people will die from the sword; fire, plague and cannon shot.*
Des habitans vn feul n'y demoura:	
Mur, fexe, temple, & vierge violee,	
Par fer, feu, pefte, cannon peuple mourra.	

If the word sex is an abbreviation of Sextus, this applies to the sack of Rome by Napoleonic troops during the reign of Pius VI, 1775–1799. But many commentators think the city may be Paris.

---

[1]*internitions.* in all other texts read as "*intentions.*"

Century III

III.LXXXV

*La cité prinſe par tromperie &
    fraude,
Par le moyen d'vn beau ieune
    attrappé:
Aſſaut donné Raubine pres de
    LAVDE.
Luy & tous morts pour auoir
    bien trompé.*

*The city is taken by trickery and
deceit, captured by means of a
handsome young man. An
assault is made by Raubine near
LAVDE, he and all of them, for
having deceived so well.*

The Robine is a tributary of the Aube. Perhaps the city lies
upon one of these rivers? There is no clear reason as to why
LAVDE should be written in capital letters.

Century III

III.LXXXVI   ★

*Vn chef d'Auſonne aux
    Eſpaignes ira,
Par mer fera arreſt dedans
    Marſeille:
Auant ſa mort vn long temps
    languira,
Apres ſa mort on verra grand
    merueille.*

*A leader from Italy will go to
Spain by sea, and he will make a
stop at Marseilles. He will linger
for a long time before dying;
after his death great wonders
will be seen.*

A ruler of a southern Italian State (or of the Two Sicilies in
particular, because that was the home of the Ausones in
Roman times), will die a lingering death at Marseilles. This
may refer to a member of the Mafia or Cosa Nostra, and may
not yet be fulfilled. Most of the places mentioned are in Mafia
country.

Century III

III.LXXXVII

Claſſe Gauloiſe n'approches de Corſegue, *Moins de Sardaigne tu t'en repentiras:* *Treſtous mourrez fruſtrez de l'aide grogne,* *Sang nagera, captif ne me croiras.*	*French fleet, do not approach Corsica; even less Sardinia, you will regret it. You will all die, the help from the Cape (comes) in vain; captive, swimming in blood you will not believe me.*

In 1655 part of the French fleet, under the command of the chevalier de la Ferrière, was sunk in the Gulf of Lyons while sailing past the islands of Sardinia and Corsica. Many lives were lost because the ships were unable to reach the shelter of the nearby Cap de Porceau. This contains a typical Nostradamus double meaning: *grogne* could mean either a cape or the snout of a pig. *Le captif* in this quatrain becomes a proper name: Jean de Rian, who had earlier been captured and taken as a galley slave by the Algerian corsairs, was the pilot of this tragic fleet. His followers called him *Le Captif.*

Century III

III.LXXXVIII

De Barſellonne par mer ſi grand armee, *Toute Marſeille de frayeur tremblera:* *Iſles ſaiſies de mer ayde fermee,* *Ton traditeur en terre nagera.*	*From Barcelona, such a great army by sea, all Marseilles will tremble with terror. The islands seized, help cut off by sea, your traitor will swim on land.*

A very accurate quatrain on the history of Marseilles and the Spanish. On February 17, 1596, Philip of Spain sent his fleet, under the command of Charles Doria, to Marseilles to divide the French interests between the Leaguers and the king. The fleet occupied the islands of Château d'If and Ratonneau and thus prevented help from coming into Marseilles by sea. A certain Charles de Casau tried to betray Marseilles to the Spanish, but was found out and assassinated by Pierre

Libertot. He was killed by the sword, drowning in his own blood, literally *en terre nagera*, swimming on land. Nostradamus always uses the second person when referring to France.

Century III

III.LXXXIX

En ce temps là ſera fruſtrée Cypres, *De ſon ſecours de ceux de mer Egee:* *Vieux trucidez, mais par meſles[1] & lyphres[2]* *Seduict leur Roy, Royne plus outragee.*	At that time Cyprus will be deprived of its help from those of the Aegean sea. Old men slaughtered; but by cannons and supplications the king is won over; the queen more outraged.

Could this quatrain refer to the Troubles in Cyprus in the 1950s, when *Enosis*, union with Greece, was the popular demand? The quatrain shows that Cyprus will not obtain complete union with Greece. The Greek king, Constantine, is misled and finally goes into exile. The queen *plus outragee* is his mother, Queen Frederika, who was greatly distressed by the family's enforced exile.

Century III

III.XC

Le grand Satyre & Tigre d'Hyrcanie, *Don preſenté à ceux de l'Occean:* *Vn chef de claſſe iſtra de Carmanie,* *Qui prendra terre au Tyrren Phocean.*	The great Satyr and Tiger of Hyrcania, a gift presented to the people of the Ocean. The leader of a fleet will come forth from Carmania and land at Phocean Tyre.

[1] *meſles*. O.F. variant of *masle*, cannon ball.
[2] *lyphres*. Gk. *lypros*, supplications, plea.

Phocea is the Latin name for Marseilles, often used by Nostradamus. But Marseilles is not situated on the Tyrrhenian sea, so Nostradamus is probably thinking of another seaport associated with the Phoenician colonists of Tyre. Both Carmania and Hyrcania were Persian provinces. But unless the events in this quatrain are intended to occur after the building of the Suez Canal, the fleet would have to cross by land. A failed quatrain, I feel.

Century III

III.XCI

L'arbre qu'eſtoit par long temps mort ſeché,
Dans vne nuict viendra à reuerdir:
Cron Roy malade, Prince pied eſtaché,
Criant d'ennemis fera voile bondir.

The tree which had been dead and withered for a long time will flourish again in one night. The Cronian king will be ill; the Prince have a damaged foot. Fear of his enemies will make him hoist sail.

The tree which sprouts again miraculously overnight is the family tree of Bourbons, when the duchesse de Berry gave birth to a son, the duc de Bordeaux, on September 29, 1820, seven months after the assassination of her husband. The duc was a sickly child and injured his foot falling from a horse in Austria, which resulted in his having a permanent limp. He went into exile, *fera voile bondir,* in 1830 with his grandfather Charles X, and despite long negotiations with Republican France, did not succeed in attaining the throne. A satisfactory quatrain.

Century III

III.XCII

Le monde proche du dernier periode,
Saturne encor tard ſera de retour:
Tranſlat empire deuers nation Brodde,
L'oeil arrache à Narbon par Autour.

The world is near its final period, Saturn will again be late on his return. The empire will shift to the Brodde nation. An eye at Narbonne is plucked out by a goshawk.

This astrological quatrain refers to the future of the African nations. *Brodde* in old French means either black or dark brown, and cannot be confused with Nostradamus' vision of Asia and Tuscany. It also contains the meaning of decadent, which certainly applies to the corruption that is rampant in most African states today.

Nostradamus speaks of an *empire tranflaté* when referring to Napoleon. Does he see the beginning of the new power of Africa starting as early as that? He states that more power will be given to the African nations before the final cycle of the world, the second millennium, occurs. He may also contain the meaning that French power will increase in Africa before this time, which it did until France left Algeria. If that is so, we are now approaching the final period.

Century III

III.XCIII

Dans Auignon tout le chef de l'empire Fera arreſt pour Paris defolé: Tricaſt¹ tiendra l'Annibalique ire, Lyon par change ſera mal conſolé.	In Avignon, the leader of all the Empire will make a stop because Paris is deserted. Tricast will contain the African anger; the Lion will be poorly consoled by the change.

The quatrain hints at a great enemy of France and possibly also of Rome, in that Avignon belonged to the Vatican until 1791. The British Lion will dislike the French presence in Africa. Perhaps one should link this quatrain with those fought by the British in Africa during the Second World War? I feel that I have not properly interpreted this quatrain and that it is of rather greater impact and futuristic. The African quatrains are always difficult. See those on AIDS, World Famine, etc.

¹*Tricaſt*. Tricasses, city of Troyes, southeast of Paris.

Century III

III.XCIIII

De cinq cens ans plus compte l'on tiendra,
Celuy qu'eſtoit l'aornement de ſon temps:
Puis à vn coup grande clarté donra,
Que par ce ſiecle les rendra treſcontens.

For more than five hundred years they will take notice of him who was the adornment of his age. Then suddenly a great revelation will be made which will make the people of that century well pleased.

Almost all commentators on Nostradamus' works have seen themselves as the source of the great revelation to be made, *à vn coup grand clarté donra*. Certainly Nostradamus' works have been in print for well over four hundred years. The great revelation I feel is not a commentator but an event which will occur during this century. An as yet unfulfilled quatrain.

Century III

III.XCV

La loy Moricque on verra deffaillir,
Apres vn autre beaucoup plus ſeductiue:
Boriſthenes premier viendra faillir,
Par dons & langue vne plus attractiue.

The Moorish law will be seen to fail, followed by another that is less pleasing. The Dnieper will be the first to give way through gifts and tongues, to another more appealing.

This must forecast the state of Communism in northern Europe. The River Dnieper is situated in the USSR. Certainly it is interesting that Nostradamus sees Russia as the first to give way. Gorbachev brought the cutting down of nuclear weapons to Europe. The *dons & langue*, sweet speeches, would apply to the summits in Iceland and Moscow all of which were initiated by the Russians. The tragedy may happen reasonably soon, when these accords break down. See I.XCI, II.LXXXIX, V.LXXVIII, VI.XXI. Nostradamus gives the accord a lifespan of between three years and seven months and thirteen years. If that is so, will Gorbachev be crushed under the machinery of Stalinist Russia? Tragic as it is, Nostradamus seems to foresee the decline of détente and a possible resumption of the Cold War. A worrying quatrain. But in IV.XCV he states the victor will be born "on American soil."

Century III

III.XCVI

Chef de Foſſan aura gorge coupee,
Par le ducteur du limier &
leurier:
Le faict patré par ceux du
mont Tarpee,
Saturne en Leo 13. de Feurier.

The leader from Fossano will have his throat cut by the man who exercised the bloodhounds and the greyhounds. The deed will be committed by those of the Tarpeian Rock, when Saturn is in Leo on February 13.

Nostradamus gives us an excellent astrological dating in line 4. Saturn rules Aquarius, so when it is in its opposite sign of Leo it should be considered maleficent. The duc de Berry was stabbed to death on February 13, 1820, when leaving the Opéra.

The reference to Fossano is more difficult. If the quatrain does refer to the duc de Berry, then he has claim to the title of duc de Fossano through his maternal grandfather who was the duc of Fossano in Sardinia. The rest then fits very well. The assassin was a certain Louvel, who worked in the royal stables, *le ducteur de limier & leurier*, and whose job was to exercise the dogs. He was a Republican, hence the reference to the Tarpeian Rock, from which Republican Rome cast criminals to their deaths (see. I.LXXXIIII).

Century III

III.XCVII

Nouuelle loy terre neufue
    occuper,
Vers la Syrie, Iudee &
    Paleſtine:
Le grand empire barbare
    corruer,
Auant que Phebés ſon ſiecle
    determine.

A new law will occupy a new land around Syria, Judea and Palestine. The great barbarian empire will crumble before the century of the sun is finished.

This is a splendidly vindicated quatrain describing the creation of the state of Israel. Barbarian in Nostradamus' terms means non-Christian. It is implied that Israel will eventually triumph over her enemies before the end of the twentieth century, the century of the sun. King Hussein of Jordan has refused to accept the Gaza Strip as being Palestinian and the Israelis through Mr. Begin have accepted the responsibility of the land they gained in the Six Days' War. This prediction seems well on the way to being fulfilled.

Century III

III.XCVIII

Deux royals freres ſi fort
    guerroyeront,
Qu'entre eux ſera la guerre ſi
    mortelle:
Qu'vn chacun places fortes
    occuperont,
De regne & vie fera leur
    grand querelle.

Two royal brothers will fight very fiercely, and the feud between them will be so deadly that both will live in fortified places. Their great quarrel will concern their lives and the kingdom.

This prediction is a great example of a prediction which will fit various historical situations. It fits the situation of Henri III, king of France, and the duc d'Alençon, 1574–1584, but it also fits the quarrel between Louis XIII and his brother the duc d'Orléans around 1632. Prophecy, like history, does repeat itself.

Century III

III.XCIX

Aux champs herbeux d'Alein & *du Varneigne,* *Du mont Lebron proche de la* *Durance,* *Camps de deux parts conflict* *fera fi aigre,* *Mefopotamie defaillira en la* *France.*	*In the green fields of Alleins and* *Verneques of the Luberon moun-* *tains near Durance, the fighting* *on both sides of the armies will be* *so bitter that Mesopotamia will* *cease to be found in France.*

Many commentators, as I have said, take Nostradamus' Mesopotamia to mean Paris, but I must confess I am not too happy with this interpretation. The villages in line 1 are situated near Nostradamus' final home in Salon-de-Provence; the Luberon mountains are near Durance. I can make nothing out of this quatrain.

Century III

III.C

Entre Gaulois le dernier *honnoré,* *D'homme ennemy fera victorieux:* *Force & terroir en moment* *exploré,* *D'vn coup de traict quand* *mourra l'enuieux.*	*The man least honored among* *the French will be victorious* *over this enemy. He explores* *strength and lands in action,* *when suddenly the envious one* *dies from the shot.*

This quatrain is usually applied to de Gaulle. The man who is assassinated is identified as Admiral Darlan, who was killed December 24, 1942. *Traict* is the usual word for an arrow shot, but could, of course, stand in for gunshot.

Century IV

IV.I

Cela du reſte de ſang non
   eſpandu,
Veniſe quiert ſecours eſtre donné.
Apres auoir bien long tẽps
   attẽdu,
Cité liurée au premier cornet
   ſõné.

The blood of the just will not be
spilled, Venice seeks for help to
be given. Having waited for a
very long time the city is handed
over at the first blast of the trum-
pet.

This probably describes the Turkish attack on Cyprus,
1560–73. Venice asked for but received little help and Cyprus
fell to the Turks after a prolonged siege in 1571.

Century IV

IV.II

Par mort la France prendra
   voyage à faire,
Claſſe par mer, marcher monts
   Pyrenées,
Eſpaigne en trouble, marcher
   gent militaire:
Des plus grand Dames en
   France emmenées.

Because of a death France will
undertake a journey, marching
over the Pyrenees, the fleet at
sea. Spain will be troubled, an
army will march; some of the
greatest ladies brought into
France.

This is quite a successful quatrain. Philip V, grandson of
Louis XIV, inherited the Spanish throne from Charles II in
1700. This was unpopular with Austria, England, Holland,
Prussia and Savoy, who formed a coalition to support the
pretentions of the Archduke Charles. The French fleet took
to sea, and the French Army crossed the Pyrenees. The War
of the Spanish Succession lasted for twelve years, 1701–1713,
and its cause was two Spanish princesses, *Des plus grand Dames
en France emmenées*, who married out of their country into the
French royal line, becoming the wives of Louis XII and Louis
XIV.

Century IV

IV.III

D'Arras & Bourges, de Brodes
    grans enſeignes,
Vn plus grand nombre de
    Gaſcons batre à pied.
Ceux long du Roſne ſaigneront
    les Eſpaignes:
Proche du mont où Sagonte
    s'aſſied.

From Arras and Bourges great
banners from the dark ones; a
greater number of Gascons will
fight on foot. Those along the
Rhône will make the Spanish
bleed, near the mountain seat of
Sagunto.

Again *Broddes*, the dark ones, appear—these mysterious dark-skinned people whom Nostradamus believed would be part of a disaster in the twentieth century. The last two lines seem to refer to the French invasion of Spain 1701. The import of Sagunto is unclear. Possibly a split quatrain?

Century IV

IV.IIII

L'impotent prince faché, plaincts
    & querelles,
De rapts & pillé, par coqz &
    par Libyques:
Grand eſt par terre par mer
    infinies voilles,
Seule Italie ſera chaſſant
    Celtiques.

The powerless prince is angered;
complaints and quarrels, rape
and pillage by the cock and the
Libyans. He is great on land,
innumerable sails at sea. By
Italy alone will the Celts be driven out.

The cock is, as always, the symbol of France. If one accepts the Libyans as the Algerian corsairs who allied with them the prince is probably a Hapsburg, possibly Duc Cosimo, who was in charge of the defense of Elba and the surrounding lands. These territories were razed to the ground in 1555. But this is, in all, an unsuccessful quatrain. The last line suggests that the French will be defeated by the Italians but be successful everywhere else. In fact, the reverse occurred. The French held their own in Italy, but were defeated in the North. An unsuccessful contemporary quatrain.

Century IV

IV.V

Croix paix, foubz vn accomply diuin verbe, *L'Eſpaigne & Gaule ſeront vnis enſemble:* *Grand clade[1] proche, & combat treſacerbe,* *Coeur ſi hardy ne ſera qui ne tremble.*	Cross, peace; under one the divine word achieved. Spain and Gaul will be united. A great disaster in close, the fighting very ferocious. No heart so brave that it will not tremble.

This seems yet another quatrain centering upon the War of the Spanish Succession, 1701–1713. Spain and France were united for a short time when Louis XIV's grandson inherited the Spanish throne. The revocation of the Edict of Nantes may be hinted at in line 1. Peace achieved under the *diuin verbe* may refer to the Papal Bull Unigenitus, issued in 1713, the year the war ended. The great disaster following the union of the countries is the War of the Spanish Succession. The last line may be self-explanatory.

Century IV

IV.VI

D'habits nouueaux apres faicte la treuue, *Malice tramme & machination:* *Premier mourra qui en fera la preuue,* *Couleur veniſe inſidiation.*	After the truce is made new clothes will be put on; malice, conspiracy and plotting. He who will prove it is the first to die, the color of Venetian treachery.

A very obscure quatrain. Perhaps the new clothes imply a new order of monks, and there is a shade of yellow-brown which is known as Venetian red.

---

[1]*clade*. L. *disaster*.

Century IV

IV.VII

*Le mineur filz du grand & hay
   Prince,
De lepre aura à vingt ans
   grande tache,
De dueil ſa mere mourra bien
   triſte & mince,
Et il mourra la où tombe cher
   lache.*

The younger son of a great and hated Prince will be greatly marked by leprosy by the time he is twenty. His mother will die of grief, very sad and thin, and he will die when the cowardly flesh vanishes (from his bones).

There is no record to date of a younger son of a royal family dying of leprosy. Perhaps this may refer to cancer or some other wasting disease, rather than leprosy.

Century IV

IV.VIII

*Le grand cité d'aſſaut prompt &
   repentin,
Surprins de nuict, gardes
   interrompus:
Les excubies & veilles ſainct
   Quintin,
Trucidés gardes & les pourtails
   rompus.*

The great city will be surprised at night by a sudden and quick assault. The guards interrupted; the watch and guards of St. Quentin slaughtered, the guards killed and the gates broken down.

St. Quentin is obviously the key word in this quatrain. There was a battle of St. Quentin in 1557 and the city was taken, not in the way Nostradamus described it, but by a seventeen-day siege. At least the prediction of the town's capture is correct. (See IV.III.)

Century IV

IV.IX

Le chef du camp au milieu de
  la preſſe,
D'vn coup de fleche ſera bleſſé
  aux cuiſſes,
Lors que Geneue en larmes &
  detreſſe,
Sera trahie par Lozan &
  Souyſſes.

The leader of the army in the
middle of the crowd is wounded
in the thighs with an arrow.
When Geneva, troubled and in
distress, is betrayed by Lausanne
and the Swiss.

This is probably another anti-Calvinist tirade by Nostradamus. He seems to forsee Lausanne and Switzerland returning
to the Roman Catholic faith with only Geneva holding out. A
completely mistaken verse.

Century IV

IV.X

Le ieune prince accuſé
  faulſement,
Mettra en trouble le camp &
  en querelles:
Meurtry le chef pour le
  ſouſtenement,
Sceptre appaiſer: puis guerir
  eſcrouelles.

The young prince, falsely
accused, will put the camp into
quarrels and trouble. The leader
is murdered for his support to
appease the crown; then he cures
the king's evil.

A pointless quatrain. A leader of an army will support a
Prince, wrongly accused of something, and lose his life as a
consequence. Both French and English kings were reported to
be able to cure scrofula, the king's evil, particularly on the day
of their coronation.

Century IV

IV.XI

*Celuy qu'aura gouuert de la
    grand cappe,[1]
Sera induict à quelque cas
    patrer:[2]
Les douze rouges viendront
    fouiller la nappe.
Soubz meurte, meurtre se
    viendra perpetrer.*

*He who will have government of
the Great Cape will be led to
execute them in some cases. The
twelve red ones will come to spoil
the cover, under murder, murder
will be perpetrated.*

A detailed quatrain. A pope will be forced into some rash
action, and then be condemned by his twelve cardinals. It is
implied that they connive at the Pope's murder. This could
possibly refer to Pope John Paul I, who reigned in 1978 for
only thirty-four days and died in mysterious circumstances in
the Vatican after a meeting with the cardinals of his curia.

John Paul I had determined to look into the scandals of the
Vatican connections with the Mafia and the powerful group of
Freemasons known as P.2. The night before his death he had
given Cardinal Villot a list of those people he wanted removed
from positions of power. The cardinal later gave false
statements to the police and press about the circumstances of
John Paul I's death. The list has not been seen since. Also,
hastily, and against all Catholic tradition, the body of the Pope
was cremated. If this is the correct interpretation, a good
quatrain. (See also X.XII, III.LXV.)

Century IV

IV.XII

*Le camp plus grand de route
    mis en fuite,
Guaires plus outre ne sera
    pourchassé:
Ost recampé, & legion reduicte,
Puis hors des Gaules du tout
    sera chassé.*

*The greatest army on the march
put to flight, will scarcely be pursued further. The army reassem-
bled and the legion reduced, they
will be driven completely out of
France.*

[1]*cappe.* Cloak, cape, standing for the Vatican.
[2]*patrer.*L. *patrare,* to execute, perform.

A general quatrain and the German invasions of the last two wars fit it most accurately. But there is nothing explicit to go on.

Century IV

IV.XIII

De plus grand perte nouuelles raportées,
Le raport fait le camp s'eftonnera:
Bandes vnies encontre reuoltées,
Double phalange grand abandonnera.

News of the great loss is brought; the report will astonish the camp. Bands unite against those who are in revolt, the double phalanx will forsake the great one.

This verse was applied by contemporaries to the 1580's, when a rumor spread through the duke of Parma's army of so great a defeat that they were completely demoralized and this enabled the Dutch to capture Antwerp for a time. A phalanx consisted of 800 men, so double this number are said to have revolted.

Century IV

IV.XIIII

La mort fubite du premier perfonnage
Aura changé & mis vn autre au regne:
Toft, tard venu à fi haut & bas aage,
Que terre & mer faudra que on le craigne.

The sudden death of the leading personage will make change, and put another to rule. Soon, but too late come to high position, of young age. By land and sea it will be necessary to fear him.

A general prophecy about a young leader who comes to power too late to alter the status quo of a country. It has fancifully been suggested that it may refer to John F. Kennedy, succeeding old General Eisenhower, whose politics had been unable to lessen world tension. During the Cuban Missile Crisis, Kennedy's power was to be feared by land and sea.

Century IV

IV.XV

D'où penſera faire venir famine,
De là viendra le reſſaſiement:
L'oeil de la mer par auare
  canine
Pour de l'vn l'autre donra
  huyle, froment.

From the place where he will think to bring famine, from there will come help. The eye of the sea, like a covetous dog. The one will give oil and wheat to the other.

This verse describes Britain's predicament during the Second World War, 1939–45, very accurately. The German blockade tried to starve Britain out (see also III.LXXI), but fortunately she received large quantities of American aid — *huyle, froment.* The "eye of the sea, like a covetous dog" is a wonderful description of U-boats, searching for British convoys through their periscopes, to hunt them down.

Century IV

IV.XVI

La cité franche de liberté fait
  ſerue,
Des profligés & reſueurs faict
  aſyle:
Le Roy changé à eux non ſi
  proterue:[1]
De cent ſeront deuenus plus de
  mille.

The free city of liberty is enslaved, it becomes the refuge of profligates and dreamers. The king changes and is not so ferocious towards them. From one hundred they will become more than a thousand.

Europe had many free cities when Nostradamus wrote. He may here be referring to Orange, which gave its name to the Dutch royal line, and did not pass to France until 1713. During Nostradamus' time it belonged to William the Silent, and line 2 may refer to it becoming a haven for Protestants, which in fact it did.

---

[1]*proterue.* L. *protervus*, violent.

Century IV

IV.XVII

Changer à Beaune, Nuy,
　　Chalons & Dijon,
Le duc voulant amander[1] la
　　Barrée[2]
Marchant pres fleuue, poiſſon,
　　bec de plõgeon,
Verra la queuë: porte ſera ſerrée.

Changes at Beaune, Nuits, Chalon and Dijon; the duke wants to
improve the Carmelites. Walking near the river, a fish, a
diving (bird's) beak, towards the
tail. The gate will be locked.

St. Theresa reformed the order of Carmelite nuns in Spain
in 1562. I can make nothing of the following lines.

Century IV

IV.XVIII

Des plus lettrés deſſus les faits
　　celeſtes
Seront par princes ignorans
　　reprouués:
Punis d'Editſ, chaſſez, comme
　　ſceleſtes,
Et mis à mort là où ſeront
　　trouués.

Some of the most learned men in
the heavenly arts will be repri-
manded by ignorant Princes.
Punished by an Edict, driven
out as scoundrels and put to
death wherever they are found.

Shades of the Inquisition linger over this verse for, in fact,
astrologers were never as grossly persecuted after Nostradamus' death as they were before. However, the witch-hunts
which bedeviled America and Europe did not occur until a
century later.

[1]*amander*. O.F. to better, to improve.
[2]*Barrée*. This was the name given to the Carmelite monks and nuns,
coming from the O.F. *barré*, motley.

Century IV

IV.XIX

Deuant Rouan d'Infubres mis le fiege,
Par terre & mer enfermés les paffages:
D'Haynault, & Flãdres, de Gâd & ceux de Liege,
Par dons laenées[1] rauiront les riuages.

The Insubrians lay siege in front of Rouen, the passages closed by land and sea. By Hainault and Flanders, by Ghent and those of Liege, through hidden gifts they will ravage the shores.

Rouen was first captured by the duke of Parma who was helping the duc de Guise against Henri de Navarre in 1592, but without a long siege. Since Milan was part of Parma's dominions, there could well have been Italians *(Infubres)* among his troops. Rouen has never since been captured by Italians; the Germans captured it in 1870 and 1940, the Americans in 1944. All the other towns mentioned in the quatrain are in the Netherlands and Flanders. Despite all this speculation, it is hard to see that this prophecy has really been fulfilled.

Century IV

IV.XX

Paix vberté[2] long temps lieu louera:
Par tout fon regne defert la fleur de lys:
Corps morts d'eau, terre là lon aportera,
Sperants vain heur d'eftre là enfeuelis.

Peace and plenty for a long time will gift the place. The fleur-de-lys is deserted throughout the kingdom. Bodies dead by water will come there to land, hoping in vain for their burial hour.

The fleur-de-lys was not the unique property of the French royal family; it was used by several others, so it is less a clue than it seems. If it does relate to France, the obvious time that

---

[1]*laenées*. L. cloak, mantle; by metaphor, hidden.
[2]*vberté*. L. *ubertas*, abundance.

it disappears from the kingdom is during the Revolution and Empire. The last two lines seem to be generalities about war and unburied dead.

Century IV

IV.XXI

Le changement ſera fort difficile,	The change will be very difficult.
Cité, prouince au change gain fera:	Both city and province will gain by it. A highly placed, prudent
Coeur haut, prudent mis, chaſſé luy habile,	man will be chased out by the cunning one. People will change
Mer, terre, peuple ſon eſtat changera.	their estate by land and sea.

If one accepts this quatrain as referring to the fall of France, it could then be applied to Marshal Pétain's policy of "centralized decentralization." The prudent man will then be de Gaulle, chased to England, and the last line would then refer to the general state of the country during the war.

Century IV

IV.XXII

La grand copie[1] qui ſera deſchaſſée,	The great army which will be driven out, will suddenly be
Dans vn moment fera beſoing au Roy,	needed by the king. The trust, promised from afar, will be bro-
La foy promiſe de loing ſera faulſée,	ken. He will see himself with nothing, in pitiful disorder.
Nud ſe verra en piteux deſarroy.	

This is such a general quatrain that these incidents may well have occurred several times. A king quarrels with an ally and suddenly finds he needs its help again. But because one of them breaks faith, the king is left powerless.

---

[1]*copie.* L. *copia,* army, troops.

Century IV

IV.XXIII

La legion dans la marine claſſe, *Calcine,[1] Magnes[2] ſoulphre, &* *poix bruſlera:* *Le long repos de l'aſſeuree place,* *Port Selyn,[3] Hercle[4] feu les* *conſumera.*	*The legion in the marine fleet will burn, lime, magnesia, sulphur and pitch. There is a long rest in a safe place. Port Selyn, Monaco will be consumed by fire.*

This is a strange and interesting quatrain. The second line appears to give us the ingredients for Greek fire, the famous "secret weapon" of the Greeks and the Byzantines. Nostradamus appears to be correct in this. The expert on ancient warfare Lt. Col. H. Hime wrote that it was the presence of quicklime which distinguished Greek fire from all other known incendiaries of the period. The mixture gave rise to heat on contact with water and thus caught fire spontaneously when wet and was used with great success in sea battles. On the other hand, if I am correct in identifying Port Selyn with Genoa, it was attacked in 1684 by the French fleet of Louis XIV, causing considerable destruction in the city.

Century IV

IV.XXIIII

Ouy ſoubs terre ſaincte dame voix *fainte,* *Humaine flamme pour diuine* *voir luire:* *Fera des ſeuls de leur ſang terre* *tainte,* *Et les ſaincts tẽples pour les* *impurs deſtruire.*	*The faint voice of a woman is heard under the holy ground. A human flame lights up for the divine voice. It will cause the earth to be stained with the blood of celibates and destroy the holy temples on behalf of the wicked.*

[1]*Calcine.* L. *calcina*, lime.
[2]*Magnes.* L. lodestone; also an abbreviation of magnesia, the usual description of Greek fire.
[3]*Port Selyn.* Genoa: it was a crescent-shaped republic and *selene* is Greek for moon.
[4]*Hercle.* L. *Herculeis Monacei*, Monaco.

This quatrain is a riddle because of the many possible interpretations of the first line. To which word does *faincte* belong? In other versions *dame* is also given as *d'aime* and *fainte* as *faincte*. The general idea seems to be the persecution of the Church, perhaps as personified by the Holy Lady of line 1. The most probable fulfillment of this quatrain would be the abolition and persecution of the clergy during the French Revolution.

Century IV

IV.XXV

Corps fublimes fans fin à l'oeil
  vifibles:
Obnubiler viendront par ces
  raifons:
Corps, front comprins, fens chief
  & inuifibles.
Diminuant les facrees oraifons.

The heavenly bodies endlessly visible to the eye come to cloud (the mind) for their own reasons. The body, together with the forehead, senses and head are all invisible, as the sacred prayers recede.

Some commentators believe this quatrain refers to the invention of the telescope, 1610, which will bring in new worlds and concepts hostile to religion. However, I believe this to be one of the "occult" quatrains, where Nostradamus is trying to describe the sensation of bodilessness which he experienced in a predictive trance, when his mind and intellect are used by the heavenly being for its own purposes. The sacred prayers of the last line are the invocations made to the spirit by Nostradamus as he gives up his being to its possession.

Century IV

IV.XXVI

Lou grand eyffame fe leuera
  d'abelhos,
Que non fauran don te fiegen
  venguddos:
Dĕuech l'ĕbousĝ, lou gach deffous
  las treilhos
Ciutad trahido per cinq lengos
  non nudos.

The great storm of bees will arise but no one will know from whence they have come. An ambush by night, the sentinel under the vines; a city handed over by five tongues, not naked.

This is the only quatrain written entirely in sixteenth century Provençal. It is also amazingly accurate. It describes Napoleon's coup d'état of 1799. The swarm of bees was Napoleon's emblem. They can still be seen on the embroideries in Josephine's house at Malmaison and at Fontainebleau. The five men, literally "babblers" *(lengos non nudos)* who handed Paris over were the members of the Directoire who were bribed, *non nudos*, to give way to Napoleon's Consulate. They were also wearing their official clothes as members of the Directoire, as opposed to their normal apparel, to give authority to their gesture.

The coup was planned the night before its execution. *Las treilhos* is probably an anagram for the Tuileries into which Napoleon moved once he had consolidated his coup. The exact French equivalent is *les treilles*. Close enough in Nostradamus' language to "Tuileries."

Century IV

IV.XXVII

Salon, Manſol, Taraſcon de *SEX. l'arc,*	*Salon, Mansol, Tarascon, the arch of SEX, where the pyramid*
Où eſt debout encor la piramide:	*is still standing. They will come*
Viendront liurer le Prince *Dannemarc,*	*to deliver the Prince of Denmark, a shameful ransom to*
Rachat honny au temple *d'Artemide.*	*the temple of Artemis.*

The complicated first line refers to St. Rémy-de-Provence where Nostradamus was born, where there stand two great historical monuments: a mausoleum with the inscription SEX. L.M. JUILEI C.F. PARENTIBIS SUIS, next to which still stands a Roman triumphal arch. (It now stands in the middle of a field with cows grazing around it.) *Mansol* is a misprint for Mausole, a priory just outside Saint Rémy. But Dannemarc and the following line I cannot decipher.

Century IV

IV.XXVIII

Lors que Venus du Sol fera couuert, *Soubs l'efplendeur fera forme occulte:* *Mercure au feu les aura defcouuert,* *Par bruit bellique fera mis à l'infulte.*	*When Venus will be covered by the sun, under the splendor will be a hidden form. Mercury will have exposed them to the fire, by a rumor of war will be affronted.*

I believe that this and four other quatrains IV.XXIX, XXX, XXXI, and XXXIII are hermetic quatrains possibly describing Nostradamus' attempts to isolate and use various materials for his occult practices. They should be read as a sequence.

Century IV

IV.XXIX

Le Sol caché eclipfe par Mercure, *Ne fera mis que pour le ciel fecond:* *De Vlcan Hermes fera faicte pafture,* *Sol fera veu pur, rutilant & blond.*	*The hidden Sun eclipsed by Mercury will be placed only second in the heavens. Hermes will be made the food of Vulcan, the Sun will be seen pure, shining and golden.*

Hermes is Quicksilver and Vulcan stands for life.

Century IV

IV.XXX

Plus vnze fois Luna Sol ne voudra, *Tous augmenté & baiffez de degré:* *Et fi baf mis que peu or on coudra,* *Qu'apres faim, pefte, defcouuert le fecret.*	*More than eleven times the Moon will not want the sun, both raised and lessened in degree. Put so low that one will sew little gold. After famine and plague the secret will be discovered.*

The Moon here stands for silver and the Sun for gold.

Century IV
IV.XXXI

La Lune au plain de nuict ſur le haut mont,
Le nouueau ſophe d'vn ſeul cerueau l'a veu:
Par ſes diſciples eſtre immortel ſemond,
Yeux au midy, en ſeins mains, corps au feu.

The moon, in the middle of the night over the high mountain; the young wise man alone with his mind has seen it. Invited by his disciples to become immortal; his eyes to the south, his hands on his breast, his body in the fire.

Does the last line suggest that Nostradamus suffers physical pain when making contact with his *diuin verbe*? Note also the position, eyes to the south and hands on his breast. This must be the pose he adopted in his study.

Century IV
IV.XXXII   ★

Es lieux & temps chair au poiſſon donra lieu,
La loy commune ſera faicte au contraire:
Vieux tiendra fort puis oſté du millieu,
Le Pánta chiona philòn mis fort arriere.

In those times and places that meat gives way to fish, the common law will be in opposition. The old (older?) will hold strong, then removed from the scene. Pânta, chiona, philôn, put far behind.

Pánta chiona philòn is the Greek for "all things held in common among friends." Communism in its most simplistic sense? Nostradamus also describes this in III.XCV, implying that the appeal of the old order will fail, as indeed it has, throughout Eastern Europe. Note Nostradamus' fear that Gorbachev may not succeed in his aims. I originally wrote in 1972, "I wonder whether this means that America and the USSR will ally?" This has now happened. (See V.LXXVIII.)

Century IV

IV.XXXIII

Iupiter ioinct plus Venus qu'à la Lune,	Jupiter joined more to Venus than to the Moon appearing in a white fullness. Venus hidden under the whiteness of Neptune, struck by Mars by the engraved wand.
Apparoiſſant de plenitude blanche:	
Venus cachée ſouz la blancheur Neptune	
De Mars frappée par la grauée branche.	

Branche is used by Nostradamus in I.II to indicate the wand he uses during his preparatory ritual for prophesying. The rest of this obscure quatrain must be allied with IV.XXVIII, XXIX, and XXX.

Century IV

IV.XXXIIII

Le grand mené captif d'eſtrange terre,	The great man led captive from a foreign land, chained in gold, offered to King Chyren. He who in Ausonia and Milan will lose the war and all his army put to fire and the sword.
D'or enchainé au Roy CHYREN offert:	
Qui dans Auſtone, Milan perdra la guerre,	
Et tout ſon oſt mis à feu & à fer.	

CHYREN is almost certainly an anagram for the Old French spelling of Henri, Henryc. The problem lies in deciding which Henri the quatrain refers to. Many commentators favor Henri IV; those of the nineteenth century in particular favor a new King Henri to come. The *CHYREN* quatrains are not particularly favorable to either idea, but it is unlikely that this is still to be fulfilled. It is probably a failed quatrain. (See II.LXXIX, VI.LXX, VIII.LIIII, IX.XXXXI.)

Century IV

IV.XXXV

Le feu eftaint, les vierges
 trahiront
La plus grand part de la bande
 nouuelle:
Fouldre à fer, lance les feulz
 Roy garderont
Etrufque & Corfe, de nuict
 gorge allumelle.

The fires put out, the virgins will betray the greater part of the new band. Lightning in the sword, lances alone will guard the king. Tuscany and Corsica, at night throats slit.

During the Empire, Tuscany and Corsica were both troubled by the French.

Century IV

IV.XXXVI

Les ieux nouueaux en Gaule
 redreffés,
Apres victoire de l'Insubre[1]
 champaigne:
Monts d'Efperie, les grands liés,
 trouffés:
De peur trembler la Romaigne
 & l'Efpaigne.

The new games are set up in Gaul after the victory of the Insubrian campaign. The mountains of Hesperia; the great ones tied and bound. Romania and Spain will tremble with fear.

Romaigne in line 4 stands for the Holy Roman Empire, i.e., Germany. The best interpretation of France's victories in Spain and in the North would be the Napoleonic campaigns.

---

[1]*Insubre*. L. *Insubria*. Italy, around Milan.

Century IV

IV.XXXVII

Gaulois par faults, monts viendra penetrer:	The Gauls will penetrate the mountains in leaps, they will occupy the great seat of Insubria. He will make his army penetrate deep (into the land). Genoa and Monaco will repulse the red fleet.
Occupera le grand lieu de l'Infubre:	
Au plus profond fon oft fera entrer,	
Gennes, Monech poufferont claffe rubre.	

In 1880, Genoa was besieged by Austria and surrendered on June 4. The British fleet, which had been helping with the blockade, attacked Monaco on May 23. Earlier that month, Napoleon made his incredible crossing of the Saint Bernard pass with an army of 40,000 men and took Milan *(Insubria)* on June 22. A very satisfactory quatrain.

Century IV

IV.XXXVIII

Pendant que Duc, Roy, Royne occupera,	While the duke occupies the king and queen, the Byzantine leader is held captive in Greece. Before the attack one will devour the other. The metal reverse will follow the train of blood.
Chef Bizant du captif en Samothrace:	
Auant l'affault l'vn l'autre mangera,	
Rebours ferré fuyura du fang la trace.	

The *rebours ferré*, metal reverse, sounds modern. Otherwise, I cannot decipher this quatrain.

Century IV

IV.XXXIX

*Les Rhodiens demanderont
 secours,
Par le neglet de ſes hoyrs
 delaiſsée:
L'empire Arabe reualera ſon
 cours,
Par Heſperies la cauſe redreſsée.*

The people of Rhodes will demand help, abandoned by the neglect of their heirs. The Arab Empire will assess its course, its cause revived again in the West.

At a time of unrest in Greece the United Arab Emirates will assess its position and be helped in some way by America. The Gulf War springs to mind. America has been selling weaponry to Iraq, and France to Iran. The United Nations, have desperately organized a cease-fire and hopefully end of the war. Probably a twentieth century quatrain.

Century IV

IV.XL

*Les forterefſes des aſſiegés ſerrés,
Par poudre à feu profondés en
 abyſme:
Les proditeurs ſeront tous vifs
 ſerrés,
Onc aux ſacriſtes n'aduint ſi
 piteux ſciſme.*

The fortress of the besieged, closed by gunpowder, sunk into the abyss. The traitors will be entombed alive. Never did so pitiful a schism happen to the sextons.

The clue to this verse lies in the last line. *Sacriſtes*, sextons are meaningless in this context. But if Nostradamus means Saxons, the Germans, associated with a schism, the breaking up of a party, this could refer indirectly to Hitler and those pitiful few of his followers who remained with him in the bunker at Berlin which was shelled by the Allies.

Century IV

IV.XLI

Gymnique[1] sexe captiue par
    hostage,
Viendra de nuit custodes
    deceuoir:
Le chef du camp deçeu par son
    langage:
Lairra à la gente, fera piteux à
    voyr.

A female captive, as a hostage,
will come by night to deceive the
guards. The leader of the camp
taken in by her words, will lead
her to the people. It will be pitiful
to see.

Too general a quatrain to be of use.

Century IV

IV.XLII

Geneue & Lãgres par ceux de
    Chatres & Dole,
Et par Grenoble captif au
    Montlimard:
Seysset, Losanne par fraudulente
    dole,
Les trahiront par or soixante marc.

Geneva and Langres through
the people of Chartres and Dôle
captured by Grenoble at Monte-
limar. Sysel, Lausanne will betray them by a fraudulent trick
for sixty gold marks.

There are too many scattered place names in both Switzerland and France to make this clear. A mark was eight ounces
of gold.

Century IV

IV.XLIII   ★

Seront ouys au ciel les armes
    battre:
Celuy au mesme les diuins
    ennemis:
Voudront loix sainctes iniustement
    debatre,
Par foudre & guerre bien
    croyans à mort mis.

Weapons will be heard fighting
in the skies. In the same year the
priests (divines) are enemies.
They will want, unjustly, to
query the holy laws. Through
lightning and war many believers put to death.

[1]Gymnique. misprint for Gk. gynique, female.

The first line definitely indicates an air battle of some kind, which should make this a twentieth century quatrain. Lightning in line 4 is probably a bombardment. But who are the priests and the believers? I don't think this can apply to the Middle East as Nostradamus would never have called Moslems *croyans*. That word is reserved strictly for Christians. This may be linked with the Millennium.

Century IV

IV.XLIIII

Deux gros de Mende, de Roudés & Milhau, Cahours, Limoges, Castres malo sepmano De nuech l'intrado, de Bourdeaux vn cailhau, Par Perigort au toc de la campano.

The two great ones of Mende, of Rodez and Milhau, Cahors and Limoges, Castres; a bad week. The entry by night. An insult from Bordeaux. Through Perigord at the peal of the bell.

A quatrain of mixed Provençal and French. Unfortunately these seem to disguise little more than the names of various towns in southern France. The tocsin singing in line 4 may be an alarm, but against what?

Century IV

IV.XLV

Par conflit Roy, regne abandonnera, Le plus grand chef faillira au besoing: Mors profligés peu en rechapera, Tous destranchés, vn en sera tesmoing.

Through a battle the king will abandon his kingdom. The greatest leader will fail in time of need. Dead, ruined, few will escape, all cut down save one who will be a witness.

This is a typical prophecy that may refer to several historical events, repeated history as it were, depending upon the reader's viewpoint. Napoleon, at Waterloo, Napoleon III and

Kaiser Wilhelm II have all been proposed as candidates. The reader can take his choice.

Century IV

IV.XLVI

Bien defendu le faict par
  excellence,
Garde toy Tours de ta proche
  ruine:
Londres & Nantes par Reims
  fera defenfe
Ne paffe outre au temps de la
  bruine.

The deed, through its excellence is strictly forbidden. Tours, beware of your future ruin. London and Nantes will make a defense through Reims. Do not venture further afield at the time of the fog.

I cannot decipher this quatrain, except that when Nostradamus uses the second person, "*Garde toy Tours*", it usually refers to France.

Century IV

IV.XLVII   ★

Le noir farouche quand aura
  effayé
Sa main fanguine par feu, fer,
  arcs tendus:
Treftout le peuple fera tant
  effrayé,
Voir les plus grans par col
  & pieds pendus.

When the ferocious dark one will have exercised his bloody hand through fire, the sword, the drawn bow, all the nation will be so terrified to see the great ones hanging by their neck and feet.

Again we have the mysterious dark-haired man, the *Brodde* of other quatrains, who appears to be terrorizing his people. He has been linked with the advent of the Third World War. I think that this quatrain has yet to be fulfilled.

Century IV

IV.XLVIII

Planure Auſonne fertile,
ſpacieuſe,
Produira taons ſi tant de
ſauterelles:
Clarté ſolaire deuiendra
nubileuſe,
Ronger le tout, grand peſte
venir d'elles.

The plains of Ansonia, rich and wide, will spawn so many gad-flies and grasshoppers that the height of the sun will be clouded over. They will devour every-thing and a great pestilence will come from them.

This may be a futuristic quatrain. At the time of writing, late 1988, there is one of the worst plagues of locusts *(sauterelles)* seen for many years in North Africa and reports have been coming in that they have been found in Sicily and even on the islands off America and England. With the appalling famine in the Sudan, maybe the swarms will turn north to Italy in search of food?

Century IV

IV.XLIX

Deuant le peuple ſang ſera
reſpandu,
Que du haut ciel ne viendra
eſloigner:
Mais d'vn long temps ne ſera
entendu,
L'eſprit d'vn ſeul le viendra
teſmoigner.

Blood will be spilled in front of the people which will not go far from high heaven. But although seen for a long time, it will not be heard. The spirit of a single man will bear witness to it.

Spilled blood is calling to the heavens for vengeance, but the bloody deed which caused it is not clear.

Century IV

IV.L

Libra verra regner les Hesperies,
De ciel & terre tenir la
  monarchie:
D'Asie forces nul ne verra
  peries,
Que sept ne tiennent par rang
  la hierarchie.

Libra will be seen to reign in the West holding the rule over the skies and earth. No one will see the strength of Asia destroyed until seven hold the hierarchy in succession.

An interesting quatrain. It states that when Libra, the Balance, rules over the Western World and therefore America, that country will be at the height of its powers. But Asian strength will be equally strong until the seventh comes. This does not mean the seventh decade so perhaps it is a seventh ruler, a change of régime? It appears from the last line that a war may occur between East and West once this seventh successor is in power. This should be linked with the quatrains of the Third Antichrist and global war towards the end of the century. "The seven" is one of the portents of the Millennium.

Century IV

IV.LI

Vn Duc cupide son ennemy
  ensuyure,
Dans entrera empeschant la
  phalange:
Hastez à pied si pres viendront
  poursuyure
Que la iournee conflite pres de
  Gange.

A duke will enter, eager to follow his enemy, hindering the phalanx. Hurrying on foot they follow so closely that the day of battle is near Ganges.

It is unlikely that *Gange* stands for the river Ganges in India as Nostradamus simply didn't take that country into his calculations, unless it comes under his sweeping term of "Asia and the East." There is a small town named Ganges near Montpellier.

Century IV

IV.LII

*En cité obseſse aux murs hommes
  & femmes,
Ennemis hors le chef preſt à ſoy
  rendre:
Vent sera fort encontre les
  gensdarmes,
  Chaſſez ſeront par chaux,
pouſſiere, & cendre.*

In the besieged city, men and women at the walls, the enemy without, the leader ready to surrender. The wind will drive strongly against the armed men. They will be driven off by lime, dust and cinders.

Another general quatrain about the besieging of a city and its attackers repelled.

Century IV

IV.LIII

*Les fugitifs & bannis reuoquez,
Peres & fils grand garniſſant les
  hauts puits:
Le cruel pere & les ſiens
  ſuffoquez,
Son fils plus pire ſubmergé dans
  le puits.*

The fugitives and the banished are recalled, fathers and sons strengthening the deep walls. The cruel father and his followers suffocated. His most wicked son drowned in the well.

Probably a failed quatrain?

Century IV

IV.LIIII

*Du nom qui onques ne fut au
  Roy Gaulois,
Iamais ne fut vn fouldre ſi
  craintif:
Tremblant l'Italie, l'Eſpaigne &
  les Anglois,
De femme eſtrangiers
  grandement attentif.*

Holding a name which never belonged to a French king, there was never so fearful a thunderbolt. Italy, Spain and the English tremble. He will be greatly attractive to foreign women.

This is a good quatrain. Napoleon brought the new name of Bonaparte to the ranks of Capet, Valois, and the other French kings. He also brought a new Christian name (there had been six Louises, two Henris, two Charleses and one François since Nostradamus' time). Napoleon caused the great upheavals that occurred in Europe—to Italy, Spain and England. He was also very enamored of both his foreign wives, Josephine, the Créole, and Marie Louise of Austria. The quatrain may possibly also hint of his Polish mistress, Marie Walewska. The reference to his name being as dreadful as a thunderbolt should be compared with IV.LXXXII, where Nostradamus refers to Napoleon as "the Destroyer."

Century IV

IV.LV

Quant la corneille *ſur tout de
     brique ioincte,
Durant ſept heures ne fera que
     crier:
Mort preſagee de ſang ſtatue
     taincte,
Tyran meurtri, aux Dieux
     peuple prier.*

When the crow will do nothing but croak for seven hours on a tower made of brick, it foretells death. A statue stained with blood, a tyrant murdered, people praying to their Gods.

Both the crow and the statue weeping blood are common omens of evil or portentous events. However, I cannot pin down anything specific in this stanza.

Century IV

IV.LVI

*Apres victoire de rabieuſe
     langue,
L'eſprit tempté en tranquil &
     repos:
Victeur ſanguin par conflict
     faict harangue,
Rouſtir la langue & la chair
     & les os.*

After the victory of the babbling tongue, the spirit is tempted by a tranquil rest. Throughout the battle the bloody victor makes speeches, roasting the tongue, the flesh and the bones.

I cannot explain this quatrain.

Century IV

IV.LVII

Ignare enuie au grand Roy
*   supportee,*
Tiendra propos deffendre les
*   escriptz:*
Sa femme non femme par vn
*   autre tentee,*
Plus double deux ne fort ne
*   criz.*

Ignorant envy, supported by the
great king, who will propose that
the writings should be forgiven.
His wife, who is not his wife,
tempted by another. No longer
will the double dealing couple
protest against it.

It has been suggested that Nostradamus is referring here to
his own writings and to Henri II's cool reception of the
Prophéties. The second woman would then be Diane de
Poitiers, who had such an enormous influence on the king's
life. There is a similar reference in VII.IX. The last line is
difficult to interpret.

Century IV

IV.LVIII

Soleil ardent dans le gosier
*   coller,*
De sang humain arroufer terre
*   Etrusque:*
Chef seille[1] d'eaue, mener son fils
*   filer,*
Captiue dame conduicte en terre
*   Turque.*

The burning sun is swallowed in
the throat; the Tuscan land
sprinkled with human blood
The chief with a pail of water,
leads his son away. A captive
lady led into Turkish hands

I cannot make anything of this, nor the quatrain following
(IV.LIX).

---

[1] *seille*. O.F. pail, bucket.

Century IV

IV.LIX

Deux assiegez en ardente ferueur,
De soif estaincts pour deux
  plaines tasses:
Le fort limé, & vn vieillart
  resueur,
Aux Geneuois de Nira monstra
  trasse.

Two besieged in a burning heat,
killed by thirst for want of two
full cups. The fort filed, and an
old dreamer will show the tracks
of Nira to the Genevans.

Century IV

IV.LX

Les sept enfans en hostaige laissés,
Le tiers viendra son enfant
  trucider:
Deux par son filz seront d'estoc
  percés,
Gennes, Florence, los viendra
  encunder.

The seven children left in hostage, the third will come to
slaughter his child. Two will be
pierced by a hook, because of his
son. He will come to strike
Genoa and Florence.

Usually the seven children in the quatrains refer to those of
Catherine de' Medicis, but the rest of the quatrain seems to
negate this.

Century IV

IV.LXI

Le vieux mocqué & priué de sa
  place,
Par l'estrangier qui le subornera:
Mains de son filz mangées
  deuant sa face,
Le frere à Chartres, Orl.
  Rouan trahyra.

The old man is mocked and deprived of his position by the foreigner who will suborn him. The
hands of his sons are devoured
before his face. He will betray his
brother at Chartres, Orléans and
Rouen.

During the Second World War, Marshal Pétain, leader of
the Vichy government, was nicknamed Le Vieux; his position
vis-à-vis the Nazis is described clearly in line 2. The hands

devoured in front of him are the destroyed forces of his régime. The brother represents the Allies, who simultaneously reached the three towns here mentioned, Chartres, Orléans and Rouen, on August 19, 1944. The régime was betrayed by Pétain to the Germans. He was deported to Sigmaringen on the very day of their liberation.

Century IV

IV.LXII

Vn coronel machine ambition,	A colonel intrigues through
Se faifira de la plus grand armée,	ambition. He will seize the greater part of the army. Against his
Contre fon prince fainte inuention,	prince a false invention; he will be discovered under his flag.
Et defcouuert fera foubz fa ramée.	

This quatrain is usually accepted as a general one applying to Oliver Cromwell, who took over the greater part of Charles I's armies and fought with them under the English flag. Cromwell certainly connived in the plotting and accusations laid against the king at his trial and execution. However, it could also be applied very neatly to Colonel Gaddafi, who overthrew King Idris of Libya in 1969.

Century IV

IV.LXIII

L'armée Celtique contre les montaignars,	The Celtic army against the people of the mountains who will be
Qui feront fceuz & prins à la lipee:	revealed and caught in a trap. The fresh bracken will soon be
Payfans frefz pouferont toft faugnars,	pressed by the peasants. They will all perish on the sword's
Precipitez tous au fil de l'efpee.	blade.

This may well refer to Marshal Villars' wide-ranging battle against the *camisard* rebels of the Cévennes who engaged him in a very efficient form of guerrilla warfare from 1702 to 1704.

Century IV

IV.LXIIII

*Le deffaillant en habit de
  bourgeois,
Viendra le Roy tempter de ſon
  offence:
Quinze ſouldartz la pluſpart
  Vſtagois,
Vie derniere & chef de ſa
  cheuance.*

*The defaulter, dressed as a citi-
zen; the king will come to try his
offense. Fifteen soldiers, for the
most part outlaws; the end of his
life and most of his estate.*

Yet another quatrain still to be unraveled.

Century IV

IV.LXV

*Au deſerteur de la grand
  fortereſſe,
Apres qu'aura ſon lieu
  abandonné:
Son aduerſaire fera ſi grand
  proueſſe,
L'Empereur toſt mort ſera
  condamné.*

*To the deserter of the great for-
tress after he has abandoned his
post, his adversary will display
such prowess that the Emperor
will soon be condemned to death.*

Napoleon III, while still Louis-Napoleon, was condemned
by the French to life detention in the fortress of Ham, but he
escaped from the castle to England on May 25, 1846. Louis
Philippe abandoned his position as king of France during the
Revolution of 1848 and Louis-Napoleon was voted Prince-
President in December of that year. He did not, however,
display great skills as an Emperor, and his policies were
responsible for the Franco-Prussian War with its consequent
disaster for the French. He died soon after the war, in 1873.
The powerful adversaries are, of course, the Russians.

Century IV

IV.LXVI

Soubz couleur faincte de fept teftes rafées *Seront femés diuers explorateurs:* *Puys & fontaines de poyfons arrouſées,* *Au fort de Gennes humains deuorateurs.*	Under the false colors of seven shaven heads several spies will be scattered. The wells and springs will be sprinkled with poisons. At the fort at Genoa they devour human flesh.

Shaven heads is often used as a synonym for the Roundheads by Nostradamus, but the situation in this quatrain does not seem to have occurred. A false prediction.

Century IV

IV.LXVII   ★

L'an que Saturne & Mars efgaux combuſt, *L'air fort feiché longue traiection:* *Par feux fecrets, d'ardeur grand lieu aduſt* *Peu pluye, vent chault, guerres, incurſions.*	In the year that Saturn and Mars are equally fiery, the air is very dry; a long meteor. From the hidden fires a great place burns with heat. Little rain, a hot wind, wars and raids.

This quatrain gives an astrological dating, common enough in Saturn and Mars. Nostradamus indicates that world drought will escalate at the time of the conjunction. It happened twice in 1985, the Ethiopian famine occurs again in 1987, and also in 1989. This fits in with sunspot activity and appears to indicate that we are approaching the worst famine of this century.

Century IV

IV.LXVIII

*En l'an bien proche non esloigné
   de Venus,
Les deux plus grans de l'Asie &
   d'Affrique
Du Ryn & Hister qu'on dira
   font venus,
Crys, pleurs à Malte & costé
   ligustique.*

*At a nearby place not far from
Venus, the two greater ones of
Asia and Africa; from the Rhine
and Hitler they will be said to
have come. Cries and tears at
Malta and the Ligurian coast.*

Venus, standing for Venice, is the clue to this quatrain as it
links Italy, *costé ligustique*, with Hitler. The two dictators, Hitler
and Mussolini, met at the Brenner Pass when they sealed the
Tripartite Pact with Asia, that is to say the Japanese. The last
line refers to the blockade of Malta by the Italians and the
trouble in the Ligurian coast to the Allied bombing of Genoa
and the bombardments by British battleships operating out of
Gibraltar.

Century IV

IV.LXIX

*La cité grande les exilés
   tiendront,
Les citadins morts meurtris &
   chassés.
Ceulx d'Aquilee à Parme
   promettront,
Monstrer l'entree par les lieux
   non trassés.*

*The exiles will hold the great
city. The citizens are dead, mur
dered and driven out. The peo
ple of Aquileia will promise
Parma to show them the entr
ance by untrodden paths.*

Although Aquileia was a great city in ancient times, by the
sixteenth century it was nothing but a village. Parma belonged
to the Papacy and became an hereditary duchy for Pope Paul
III's bastard in 1545.

Century IV

IV.LXX

Bien contigue des grans monts Pyrenees,
Vn contre l'aigle grand copie addreſſer:
Ouvertes vienes, forces exterminees,
Que iuſque à Pau le chef viendra chaſſer.

Very near the great mountains of the Pyrenees a man will raise a great army against the Eagle. Veins will be opened, strength disappears. The leader will chase them as far as Pau.

This quatrain describes Wellington's approach to France through Portugal and Spain where he is to confront the Eagle, Napoleon. The opened veins probably mean the lost supply lines of the French when they were driven back as far as Pau. Despite the French victory at Toulouse, it was of uncertain value to Napoleon.

Century IV

IV.LXXI

En lieu d'eſpouſe les filles trucidées,
Meurtre à grand faulte ne ſera ſuperſtile:[1]
Dedans le puys veſtules inondées,
L'eſpouſe eſtaincte par hauſte d'Aconile.[2]

Instead of a bride, girls are slaughtered, murder so wicked there will be no survivors. The Vestals are drowned in the wells, the bride killed by a draught of Aconite.

Aconite is a classic poison distilled from monkshood and wolfsbane. Otherwise the quatrain is completely obscure.

---

[1] *ſuperſtile.* misprint for *supersite,* survivor.
[2] *Aconile.* misprint for aconite.

Century IV

IV.LXXII

*Les Artomiques par Agen
  & l'Eftore,
A sainct Felix feront leur
  parlement:
Ceux de Basas viendront à la
  mal'heure,
Saisir Condon et Marsan
  promptement.*

*The Artomiques through Agen
and Lectoire will hold their parlement at St. Felix. The people of
Bazas will arrive at an unfortunate time to seize Condon and
Maisan promptly.*

What "the Artomiques" means is not certain. *Artos* means bread in Greek, but there is also a strong resemblance to the modern word "atomic."

Century IV

IV.LXXIII

*Le nepueu grand par forces
  prouuera,
Le pache fait du coeur
  pufillanime:
Ferrare & Ast le Duc
  efprouuera,
Par lors qu'au soir fera le
  pantomine.*

*The nephew shall prove by great
strength the crime committed by a
cowardly heart. The duke will
test Ferrara and Asti; then,
when the comedy takes place in
the evening.*

The nephew in this case is almost certainly the duc de Berry, who was assassinated when he left the Opéra on the evening of February 13, 1820. The other nephew who benefits from this deed became Napoleon III, who later succeeded to the French throne because of the death of his cousin, the direct male heir. (See also I.LXX-XIIII and III.XCVI.)

Century IV

IV.LXXIIII

*Du lac lyman & ceux de
    Brannonices,[1]
Tous assemblez contre ceux
    d'Aquitaine
Germains beaucoup, encor plus
    Souisses,
Seront defaictz auec ceux
    d'Humaine.[2]*

*The people of Lake Geneva and
Mâcon all gathered against
those of Aquitaine. Many Germans, even more Swiss, will be
routed together with those of
Maine.*

It is just possible that with *Humaine* in line 4 Nostradamus is referring to the Humanists, whom he regarded as responsible for the Protestant Reformation in Switzerland. But the variant, *ceux de Maine*, which occurs in many editions does not fit in with this explanation. A confusing quatrain.

Century IV

IV.LXXV

*Prest à combatre fera defection.
Chef aduersaire obtiendra la
    victoire.
L'arrieregarde fera defension,
Les defaillans mort au blanc
    territoire.*

*He who was ready to fight will
desert, the chief adversary will
win the victory. The rear guard
will raise a defense. The falterers
dying in a white country.*

Marshal Grouchy is the deserter mentioned in the first line. During the Battle of Waterloo, 1815, he was the commander of the French cavalry. His orders from Napoleon were delayed by twelve hours, but even when he received them, Grouchy did not obey them. The great adversary of the French is, of course, Wellington. The famous stand of Napoleon's Imperial Guard is described in line three. They fought to the last man. The *blanc territoire* may be an indirect reference to Napoleon's retreat from Moscow in 1812, and also a direct one to the sign of the white cockade of the Bourbons. It was written in

[1]*Brannonices.* L. people from Mâcon and around.
[2]*Humaine.* Variant, *ceux de Maine.*

contemporary reports that, at Napoleon's capture, so many
people in Paris sported white cockades that it looked as though
there had been a fall of snow.

Century IV

IV.LXXVI

Les Nictobriges[1] par ceux de
    Perigort,
Seront vexez tenant iufques au
    Rofne:
L'affocié de Gafcons & Begorne,
Trahir le temple, le prebftre
    eftant au profne.

*The people of Agen by those of
Périgord will be troubled as far
as the Rhône. The association of
Gascons and Bigone betrays the
Church, while the priest is giv-
ing his sermon.*

Both Agen and Périgord are about two hundred miles from
the Rhône. Bigone is a Gascon town, but also the rallying cry
of Henri IV's Huguenots was Bigorre. The verse is probably
hinting at the Protestant-Catholic conflict in France during the
sixteenth century.

Century IV

IV.LXXVII

SELIN monarque l'Italie
    pacifique,
Regnes vnis Roy chreftien du
    monde:
Mourant voudra coucher en
    terre blefique[2]
Apres pyrates auoir chaffé de
    l'onde.

*Selin King, Italy peaceful, king-
doms united by the Christian
king of the world. When he dies,
he will want to lie in Blois territory having chased the pirates
from the sea.*

It was upon this quatrain that many nineteenth century
Royalists built their hope of a new, great French king who
would come and change the face of Europe. The key to the
quatrain is the word *SELIN*. It is derived from the Greek

[1]*Nictobriges.* the people around Agen.
[2]*blefique.* L. *Blesa; Blois.*

Selene, meaning the moon or the goddess Diana. I think that Nostradamus and some of his interpreters were completely mistaken about this series of quatrains. Nostradamus probably intended them for Henri II and Diane de Poitiers. Not even prophets are loath to flatter their superiors and Catherine de' Medicis would certainly have interpreted this quatrain in her husband's favor. Henri II had adopted the moon as his device.

Put into a modern context, these predictions seem unlikely to succeed. The notion of a Christian king governing the world seems impossible in modern terms.

Century IV

IV.LXXVIII

La grand armee de la pugne ciuile,	The great army of the civil war. Parma taken at night by foreigners. Seventy-nine murdered in the town, the foreigners all put to the sword.
Pour de nuict Parme à l'eſtrange trouuée,	
Septante neuf meurtris dedans la ville,	
Les eſtrangiers paſſez tous à l'eſpee.	

Parma was an Italian Duchy and an ally of the French, so the Spanish are probably the foreign invaders.

Century IV

IV.LXXIX

Sang Royal fuis, Monhurt, Mas, Eguillon,	Flee, royal blood, Montheurt, Mas and Aiguillon. The Landes will be full of people from Bordeaux. Navarre, Bigorre, points and spurs; deeply hungry they devour the acorns of the cork oak.
Remplis ſeront de Bourdelois les landes,	
Nauarre, Bygorre poinctes & eguillons,	
Profondz de faim vorer de liege glandes.	

These places are all situated in southwest France and probably have some connection with IV.LXXVI. As I mentioned before, *Bigorre* was also the rallying cry of the Huguenot Protestants.

Century IV

IV.LXXX

Pres du grand fleuue grand
   foſſe, terre egeſte,
En quinze pars sera l'eau
   diuiſee:
La cité prinſe, feu, ſang, cris
   conflict mettre
Et la plus part concerne au
   colliſee.[1]

Near the river a great trench,
earth excavated. The water will
be divided into fifteen parts. The
city taken, fire, blood, cries and
battle given; the greater part
concerned with the collision.

James Laver says that this is the quatrain that persuaded the
nineteenth century commentator the Abbé Torné to insist that
France erect the infamous Maginot Line, which eventually fell
so quickly to the Germans. In the late 1920s the French
Minister of Defense decided to build the Line, because he was
convinced that the next German invasion would come through
Switzerland. The wall cost two million dollars a mile to build.
Its existence caused a strong sense of false security in France
during the rise of Hitler. The river in the first line is the Rhine.
Hitler partially ignored the Maginot Line and advanced from
other directions, thus fulfilling lines 3 and 4. The collision
becomes the series of battles fought in France during the
Second World War.

Century IV

IV.LXXXI

Pont on fera promptement de
   nacelles,
Paſſer l'armee du grand prince
   Belgique:
Dans profondrés[2] & non loing
   de Brucelles,
Outre paſſés, detrenchés ſept à
   picque.

A bridge will quickly be built
from boats to enable the army of
a great Belgian Prince to cross.
Poured inside, not far from
Brussels; having passed over,
seven will be out down by a pike.

[1]colliſee. L. collisus, clash.
[2]profondrés. L. profondatus, poured forth.

At the time Nostradamus wrote, the word Belgian was archaic and could only refer to Philip II, who had been given the territory by the Emperor Charles V in 1554. An attack on Northern France, across the river Scheldt (lines 1 and 2), was made in the 1560s.

Century IV

IV.LXXXII

Amas s'approche venant d'Esclauonie, *L'Oleſtant vieux cité ruynera:* *Fort deſolee verra ſa Romanie.* *Puis la grand flamme eſtaindre ne ſçaura.*	A mass (of men) will draw near coming from Slavonia. The Destroyer will ruin the old city. He will see his Romania quite deserted, then will not know how to extinguish the great flame.

This must refer to Napoleon's retreat from Moscow in 1812–13, when the *grande armée* fled during that bitter winter. *Oleſtant* means "Destroyer" and Nostradamus refers to Napoleon as this in IV.IIII when he calls him the dreadful thunderbolt, *Vn fouldre si craintif*. The old city is Moscow, razed to the ground by fire. Romania has been used in the *Prophéties* to indicate Rome. Napoleon's younger son had just been made King of Rome and his empire did not last long. Perhaps one may understand the great flame, *grand flamme*, as a metaphor for the wars initiated by Napoleon and which gathered in momentum to eventually defeat him. I do not think that this implies Romania in 1990.

Century IV

IV.LXXXIII

Combat nocturne le vaillant capitaine, *Vaincu fuyra peu de gens profligé:* *Son peuple eſmeu, ſedition non vaine,* *Son propre filz le tiendra aſſiegé.*	In a night battle the brave captain is overcome and flees, ruined by a few men. His people are moved, successfully pleading, his own son will keep him besieged.

A quatrain with too many generalities to make it coherent.

Century IV

IV.LXXXIIII

Vn grand d'Auxerre mourra
   bien miſerable,
Chaſſé de ceux qui ſoubs luy ont
   eſté:
Serré de chaines, apres d'vn
   rude cable,
En l'an que Mars, Venus, &
   Sol mis en eſté.

An important man from Auxerre
will die very wretchedly, driven
out by the people under him.
Bound in chains, and then with
a long-lasting rage in the year
that Mars, Venus and the Sun
are in conjunction in the summer.

A quatrain with plenty of clues but it is insoluble. Who is the
man from Auxerre? This astrological conjunction is very rare,
so this quatrain may just possibly be unfulfilled to date.

Century IV

IV.LXXXV

Le charbon blanc du noir ſera
   chaſſé,
Priſonnier faict mené au
   tombereau:
More Chameau ſus piedz
   entrelaſſez,
Lors le puiſné ſillera l'aubereau.

The white charbon is driven out
by the black: made a prisoner,
led to the tumbril. His feet are
tied together like a rogue, when
the last born will let stop the falcon.

This is a complicated quatrain. Nostradamus as a plague
doctor treated the disease which was known at that time as le
charbon because of the black pustules it raised on the body and
referred to it as such. But many commentators interpret
charbon as an anagram for Bourbon and noir as the usual
anagram for king, roi. It must be remembered that most
anagrams of Nostradamus' period involved an extra letter to
further confuse the issue. White was the color of the Bourbon
king's standard. Louis XVI was the last Bourbon king before
the Revolution. He was imprisoned in the Temple and taken
to his death in a cheap carriage. His wife, Marie Antoinette,
was dragged through the streets on a tumbril on January 27,
1793. The last line implies that his heir, Louis XVII, about
whom there has been so much speculation, may have escaped

from his cell in the Temple. For a while the eleven-year-old Louis was placed under the "protection" of Simon the Cobbler who had been given instructions by the *procureur* of the Commune to "humble" the Prince. In December, 1794, Louis was examined by a Dr. Harmand, who noted tumors on his left arm and swollen knees. But when Louis' death was announced in 1795, the body shown to the public was so disfigured that identification was impossible. Louis was the second-born of the family. His elder brother Charles died in 1795.

Century IV

IV.LXXXVI

L'an que Saturne en eau sera conioinct,
Auecques Sol, le Roy fort &
puissant:
A Reims & Aix sera reçeu &
oingt,
Apres conquestes meurtrira innocens.

In the year when Saturn is in conjunction with Aquarius with the Sun, the very powerful king will be received and anointed at Reims and Aix. After conquests he will murder innocent people.

The astrological conjunction in lines 1 and 2 is reasonably rare. Reims is the traditional site for the coronation of French kings and Aix the coronation site for the German and Holy Roman Emperors. No king has been crowned in both places since Nostradamus wrote this. This is another of the quatrains used by French Royalists to predict the return of the French royal line. (See IV.LXXXVII.) A failed quatrain.

Century IV

IV.LXXXVII

Vn filz du Roy tant de langues aprins,
A son aisné[1] au regne different:
Son pere beau[2] au plus grand filz comprins
Fera perir principal adherant.

The son of a king, so many languages learned, is different from his predecessor in the kingdom. His father-in-law, understanding his elder son well, will cause the main adherent to perish.

[1]*aisné.* elder or predecessor.
[2]*pere beau.* father-in-law or handsome father.

This quatrain implies that the younger son of a king will take over the kingdom, the elder, legitimate heir having been removed from the succession by his father (in-law?).

Century IV

IV.LXXXVIII

Le grand Antoine du nom de faict sordide
De Phthyriase à son dernier rongé:
Vn qui de plomb voudra estre cupide,
Passant le port d'esleu sera plongé.

Anthony, great in name, base in his actions, at the end will be riddled with consumption. One who is eager for lead, passing the harbor will be drowned by the elected one.

In this quatrain we have a specific name and a specific illness. *Phthiriase* is either consumption, *Phthisis*, or *Phthiriasis*, which means someone suffering from lice. Pediculosis is an illness caused by lice. Who the Anthony may be is unclear.

Century IV

IV.LXXXIX

Trente de Londres secret coniureront,
Contre leur Roy sur le pont l'entreprinse,
Luy, fatalites la mort degousteront,
Vn Roy effleu blonde, natif de Frize.

Thirty Londoners will secretly conspire against their king, the enterprise on the sea. He and his followers will not like death. A fair king elected, a native of Friesland.

This is a good prediction of the Glorious Revolution of 1688–89. The Dutch William III insisted that those English lords who supported him should sign a document to ensure their loyalty to him. There were certainly a number of conspirators who crossed the sea to Holland and back before William was prepared to sail with his fleet. Those who dislike death, *la mort degousteront*, are James II and his supporters, who decide to flee rather than fight it out once the duke of

Marlborough, who led the English army, deserted their cause. William III came from Friesland. What makes this prophecy so interesting is that there was no possibility of a Dutch candidate for the English throne while Nostradamus was alive.

Century IV

IV.XC

Les deux copies aux murs ne pourront ioindre,
Dans cest instant trembler Milan, Ticin:
Faim, soif, doubtance si fort les viëdra poindre,
Chair, pain, ne viures n'auront vn seul boucin.

The two armies cannot join up at the walls. At that time Milan and Pavia tremble. Hunger, thirst and drought will weigh on them so much. They will not have a scrap of meat, bread nor supplies.

A failed quatrain. It seems unlikely that line 1 could refer to the twentieth century.

Century IV

IV.XCI

Au duc Gaulois contrainct battre au duelle,
La nef Mellele monech n'approchera,
Tort accusé, prison perpetuelle,
Son fils regner auant mort taschera.

For the French duke compelled to fight in a duel, the ship Mellele will not approach Monaco. Wrongly accused, perpetually imprisoned, his son will attempt to reign before his death.

Mellele may be a corruption of Melilla, a Moroccan seaport, but it does not seem to fit into this context. This quatrain may have a connection with IV.LXXXIII? The last lines are very similar.

Century IV

IV.XCII

*Tefte tranchee du vaillant
  capitaine,
Sera gettee deuant fon
  aduerfaire:
Son corps pendu de la claffe à
  l'antenne,
Confus fuira par rames à vent
  contraire.*

*The head of the brave captain,
cut off, will be thrown down in
front of his adversary. His body
hung from the mast of the ship.
Confused, he will flee using oars
in a contrary wind.*

It is interesting that Nostradamus again uses the word
antenne instead of *mât*, for the ship's mast. Is he using it to
indicate complex equipment with which he was not familiar?
It might possibly be a radio mast or radar equipment which
cover much of the surface of modern ships.

Century IV

IV.XCIII

*Vn ferpent veu proche du lict
  royal,
Sera par dame nuict chiens
  n'abayeront:
Lors naiftre en France vn
  Prince tant royal,
Du ciel venu tous les Princes
  verront.*

*A serpent will be seen near the
royal bed by a lady at night. The
watchdogs will not bark. Then in
France will be born a prince so
royal, that all the princes will see
him as a gift from heaven.*

This quatrain refers to the birth of the comte de Chambord,
1820–83. The duchesse de Berry gave birth to her son seven
months after her husband's assassination. The legitimacy of
the birth was contested by the duc d'Orléans (the snake), who
had right of entry to the duchesse's rooms, so the watchdogs
were not alerted. The birth of a grandson to Charles X caused
great rejoicing and the child was nicknamed *Dieudonné*, a gift
from heaven, as Nostradamus so rightly puts it, *Du ciel venu*.

Century IV

IV.XCIIII

Deux grans freres feront chaſſez d'Eſpaigne,
L'aiſné vaincu ſous les monts Pyrenees:
Rougir mer, roſne, ſang lemam d'Alemaigne,
Narbon, Blyterre, d'Agath.[1] contaminees.

Two great brothers will be driven out of Spain, the elder beaten beneath the Pyrenean mountains. The sea is reddened. Rhône, blood in Lake Geneva from Germany. Narbonne and Beziers contaminated by Agde.

This detailed quatrain contains five separate predictions:

1. Exile for two Spanish leaders.
2. Defeat for one of them near the Pyrenees.
3. A bloody naval battle.
4. An attack against Geneva from Germany.
5. A possible plague spreading from Agde to local towns. (See VIII.XXI.)

Century IV

IV.XCV

Le regne à deux laiſſé bien peu tiendront,
Trois ans ſept mois paſſés feront la guerre
Les deux veſtales contre rebelleront,
Victor puis nay en Armonique terre.

The rule left to two, they will hold it for a very short time. Three years and seven months having passed they will go to war. The two vestals will rebel against them. The victor then born on American soil.

If in this quatrain one takes the two rulers to be world powers, it implies that three years and seven months after the final signing of the INF Treaty by the Soviet Union and the USA, an alliance Nostradamus predicts elsewhere, those powers will go to war against Asia, possibly the Moslem fundamentalists who are now appearing everywhere. "*Veſtales*" in line 3

---

[1]*Agath.* L. Agde.

is probably a corruption of "vassals," two smaller countries who disagree with the treaty and remain neutral. See also III.LX and IV.L for further details and dating. This is also an indirect reference to the age of glasnost.

Century IV

IV.XCVI

La foeur aifnée de l'ifle
  Britannique,
Quinze ans deuant le frere
  aura naiffance:
Par fon promis moyennant
  verrifique,
Succedera au regne de balance.

The elder sister of the island of Britain will be born fifteen years before her brother. Because of his promise proving to be true, she will succeed to the kingdom of the Balance.

Mary was the elder sister of James III, who never came to the English throne. On her accession she was twenty-six, not fifteen years older than her brother. Mary inherited the throne because of promises she and her husband, William of Orange, made to the English Parliament. The Balance is the zodiac sign of Libra, which Nostradamus seems to apply here to England, although many astrologers apply it to Austria and Savoy. But it also governs trading nations, of which Britain was certainly one. It is important to note that Nostradamus speaks of the British isles, *l'ifle Britannique*, which immediately dates the quatrain as after 1603. A satisfactory quatrain.

Century IV

IV.XCVII

L'an que Mercure, Mars,
  Venus, retrograde,
Du grand Monarque la ligne
  ne faillit:
Efleu du peuple l'vfitant[1] pres de
  Gagdole,[2]
Qu'en paix & regne viendra
  fort enuieller.

In the year that Mercury, Mars and Venus are retrograde, the family line of the great Monarch will not fail. Elected by the Portuguese people near Cadiz, who in peace will grow very old in his kingdom.

[1] *vfitant*. probable misspelling of *Lufitan*, Portuguese.
[2] *Gagdole*. probable misspelling for *Gades*, Cadiz. The existing reading doesn't even rhyme and is obviously incorrect.

This quatrain may refer to the Portuguese succession and is dated by the conjunction in line 1. It also seems to imply that the Portuguese royal line are elected in Spain, but this never happened. Philip II of Spain seized the Portuguese throne and held it until 1621, followed by his son Philip III, until the Portuguese rose in revolt against the Spanish in 1640.

Century IV
IV.XCVIII

Les Albanois paſſeront dedans Rome,
Moyennant Langres demipler¹ affublés,
Marquis & Duc ne pardonnes à homme,
Feu, ſang, morbilles² point d'eau, faillir les bleds.

The people of Alba will cross into Rome; by means of Langres the multitude are weakened. The Marquis and the Duke will spare no man. Fire, blood and small-pox, no water, the crops will fail.

The word *Albanois* is hard to interpret here. It probably stands for the troops of the duke of Alba, but Albania is also a possibility. The many disasters are obscure. Langres is in Champagne. (See VII.IIII.)

Century IV
IV.XCIX

L'aiſné vaillant de la fille du Roy,
Repouſſera ſi profond les Celtiques:
Qu'il mettra foudres, combien en tel arroy
Peu & loing puis profond és Heſperiques.

The brave eldest son of a king's daughter will drive the Celts back very far. He will use thunderbolts, so many in such an array, few and distant, then deep into the West.

---

¹*demipler*. A word invented by Nostradamus. Probably derived from the Greek, *demiſpleres*, multitude.
²*morbilles*. O.F. smallpox.

The second part of this quatrain seems to indicate an intercontinal ballistic missile attack which will penetrate deep into the West. Could this be a possible foretaste of the Third World War?

Century IV

IV.C

*De feu celeſte au Royal edifice,
Quant la lumiere de Mars
   defaillira:
Sept mois grãd guerre, mort
   gent de malefice,
Rouen, Eureux au Roy ne
   faillira.*

Fire will fall from the sky on the royal building when the light of war is weakened. For seven months a great war, people dead through evil. Rouen and Evreux will not fail their king.

During the siege of Paris during the Franco-Prussian War, the royal palace, the Tuileries, was destroyed by cannon fire. The glory of the Bonaparte family was weakened and almost ended by the war. Napoleon III was to die two years later and from then on France remained a Republic. The Franco-Prussian War did last for seven months, July, 1870 to February, 1871, an accurate prediction. The Norman towns in the last line remained loyal to the king and wanted to restore the monarchy through the National Assembly. Successful.

Century V

V.I

*Avant venue de ruine Celtique,
Dedâs le têple deux
   parlementeront
Poignard coeur, d'vn monté au
   courſier & picque,
Sans faire bruit le grand
   enterront.*

Before the ruin of the Celtish one, two will talk within the temple. Scarred to the heart by one riding on a charger with a lance, they will bury the great one secretly.

There has always been much speculation about the fate of the Celtic French king enclosed within the Temple, Louis XVII, the second son of Louis XVI and Marie Antoinette. Louis XVI and his family were housed in the Temple in 1792, when the Revolutionary mob appeared to be getting out of control. The fate of the whole royal family was debated by the newly formed French Legislative Assembly, *parlementeront*. It is not known exactly how Louis XVII died. He was put into the charge of a local cobbler and treated very severely, under the orders of the local Commune. But at the time of his supposed death, the body produced to the public could not be identified, even by autopsy. Nostradamus clearly believed Louis died in line 4, *le grand enterreront*. Line 3 seems to describe his killer as a soldier. The young king was treated appallingly while in prison, separated from his mother and sisters and half-entombed for months in the dark, like a wild beast. Some record his body as being found dead among his own excrement. He was declared to be seriously ill in May, 1785, and his death was announced the following June. During the next forty years, several pretenders came forward claiming to be the young prince but if Nostradamus is correct, the prince was buried at the Church of Sainte Marguerite on June 10, as was officially announced, without even a headstone to mark the spot, *sans faire bruit*. A complicated but immensely interesting quatrain.

Century V

V.II

Seps coniurés au banquet feront luire,
Contre les trois le fer hors de nauire:
L'vn les deux claſſes au grand fera conduire,
Quant par le mail. Denier au front luy tire.

Seven conspirators at a banquet will flash their weapons against the three who come from the ship. One of the two will take the fleet to the leader, when the last one will shoot him through the forehead, piercing his armor.

I cannot decipher this quatrain.

Century V

V.III

*Le successeur de la Duché
    viendra,
Beaucoup plus outre que la mer
    de Tosquane:
Gauloise branche la Florence
    tiendra,
Dans son giron d'accord
    nautique Rane.*[1]

*The successor to the dukedom
will come from far beyond the sea
of Tuscany. A French branch
will hold Florence, in its wake
an agreement with the nautical
force.*

This quatrain probably applies to the duc de Lorraine, who
was given the Duchy of Tuscany in 1737. Until then it had
belonged to Italians, from Alessandro de' Medicis in 1531 to
the death of Gian Gastone in 1737. It remained in the
Lorraine family until 1859, except during the French Revolution when it belonged to Napoleon and the French. The
reference to a nautical force is unclear. If one accepts the
translation of *Rane* as frog, it could refer to the myth in which
the earliest inhabitants of Tuscany were turned into frogs by
Bacchus, which simply reinforces the identity of the particular
Duchy referred to in the quatrain.

Century V

V.IIII

*Le gros mastin de cité deschassé,
Sera fasché de l'estrange alliance,
Apres aux champs auoir le cerf
    chassé,
Le loup & l'Ours se donront
    defiance.*

*The great mastiff is driven out of
the city, angered by the foreign
alliance. Later, having chased
the stag to the field, the wolf and
the bear will defy each other.*

The mastiff in French is also known as *le dogue anglais*, and
England is therefore probably intended in line 1. Angered by
a foreign treaty, the English chase the stag to the battlefield,
where the wolf (Italy, from the legend of Romulus and Remus)

[1]*Rane.* L. *rana*, frog. Probably a misprint for *rame*, oar, and by
extension, fleet.

and the Bear (Russia) are defying each other. This appears to
refer to the Second World War, when the Russians entered
the war as British allies.

Century V

V.V

*Souz ombre faincte d'ofter de
  feruitude,
Peuple & cité l'vfurpera luy
  mefmes:
Pire fera par fraux de ieune
  pute,
Liuré au champ lifant le faux
  proefme.*

*Beneath the faint shadow of
removing servitude, the people
and the city will usurp power for
themselves. He will do worse
because of the trickery of a young
whore, delivered in the field,
reading the false promise.*

The shadow or attempt to remove servitude in a city refers
to the French Revolution, which started in Paris. However,
revolutionary rule was just as authoritative as that of Louis
XVI, whom it usurped, albeit in a different way. The people
of Paris took over the government of their city after the
storming of the Bastille on July 14, 1789. The so-called whore
who made things worse is Marie Antoinette, who enraged the
populace by her extravagance and in particular by the affair
of the diamond necklace, a fraudulent deal of which she was
unjustly accused. Although she was certainly innocent of this
particular incident, it damaged her popularity beyond repair.
When she and Louis were later caught trying to go to Saint
Cloud in 1792, the family were turned back by the crowd who
said to Louis "we love you alone." The false promises were
those given by the king when he promised not to attempt to
escape from the Temple where he and his family had been
placed to protect them from the wrath of the populace. They
attempted to escape to Varennes in 1792 and were caught.
(See the remarkable quatrains IX.XX and IX.XXXIIII.)

Century V

V.VI

Au roy l'Augur ſur le chef la
  main mettre,
Viendra prier pour la paix
  Italique:
A la main gauche viendra
  changer le ſceptre
De Roy viendra Empereur
  pacifique.

The Augur will put his hand on
the king's head and pray for
peace in Italy. The scepter will be
changed to his left hand, from
the king will proceed a peaceful
Emperor.

The Pope, *Augur*, was godfather by proxy to the son of Louis
Napoleon, later Napoleon III, who was not popular in his
dealings with Italy and the Vatican because the Roman
Revolutionaries felt he was too accommodating. The changing
of the scepter probably refers to Napoleon III's underhand
manipulation of the Revolution in France in 1848 and to the
fact that he declared himself Emperor on December 2, 1851.
The fact that Nostradamus refers to his being a peaceful
Empire ties in well with the famous statement Napoleon III
made on attaining power: "*L'Empire, c'est la paix.*" The art of
Empire is peace. A good quatrain.

Century V

V.VII

Du Triumuir ſeront trouuez les
  os,
Cherchant profond threſor
  aenigmatique:
Ceux d'alentour ne ſeront en
  repos.
Ce concauer marbre & plomb
  metallique.

The bones of the Triumvir will
be found by those searching for a
deep and enigmatic treasure.
Those around will not be peaceful. The hollow is of marble and
metallic lead.

Triumvir is the key word to this quatrain. After the coup
d'état of the 18 Brumaire when Napoleon attained power, he
reduced the five members of the Directoire to three, and made
himself First Consul. Later, Louis Philippe attempted to revive
his waning popularity when he brought back Napoleon's ashes

(les os) from St. Helena and interred them at Les Invalides. The treasure Louis Philippe was vainly searching for was Napoleon's popular appeal. The restless people are the Bonapartistes, who were politically encouraged by this act and insisted on physically helping in the task of burying the Imperial ashes. The coffin itself was of lead, *plomb metallique.*

Century V

V.VIII

Sera laiſſé le feu vif, mort caché,
Dedans les globes horrible
eſpouuentable,
De nuict à claſſe cité en poudre
laſché,
La cité à feu, l'ennemy
fauorable.

There will be let loose living fire and hidden death, fearful, inside terrifying globes. By night the city will be reduced to rubble by the fleet, the city in flames, helpful to the enemy.

This probably refers to the Second World War, rather than Vietnam or Korea, although it might equally be applicable to the Iran-Iraq War or the war in Afghanistan, because of the reference to a city. It almost certainly refers to a war or wars in the twentieth century, characterized by the use of bombs and rocketry, *globes horrible eſpouuentable.* Ships are also used in this battle to bombard a city which, when it erupts in flames, is helpful as a target to enemy aircraft.

Century V

V.IX

Iuſques au fonds la grand arq
demolue,
Par chef captif, l'amy anticipé:
Naiſtra de dame front face
cheuelue,
Lors par aſtuce Duc à mort
attrapé.

At the foot of the great fallen arch, by the captured chief the friend forestalled. A woman will bear a son, his face and forehead covered with hair. Through cunning the duke then escapes death.

These first two lines are believed by most commentators to refer to the assassination attempt made upon Napoleon III in

1858. He had been involved in the Italian revolutionary movement as a young man. But after he came to power in France the Italians felt he had betrayed their cause and four of them attempted to assassinate him as he left the Opéra on the night of January 14, 1858. This seems a favorite place for assassinations—see Nostradamus' references to the murder of the duc de Berry at the Opéra on February 13, 1820 (I.LXXXIIII, III.XCVI, IV.LXXIII). The plot against Napoleon III was led by Count Orsini. The building was damaged, but did not collapse, although various bystanders were killed. The captured friend was Pieri, a friend of Orsini's, who was arrested before the explosion. Napoleon III was only slightly hurt, *à mort attrapé*. The third line is completely obscure. But line 4 seems to imply that Napoleon III escaped death through foreknowledge, possibly due to Pieri's arrest. The following quatrain appears to follow immediately upon this one.

Century V

V.X

Vn chef Celtique dans le conflict blefsé,	*A French leader wounded in the conflict sees his subjects struck dead near the theater. Hustled by enemies, with bloody wounds, he will be saved from the four by unknown people.*
Aupres de caue voyant fiens mort abbatre:	
De fang & playes & d'ennemis preffé,	
Et fecourus par incognus de quatre.	

As stated in V.IX there was an attempt to assassinate Napoleon III with a bomb outside the Paris Opéra. *Cavea* (*cave*) is the Latin word for theater. The four conspirators were Orsini, Pieri, Gomez and Rudio. The unknown people *fecourus par incognus* are the innocent bystanders who unwittingly sheltered the king from the blast.

Century V

V.XI

Mer par ſolaires ſeure ne paſſera,
Ceux de Venus tiendront toute
l'Affrique:
Lur regne plus Saturne
n'occupera,
Et changera la part Aſiatique.

Those of the sun will not cross
the sea in safety. The people of
Venus will hold the whole of
Africa. Then Saturn occupies
their kingdom no longer and a
part of Asia will change.

The flag of Japan is that of the sun, and the country is known as the Land of the Rising Sun. This quatrain describes Japan's position during the Second World War, between 1941 and 1945. Her ships will not be safe once she enters the war on the side of the Germans and causes a shift in Asian politics, with China joining up with the Allied Powers in 1941. The people of Venice (Venus is a common corruption in the *Prophéties* for the name of this city) stand for Italy and are fighting with Rommel in Northern Africa. The malign influence of Saturn upon Italian affairs causes them to withdraw from the war in 1943.

Century V

V.XII

Aupres du lac Leman ſera
conduite,
Par garſe eſtrange cité voulant
trahir:
Auant ſon meurtre à Auſpourg
la grand ſuitte
Et ceux du Rhyn la viendront
inuahir.

Near Lake Geneva he will be led
by a woman who wants to betray
the foreign city. Before the death
a great retinue will come to
Augsburg. They will come to
invade the people of the Rhine.

Augsburg is the key word in this quatrain. The Battle of Augsburg in 1636, during the Thirty Years' War, forced the retreat of Bernhard, duke of Saxe-Weimar, across the Rhine. This left southern and central Germany exposed to the attacks of the Hapsburg armies of the Holy Roman Emperor, Ferdinand II. Augsburg fell to Ferdinand, as did other towns along the Rhine near the Swiss border. The spelling of

Aufpourg by Nostradamus is a typical pun, containing elements of both the words *Augsburg* and *Hapspurg*. The puzzle is the young woman of line 2.

Century V

V.XIII

Par grand fureur le Roy Romain Belgique	In a great rage the Roman king will wish to trouble Belgium with barbarian warriors. In a gnashing fury he will chase the Libyan people from Hungary as far as Gibraltar.
Vexer vouldra par phalange barbare:	
Fureur grinſſeant chaſſera gent Lybique	
Deſpuis Pannons[1] iuſques Hercules la hare.[2]	

This quatrain also applies to the Thirty Years' War. Philip of Spain and the Holy Roman Emperor, Ferdinand II, were allied against Denmark, Saxony and Sweden. In 1648, the Treaty of Westphalia recognized the republic of the United Netherlands, part of which is now modern Belgium. The barbarian *phalange* are the Protestant German powers. The Thirty Years' War started as a revolt in Bohemia and spread as far as Gibraltar when France and Spain refused to recognize the 1648 treaty and continued to fight until the Treaty of the Pyrenees in 1659.

Century V

V.XIIII

Saturne & Mars en leo Eſpagne captifue,	Saturn and Mars in Leo, Spain is captive, taken in battle by a Libyan leader. Near to Malta (the knights of Rhodes) captured alive, and Roman power smitten by the cock.
Par chef Lybique au conflict attrapé,	
Proche de Malthe, Heredde prinſe viue,	
Et Romain ſceptre ſera par coq frappé.	

[1] *Pannons.* L. Panonia, now Hungary.
[2] *hare.* misprint for *bare*, pillars (of Hercules), Gibraltar.

This is a mixed quatrain; referring to two separate events. The only time that Spain can really be considered as a captive country was during the Peninsular War of 1807–8 when Napoleon's troops occupied both Spain and Portugal. The resistance of the Spanish patriots led the British to send in an army under Sir Arthur Wellesley, who, after five years of fighting, succeeded in driving out the French. The rest of the quatrain refers to events which occurred ten years earlier. The first action of Napoleon's Egyptian campaign in 1798 was the capture of Malta from the Knights of Rhodes. Finally, at the Treaty of Tolentino the Pope ceded part of the Vatican and Church States to the Cock, the symbol for France.

Century V

V.XV

En nauigant captif prins grand pontife,	While traveling the great Pope will be captured. Great prepara-
Grans aprets faillir les clercz tumultuez:	tions by the troubled clerks will fail. The second elected being
Second esleu absent son bien debise,	absent, his power declines. His favorite bastard put to death.
Son fauory bastard à mort tué.	

Pope Pius VII, who had traveled to France in 1804 to crown Napoleon, was taken prisoner by the French in 1808. He was the second Pope to be hurt by Napoleon, the first being Pius VI, who died in exile at Valence. The trouble among the clergy, *clercz tumultuez*, describes the religious discontent in France after the abolition of the established Church. Most commentators interpret the bastard in line 4 as Napoleon, who inherited a crown that was not rightfully his and who, having received favors from the Pope, sacks Rome in 1808, and imprisons the pontiff, although the death of his predecessor, Pius VI, was directly caused by his imprisonment by Napoleon.

Century V

V.XVI

A *son hault pris plus la lerme*
sabee.
D'humaine chair par mort en
cendre mettre,
A l'isle Pharos par croisars
perturbee,
Alors qu'à Rodes paroistra dur
espectre.

The tears of the Sabines will no
longer be of value. Human flesh
is put to death, burned to ashes.
The island of Pharos disturbed
by men of the cross, when at
Rhodes a dreadful sight is seen.

This quatrain appears to implicate Italy with the pogroms
against the Jews during the Second World War ("the men of
the cross," the swastika). Cremation was anathema to a
sixteenth century Jew or Christian. Pharos is an island
opposite Alexandria and may be used to indicate Tobruk,
which is close by and which Nostradamus mentions in
I.XXVIII. Tobruk was troubled several times by the Nazis as
the battles in the African desert waged between the Allies and
Rommel. The *dur espectre* at Rhodes would be the invasion of
Greece by Mussolini in 1940, followed by the Germans in
1941. Despite British evacuations of Greece, the Germans
claimed 270,000 prisoners. About 70,000 people are believed
to have been killed.

Century V

V.XVII

De *nuict passant le roy pres*
d'vne Andronne,
Celuy de Cipres & principal
guette:
Le roy failli la main fuict long
du Rosne,
Les coniurés l'iront à mort
mettre.

The king, passing at night
through a narrow lane, the man
from Cyprus is the main guard.
The king dies, the hand flees the
length of the Rhône. The conspirators will put him to death.

Cyprus belonged to Venice until 1571, but the location of
this conspiracy is obscure.

Century V

V.XVIII

De dueil mourra l'infelix
profligé,
Celebrera fon vitrix l'hecatombe:
Priftine loy franc edict redigé,
Le mur & Prince au feptiefme
iour tombe.

The wretched man, destroyed, will die of grief. His victorious consort will celebrate the ceremonies. Former laws, free edicts are drawn up. Both the prince and the wall fall on the seventh day.

I cannot decipher this quatrain.

Century V

V.XIX

Le grand Royal d'or, d'aerain
augmenté,
Rompu la pache,[1] par ieune
ouuerte guerre:
Peuple affligé par vn chef
lamenté,
De fang barbare fera couuerte
terre.

The great golden royal, augmented by money, breaks the covenant. The war is started by the young man. The people are afflicted by a lamented leader. The land will be covered with barbarian blood.

Another indecipherable quatrain.

Century V

V.XX

Dela les Alpes grand armée
paffera,
Vn peu deuant naiftra monftre
vapin:
Prodigieux & fubit tournera,
Le grand Tofquan à fon lieu
plus propin.

A great Army will cross over the Alps. A short time before a wretched monster will be born. In a strange way, suddenly the great Tuscan will return to his native land.

---

[1] *pache.* A. Pr. treaty, covenant.

The great army crossing the Alps is that of Napoleon III, who achieved this against Austria in 1859. The evil monster would then be, as always in Nostradamus, a Revolution—this time in Italy, led by Garibaldi. It is interesting to note that one of the first results of the 1854 campaign was to drive the grand duke of Tuscany, Leopold II, from Florence. He was a Hapsburg and retired to Austria, *son lieu plus propin*, to escape the Italians, thus fulfilling the prediction in line 4.

Century V

V.XXI

Par le trespas du monarque latin,
Ceux qu'il aura par regne secouruz:
Le feu luyra, diuisé le butin,
La mort publique aux hardis incoruz.

By the death of the Latin king; those whom he will have assisted during his reign. The fire glows, the booty, is shared out. Public death for the bold incursors.

The Latin monarch is difficult to interpret. If it stands for Latium, it represents the Pope. Could Nostradamus be referring to Mussolini and the Fascists?

Century V

V.XXII

Auant qu'à Rome grand aye rendu l'ame,
Effrayeur grande à larmée estrangere:
Par Esquadrons, l'embusche pres de Parme,
Puis les deux rouges ensemble feront chere.

Before the great man gives up his soul at Rome, there is much fear among the foreign army. The ambush by the squadrons takes place near Parma. Then the two red ones will feast together.

This seems, together with V.XXIII, to be a futuristic quatrain. Sometimes before the death of a pope there will be a war abroad, *estrangere*. The two red ones who feast together would mean in modern terminology Russia and the People's

Republic of China. This may then well occur after the breakdown of the alliance between the USA and the USSR (which Nostradamus tells us may last for three years and seven months). Otherwise the *deux rouges* may refer to terrorist régimes such as that of Colonel Gadaffi, the North Koreans, or even the private army of Abu Nidal, which is an extreme terrorist element supported by Gadaffi.

Century V

V.XXIII

Les deux contens ſeront vnis enſemble,
Quant la pluſpart à Mars ſeront conioinct:
Le grand d'Affrique en effraieur & tremble:
DVVMVIRAT par la claſſe deſioinct.

The two contented men are united together when most (planets) are in conjunction with Mars. The African leader trembles in terror. The twin alliance scattered by the fleet.

Nostradamus elsewhere describes the USA and the USSR as *vnis enſemble*, probably while honoring the INF Treaty signed by Reagan and Gorbachev. But war soon breaks out again, possibly the war of the Third Antichrist, the man known as *Brodde*, which troubles even Africa. It appears that naval interference is partly the reason for the breaking of the alliance. Will the American and the Soviet fleets have a serious confrontation in the Gulf?

Century V

V.XXIIII

Le regne & loy ſouz Venus eſleué,
Saturne aura ſus Iupiter empire:
La loy & regne par le Soleil leué,
Par Saturnins endurera le pire.

The kingdom and law raised under Venus, Saturn will dominate Jupiter. Law and Empire raised by the Sun will endure the worst through the Saturnine people.

Venus and Saturn dominating Jupiter is obviously yet another astrological dating, but unfortunately Nostradamus is

seldom specific enough to enable one to use the astrological
clues. The quatrain bears some resemblance to V.XI, but I
believe it relates to the preceding quatrain. The Sun might also
stand for Charles V or even the Catholic Church. It is a very
difficult quatrain to decipher.

Century V

V.XXV

Le prince Arabe Mars, Sol,
*   Venus, Lyon,*
Regne d'Eglise par mer
*   succombera:*
Deuers la Perse bien pres d'vn
*   million,*
Bisance, Egypte, ver. serp.[1]
*   inuadera.*

The Arab Prince, Mars, the
Sun, Venus and Leo, the rule of
the Church will succumb to the
sea. Towards Persia very nearly
a million men will invade Egypt
and Byzantium, the true serpent.

When Mars, the Sun and Venus are in conjunction with Leo,
the following predictions are forecast about the Middle East,
Arabia. It will attack Persia (Iran), Egypt, Constantinople and
the navies of Christendom. This conjunction last took place on
August 21, 1987, so it may well refer to the Gulf wars, and to
the various other troubles in the Middle East. The navies
would be the UK, Italian, American and Soviet fleets which
are at present patrolling the Gulf. This all occurs at a time
when religion is losing its hold upon humanity, although one
must not deny the possibility of various Antichrists, the false
Messiahs who make claims worldwide. Nostradamus would
have regarded the Moslem Azerbaijanis as false Messiahs, and
their country borders on Iran.

The total of a million men was an incredible number in
Nostradamus' day, when the world population was obviously
much smaller. But the Biblical King of the East claims to
invade the Soviet Middle East with an army of 2,000,000 men.
It is worth noting that in 1961 China's leaders boasted that
they could mobilize an army of 2 billion soldiers. An uneasy
quatrain.

---

[1]*ver. serp.* Suggested interpretation, *vera serpens*, true serpent.

Century V

V.XXVI

La gent esclaue par vn heur martial,
Viendra en haut degré tant esleuee:
Changeront prince naistre vn prouincial,
Passer la mer copie aux monts leuee.

The Slav people, through fortune in war, will become elevated to a high degree. They will change their prince, born of the provinces. An army raised in the mountains to cross over the sea.

The word *esclaue* may mean Slav or slave. The Russians were not regarded as Slavs in Nostradamus' day; this word was reserved for the people of the Balkans. The Greeks, who were partially Slav, rose against the Turks and landed troops at Smyrna in 1919, remaining there until 1922. They changed their king, as Nostradamus predicted.

King Constantine was exiled in 1917, recalled in 1920 and sent into exile again in 1922. Although he was born in Athens, he was of German origin. His rival was Premier Venizelos from Crete. The same fate was to befall Constantine's son, who is now in permanent exile in Britain.

Century V

V.XXVII

Par feu & armes non loing de la marnegro,
Viendra de Perse occuper Trebisonde:
Trembler Phatos Methelin, Sol alegro,
De sang Arabe d'Adrie couuert onde.

With fire and weapons, not far from the Black Sea, he will come from Persia to occupy Trebibond. Pharos and Mytilene tremble. The Sun is bright, the Adriatic Sea covered with Arab blood.

This quatrain appears to link up with V.XXV. What is not clear is whether the conquerors are the Arabs or the Iranians. In the light of present events, it appears to be the former, the Iraqis, but the peace settlement is extremely delicate at this time, with the Iranian army poised near the border of Turkey, driving the Kurds from Iraq in hundreds of thousands, suffering from the effects of chemical warfare.

Pharos is an island off Alexandria and Mytilene is the Greek island of Lesbos. Nostradamus seems convinced in so many quatrains that Greece will be drawn into this Middle Eastern War.

Century V

V.XXVIII

Le bras pendu & la iambe liée,	*His arm hung and leg tied, pale-*
Viſaige paſle au ſeing poignard	*faced with a dagger hidden in*
caché:	*his breast. Three will be sworn in*
Trois qui ſeront iurez de la	*the crowd. Against the great one*
meſlee,	*of Genoa the blade will be*
Au grand de Gennes sera le fer	*drawn.*
laſché.	

Genoa is the key word in this quatrain, which speaks of the threat of assassination. King Umberto of Italy (which included Genoa) was assassinated by an unemployed smith named Acciartio on July 29, 1900. But Nostradamus implies that the assassin will be bound up in some way. This was not the case, so it is possible that this refers to some other assassination. The king was stabbed with a dagger.

Century V

V.XXIX

La liberté ne ſera recouuree,	*Liberty will not be regained. It*
L'occupera noir fier vilain	*will be occupied by a black,*
inique:	*proud, villainous and unjust*
Quand la matiere du pont ſera	*man. When the subject of the*
ouuree,	*Pope is opened by Hitler, the*
D'Hiſter, Veniſe faſchee la	*republic of Venice will be*
republique.	*angered.*

This quatrain describes Mussolini's intrigues to secure an alliance with Hitler between the years 1934 and 1938. Hitler and Mussolini met at Venice. Notice how accurate the details

are in this quatrain. The adjective black can refer both to the
Fascisti, the Blackshirts, and to Hitler himself. Both Pope Pius
XI and Pius XII played a predominant part in this situation.
Pius XI, as secretary of state, played a major part in securing
a treaty with Nazi Germany in 1933. He also refused to
excommunicate either Hitler or Mussolini. Pius XII continued
this policy of remaining on good terms with the Fascists. He
refused to condemn Germany's invasion of Poland. The
Vatican was known as a notorious escape route for German
war criminals. An unpleasant, if accurate, quatrain.

Century V

V.XXX

*Tout à l'entour de la grande
   cité,
Seront foldats logez par champs
   & villes:
Donner l'affaut Paris, Rome
   incité,
Sur le pont[1] lors fera faicte
   grand pille.*

*Soldiers will be billeted in fields
and towns all around the great
city. Paris will make the assault,
Rome incited. There will be
great pillage made against the
pontiff.*

Rome was sacked twice by the French, in 1797 and 1808.
The pillage refers to the fact that the Pope was forced to cede
part of the Papal States in 1797 which were incorporated into
the Republic of France in 1809.

Century V

V.XXXI

*Par terre Attique chef de la
   fapience,
Qui de prefent eft la rofe du
   monde:
Pont ruiné & fa grand
   preeminence,
Sera fubdite & naufrage des
   vndes.*

*From the land of Attica, source
of all wisdom, which presently is
the rose of the world. The Pontiff
ruined, its great pre-eminence
will be subjected and wrecked
beneath the waves.*

[1]*pont.* Normal Nostradamus shorthand for *Pontifex*, Pontiff, Pope.

This is the third successive quatrain mentioning Greece, a pope and disaster at sea. It seems to follow the sequence starting at V.XXVII, but I cannot elucidate further.

Century V

V.XXXII

*Où tout bon eſt tout bien Soleil
    & Lune,
Eſt abondant ſa ruine s'approche:
Du ciel s'aduance vaner ta
    fortune,
En meſme eſtat que la ſeptieſme
    roche.*

Where all is good and all abundant, in the Sun and Moon its ruin approaches. It comes from heaven as you boast of your fortune, in the same state as the seventh rock.

James Laver suggests that this refers to the Franco-Prussian War, 1870–1871. Nostradamus applies the singular "*ta*" *fortune* only to France. When France is at the height of her fortune (the *Exposition Universelle* in 1867), then the Prussians will gather to declare war. Laver interprets the seventh rock as a reference to the desolation of the seventh rock in the Apocalypse but I feel that it is more likely to stand for one of the seven hills of Rome. The difficulty is to fit the Papacy into this interpretation.

Century V

V.XXXIII

*Des principaux de cité rebellee,
Qui tiendront fort pour liberté
    rauoir:
Detrencher maſles, infelice meſlee,
Crys hurlemens à Nantes piteux
    voir.*

Some of the principal citizens of the rebellious city, will try hard to regain their liberty. The men are cut up, unhappy confusion. Cries, groans at Nantes, pitiful to see.

The atrocities at Nantes in 1793 were known as the Noyades. They were committed by excessive revolutionaries and are surely the subject of this quatrain. In 1793, the citizens of the town had allied themselves with neighboring districts and declared a Central Assembly of Resistance to Oppression. But the National Convention soon broke up this counterrevolutionary activity. Over one thousand citizens were guillotined, *detrencher mafles*, others were tied, face to face, naked, placed into boats which were rowed to the middle of the river Loire and scuttled. These wretched victims were coolly watched by their killers as they drowned in a threshing mass of bodies.

Century V

V.XXXIIII

Du plus profond de l'occident Anglois.
Où eft le chef de l'ifle Britannique:
Entrera claffe dans Gyronde par Blois,
Par vin & fel, feux cachez aux barriques.

From the deepest part of the English West where is the leader of the British Isles. A fleet will enter Gironde through Blois, through wine and salt, fires hidden in casks.

The words "British Isles" firmly place this quatrain as later than 1604. The west of England is puzzling. The Duchy of Cornwall belongs, by tradition, to the Prince of Wales, who shall probably become king, although Nostradamus states elsewhere that Prince Charles will be the last of the royal or reigning line. Wine and salt are French metaphors for taxation, especially the latter, known as the *gabelle*. The fires hidden in casks resemble the globes of fire which Nostradamus frequently uses to describe weapons such as bombs or rockets. So this quatrain may possibly have yet to be fulfilled.

Century V

V.XXXV

Par cité franche de la grand mer Seline,
Qui porte encores à l'eftomach la pierre:
Angloife claffe viendra foubs la bruine
Vn rameau prendre, du grand ouuerte guerre.

For the free city of the great crescent sea which still carries the stone in its stomach. An English fleet will come in under the mist to seize a branch. War started by the great one.

This quatrain may relate to the preceding one because of the use of the word English. But an English fleet having a series of protracted encounters with invaders seems to relate it to the past. The crescent sea normally stands for the sea of Genoa in Nostradamus, but the whole quatrain seems improbable.

Century V

V.XXXVI

De ſoeur le frere par ſimulte
  faintiſe,
Viendra meſler roſee en myneral:
Sur la placente¹ donne à vielle
  tardifue,
Meurt, le gouſtant ſera ſimple &
  rural.

The sister's brother, through feigned deceit will come and mix dew with the mineral. On the cake given to the slow old woman who dies testing it. She will be simple and rustic.

A classic case of a woman killed by poison given on a cake. The only other clue I can offer is that *roſee*, dew, may stand for the Latin *rosarus*, poison extracted from the laurel rose.

Century V

V.XXXVII

Trois cents ſeront d'vn vouloir
  & accord,
Que pour venir au bout de leur
  attaincte:
Vingts mois apres tous &
  records,
Leur Roy trahi ſimulant haine
  faincte.

Three hundred will be of one accord and in agreement to arrive at the execution of their end. Twenty months later, after all remembrance, their king is betrayed, feigning a holy hatred.

I cannot decipher this quatrain.

¹*placente*. L. *placenta*, a cake

Century V

V.XXXVIII

*Ce grand monarque qu'au mort
  ſuccedera,
Donnera vie illicite & lubrique,
Par nonchalance à tous
  concedera,
Qu'à la parfin faudra la loy
  Salique.*

He who succeeds upon the death
of a great king will lead an illicit
and debauched life. Through
carelessness he will give way to
all so that in the end Salic law
will fail.

Salic law prevailed in France: it prohibited the accession of women to the throne. Louis XV succeeded his great-grandfather (great in both senses), and led a life of extreme debauchery and irresponsibility. An example of this was his famous seraglio at the Parc des Cerfs, and of course, the influence of Madame de Pompadour. The *Encyclopaedia Britannica* says that it is "difficult to find a European king whose life shows such a record of vulgar vice." His carelessness in state affairs led to the bankruptcy of France and was partially responsible for the trouble which came to a head under the Revolution.

Louis XV was succeeded by his ill-fated son, Louis XVI. Some historians might accept the view that both these French kings were effectively ruled by the women in their life, Louis XV by Mme. de Pompadour and Mme. du Barry; Louis XVI by his wife, Marie Antoinette. I personally think that the latter had little decisive effect upon her weak and inconsiderate husband in his role as king.

Century V

V.XXXIX

*Du vray rameau de fleur de lys
  iſſu,
Mis & logé heritier d'Hetrurie:
Son ſang antique de longue
  main tiſſu,
Fera Florence florir en
  l'armoirie.*

Issued from the true branch of
the fleur-de-lys, placed and
lodged as heir to Etruria. His
ancient family line woven by
many lands will make the armorial bearings of France flower.

The comte de Chambord was the heir to Charles X and his
legitimacy was questioned by the duc d'Orléans at his birth.
(See IV.XCIII.) His mother, the duchesse de Berry, took her
son with her into exile to Venice. Etruria here stands for Italy.
In 1846 he married in Venice the daughter of Duke Francis
IV of Florence. The fleur-de-lys is part of the arms of the
house of Florence as well as the French royal line, and their
marriage caused their united family lines to flower. A happy
quatrain.

Century V

V.XL

Le sang royal sera si tresmeslé,
Contraint seront Gaulois de
l'Hesperie:
On attendra que terme soit
coulé,
Et que memoire de la voix soit
perie.

*The Royal blood will be very
mixed, the French will be restrained by the West. They will
wait until his term of office is
ended and the memory of his
voice has perished.*

Line 1 probably indicates that the French royal line will be
much diminished, that is, not in power any longer. This brings
the quatrain into the twentieth century, which is reinforced by
the line *que terme soit coulé*, implying an elected office dependent
upon a vote or something similar. The one Frenchman who
really interfered effectively with Western politics was, of
course, General de Gaulle. Once his term of office and
influence ended with his death, his policy, the famous *Non*,
was soon forgotten.

Century V

V.XLI

Nay souz les vmbres & iournee
nocturne
Sera en regne & bonté
souueraine:
Fera renaistre son sang de
l'antique vrne,
Renouuellant siecle d'or pour
l'aerain.

*Born beneath the shadows on a
dark day he will be sovereign
both in his rule and goodness.
He will cause his blood to revive
the ancient urn, renewing the
century of gold for one of brass.*

Line 4 is the only clue which possibly indicates that this quatrain belongs to the twentieth century, during which all gold coinage disappeared among most nations to be replaced by brass coins. So it is possible that this is a futuristic quatrain.

Century V

V.XLII

Mars esleué en son plus haut befroy,[1]
Fera retraire les Allobrox[2] de France:
La gent Lombarde fera si grand effroy,
A ceux de l'Aigle comprins souz la balance.

A warlike man raised to the heights will bring about the return of Savoy to France. The people from Lombardy will cause such fear to those of the Eagle, included under the Balance.

Napoleon III and Cavour of Italy agreed between them that in return for French assistance in driving out the Austrians (Libra) from Italy, Savoy should be returned to France. This was done on March 22, 1860. It is the only time that this has occurred since Nostradamus' day.

Century V

V.XLIII

La grande ruine des sacrez ne s'esloigne,
Prouence, Naples, Sicille, Seez & Ponce:
En Germanie, au Rhin & la Cologne,
Vexez à mort par tous ceux de Magonce.[3]

The great ruin of the clergy is not far off, Provence, Naples, Sicily, Sees and Pons. In Germany at the Rhine and Cologne; vexed to death by those of Maine.

In this far-reaching quatrain Nostradamus seems to imply that Mainz and the other places mentioned would turn

---

[1] *befroy.* literally a belfry.
[2] *Allobrox.* The Allobroges occupied what is present-day Savoy.
[3] *Magonce.* L. *Maguntiacum,* Mainz or Mayence.

Protestant, possibly because Mainz was the center of Gutenberg's city and the original center of printing with all its inherent dangers as it was still regarded uneasily by the Church. A totally unsuccessful quatrain.

Century V

V.XLIIII

Par mer le rouge sera prins de pyrates,
La paix sera par son moyen troublee:
L'ire & l'auare commettra par fainct acte
Au grand Pontife. fera l'armee doublee.

On the sea the red one will be taken by pirates and because of his method there will be a troubled peace. He will reveal anger and greed through a false act. The army of the great pontiff will be doubled.

There is no record of this quatrain's being fulfilled. There has never been a record of a Cardinal, *le rouge*, being captured by pirates. The Pope still had an army in the sixteenth century.

Century V

V.XLV

Le grand Empire sera tost desolé,
Et translaté pres d'arduenne silue:
Les deux bastardz par l'aisné decollé,
Et regnera Aenodarb, nez de milue.

The great Empire will soon be desolated and changed near the forest of Ardennes. The two bastards will be beheaded by the oldest. Aenobarbe, the hawk-nosed one, will rule.

The French Empire was lost to the Germans in 1940 and there were bloody battles among the forests of the Ardennes, both then and 1944–45. The two bastards may be the two "unworthy" French generals who let the Germans through after the Battle of Sedan, 1940; they were André Georges Corap of the French Ninth Army and his second-in-command, Henri Giraud, who was taken prisoner. The *aisné*, the commander-in-chief, Maxime Weygand, then took over, but the Allies had already lost. The hawk-nosed man may refer to General de Gaulle, but Nostradamus usually places Aenobarbe with *Brodde* in Africa. De Gaulle, together with the 4th Armored Division, was the only French general who put up any resistance to the Germans at Montcornet. Dunkirk followed upon this crushing defeat. The problem in this quatrain is Aenobarbe. Possibly I am mistaken and this quatrain relates to Africa during the next decade. There are several other quatrains which mention this mysterious Aenobarbe, so far unidentified.

Century V

V.XLVI

*Par chapeaux rouges querelles
  & noueaux ſciſmes
Quant on aura eſleu le
  Sabinois:
On produira contre luy grans
  ſophiſmes,
Et ſera Rome leſee par Albanois.*

Quarrels and new schisms by those of the red hats when the Sabins will have been elected. They will produce great sophisms against him. Rome will be injured by those of Albania.

In Nostradamus' terminology *chapeaux rouges* always stands for the cardinals of the Roman Catholic Church. He says they will be divided when they elect someone from the Northeast of Rome, *Sabinois*. But the Albanians pose a problem. Albania in the twentieth century is a blocked, Communist state with strong links to the People's Republic of China. Perhaps this is a futuristic quatrain referring to the present Pope or his successor?

Century V

V.XLVII

*Le grand Arabe marchera bien
  auant,
Trahy ſera par les Biſantinois:
L'antique Rodes luy viendra au
  deuant,
Et plus grand mal par auſtre
  Pannonois.*

The great Arab will march well ahead. He will be betrayed by the Turks. Ancient Rhodes will come forward to meet him and greater harm through the other Hungarians.

This seems another futuristic quatrain. If the great Arab is Gadaffi or his deputy Abu Nidal, they will get into trouble with the Turks. At the moment the Turks are in danger of being dragged into the residue of the Gulf War, with the Iraqis having driven the Kurds by the hundred thousand as refugees into Turkey. Again there is this continual complication of Greece which I cannot decipher. The Hungarians, *Pannonois*, stand for the Communist influence in this situation. A quatrain, I imagine, soon to be clarified and fulfilled.

Century V

V.XLVIII

Apres la grande affliction du
  sceptre,
Deux ennemis par eux seront
  defaictz:
Classe d'Affrique aux Pannons
  viendra naistre,
Par mer & terre seront horribles
  faictz.

After the great affliction of the scepter two enemies will be defeated by them. A fleet from Africa will come forth to the Hungarians. Dreadful deeds will occur on land and sea.

This seems to be a continuation of the last quatrain. Again a fleet, Africa and the Communist satellite countries. Probably a quatrain still to be fulfilled. De Klerk of South Africa visited Hungary in early 1990, the first recognized state visit involving the two countries.

Century V

V.XLIX

Nul de l'Espaigne mais de
  l'antique France
Ne sera esleu pour le tremblant
  nacelle,
A l'ennemy sera faicte fiance,[1]
Qui dans son regne sera peste
  cruelle.

Not from Spain but from ancient France will he be elected for the trembling ship. He will make a promise to the enemy who will cause great devastation during his reign.

[1]*fiance*. O.F. assurance, promise.

This must be a futuristic quatrain if it is correct, because since Nostradamus' time until 1978 when the Polish John Paul II was elected, we have had only Italian popes. When the Church is in a troubled state, *tremblant nacelle*, it appears there will be two main candidates for the Papacy, one Spanish and one French. The French candidate will be elected. He will try to compromise with his enemy, presumably Communism, with remarkably little success.

The Irish prophet, Malachy, whose original manuscript works are kept hidden in the Vatican, gives us only two more popes until the Millennium. He ascribes to the next Pope the motto *Gloria Olivae*, the Glory of the Olive. The olive branch is the universal symbol of peace but presumably in Nostradamus' view, this Pope's essays towards peace will be unsuccessful.

The Benedictines have always claimed through tradition that this next Pope will come from their order. Another name for the Benedictines is the Olevitians. It will be interesting to see. (See also V.XLVI and V.LXXVIII.) It is worth noting that the only Benedictine cardinal in the Curia at the moment is the English Cardinal Hume. The last English Pope was Nicholas Breakspear.

There is a remote chance that this quatrain refers to the present Pope, John Paul II, who was born in southwestern Poland, an area which once formed the boundary of Charlemagne's empire. Another of the candidates at his election was from South America, in Nostradamus' time largely a property of Spain.

It was shortly after John Paul II acceded to the Papacy that AIDS, Auto-Immune Deficiency Syndrome, became a world issue. Perhaps this is the "great plague" and "the enemy within" which Nostradamus refers to repeatedly during this Papacy. He correctly dates John Paul II's accession to the Papacy as during the time of Halley's Comet. (See II.XV, III.LXXV, VI.V,IX.LV.) Nostradamus also predicts that John Paul II will be assassinated. There have so far been two unsuccessful attempts on his life. (See II.XV, II.XCIII.)

Century V

V.L

L'an que les freres du lys feront en aage, *L'vn d'eux tiendra la grande Romanie:* *Trembler les monts, ouuert Latin paffage* *Pache macher, contre fort d'Armenie*	The year that the brothers of the lily come of age one of them will hold great Romania. The mountains tremble, a Latin passage is opened. A treaty to march against the fort of Armenia.

A difficult quatrain. In V.XCIIII Armenia is connected with Hitler and the Second World War. The rest is unclear.

Century V

V.LI

La gent de Dace,[1] d'Angleterre & Polonne *Et de Boefme[2] feront nouuelle ligue:* *Pour paffer outre d'Hercules la colonne,* *Barcins,[3] Tyrrens[4] dreffer crue le brique.[5]*	The people of Dacia, England, Poland and Czechoslovakia will form a new alliance, in order to pass beyond the Straits of Gibraltar. The Spanish and the Italians will hatch a cruel plot.

One of Nostradamus' more interesting predictions. In March, 1939, Britain allied with the Balkan countries. It was the British support of Poland that motivated the Second World War in September, 1939. It was essential to keep the Mediterranean, *outre d'Hercules la colonne*, open for shipping Allied troops and vital supplies. The Italians were Hitler's natural allies under Mussolini and although Spain remained technically neutral, she was definitely biased towards Nazism.

---

[1] *Dace*. Now part of Romania.
[2] *Boefme*. Modern Czechoslovakia.
[3] *Barcins*. L. *Barcino*, Barcelona, by extension Spain.
[4] *Tyrrens*. L. Tuscans, by extension Italy.
[5] *crue le brique*. printer's error for *cruele brigue*.

Century V

V.LII

Vn Roy ſera qui donra l'oppoſite,
Les exilez eſleuez ſur le regne:
De ſang nager la gent caſte[1]
* hyppolite,[2]*
Et florira long temps ſoubs telle
* enſeigne.*

There will be a king who will give opposition, the exiles elected over the kingdom. The chaste, poor ones swim in blood and he will flourish for a long time under this standard.

A king who will tyrannize over a rule of bloodshed. Unfortunately there is nothing specific to work on.

Century V

V.LIII   ★

La loy du Sol, & Venus
* contendens,*
Appropriant l'eſprit de prophetie:
Ne l'vn ne l'autre ne feront
* entendus,*
Par Sol tiendra la loy du
* grand Meſſie.*

The law of the Sun contending with Venus, appropriating the spirit of prophecy. Neither the one nor the other will be understood. The law of the great Messiah retained through the Sun.

This relates to Nostradamus' Jewish beliefs, that the law of the Messiah, the Second Coming which was prophesied in the Book of Enoch, will occur in the century of the Sun, the twentieth century. The prophecy referred to is probably Biblical. See the introductory material for a discussion of Jewish influences on Nostradamus' views concerning the Millennium. Most people certainly do not believe in a Second Coming at the end of this century, *Ne l'vn ne l'autre ne seront entendus.* However, it is difficult to reconcile this with Nostradamus' conviction that the Third Antichrist will come before the end of the next decade.

---

[1]*caſte*. L. chaste, pure.
[2]*hyppolite*. Gk. *hyppolitos*, poor, mean, little.

Century V

V.LIIII

Du pont Euxine, & la grand
    Tartarie,
Vn roi sera qui viendra voir la
    Gaule
Transpercera Alane &
    l'Armenie,
Et dans Bisance lairra sanglante
    Gaule.

From beyond the Black Sea and great Tartary, there will be a king who will come to see France. He will pass through Alania and Armenia, leaving his bloody rod in Byzantium.

The mention of a man from the East wielding a bloody rod also occurs in II.XXIX. Nostradamus is definite that the Third Antichrist will appear towards the end of this century and that he will come from Asia (beyond Tartary, which is China). His route appears to go through southern Russia (Alania, and Armenia) around the Balkan peninsula to Turkey, Constantinople. The rod may stand for red power or a bloody weapon. Definitely a quatrain of the future.

Century V

V.LV

De la felice Arabie contrade,[1]
Naistra puissant de loy
    Mahometique:
Vexer l'Espaigne conquester la
    Grenade,
Et plus par mer à la gent
    Lygustique.[2]

In the fortunate country of Arabia will be born one powerful in the laws of Mahomet. He will trouble Spain and conquer Granada as well as most of the Ligurian nation from the sea.

This appears to be a failed or retroactive prediction. Granada, Spain, was last lost to the Arabs in 1492. There has never been another conquest of Spain, let alone Italy, by the Arabs since Nostradamus' day.

---

[1]*contrade*. A. Pr. *contrada*, country.
[2]*Lygustique*. The Ligurians came from around Genoa, therefore Italy.

Century V

V.LVI

*Par le trespas du tresuieillart
    pontife,
Sera esleu Romain de bon aage:
Qu'il sera dict que le siege
    debiffe,
Et long tiendra & de picquant
    ouurage.*

*Through the death of the very
old Pope will be elected a Roman
of good age. It is said of him that
he weakens the (Holy) Seat, but
he will hold it with long and
painful effort.*

The old Pope who dies is probably Pope John XXIII, a very popular Pontiff. It was under him that the Second Vatican Council was convened. He tried to bring the Church out of its elitist stance and lead it towards a more democratic role. Sadly, he died after only four years in office.

He was succeeded by the worldly, strictly orthodox Pope Paul VI, under whose tenure the Vatican went through a series of severe political and financial scandals, *long tiendra & de picquant ouurage*. Paul VI certainly weakened the Vatican's position when it was revealed that he was a close friend of the Sicilian banker Michele Sindona, believed to be a member of the Mafia, who in fact became an adviser to the Vatican Bank. This led to the scandal of the P2 Freemasons' Lodge and various suicides and murders, perhaps the most well-known being the mysterious death of Roberto Calvi under Blackfriars Bridge, London, in June, 1982. Paul VI died in 1978, to be succeeded for thirty days by Pope John Paul I, whose untimely and mysterious death was almost certainly due to his attempt to rectify the situation created by his predecessor.

Century V

V.LVII

*Iſtra du mont Gaulſier &
  Auentin,
Qui par le trou aduertira
  l'armée:
Entre deux rocs ſera prins le
  butin,
De SEXT. manſol fallir la
  renommee.*

*There will go forth from Mont-
golfier and Aventine, one who
through a hole will warm the
army. The booty will be taken
between two rocks. The renown
of Sextus the Celibate will fail.*

This is a gift of a quatrain, which has two unmistakable key
words, Montgolfier and Sextus. Montgolfier is remembered in
the public mind for only one thing—his invention, together
with his brother, of the hot air balloon. In 1793 they made a
triumphant ascent over Paris. The following year it was used
to help a scouting party, *qui par le trou aduertira l'armée*, at the
Battle of Fleurus. The French victory at Fleurs, partly based
on the Montgolfiers' information, was the turning point in the
first coalition phase of the Revolutionary Wars, paving the way
for the sack of Rome and the Aventine.

The word *manſol* is derived from the Latin *manus solus*, he
who remains alone, that is, celibate. Nostradamus elsewhere
calls monks and priests *les seuls. SEXT.* is an abbreviation of
Sextus, the sixth, and Pius VI, who was in the Vatican at that
time, was later captured by Napoleon during the sack of
Rome. By the earlier Treaty of Tolentino, 1797, Pius VI was
deprived of much of his lands, the rocks upon which his power
was based, *entre deux rocs ſera prins le butin*. A highly elaborate
and accurate quatrain.

Century V

V.LVIII

De l'aqueduct d'Vticenſe,
    Gardoing,
Par la foreſt & mont
    innacceſſible:
En my du pont ſera taſché au
    poing,
Le chef nemans qui tant ſera
    terrible.

*By the aqueduct of Uzès by
Gard, through the forest and the
inaccessible mountain. In the
middle of the bridge he will be
cut in the hand. The chief of
Nîmes will also be very terrible.*

The thing for which Uzès is most famed is its Roman
aqueduct, which extended from Uzès to Nîmes. In 1627 the
duc de Rohan tried to support his fellow Calvinists who were
besieged at Nîmes, and he moved in his supporting artillery
by means of the aqueduct. Line 3 describes the actions of some
of Rohan's soldiers, who cut some of the supports of the
aqueduct at Gard to widen the path for the cannon to be
brought up. Rohan was put in command when he arrived at
Nîmes, *le chef nemans*. An impressive and accurate quatrain.

Century V

V.LIX ★

Au chef Anglois à Nymes trop
    ſeiour,
Deuers l'Eſpaigne au ſecours
    Aenobarbe:
Pluſieurs mourront par Mars
    ouuert ce iour,
Quant en Artois faillir eſtoile en
    barbe.

*The English chief stays too long
at Nîmes towards Spain, Aenobarbe to the rescue. Many will
die through war started on that
day when a bearded star falls in
Artois.*

Again, the ubiquitous and as yet identified Aenobarbe,
whom elsewhere Nostradamus links with the coming of the
Third Antichrist. He is linked with war, the geographical limits
are not defined, and with a comet—all standard warnings for
the Antichrist and the coming Millennium. An unsolved and
futuristic quatrain.

Century V

V.LX

*Par teſte raſe viendra bien mal
  eſlire,
Plus que ſa charge ne porte
  paſſera:
Si grand fureur & raige fera
  dire,
Qu' à feu & ſang tout ſexe
  trenchera.*

*Through the shaven heads he
will be seen to be wrongly elected,
burdened with a load he cannot
carry. He will be made to proc-
laim with such great fury and
rage that all of a sex will be
slaughtered into pieces in fire
and blood.*

Some commentators apply this quatrain either to Napoleon
or to the popes whose heads were shaven as they were monks.
But I think it is far more appropriate when applied to
Cromwell. As Nostradamus says, Cromwell was elected to
power, "wrongly" in that he did not rule by divine right. The
fury and rage that cover the population refers to the Civil War
between the Cavaliers and the Roundheads, *teſte raſe*, which was
a war of both politics and religion. Since fighting armies were
composed of men (*ſang tout ſexe*), great numbers lost their lives
during the Protectorate and there were many deaths by fire
and beheading, the latter including Charles I, of people who
would not change sides and stuck to their beliefs. Comparatively few women and children were victims of these excesses.

Century V

V.LXI

*L'enfant du grand n'eſtant à ſa
  naiſſance,
Subiuguera les hauts monts
  Apennis:
Fera trembler tous ceux de la
  balance,
Et des monts feux iuſques à
  mont Senis.*

*The child of the great man, not
through his birth, will subjugate
the high Apennine mountains.
He will make all those under the
Balance tremble, fire from the
mountains as far as Mount
Cenis.*

The nearest person who seems to fulfill this quatrian is
Eugène de Beauharnais, the son of Josephine and stepson of
Napoleon. Nostradamus says that this adopted son of a French

ruler will vex the Hapsburgs of Austria (Libra), both in Spain
and Italy. In this the prophet was only half correct. Napoleon
went forth and conquered and made Eugène ruler of Italy.

Century V

V.LXII

Sur les rouchers sang on les verra plouuoir,	Blood will be soon to rain on the rocks, Sun in the East, Saturn in
Sol Orient, Saturne Occidental:	the West. War near Orgon. A
Pres d'Orgon guerre, à Rome grand mal voir,	great evil seen near Rome. Ships sunken and the trident taken.
Nefs parfondrees & prins le Tridental.[1]	

This must be a futuristic quatrain leading to the Millennium.
As I say in my discussion of the Jewish sources for the
Millennium, seven great disasters have to accumulate and
come together to give warning of its actual coming and of the
Third Antichrist. Phenomena such as showers of blood,
Saturn in a bad aspect and war together with some great evil
affecting the Vatican and the Papacy and a naval war are all
portents. Nostradamus intended the reader to take note of
these events and try to halt them, but the way the world is
going this tragically seems unlikely.

Century V

V.LXIII

De vaine emprise l'honneur indue plaincte,	From the useless enterprise honor and undeserved com-
Galiotz errans par latins froit, faim, vagues	plaint. Boats wandering among the Latins, cold, hunger and
Non loing du Tymbre de sang la terre taincte	waves (storms). Not far from the Tiber the land is stained with
Et sur humains seront diuerses plagues.	blood and there will be several plagues upon mankind.

---

[1]*Tridental.* One who holds the trident, i.e. power over the seas.

This quatrain seems in some areas to continue the preceding one, V.LXII. Again we have a fleet in trouble around Italy, the river Tiber stained with blood and plagues throughout the world. At the moment we are cursed with various wars, famine, floods and disease throughout Africa and parts of the East and these troubles seem to be mounting daily. It does seem we are leading up to Nostradamus' vision of the Millennium in every sense. See the introductory material.

Century V

V.LXIIII

Les assemblés par repoz du grand nombre,	*Those assembled through the calm of the great number, coun-*
Par terre & mer conseil contremandé:	*termanded by land and sea. Near Autonne, Genoa, the sha-*
Pres de l'Autonne Gennes, Nice de l'ombre	*dow of Nice. Revolution against the leaders through fields and*
Par champs & villes le chef contrebandé.	*towns.*

Autonne is one of Nostradamus' unsolved anagrams. It is written *Antonne* in some editions. The nearest phonetic equivalents are Nentone or Antipolis (Antibes), but this does not clarify the meaning. It is probably a failed quatrain of events occurring in the nineteenth century.

Century V

V.LXV

Subit venu l'effrayeur sera grande,	*Suddenly appeared, the terror will be great, hidden by the*
Des principaux de l'affaire cachés:	*ringleaders of the situation. The women on (of) the charcoal will*
El dame en braise plus ne sera en veue	*no longer be seen. Thus, little by little, the great ones will be*
Ce peu à peu seront les grans fachés.	*angered.*

I cannot decipher this quatrain.

Century V

V.LXVI

Soubs les antiques edifices veſtaulx,	Under the ancient buildings of the vestals not far from the ruin
Non eſloignez d aqueduct ruyne:	of the aqueduct. There will be
De Sol & Lune ſont les luiſans metaulx,	glittering metals of the Sun and the Moon, the golden Trojan
Ardante lampe Traian d'or burine.	lamp, burning, pillaged.

The commentator Jaubert suggests that this quatrain refers to the convent of St.-Sauveur-de-la-Fontaine, at Nîmes, which was built upon the site of a temple to the goddess Diana, the Moon, and that valuable treasures of gold and silver will be dug up, including a golden lamp. The aqueduct could place the quatrain at Nîmes, but I do not feel able to follow this interpretation further.

Century V

V.LXVII

Quand chef Perouſe n'oſera ſa tunique	When the great head of Perugia dare not risk his tunic, without
Sens au couuert tout nud s'expolier:	any cover, and strip himself completely naked. The seven aristoc-
Seront prins ſept faict Ariſtocratique,	rats will be taken; father and son dead through a wound in the
Le pere & fils mors par poincte au colier.	throat.

The head of Perugia in this case was the Pope, Sixtus V, who had excommunicated Henri de Navarre in 1595, and was reluctant to do the same to Henri III of France and thus risk losing France, *tout nud s'expolier*. The Pope was finally forced to act in 1589, but he did not dare release his Catholic subjects from their oath of allegiance, because the Papacy had already lost the revenues of England and Northern Europe to Protestantism.

The seven are again the children of Catherine de' Medicis. Their father, Henri II, was already dead from a wound in the

throat (I.XXXV) and his last ruling son, the sixth Medicis
child, Henri III, was to die from stab wounds, but in the
stomach, not the throat (see I.XCVII) in 1589. An interesting
quatrain, if somewhat convoluted.

Century V

V.LXVIII

*Dans le Danube & du Rhin
    viendra boire,
Le grand Chameau ne s'en
    repentira:
Trembler du Rofne & plus fort
    ceux de Loire,
Et pres des Alpes coq le
    ruinera.*

*The great Camel will come to
drink of the Danube and the
Rhine and will not repent of it.
Those of the Rhône tremble and
even more so those of the Loire.
Near the Alps the cock will ruin
him.*

The great camel, appearing also in IV.LXXV and VI.LV, is
a complete enigma. It appears that this person sweeps aside
German opposition but gets his comeuppance in France.
Shades of Hitler perhaps? I think that this quatrain refers, as
do the others, to past events. Nostradamus was wrong in this
case.

Century V

V.LXIX

*Plus ne fera le grand en faux
    fommeil,
L'inquietude viendra prendre
    repoz:
Dreffer phalange d'or, azur, &
    vermeil,
Subiuguer Affrique la ronger
    iufques oz.*

*The great one will remain no
longer in a false sleep. Unease
will take the place of repose. A
phalanx of gold, blue and vermi-
lion will be drawn up to subdue
Africa, and gnaw it to the very
bone.*

Louis Philippe usurped the French crown of his nephew in
1830, having waited for an opportune moment, line 2. He was
the first legitimate Bourbon to accept the tricolor of red, white
and blue, as the royal standard. The French conquest of

Algeria happened in the same year that he snatched the throne. Nostradamus says that the standard is gold, red and blue, line 3. James Laver makes a charming comment: "The old eyes of the prophet may be pardoned for being slightly colour blind." Gold as well was the symbol of royalty and power so perhaps it is understandable.

Century V

V.LXX

Des regions ſubiectes à la Balance,	Some of the regions subject to the Balance will trouble the moun-
Feront troubler les monts par grande guerre	tains with a great war. The entire sex will be captured,
Captifz tout ſexe deu & tout Biſance,	endebted, with all Byzantium. At dawn they will call from land to
Qu'on criera à l'aube terre à terre.	land.

The Balance, Libra, stands normally for Austria and Savoy in Nostradamus' writing, and he also applies it to England and trading nations which are governed by Libra. He appears to think that Austria will overthrow the Ottoman Empire. It is possible that the Austrian troubles in the Balkans during the early 1900s are hinted at in this verse. It might also hint at new developments in the wake of perestroika.

Century V

V.LXXI

Par la fureur d'vn qui attendra l'eau,	By the fury of one who will wait for the water; by the great rage
Par la grand raige tout l'exercite eſmeu:	that moves all the army. Seven- teen boats are loaded with
Chargé des nobles à dix-ſept bateaulx,	nobles. The messenger arrives too late along the Rhône.
Au long du Roſne, tard meſſagier venu.	

This quatrain has been tentatively applied to every would-be invader of Britain *qui attendra l'eau*, who would cross the Channel, including Napoleon, Hitler, etc. I cannot decide to whom it actually refers.

Century V

V.LXXII

Pour le plaiſir d'edict voluptueux,	*For the pleasure of the edict of vice, poison will be mixed with*
On meſlera la poyſon dans l'aloy:	*the law. At court, Venus will be*
Venus ſera en cours ſi vertueux,	*so virtuous, that all the glory of*
Qu'obfuſquera du ſoleil tout à loy.	*the sun will be obscured by it.*

A difficult quatrain but possible to solve if one accepts that the glory of the sun refers to the Sun King, Louis XIV, and the Edict of Poitiers, 1577, greatly disapproved of by Nostradamus because it legalized Calvinism and allowed the clergy to marry.

At this time the court of Henri III, Louis XIV's predecessor, was very depraved. His openly flaunted homosexuality and interest in public self-flagellation greatly offended France, and his *mignons* acquired not only power but also great wealth. Henri was reputed to have a familiar sorcerer named Tarragon.

Century V

V.LXXIII

Perſecutee ſera de Dieu l'Eglife,	*The Church of God will be perse-*
Et les ſainctz temples ſeront expoliez:	*cuted and the holy temples will be pillaged. The mother will put*
L'enfant la mere mettra nud en chemiſe,	*away the child, naked in a shift.*
Seront Arabes aux Polons raliez.	*The Arabs will ally with the Poles.*

Presumably the clue to this quatrain lies in line 4, but I cannot see either the Polish government or Solidarity linked with the Arabs, who normally stand for terrorism. It may possibly be a futuristic quatrain.

Century V

V.LXXIIII

De ſang Troyen[1] naiſtra coeur
  Germanique
Qu'il deuiendra en ſi haute
  puiſſance:
Hors chaſſera gent eſtrange
  Arabique
Tournant l'Egliſe en priſtine
  preeminence.

Of Trojan blood he will be born with a German heart and will rise to very great power. He will drive out the foreign Arabic nation and return the Church to her early glory.

Trojan blood in Nostradamus' predictions stands for French royal blood, a reference to the ancient myth that the line was descended from Priam, king of Troy. But a French king with German ancestry who will control the Arabs and restore the Roman Catholic Church to its former power? Unlikely. A failed quatrain.

Century V

V.LXXV

Montera haut ſur le bien plus à
  dextre,
Demourra aſſis ſur la pierre
  quarree:
Vers le midy poſé à la feneſtre,
Baſton tortu en main, bouche
  ſerree.

He will rise high over his wealth, more to the right-hand side he will remain seated on the square of stone. Towards the south, placed at the window, a crooked staff in his hand, his mouth sealed.

I cannot help with this quatrain except to mention that a *baston tortu*, a crooked staff, normally refers to a bishop's crook and possibly by extension to that of a pope.

[1] *ſang Troyen*. The myth by which the French royal line were descended from Francus, son of Priam of Troy.

Century V

V.LXXVI

*En lieu libere tendra ſon
     pauillon,
Et ne voudra en citez prendre
     place:
Aix, Carpen l'iſle volce, mont
     Cauaillon,
Par tous ſes lieux abolira ſa traſſe.*

*In a free place he will pitch his
tent, he will not want to stay in
the cities. Aix, Carpentras, L'isle
Vaucluse. Montfavet, Cavaill-
lon. In all these places he will
abolish his trace.*

All the places mentioned are near Nostradamus' home in
Salon-de-Provence.

Century V

V.LXXVII

*Tous les degrez d'honneur
     Eccleſiaſtique,
Seront changez en dial
     quirinal:
En Martial quirinal flaminique,
Puis vn Roy de France le
     rendre vulcanal.*

*All degrees of ecclesiastical
honor will be changed to Jupiter
and Quirinus. A priest of Quirinus in martial guise. Then a
king of France will make him a
man of Vulcan.*

I cannot decipher this quatrain. It implies that Roman
ecclesiastical honors revert to paganism. Other than this, I can
go no further. It may be linked with the twentieth century
decline of religious beliefs. Or it may have some connections
with militant Islam.

Century V

V.LXXVIII

*Les deux vnis ne tiendront
     longuement,
Et dans treze ans au Barbare
     Satrappe:
Aux deux coſtez seront tel
     perdement,
Qu'vn benyra le Barque & ſa
     cappe.*

*The two will not remain allied
for long. Within thirteen years
they give into barbarian power.
There will be such a loss on both
sides, that one will bless the Barque (of Peter) and its leader.*

I feel the clue to this quatrain lies in II.LXXXIX when Nostradamus writes of the day the "two great leaders will be friends," and this is reported "to the man of blood," the Antichrist. He gives differing views on the length of the alliance between the two great powers, the USA and USSR, with the commencement of the INF Treaty. In another quatrain he says it will last only "three years and seven months" (IV.XCV). In VIII.LXXVII he states the war which results as the breakdown of this alliance will last for twenty-seven years and will be initiated by the Third Antichrist. This dating would bring us past the Millennium. Nostradamus is somewhat confused as to exact date of the alliance and war, but definite that they will occur. Why the then Pope, the final Pope if we believe Nostradamus and Malachy, should be blessed for his actions remains to be seen, because in other quatrains Nostradamus implies that he will flee Rome.

Century V

V.LXXIX

La facree pompe viendra baiffer les aifles,	The sacred pomp will come to lower its wings at the coming of
Par la venue du grand legiflateur:	the great lawgiver. He will raise the humble and trouble the rebel-
Humble haulfera vexera les rebelles,	lious. His like will not appear again on earth.
Naiftra fur terre aucun aemulateur.	

The generalities of this quatrain seem most applicable to Napoleon. He treated both the Church and the Vatican with arbitrary power. He originated France's present legal system, the Code Napoléon. He raised the lowly to aristocracy and was brutal in his stamping out of rebellion. Line 4 is an exaggeration, but he was a great dictator, although different in mould from his successor, Hitler.

Century V

V.LXXX

*Logmion grande Biſance
  approchera,
Chaſſé ſera la barbarique ligne:
Des deux loix l'vne l'eſtinique[1]
  lachera,
Barbare & franche en
  perpetuelle brigue.*

Ogmios will approach great
Byzantium. The barbarian
league will be driven out. Of the
two laws the pagan one will fail,
barbarian and freeman in perpetual struggle.

Ogmios is the key word in this quatrain, which I cannot
decipher in this context. Ogmios was the Celtic Hercules. He
appears elsewhere in the quatrains, equally mysterious.

Century V

V.LXXXI

*L'oiſeau royal ſur la cité ſolaire,
Sept moys deuant fera nocturne
  augure:
Mur d'Orient cherra tonnerre
  eſclaire,
Sept iours aux portes les
  ennemis à l'heure.*

The royal bird over the city of the
sun will give a nightly warning
for seven months. The wall in
the East will fall; thunder and
lightning. In seven days the enemies (arrive) directly at the
gates.

The royal bird is usually an eagle, here flying over either
Paris, the City of the Sun, or Rome, the City of Light, as an
omen of disaster to come. Earlier commentators have identified the wall in the East as the Maginot Line, the fall of France,
and the Blitzkrieg as the seven days (the crucial period of
which was June 5–11, 1940). However, it may well refer to the
Berlin Wall.. Nostradamus indicates that the wall will come
down eventually, or allow entry, *aux portes les ennemis,* but that
other natural disasters, symbolized by thunder and lightning,
will follow in the wake of this event.

---

[1]*eſtinique.* L. *ethnicus,* pagan.

Century V

V.LXXXII

*Au conclud pache[1] hors de la
    fortereſſe,
Ne ſortira celuy en deſeſpoir mis:
Quant ceux d'Arbois, de
    Langres, côtre Breſſe,
Auront mont Dolle, bouſcade[2]
    d'ennemis.*

At the conclusion of the treaty he
will not go outside the fortress,
overcome with despair. When the
people of Arbois, Langres,
against Bresse will have an
enemy ambush the mountains of
Dôle.

I cannot interpret this quatrain.

Century V

V.LXXXIII

*Ceux qui auront entreptins
    subuertir,
Nompareil regne puiſſant &
    inuincible:
Feront par fraude, nuictz trois
    aduertir,
Quant le plus grand à table
    lira Bible.*

Those who will have an under-
taking to subvert an unparalle-
led kingdom, powerful and
invincible. They will deceive,
warn for three nights, when the
most important one will read his
Bible at the table.

This is a propagandist quatrain and could have many
applications since Nostradamus' time. The reference to the
Bible probably inclines the prophecy towards the Protestant
Huguenots. Otherwise it is too general to place.

[1]*pache*. A.Pr. treaty
[2]*bouſcade*. A.Pr. ambush.

Century V

V.LXXXIIII

Naiſtra du gouphre & cité
  immeſuree,
Nay de parents obſcurs &
  tenebreux:
Qui la puiſſance du grand roy
  reueree,
Voudra deſtruire par Rouan &
  Eureux.

*He will be born of the gulf and
the immeasurable city, born of
dark and obscure parents. He
will wish to destroy the power of
the great, revered king through
Rouen and Eureux.*

Apart from the fact that Rouen and Evreux are linked in
IV.C as loyal to Napoleon III and the monarchy, I cannot
decipher this quatrain further.

Century V

V.LXXXV

Par les Sueues[1] & lieux
  circonuoiſons,
Seront en guerre pour cauſe des
  nuees:
Gamp marins locuſtes & couſins,
Du Leman fautes, ſeront bien
  deſnuees.

*Through the Swiss and the sur-
rounding areas they will war
because of the locusts. A swarm
of marine locusts and mos-
quitoes(?). The faults of Geneva
will be laid quite bare.*

The Swiss fail, that is the League of Nations (see I.XLVII)
and the result is the Second World War. Locusts and their
"like" are usually planes or weapons of destruction in Nostradamus' vocabulary, but the geographical location makes it
unlikely that one might take them literally, as in this case.

---

[1] *Sueues.* L. *Suevi*, ancestors of the German Swiss.

Century V

V.LXXXVI

Par les deux testes, & trois bras
separés,
La cité grand par eaux sera
vexee:
Des grands d'entre eux par exil
esgarés,
Par teste perse Bisance fort pressee.

Divided by two heads and three arms, the great city will be troubled by water. Some of the great men among them wander in exile. Byzantium is hard pressed by the leader of Persia.

The two heads and three arms probably stand for the river Seine, which troubles the great city of Paris by flooding. This occurred reasonably frequently during the seventeenth and eighteenth centuries, particularly in the earlier part of the former when the Turks (Byzantium) were hard pressed by Persia. There was further fighting in the East during the first part of the eighteenth century. Not a very convincing quatrain in all.

Century V

V.LXXXVII

L'an que Saturne hors de
seruage,
Au franc terroir sera d'eau
inundé:
De sang Troyen sera son mariage,
Et sera seur d'Espaignols
circundé.

In the year that Saturn is freed from servitude the Frankish territory will be inundated by water. His marriage will be of Trojan blood and he will be closely encircled by the Spaniards.

The only clear fact here is that Nostradamus foresees someone of French royal blood marrying a Spaniard. I am tempted to think that this is a retroactive quatrain referring to the marriage of Elisabeth, daughter of Henri II and Catherine de' Medicis, to Philip II of Spain, his third wife after Mary Tudor of England. As I have said elsewhere, even prophets needed to be right from time to time in contemporary eyes. There was certainly great flooding in the Midi and around Marseilles in 1554, the worst for many years, possibly linking up with line 2.

Century V

V.LXXXVIII

Sur le ſablon par vn hideux deluge,
Des autres mers trouué monſtre marin:
Proche du lieu ſera faict vn refuge,
Tenant Sauone eſclaue de Turin.

Through a dreadful flood a marine monster will be found on the sand from other seas. A refuge will be made near the place, holding Savona slave to Turin.

The only fact I can contribute toward the interpretation of this quatrain is that in 1815 Savona, which was part of the Genoa, was given to the house of Savoy, to which Turin also belonged. There is no record of a sea monster. Perhaps it is a metaphor?

Century V

V.LXXXIX

Dedans Hongrie par Boheme, Nauarre,
Et par banniere faincts ſeditions:
Par fleurs de lys pays portant la barre,
Contre Orléans fera eſmotions.

Into Hungary through Bohemia and Navarre, by the banner feigned seduction. The country of the fleur-de-lys carrying the bar. They will cause disturbances against Orléans.

The family whose arms carried the fleur-de-lys with a diagonal bar at each corner were the Bourbons. The junior branches who acquired the throne, such as the Vendômes and the Condés, simply had a diagonal bar in the center of their shields. Nostradamus appears to be describing an expedition into Bohemia and Hungary led by one of the French royal line, possibly a Bourbon Vendôme of Navarre? It is all very obscure and appears to be unfulfilled and probably a failed quatrain.

Century V

V.XC

★

Dans les cyclades, en perinthe *& lariſſe,* *Dedans Sparte tout le* *Pelloponneſſe:* *Si grand famine, peſte par faux* *conniſſe,[1]* *Neuf mois tiendra & tout le* *cherronneſſe.*	*In the Cyclades, in Perinthus and Larissa, in Sparta and all of the Peloponnese, a very great famine, plague through false dust. It will last nine months throughout the whole peninsula.*

False dust implies a chemical agent of some kind. Is Nostradamus trying to imply here that the plague and famine are artificially introduced? There appears to be a widespread disaster throughout the whole of Greece and the southern Balkans. This quatrain may tie in with those that predict trouble in the Middle East. Perhaps it may be a reference to the deaths of many thousands of Turkish and Iraqi Kurds in 1988.

Century V

V.XCI

Au grand marché qu'on dict des *menſongiers,* *Du tout Torrent[2] & champ* *Athenien:* *Seront ſurprins par les cheuaux* *legiers,* *Par Albanois Mars, Leo, Sat.* *vn verſien.[3]*	*At the great market, called that of the liars, all of Torrent and the field of Athens. They will be surprised by the light armed horses, by the Albanians, when Mars is in Leo and Saturn in Aquarius.*

Yet another reference to an unlikely attack from Albania at the conjunction mentioned. This, like most of Nostradamus' astrological datings, is not specific enough to place. Perhaps he was still protecting himself from the French Inquisition. It is very irritating not to be able to be more specific.

[1]*conniſſe*. Difficult word, possibly from Gk. *konis*, dust, or L. *connıssus*, exerted.
[2]*Torrent*. It is unclear whether this is a proper name or not.
[3]*verſien*. *Verseau*, Aquarius.

Century V

V.XCII

Apres le ſiege tenu dixſept ans,
Cinq changeront en tel reuolu
terme:
Puis ſera l'vn eſleu de meſme
temps,
Qui des Romains ne ſera trop
conforme.

After the See (seat) has been held for seventeen years, five will change within the same period of time. Then one will be elected at the same time who will not be too agreeable to the Romans.

Nostradamus says that after a pope has ruled for seventeen years there will be five popes during the next seventeen. If he is slightly out in his calculations, this might apply to Pius XII, who was in the Vatican for nineteen years. Since then we have had John XXIII, 1958–63, Paul VI, 1963–78 and John Paul I, 1978, with Pope John Paul II presently occupying the papal throne. So we have only one more pope to go, then *"Gloria Olivae"* of Malachy. The timing is slightly wrong, but we have had four popes in twenty years, quite a rapid turnover for the Vatican. John Paul II has now been on the papal throne for ten years. It will be interesting to see what his successor may bring.

Century V

V.XCIII

Soubs le terroir du rond globe
lunaire,
Lors que ſera dominateur
Mercure:
L'Iſle d'Eſcoſſe fera vn luminaire,
Qui les Anglois mettra à
deſconfiture.

Under the land of the round moonlike globe when Mercury is at the height of his powers. The island of Scotland will produce a leader who will put the English into confusion.

Most commentators apply this quatrain to Charles I because he was born in Scotland before the Stuarts came to the English throne. But it seems to me to be more applicable to Bonnie Prince Charlie, who did put the English into confusion for a while when his army marched as far south as Derby.

Century V

V.XCIIII

Tranſlatera en la grand Germanie,
Brabant & Flãdres, Gand, Bruges, & Bolongne:
La traiſue ſainte, le grand duc d'Armenie,
Aſſaillira Vienne & la Coloigne.

He will change into the Greater Germany Brabant and Flanders, Ghent, Bruges and Boulogne. The truce feigned, the great duke of Armenia will assault Vienna and Cologne.

Greater Germany, is, of course, the Third Reich. Hitler assimilated all the countries mentioned during his invasion of Europe. The feigned truce may describe the German invasion of Poland under the guise of help, which elsewhere Nostradamus described as *ſimilé ſecours*. Armenia is Russia which, once allied with the West, moved troops southwards into Germany. (See I.XXXIIII, III.XXXV, LIII, LXI, IV.XL, LXVIII, IX.XC.)

Century V

V.XCV

Nautique rame inuitera les vmbres,
Du grand Empire lors viendra conciter:
La mer Aegee des lignes lesencombres,
Empeſchant l'onde Tirreme defflotez.

The nautical oar will invite the shadows and then come to provoke the great Empire. In the Aegean Sea the remains of (bits of) wood obstruct the Tyrrhenian Sea and impede it.

A fleet *(nautique rame)* will trouble an Empire, but whether the French or Roman empire is not clear. The end result is the destruction of the empire in Greek waters.

Century V

V.XCVI

Sur le milieu du grand monde
  la rose,
Pour nouueaux faicts sang
  public espandu:
A dire vray on aura bouche
  close,
Lors au besoing viendra tard
  l'attendu.

The rose upon the middle of the world. Because of new deeds public blood is shed. To speak the truth they will have closed mouths. Then, at the time of need the awaited one will come late.

I cannot decipher this quatrain. The key probably lies in line 1.

Century V

V.XCVII

Le nay difforme par horreur
  suffoqué,
Dans la cité du grand Roy
  habitable:
L'edict seuere des captifs
  reuoqué,
Gresle & tonnere, Condon
  inestimable.

One born deformed, suffocated through honor in the city inhabited by the great King. The severe edict of the captives is revoked, hail and thunder. Condom too powerful.

This quatrain can be dated by line 2 as occurring before the French Revolution. There were no great kings after that. Commentators have suggested it may refer to the mysterious Man in the Iron Mask, the reputed son of the queen and Cardinal Mazarin. But there is no evidence that this mysterious prisoner, in his mask of velvet, not iron, was deformed, or that he was suffocated. Line 3 may refer to the Edict of Nantes, 1598, and be a point for dating the quatrain. Unsatisfactory.

Century V

V.XCVIII

*A quarante huict degré
climaterique,
A fin de Cancer ſi grande
ſeichereſſe:
Poiſſon en mer, fleuue, lac cuit
hectique,
Bearn, Bigorre par feu ciel en
deſtreſſe.*

At the forty-eighth degree of the climacteric, the end of Cancer, there is a very great drought. Fish in the sea, river and lake hectically boiled. Bearn and Bigorre in distress from fire in the sky.

The "forty-eighth degree of the climacteric" may mean 48° latitude, which runs through France near Rennes, Orléans and Langres. A drought is predicted as occurring after July 22, when the Sun leaves Cancer. There is another reference to fish cooking in the sea in II.III. Fire in the sky may either be some form of freak electrical storm or Nostradamus' usual reference to an attack by bombs or rockets. Since such a situation seems unlikely to be confined to France alone I think I have probably misinterpreted the 48° of the climacteric. This may well be a futuristic quatrain.

Century V

V.XCIX

*Milan, Ferrare, Turin, &
Aquilleye,
Capne Brundis vexés par gent
Celtique:
Par le Lyon & phalange
aquilee
Quant Rome aura le chef vieux
Britannique.*

Milan, Ferrare, Turin and Aqualia, Capua and Brundis vexed by the Celtic nation. By the lion and his eaglelike phalanx, when Rome will hold to the old British chief.

Cardinal York, the last of the Stuarts, true heirs to the British throne, died in Rome in 1807. By that time all the places mentioned had been conquered by the Imperial Eagle of France, by Napoleon. A good, simple quatrain.

Century V

V.C   ★

Le boutefeu par ſon feu attrapé,   The incendiary trapped in his
De feu du ciel à Carcas &   own fire. Five from the sky at
   Cominge: Carcassonne and Comminges.
Foix, Aux,Mazere, haut vieillart   Foix, Auch and Mazeres; the
   eſchappé,   important old man escaped,
Par ceux de Haſſe, des Saxons   through those of Hesse, Thur-
   & Turinge.   ingia and some Saxons.

Yet another reference to fire in the sky, perhaps bombs or
rockets, this time in southwestern France. (See V.XCVIII.)
Not many of the German forces got this far south even during
the Second World War, so this quatrain also may not yet be
fulfilled.

Century VI

VI.I

Autour des māts Pyrenees grās   Around the Pyrenean mountains
   amas   a great throng of foreign people
De gent eſtrange ſecourir roy   will help the new king. Near the
   nouueau: temple of Mas by the Garonne, a
Pres de Garonne du grand   Roman leader will fear the one
   temple du. Mas,   on the water.
Vn Romain chef le craindra
   dedans l'eau.

The Mas d'Agenais has many famous Roman antiquities
which Nostradamus would have known of when he lived at
Agen with his first wife and as a friend of Scaliger. But the
Roman chief fearing a naval commander is unclear.

Century VI

VI.II

En l'an cinq cens octante plus & moins,	In the year five hundred and eighty more or less, one will await a very strange century. In the year seven hundred and three, the skies are witness that several kingdoms, between one to five will be changed.
On attendra le siecle bien estrange:	
En l'an sept cens, & trois cieux en tesmoings.	
Que plusieurs regnes vn à cinq feront change.	

This is a daring quatrain in which Nostradamus gives the reader two dates, 1580 and 1703. As I have explained elsewhere, it was common in the fifteenth and sixteenth centuries to give dates leaving out the year 1000. Tombstones of the period give ample evidence of this, both in Britain as well as on the Continent. (See II.LI for the famous quatrain dating the Fire of London in the same manner.)

In 1580, soon after Nostradamus' death, France was torn by yet another civil war, known as the Seventh War, and things looked grim for the country as a whole. But by 1703, Louis XIV was defying Europe and fighting the War of the Spanish Succession. The five kingdoms were probably those of the Two Sicilies, Milan, the Netherlands, the Americas and Spain, the last of which was inherited by a Frenchman, Philip V, the grandson of Louis XIV. A good, realistic quatrain.

Century VI

VI.III

Fleuue qu'esprouue le nouueau nay Celtique,	The river is attempted by the newborn French heir. There will be great discord among the Empire. The young prince will remove peace from the crown and scepter because of the ecclesiastics.
Sera en grande de l'Empire discorde:	
Le ieune prince par gent ecclesiastique,	
Ostera le sceptre coronal de concorde.	

Garencières produces a legend that in former times new-born heirs to the French throne were put on a target and made to swim up the Rhine to see if they were lawfully begotten or not. Unfortunately, I can find no other reference to this tale. The word "Empire" dates the quatrain as post-1798. Napoleon, by his forcing Pope Pius VII to crown him at his coronation and imprisoning his predecessor Pius VI at Valence, may be a more likely interpretation of the last two lines.

Century VI

VI.IIII

Le Celtiq fleuue changera de riuaige,	The French river will change course and no longer surround the city of Agrippina. All changed except the old language, Saturn in Leo, Mars plundering in Cancer.
Plus ne tiendra la cité d'Agripine:[1]	
Tout tranſmué ormis le vieil langaige,	
Saturne, Leo, Mars, Cancer en rapine.	

After the Franco-Prussian War and the surrender of Alsace and Lorraine to the Germans, the Rhine, the French river, was no longer the border between France and Germany. The old language that remained must be German. Everything else was changed by the war. As usual, the astrological dating is not detailed enough to determine the exact time of this quatrain, although Saturn is always a bad aspect and Mars stands for war.

---

[1]*Agripine.* L. *Colonia Agrippina,* now Cologne.

Century VI

VI.V

Si grand famine par vnde
  peſtifere.
Par pluye longue le long du
  polle arctique:
Samarobryn cent lieux de
  l'hemiſphere,
Viuront ſans loy exempt de
  pollitique.

A very great famine (caused) by a plague-ridden wave will extend through long rain the length of the Arctic pole. Samarobrin, one hundred leagues from the hemisphere. They will live without law, exempt from politics.

This quatrain is of great importance. The word *Samarobrin* seems to have two meanings here. Initially I believed it to derive from the Russian words *samo*, self, and *robin*, operator, that is, a self-operating machine in space, such as the Russians' Mir Satellite. But Nostradamus links this with a plague which will cover the earth, in particular the Northern Pole. Two new drugs have appeared which may be helpful in the treatment of the worldwide scourge of AIDS. They are suramin and ribavirin. Together they form a word similar to *Samarobrin*. Perhaps the remedy for AIDS will be produced in a sterile laboratory circling the earth? Certainly AIDS is the plague of the latter half of the twentieth century and the description of a space station can only confirm the dating. It is important to remember that Nostradamus was a qualified plague doctor who would understand a disaster like AIDS. The last line is unclear. Does it refer to the victims who are struck down regardless of political stance or to the fact that the astronauts working in the space station are out of the hands of the law and politics, in another dimension? A very thought-provoking quatrain.

Century VI

VI.VI

Apparoiſtra vers le Septentrion,
Non loing de Cancer l'eſtoille
  cheuelue:
Suze, Sienne, Boece, Eretrion,
Mourra de Rome grand, la
  nuict diſperue

He will appear towards the North, not far from the bearded star in Cancer. Susa, Siena, Boetia, Eretria; the great man of Rome will die, the night dispersed.

One can place this great man of Rome by his successor Pope Leo XIII, whose family's coat of arms contains a bearded star, a comet, *l'eſtoille cheuelue*. Leo was also called *"Lumen in Caelo"* by the prophet Malachy. His predecessor was Pius IX, who died in 1878. I cannot relate the place names to any particular event.

Century VI

VI.VII

Norneigre & Dace, & l'iſle Britannique,	Norway, Dacia and the British Isles will be troubled by the
Par les vnis freres ſeront vexées:	united brothers. The Roman
Le chef Romain iſſu de ſang Gallique	leader, sprung from French blood and the forces thrust back
Et les copies aux foreſtz repoulſées.	into the forests.

This quatrain strongly resembles V.LI, where Hitler and Mussolini are described as the united brothers or allies who trouble Norway, Romania (Dacia) and Great Britain during the Second World War. The forces in the forests presumably refer to the famous Resistance movement, the *Maquis*, which caused great trouble for the Nazis.

Century VI

VI.VIII

Ceux qui eſtoyent en regne pour ſçauoir,	Those who were in the kingdom for knowledge will become
Au Royal change deuiendront apouuris:	impoverished by a royal change. Some exiled without support,
Vns exilez ſans appuy, or, n'auoir,	having no gold, neither learning nor the learned will be held of
Lettrez & lettres ne ſeront à grand pris.	much value.

I feel that this is a general comment by Nostradamus on his belief that learning would decline during a period after his death. Knowledge will not be respected and scholars sent into exile.

Century VI

VI.IX

Aux ſacrez temples ſeront faicts
  eſcandales,
Comptez ſeront par honneurs &
  louanges
D'vn que on graue d'argent,
  d'or les medalles,
La fin ſera en tormens bien
  eſtranges.

In the sacred temples scandals
will be committed. They will be
thought of as honors and praise-
worthy by one whom they
engrave on silver, gold and
medals. The end will be
(achieved) in very strange torments.

John Hogue relates this quatrain to the Papacy but personally I cannot connect the quatrain with anything to do with
the Vatican. I can see why he wishes to interpret line 1 as the
Vatican and line 3 as memorabilia of the Pope, but it does not
feel to me to be Nostradamus' line of thought. Also, where
does line 4 fit in? The Pope's possible assassination is predicted
elsewhere by Nostradamus.

Century VI

VI.X

Vn peu de temps les temples des
  couleurs
De blanc & noir des deux
  entremeſlée:
Rouges & iaunes leur
  embleront les leurs.
Sang, terre, peſte, faim, feu,
  d'eau affollée.

In a short time the colors of the
temples, the two will be inter-
mingled with black and white.
The red and yellow ones will
carry off their (possessions).
Blood, earth, plague, hunger,
fire, maddened by thirst.

This sounds like a quatrain relating to the Millennium.
Religion will become confused, unable to distinguish between
right and wrong, *de blanc & noir*. The red and yellow people
may well then refer to the Russian Communists and the
Chinese who, when they carry the day, bring in their wake all
the plagues, famines and wars that are forecast.

Century VI

VI.XI

Des sept rameaux à trois seront reduicts, *Les plus aisnez seront surprins par mort,* *Fratricider les deux seront seduicts,* *Les coniurez en dormans seront morts.*	The seven branches will be reduced to three, the elder ones will be surprised by death. Two will be attracted towards fratricide. The conspirators will die while asleep.

This is a good quatrain. The seven children of Catherine de' Medicis were reduced to three in 1575 when only Henri III, the duc d'Alençon and Marguerite de Navarre remained alive. Henri III and his brother were involved in a series of campaigns against the Guises, their first cousins. Finally the duc d'Alençon allied himself with the Guises, hoping to take the throne from his brother (*Fratricider*). Both the Guise brothers, probably the most powerful men in France after the king, were murdered at Blois in the early morning of 1558. (See II.XVIII, III.LI.)

Century VI

VI.XII

Dresser copies pour monter à l'Empire, *Du Vatican le sang Royal tiendra:* *Flamans, Anglois, Espaigne auec Aspire,[1]* *Contre l'Italie & France contendra.*	To raise forces to ascend to Empire the royal blood of the Vatican will hold fast. Flemish, English, Spain with Aspire. He will fight against France and Italy.

This is an interesting quatrain, as Nostradamus visualizes Europe in definitive modern terms, not contemporary ones. Italy did not exist as a nation until 1870. The Flemings were a Hapsburg dependency until the creation of modern Belgium.

[1] *Aspire.* Uncertain. Possible Speyer or Spires?

This prediction makes three main points: Firstly, there will be an attempt to gain the Imperial throne (Holy Roman Empire?); secondly, a pope, possibly with French blood, which Nostradamus predicts in V.XLIX; whose alliance would be moved to the Vatican against his own country; thirdly, the Hapsburgs and the English will ally against France and Italy. The first and last predictions occurred during the Napoleonic Wars. A succinct commentary about the nineteenth century European political scene.

Century VI

VI.XIII

Vn dubieux ne viendra loing
  du regne,
La plus grand part le voudra
  souftenir:
Vn Capitole[1] ne voudra point
  qu'il regne,
Sa grande charge ne pourra
  maintenir.

The doubtful one will not come far from the kingdom, the greater part will wish to support him. A pope will not want him to reign. He will not be able to bear his great burden.

Apart from papal interference in European politics, I cannot clarify this. Many commentators apply it to the fall of the House of Savoy, at that time the rulers of Italy.

Century VI

VI.XIIII

Loing de fa terre Roy perdra la
  bataille,
Prompt efchappé pourfuiny
  fuiuant prins,
Ignare prins foubs la doree
  maille.
Soubs fainct habit & l'ennemy
  furprins.

Far from his country a king will lose the battle. Quickly escaped, he is followed and retaken. The ignorant one taken under the golden chain mail, under a false garment. The enemy is surprised.

[1]*Capitole*. Probably standing for the Pope, as the Capitol was the Roman Citadel.

This is yet another quatrain to support a romantic theory such as V.I, when the king, Sebastian of Portugal, decided to raise a Crusade in 1578, despite the objections of the Pope and the Spanish king.

After all, the age of Crusades was long past. But Sebastian crossed to Morocco in 1578 and attacked the army of the king of Fez and was obliterated at the Battle of Kasr Al-Kabir. He was reported killed but there were strong and persistent rumors that he had escaped. Nostradamus implies he did so by covering his golden chain mail with a more humble garment. Although the Moors discovered this and recaptured him, for political reasons they did not release the information. Nostradamus, for once, gives us a new slant upon history!

Century VI

VI.XV

Deſſoubs la tombe ſera trouué le   Under the tomb will be found a
Prince,   prince, who will take him above
Qu aura le pris par deſſus   Nuremberg. The Spanish king,
Nuremberg: thin in Capricorn, deceived and
L'Eſpaignol Roy en Capricorne   betrayed by the great Wittenberg.
mince,
Fainct & trahy par le grand
Vvitemberg:

I cannot make head or tail of this quatrain. Wittenberg refers to the first printing of the Bible and Luther but I see no connection with Nuremberg and a Spanish king.

Century VI

VI.XVI

Ce que rauy ſera du ieune   That which the young hawk will
Milue,   carry off by the Normans of
Par les Normans de France &   France and Picardy. The black
Picardie: ones of the temple of the Black
Les noirs du temple du lieu de   (forest?) wood, will make an inn
Negriſilue   and fire at Lombardy.
Feront aulberge & feu de
Lombardie.

The black ones are almost certainly the Benedictines, who were also known as the Black monks. They did have a monastery at Hauenhalb in the Black Forest. But I am afraid the quatrain remains to be deciphered. It may be a failed quatrain.

Century VI

VI.XVII

Apres les limes bruſlez les aſiniers,
Contraints feront changer habits diuers:
Les Saturnins bruſlez par les meuſniers,
Hors la pluſpart qui ne ſera couuers.

After the penances are burned the ass drivers will be forced to change into different clothing. Those of Saturn, burned by the milkers. But the greater part excepted, it will not be covered.

I cannot decipher this quatrain.

Century VI

VI.XVIII

Par les phiſiques le grand Roy delaiſſé,
Par fort non art de l'Ebrieu eſt en vie,
Luy & ſon genre au regne hault pousé,
Grace donnee à gent qui Chriſt enuie.

The great king deserted by the physicians lives through chance, not the skill of the Jew. He and his people placed high in the realm. Pardon given to the race which denies Christ.

This may be one of Nostradamus' very rare revelations about his private life as a crypto-Jewish doctor. He seems to envisage the Jews being restored to their due place in the realm and pardoned. Presumably the latter meant giving them the right to practice the Jewish faith openly. But sadly, the future would bring the Nazis and other similarly thinking political parties, and these prejudices are only now beginning to fade.

Century VI

VI.XIX

La vraye flamme engloutira la
  dame,
Que voudra mettre les Innocens
  à feu:
Pres de l'affaut l'exercite
  s'enflamme,
Quant dans Seuille monſtre en
  boeuf ſera veu.

*The true flame will swallow up
the woman who wants to put the
Innocents to the fire. Near the
assault the army is inflamed,
when in Seville a gigantic (monstrous) ox will be seen.*

The last line may be a reference to the Spanish passion for
bull-fighting but the rest of the quatrain remains completely
indecipherable.

Century VI

VI.XX

L'vnion ſaincte ſera peu de
  durée,
Des vns changés reformés la
  pluſpart:
Dans les vaiſſeaux ſera gent
  endurée,
Lors aura Rome vn nouueau
  liepart.

*The feigned union will last a
short time, some changed, the
greater part reformed. People
will be suffering in the vessels
when Rome has a new Leopard.*

In heraldry a Leopard is a lion walking to the left with its
head turned left to face the spectator. Possibly the last line is
dated to a time when a pope has a leopard in his coat of arms,
but since Nostradamus predicts that there will be only one
other pope before the Millennium, this is unlikely. The nearest
I can come to this is John XXIII, who had a winged leopard
on the top of his armorial shield. His dates were 1958–63, so
he does not seem to fit into this quatrain. Probably a failed
prediction.

Century VI

VI.XXI

Quant ceux du polle artiq vnis enfemble,
En Orient grand effraieur & crainte:
Efleu nouueau, fouftenu le grand tremble,
Rodes, Bifance de fang Barbare taincte.

When those of the Northern Pole are united together, in the East will be great fear and dread. A new man elected supported by the great one who trembles. Both Rhodes and Byzantium will be stained with barbarian blood.

This quatrain must be linked with VI.V, which also indicates that the people of the Northern Pole will be united both in the fear and dread of the new twentieth century plague, AIDS. They are united in a search for a cure, possibly through the two anti-virus drugs suramin and ribavirin, which Nostradamus seems to believe will be finally developed in a sterile space station. He is not very optimistic about the length of time this search will take. (See III.LXXV.) "Relief near at hand" is probably AZT, "but remedies far away."

This quatrain may also have a second meaning referring to the new rapproachment between Bush and Gorbachev, *ceux du polle artiq vnis enfemble.*

AIDS started to come to the notice of the world around 1978, when Pope John Paul II was elected, *"Efleu nouuueau."*

The barbarian blood in Greece and Turkey may indicate further wars in the Middle East, possibly the blood of the Kurds have been fleeing to Iraq in their hundreds of thousands. To Nostradamus they would appear as barbarians.

Century VI

VI.XXII

Dedans la terre du grand temple celique,
Nepueu à Londres par paix faincte meurtry:
La barque alors deuiendra fcifmatique,
Liberté faincte fera au corn & cry.

In the land of the great heavenly temple, a nephew is murdered at London through a false peace. The ship will then be schismatic; false liberty will be shouted abroad.

An odd quatrain. The nephew of a ruler is asked to come to London on a peace treaty and then murdered. This rules out the Scottish pretenders. When this happens there will be a schism at the Vatican. Could this refer to the denounced Archbishop Lefèbvre? It is a most frustrating quatrain, possibly futuristic since Lefèbvre was excommunicated only in 1988.

Century VI

VI.XXIII

D'esprit de regne munismes descriées,	Defenses undermined by the spirit of the kingdom, people will
Et feront peuples esmeuz contre leur Roy:	be stirred up against their king. A new peace is made, holy laws
Paix, faict nouueau, sainctes loix empirées,	become worse. Never was Paris in so much trouble.
Rapis onc fut en si tresdur arroy.	

Rapis is Nostradamus' standard anagram for Paris, and is accepted as such by all commentators. This quatrain is full of generalities, most of which best apply to the French Revolution: new peace, new laws, and the religious element of society controlled rigidly by the state. During the Terror, Paris was in a state of anarchy.

Century VI

VI.XXIIII

Mars & le sceptre se trouuera conioinct,	Mars and the Scepter will be in conjunction, a calamitous war
Dessoubz Cancer calamiteuse guerre:	under Cancer. A short time afterwards a new king will be
Vn peu apres sera nouueau Roy oingt,	anointed who will bring peace to the earth for a long time.
Qui par long temps pacifiera la terre.	

The scepter here stands for Jupiter and, according to Wölner, the only time this conjunction will appear is on June

21, 2002. Before this there will be a dreadful war, probably starting under the sign of Cancer, June 22 to July 23. But, for the first time in the quatrains, Nostradamus allows that a period of peace may follow the war. If Wölner's dating of the conjunction is correct, there is a future for the world after the Millennium. He appears to be hedging his bets.

Century VI

VI.XXV

Par Mars contraire fera la monarchie,
Du grand pefcheur en trouble ruyneux:
Ieune noir[1] rouge prendra la hierarchie,
Les prodicteurs iront iour bruyneux.

With Mars adverse the monarchy of the great fisherman will be in ruinous trouble. The young, red king will take over the government. The traitors will act on a misty day.

The great fisherman is, of course, the Pope, "the fisher of men." This quatrain probably dates to a period when the Vatican had its own army. It was defeated between 1796 and 1815 by Napoleon and was again in trouble in 1860–70. The young king with Socialist leanings, *rouge*, stands for Victor Emmanuel and the ensuing Italian Revolution.

Century VI

VI.XXVI

Quatre ans le fiege quelque peu bien tiendra,
Vn furuiendra libidineux de vie:
Rauenne & Pife, Veronne fouftiendront,
Pour efleuer la croix de Pape enuie.

For four years the seat be held for some little good. One will succeed to it who is libidinous in life; Ravenna and Pisa, Verona will support him, desirous of elevating the Papal Cross.

---

[1]*noir.* usual anagram for *roi* and makes much better sense in this context.

A good pope will after four years be succeeded by a more worldly one. This could most suitably apply to the popular John XXIII, who reigned for less than five years. His successor was the worldly, politically minded Paul VI. Paul gained great support from the main Italian cities, being involved with Michele Sindona, the Sicilian banker who has been linked with the Mafia and the Banco Ambrosiano. The near-collapse of one of Sindona's banks, the Ambrosiano, exposed a vast network of corruption, fraud and murder—all made feasible through Vatican financing. As to Paul VI being *libidineux de vie*, he was widely reputed to have a homosexual lover. He did, however, keep the Papacy for fifteen years, 1963–1978.

Century VI

VI.XXVII

Dedans les iſles de cinq fleuues
    à vn,
Par le croiſſant du grand Chyren
    Selin:
Par les bruynes de laer fureur
    de l'vn,
Six eſchapés, cachés fardeaux de
    lyn.

Within the islands of five rivers
to one, by the crescent of the
great Chyren Selin. Through the
mists in the air, the fury of one.
Six escaped, hidden in bundles
of flax.

This must be connected in some way with the other Chyren quatrains, but the text is impenetrable.

Century VI

VI.XXVIII

Le grand Celtique entrera
    dedans Rome,
Menant amas d'exilés &
    bannis:
Le grand paſteur mettra à mort
    tout homme,
Qui pour le coq eſtoient aux
    Alpes vnis.

The great Celt will enter Rome,
leading a crowd of exiled and
banished. The great pastor will
put to death every man who was
united over the Alps for the
Cock.

The great Celt, a Frenchman, may be a reference to Napoleon's conquest of Rome and the subsequent return of Pope Pius VII with his clergy who had been imprisoned in France. But line 3 is totally incorrect, as Pius VII was extremely kind to his ex-captors and their adherents until his death in 1823.

Century VI

VI.XXIX

La vefue faincte entendant les nouuelles, *De fes rameaux mis en perplex & trouble:* *Qui fera duict appaifer les querelles,* *Par fon pourchas des razes fera comble.*	The holy widow hearing the news of her offspring in trouble and distress. He who will be led to calm the quarrels by his pursuit will make the shaven heads pile up.

The widow, Catherine de' Medicis, will learn much of the problems and troubles of her children, in particular of the massacre of Saint Bartholemew and the murders of the duc de Guise and his brother, by her son Henri III. All these actions created civil unrest and led to the eventual religions and civil wars between the Leaguers and the Huguenots, *razes*.

Century VI

VI.XXX

Par l'apparence de faincte faincteté, *Sera trahy aux ennemis le fiege:* *Nuict qu'on cuidoit dormir en feureté,* *Pres de Braban marcheront ceux du Liège.*	By the appearance of simulated holiness, the Seat will be betrayed to the enemies in the night when they thought to sleep safely. The people of Liège will march near Brabant.

Liège was a province east of Brabant in the Netherlands. Normally Nostradamus uses the word Seat to indicate the Papal See, the Vatican, but here it is difficult to be certain.

Century VI

VI.XXXI

Roy trouuera ce qu'il desiroit
tant,
Quand le Prelat sera reprins à
tort:
Responce au duc le rendra mal
content,
Qui dans Milan mettra plusieurs
à mort.

The king will find that which he
desires so greatly, when the Prelate will be wrongly taken. The
reply to the Duce will make him
angry. In Milan he will put
several to death.

The king of Italy, Umberto, achieves his desire when he
angers the Duce, Mussolini. The executions at Milan probably
refer to the deaths of Ciano and others. The Pope, wrongly
taken, might be understood as the Vatican, a neutral city,
completely surrounded by a hostile, Fascist Italy during the
Second World War.

Century VI

VI.XXXII

Par trahyson de verges à mort
battu,
Prins surmonté sera par son
desordre:
Conseil friuole au grand captif
sentu,
Nez par fureur quant Berich
viendra mordre.

Beaten to death by rods for
treason. Captured, he will be
overcome because of his disorder.
Frivolous advice is handed to the
great captive, when Berich
comes to bite his nose in a rage.

The solution to this quatrain lies in the as yet unsolved
Berich, probably an anagram.

Century VI

VI.XXXIII

Sa main derniere par Alus
sanguinaire,
Ne se pourra par la mer
guarentir:
Entre deux Fleuues craindre
main militaire,
Le noir l'ireux le fera repentir.

His hand finally through the bloody Alus, he will be unable to protect himself by sea. Between two rivers he will fear the military hand. The black and angry one will make him repent of it.

Alus is another unsolved mystery and an interesting one. It (he?) appears to connect with the fearsome Mabus of II.LXII. Is Alus the precursor of the Antichrist, whose hand finally acts through the bloody Alus? There is the repetition of the word *main* in connection with both. Or it may be an approximation of the Antichrist himself, tying up with the cryptic quatrain II.XXVIII where Nostradamus seems to be trying to give the letters which make up the name of the third Antichrist. See also I.L, II.LXXXIX, VIII.LXXVII and X.LXXII.

Century VI

VI.XXXIIII

De feu volant la machination,
Viendra troubler au grand chef
assiegez:
Dedans sera telle sedition,
Qu'en desespoir seront les
profligez.

The machine of flying fire will come to trouble the great besieged chief. Within there will be such sedition that those abandoned will be in despair.

The first line of the quatrain is very striking; it describes a probable rocket attack, which places the quatrain in this century. Unfortunately, there are many recent and current situations to which this prediction could apply and it is too general otherwise to offer a clue.

Century VI

VI.XXXV

*Pres de Rion[1], & proche à
    blanche laine,
Aries, Taurus, Cancer, Leo, la
    Vierge,
Mars, Iupiter, le Sol ardra
    grand plaine,
Bois & citez, lettres cachez au
    cierge.*

Near the Bear and close to the
white wool, Aries, Taurus, Cancer, Leo, Virgo, Mars, Jupiter,
the Sun will burn the great
plain, woods and cities. Letters
hidden in the candle.

I wonder whether the white wool might stand for the Milky
Way? Otherwise Nostradamus gives such a plethora of planets
and constellations that it is difficult to know what he intended,
other than in line 3, where he predicts an extreme drought
throughout both city and countryside.

Century VI

VI.XXXVI

*Ne bien ne mal par bataille
    terreſtre,
Ne paruiendra aux confins de
    Perouſſe:
Rebeller Piſe, Florence voir mal
    eſtre,
Roy nuict bleſſé ſur mulet à noire
    houſe.*

Neither good nor evil from the
earthly battle will come to the
borders of Perugia. Pisa to rebel,
Florence seen to be upon bad
(times). A king on a mule
wounded by night, to the black
cover.

I cannot penetrate the convolutions of this quatrain except
to state that all the places mentioned are in Italy or were parts
of the Italian States.

---

[1]*Rion.* Misprint for *Trion,* L. *Triones,* the Constellation of the Bear.

Century VI

VI.XXXVII

L'oeuure ancienne ſe
paracheuera,
Du toict cherra ſur le grand
mal ruyne:
Innocent faict mort on accuſera:
Nocent caiché taillis à la
bruyne.

The ancient work will be accomplished and from the roof evil ruin will fall on the great man. Being dead, they will accuse an innocent of the deed. The guilty one hidden in the misty woods.

This detailed prophecy seems likely to have been fulfilled. A great man will be murdered and an innocent person accused of the deed while the guilty person remains hiding out in the woods.

Century VI

VI.XXXVIII

Aux profligez de paix les
ennemis,
Apres auoir l'Italie ſuperee:
Noir ſanguinaire, rouge ſera
commis,
Feu, ſang verſer, eaue de ſang
couloree.

The enemies of peace, the dissolute ones, having overcome Italy the bloody, black one will be seen red; fire, bloodshed, water colored with blood.

The color red probably stands for blood and revolution, although red did not contain this meaning until late eighteenth century. Before then it was used to refer to the Spanish or to the cardinals of the Catholic Church. Like many of Nostradamus' concepts, this metaphor is surprisingly modern.

Century VI

VI.XXXIX

*L'enfant du regne par
    paternelle prinſe,
Expolié ſera pour deliurer:
Aupres du lac Traſimen l'azur
    prinſe,
La troupe hoſtaige pour trop
    fort s'enyurer.*

*The child of the kingdom,
through his father's capture, will
be deprived to deliver him. Near
Lake Trasimene the azure captive, in order that the hostage
troop may become very drunk.*

An impenetrable quatrain.

Century VI

VI.XL

*Grand de Magonce pour
    grande ſoif eſtaindre,
Sera priué de ſa grand dignité:
Ceux de Cologne ſi fort le
    viendront plaindre,
Que le grand groppe au Ryn
    ſera getté.*

*To quench the great thirst the
great one of Mainz will be deprived of his great dignity. Those
from Cologne will come to complain so strongly, that the great
rump will be thrown into the
Rhine.*

The archbishop of Mainz was one of the Electors of the
Empire. Mainz was captured by the French during the
Revolution and ceded by the Treaty of Campoformio to the
French. However, the Elector held his title until the Empire
formally ended in 1806. The archbishop of Cologne was also
an Elector but his office was abolished three years earlier, in
1803, so he had every right to complain.

Century VI

VI.XLI

Le second chef du regne d'Annemarc,
Par ceux de Frise & l'isle Britannique,
Fera despendre plus de cent mille marc,
Vain exploicter voyage en Italique.

The second leader of the kingdom of Annemarc, through those of Frisia and the British Isles will spend more than one hundred thousand marks, attempting in vain a voyage to Italy.

A difficult quatrain, but made interesting by the fact that at the time of Nostradamus' writing, England and Frisia had the same ruler, Philip II of Spain, husband of Mary Tudor. In IV.LXXXIX Nostradamus foresees William of Orange, a Frisian, attaining the English throne. This may be a better interpretation since the British Isles, as opposed to England, did not come into existence until 1604. But a problem remains with the uninterpreted Annemarc (Denmark?), as also in IV.XXVII.

Century VI

VI.XLII

A logmyon[1] sera laissé le regne,
Du grand Selin qui plus fera de faict:
Par les Italies estendra son enseigne,
Regisera par prudent contrefaict.

To Ogmios the kingdom of the great Selin will be left who will do even more. He will extend his banner throughout Italy and it will be ruled by careful forgery.

The enigmatic Ogmios also appears in V.LXXX, VI.LXI, IX.LXXXIX, but his true identity has never been deciphered other than the probability that he was the Celtic equivalent of Hercules.

---

[1]*Logmyon.* Misprint for Ogmios, the Celtic Hercules.

Century VI

VI.XLIII

Long temps ſera ſans eſtre habitée, *Où Signe & Marne autour vient arrouſer:* *De la Tamiſe & martiaux tentée,* *Deceux les gardes en cuidant repouſer.*	*For a long time it will remain uninhabited around where the Seine and Marne come to gush forth. Tried by the Tamise and soldiers, the guards deceived in believing it rebuffed.*

It appears that the city between the Seine and the Marne which Nostradamus envisages here is Paris. The Tamise could mean the Thames in London or a town of the same name near Antwerp.

Century VI

VI.XLIIII ★

De nuict par Nantes L ris[1] apparoiſtra, *Des artz marins ſuſciteront la pluye:* *Arabiq goulfre grand claſſe parfondra,* *Vn monſtre en Saxe naiſtra d'ours & truye.*	*By night the rainbow will appear near Nantes, the marine arts will raise up rain. In the Arabian Gulf a great fleet will flounder. In Saxony, a monster will be born of a sow and a bear.*

This quatrain may apply to the twentieth century for two reasons. In 1947, scientists discovered how to produce artificial rain (line 2); there is no actual Gulf of Arabia but the Gulf War between Iran and Iraq has been raging for most of this decade. The last line must refer to the dissension in East Germany and Russia ("l'ours").

---

[1] *L ris*. Obvious misprint for *l'iris*, the rainbow.

Century VI

VI.XLV

*Le gouuerneur du regne bien
  ſçauant,
Ne conſentir voulant au faict
  Royal:
Mellile claſſe par le contraire
  vent,
Le remettra à ſon plus deſloyal.*

The very learned governor of the kingdom does not wish to consent to the Royal deed. The fleet at Melilla by a contrary wind, will deliver him back to his most disloyal one.

Melilla is in Spanish Morocco and from this some commentators refer to this quatrain to the Spanish Civil War.

Century VI

VI.XLVI

*Vn iuſte ſera en exil renuoyé,
Par peſtilence aux confins de
  Nonſeggle,
Reſponce au rouge le fera
  deſuoyé,
Roy retirant à la Rane & à
  l'aigle.*

A just one will be sent back into exile through pestilence to the confines of Nonseggle. His reply to the red one will mislead him. The king withdraws to the Frog and the Eagle.

Nonſeggle remains an unsolved proper name or anagram. The frog also appears in quatrains V.III and V.XCV. It is just possible that the first line may refer to Louis XVIII during the Hundred Days, but the rest remains obscure.

Century VI

VI.XLVII

*Entre deux monts les deux
  grans aſſemblés
Delaiſſeront leur ſimulté ſecrette:
Brucelle & Dolle par Langres
  acablés,
Pour à Malignes executer leur
  peſte.*

The two great ones assembled between two mountains, will give up their secret quarrel. Brussels and Dôle overcome by Langres in order to execute their pestilence at Malines.

Brussels, Dôle and Malines were all in the Spanish Netherlands. This quatrain may therefore be a failed prediction in
that Nostradamus predicts their being conquered by France
(Langres).

Century VI

VI.XLVIII

La sainteté trop saincte &
seductiue,
Accompaigné d'vne langue
diserte:
La cité vieille & Parme trop
hastiue,
Florence & Sienne rendront
plus desertes.

The holiness, too false and too
attractive, is accompanied by an
eloquent tongue. The old city,
Parma, too hasty. They will
make Florence and Siena even
more deserted.

I can make nothing of this quatrain.

Century VI

VI.XLIX

De la partie de Mammer grand
Pontife,
Subiuguera les confins du
Dannube:
Chasser les croix par fer raffe ne
riffe,
Captifz, or, bagues plus de cent
mille rubes.

The great pontiff by the warlike
party will subjugate the borders
of the Danube. The cross pur-
sued by hook or by crook. Cap-
tives, gold, jewels, more than one
hundred thousand rubies.

The cross, described by Nostradamus as *raffe ne riffe*, is an
expression which can mean by hook or by crook, and also by
extension crooked. The crooked cross can only be the swastika.
Hitler's party originated in Austria, the Danube. Line 4 is
horribly reminiscent of the millions of pounds of personal
gold, jewelry and possessions which were stolen by the Nazis,
particularly when their victims arrived at the concentration
camps. The exact meaning of the position of the Pope in line
1 is not clear, but although the Vatican remained technically

neutral, it favored the Fascisti under Pius XI and its position on helping the Germans was ambiguous under Pius XIII, who was criticized for not excommunicating Hitler and for giving Nazi officers refuge in the Vatican towards the end of the war, and afterwards.

Century VI

VI.L

Dedans le puys feront trouués les oz,
Sera l'inceft commis par la maratre;[1]
L'eftat changé on querra bruict & loz,
Et aura Mars attendant pour fon aftre.

The bones will be found inside the walls. It will be incest committed by the stepmother. The State changed one will seek praise and renown. He will have Mars attendant as his star.

An indecipherable quatrain.

Century VI

VI.LI

Peuple affemblé, voir nouueau expectacle,
Princes & Roys par plufieurs affiftans:
Pilliers faillir, murs, mais comme miracle
Le Roy fauué & trente des inftans.

The people gathered to see a new sight. Princes and kings (are) among many onlookers. The pillars, walls fall, but as if by a miracle the king and thirty of those present are saved.

This is the verse which caused the Swiss astrologer Ernst Krafft, who was working for Goebbels's Propaganda Ministry, to telegraph Hitler that an assassination attempt would be made upon him while he attended a meeting in November, 1939. In fact, it was organized by the party of von Stauffen-

[1]*maratre.* more likely in this concept to mean stepmother than mother, because of the incest theme.

berg, who was caught and executed when he attempted a
similar attempt in 1944. The bomb was hidden in a pillar
behind the rostrum and in fact it was by sheer chance that
Hitler and some of his party left unexpectedly early. This
prediction gained Krafft great credibility at the time, but his
refusal to produce interpretations to order ended tragically
with his early death in a concentration camp in 1941.

Century VI

VI.LII

En lieu du grand qui sera condemné,	*In the place of the great one who will be condemned, he is outside*
De prison hors son amy en sa place:	*the prison, his friend in his place. The Trojan hope for six*
L'espoir Troyen en fix moys ioinct, mort nay,	*months joined, born dead. The Sun in Aquarius, the rivers will*
Le Sol à l'urne feront prins fleuues en glace.	*be frozen.*

This is another of Nostradamus' tantalizing quatrains, in
which he contradicts the little that is known of an historical
mystery, the fate of the child King Louis XVII (see V.I). Here
it is implied that another child died in 1795 and his body was
substituted for that of the king. It must be remembered that
no certain identification could be made of the corpse, even
after an autopsy. The Trojan blood refers, as always, to the
French royal line, from the myth that they were descendants
of Francis, son of King Priam of Troy. Line 3 is difficult to
interpret. Does it refer to the death of the false kind after six
months, which could have been very possible, or to the death
of the real king six months after his escape? The Sun is in
Aquarius from mid-February until mid-March. The dauphin's
death was officially reported on June 8, 1795, but due to the
state of the corpse, it could easily have occurred earlier. An
interesting quatrain. Although technically king, the dauphin
was never crowned and so was normally referred to by that
title.

Century VI

VI.LIII

Le grand Prelat Celtique à Roy suspect,	The great French prelate suspected by the king, will flee from his realm by night. Through a duke fertile (favorable?) to his great king, Britain Byzantium as far as Cyprus and Tunis are undiscovered.
De nuict par cours sortira hors du regne:	
Par duc fertile à son grand Roy, Bretaigne,	
Bisance à Cipres & Tunes insuspect.	

This confused and probably failed quatrain appears to indicate that a French cardinal or bishop will flee to England and from there to Tunis via Constantinople and Cyprus.

Century VI

VI.LIIII

Au poinct du iour au second chant du coq,	At daybreak at second cockrow, those of Tunis, Fez and of Bougie. The Arabs captured by the king of Morocco in the year 1607 by the Liturgy.
Ceulx de Tunes, de Fez, & de Bugie:	
Par les Arabes captif le Roy Maroq,	
L'an mil six cens & sept, de Liturgie	

This quatrain appears to be one of Nostradamus' complete failures, date notwithstanding. He seems to envisage the fall of the Ottoman Empire through a new European king, and in Asia through new Persian and Arab empires. The only enigma is what Nostradamus means by "the Liturgy." It may be an equivalent of Anno Domini, but Nostradamus was usually more convoluted than that.

Century VI

VI.LV

Au chalmé Duc, en arrachant l'eſponce, *Voile Arabeſque voir, ſubit deſcouuerte:* *Tripolis Chio, & ceux de Trapeſonce,* *Duc prins, Marnegro & la cité deſerte.*	*The becalmed duke drawing up the contract, an Arabian sail is seen, a sudden discovery. Tripolis, Chios and those from Trabazon. The duke captured, the Black Sea and the city deserted.*

The only certainty in this quatrain is that the action takes places in Asia Minor, the Black Sea and the Aegean (Chios).

Century VI

VI.LVI

La crainte armee de l'ennemy Narbon, *Effrayera ſi fort les Heſperiques:[1]* *Parpignan vuide par l'aueugle darbon,[2]* *Lors Barcelon per mer donra les piques.*	*The dreaded army of the enemy Narbonne will greatly terrify the Hesperians. Perignon is empty through the blind of Arbon, then Barcelona will take up her weapons by sea.*

It appears that in this quatrain the Spaniards are being terrified by the French from Narbonne. Narbonne is only forty miles north of Perpignan, while Barcelona, about a hundred miles to the south, is sending supplies and weapons by sea. Perpignan was besieged by the French for a short time in 1597.

---

[1]*Heſperiques*. Spanish, Western or American.
[2]*darbon*. of Arbon, possibly somewhere in France or Switzerland.

Century VI

VI.LVII

Celuy qu'estoit bien auant dans le regne,	*He who was well to the front in the kingdom having a red chief*
Ayant chef rouge proche à la hierarchie:	*close to the seat of power. Harsh and cruel, he will make himself*
Aspre & cruel, & se fera tant craindre,	*most greatly feared. He will succeed to the sacred monarchy.*
Succedera à sacré monarchie.	

A cruel cardinal, or less likely a bishop, will greatly influence his king. He eventually succeeds to the throne. It is difficult to know whom in particular Nostradamus had in mind. Obvious possibilities such as Mazarin and Richelieu do not fit the last line of the quatrain. They were the éminences grises behind the throne. In modern-day context, an unlikely and probably failed quatrain.

Century VI

VI.LVIII

Entre les deux monarques esloignez,	*Between the two distant monarchs, at a time when the*
Lors que le Sol par Selin clair perdue:	*dear Sun is lost by Selin. Great enmity between two indignant*
Simulté grande entre deux indignez,	*ones, so that liberty is restored to the islands and to Siena.*
Qu'aux Isles & Sienne la liberté rendue.	

This quatrain is contemporary with Nostradamus' lifetime. The Sun and the chariot of Apollo were the devices of Philip II of Spain. The moon, *Selin*, was that of Henri II of France, partly to honor his mistress, Diane de Poitiers. Nostradamus seems to envisage that France will conquer the Hapsburgs. All that occurred during this period was that the French held Siena and they were also attempting to conquer Corsica. The restoration of Liberty in line 4 is ambiguous. Does it mean the arrival or the withdrawal of the French? Nostradamus is usually more patriotic than this. If it were not for the first two lines I might be inclined to date this quatrain during the Napoleonic period.

Century VI

VI.LIX

Dame en fureur par rage d'adultere,
Viendra à son Prince coniurer non de dire:
Mais bref cogneu sera le vitupere,
Que seront mis dixsept à martire.

The lady, furious in an adulterous rage, will conspire against her prince, but not speak to him. However, the culprit will soon be known so that seventeen will be martyred.

An incomprehensible quatrain.

Century VI

VI.LX

Le Prince hors de son terroir Celtique
Sera trahy, deceu par interprete:
Rouan, Rochelle par ceux de l'Armorique
Au port de Blaue deceus par moyne & prebstre.

The prince, outside his French territory will be betrayed; deceived by the interpreter. Rouen, La Rochelle, by those of Brittany at the port of Blaye deceived by monk and priest.

Nothing remotely relating to this quatrain has occurred to date and I am under the impression that it is a failed quatrain.

Century VI

VI.LXI

Le grand tappis plié ne monstrera,	Folded, the great carpet will not show except by halves the greater part of its history. Driven far out of the kingdom he will appear harsh, so that each one will believe in his warlike act.
Fors qu'à demy la pluspart de l'hiſtoire:	
Chaſſé du regne loing aſpre apparoiſtra	
Qu'au faict bellique chaſcun le viendra croire.	

Yet another quatrain I cannot unravel.

Century VI

VI.LXII

Trop tard tous deux les fleurs feront perdues,	Too late, both of the flowers will be lost, the snake will not want to act against the law. The forces of the Leaguers, confounded by the French. Savona, Albenga, great martyrdom through Monaco.
Contre la loy ſerpent ne voudra faire:	
Des ligueurs forces par gallots[1] confondues,	
Sauone, Albingue par monech grand martyre.	

Yet another erroneous quatrain. Nostradamus seems to envisage a League conspiring against the French, but the French emerge victorious. But Monaco was bound to the Spanish by treaty and Savona and Albenga belonged to Genoa. The League was probably one of the sixteenth century Italian Leagues, but none of this happened.

[1]*gallots.* O.F. a Gallic or French man.

Century VI

VI.LXIII

La dame ſeule au regne
  demeuree,
L'vnic eſtaint premier au lict
  d'honneur:
Sept ans ſera de douleur
  exploree,
Puis longue vie au regne par
  grand heur.

*The lady left alone in the king-
dom, her only (spouse) first dead
on the bed of honor. For seven
years she will weep with grief,
then a long life for the good fortune of the kingdom.*

Nostradamus may have been somewhat prejudiced in this
quatrain as he knew Catherine de' Medicis well and their
relationship continued until his death in 1566. But the queen
certainly lived for the good of her adopted country. Every time
the king, or his sons, were in need of money, it was Catherine
who was sent to beg for it from the Parlement de Paris, and
she was always successful. It was she, too, who recognized and
tried to avert the terrible religious wars that racked France
during the reigns of her three sons. She was a far better
political animal than any of the Valois.

She left off mourning for her late husband, Henri II, on
August 1, 1566, after seven years. She acted as regent under
François II and Charles IX, but age and illness reduced most
of her power during the reign of her third son, Henri III.

Century VI

VI.LXIIII

On ne tiendra pache aucune
  arreſté,
Tous receuans iront par
  tromperie:
De paix & trefue, terre & mer
  proteſté,
Par Barcelone claſſe prins
  d'induſtrie.

*They will not keep any peace
agreed upon, all the receivers
will go through deceit. In peace
and truce, land and sea having
protested, the fleet is seized with
skill by Barcelona.*

I know of no fleet seized in these cirumstances in Barcelona.

Century VI

VI.LXV

Gris & bureau¹ demie ouuerte guerre,
De nuict feront affaillis & pillez:
Le bureau prins paffera par la ferre,
Son temple ouuert, deux au plaftre grillez.

Gray and brown in half declared war at night they will be besieged and pillaged. The captured, brown one will pass through the prison, his temple opened, two shipped in the plaster.

It is likely that here Nostradamus was describing a feud between two monastic orders, *gris & bureau*. Some of the Franciscans wore brown habits, although many their subsidiary orders wore gray, as did the Dominicans. The last line appears incomprehensible.

Century VI

VI.LXVI

Au fondement de la nouuelle fecte,
Seront les oz du grand Romain trouués,
Sepulchre en marbre apparoiftra couuerte,
Terre trembler en Auril, mal enfouetz.

At the founding of a new seat the bones of the great Roman will be found. A sepulcher, covered in marble will appear. The earth will quake in April, badly buried.

The great Roman is presumably a pope, and in this context the bones probably refer to the tomb of Saint Peter. Nostradamus says it will be found in April. (See II.LXV.) Some sixty-five years ago a grave was found and declared to be that of Saint Peter, but many people remain unconvinced, as indeed, does Nostradamus. There is a very old legend that Peter actually died in Alexandria, Egypt.

¹*bureau*. O.F. variant of *burel*, brown.

Century VI

VI.LXVII

Au grand Empire paruiendra tout vn aultre *Bonté diſtant plus de felicité:* *Regi par vn iſſu non loing du peaultre,* *Corruer regnes grande infelicité.*	*Quite a different man will attain to the great Empire, distant from kindness, more so from happiness. Ruled by one not long raised from his bed, the kingdom rushes to great misfortune.*

Line 3 may be interpreted in two ways. Either the Emperor is but a very young child, not long having left the cradle, or he is a man who lived a very debauched life, as *peaultre* also means a brothel. It just possibly may refer to Napoleon, ruled by his Empress Josephine. He certainly put France into dreadful difficulties.

Century VI

VI.LXVIII

Lors que ſoldatz fureur ſeditieuſe, *Contre leur chef feront de nuict fer luire,* *Ennemy d'Albe ſoit par main furieuſe,* *Lors vexer Rome & principaux ſeduire.*	*When the soldiers rise up in a treacherous fury at night to fight against their leader. The enemy of Alba with furious hand, then troubles Rome and wins over the Principals.*

This prediction was probably meant for the near future, the sixteenth century and the duke of Alva (Alba). Nostradamus correctly foresees him trying to suppress a revolt in the Spanish army, which he did soon afterwards in the Netherlands.

Century VI

VI.LXIX

La pitié grande ſera ſans loing tarder,
Ceux qui dõnoient ſeront contrains de prẽdre.
Nudz affamez de froit, ſoif, ſoy bander,
Les monts paſſer commettant grand eſclandre.

A very great sadness will arrive before long. Those who give will be forced to take. Naked, starving with cold and thirst, they band together to cross the countries causing a great scandal.

France disbanded and disestablished the Catholic clergy in 1792, which left many priests in really wretched circumstances. Instead of supporting themselves through their duties to their parishioners, they were constrained to beg to stay alive. Many of them did join up in a band and crossed the Alps to ask help from the Vatican. Their plight was scandalous by any standards.

Century VI

VI.LXX

Au chef du monde le grand Chyren ſera,
Plus oultre[1] apres aymé, craint, redoubté:
Son bruit & loz les cieux ſurpaſſera,
Et du ſeul titre victeur fort contenté.

The great Chyren will be chief of the world after "plus oultre," loved, feared and dreaded. His fame and praise go beyond the heavens and he will be greatly satisfied with the sole title of victor.

Here again we have the enigmatic Chyren, the anagram of the older French spelling of Henri, Henryc. This quatrain implies that Chyren will be even greater than the Emperor Charles V. It is tempting to equate Chyren with Henri IV de Navarre but some of the other Chyren quatrains will not

---

[1]*"Plus oultre Carol Quint"* was the device of the Emperor Charles V. *Plus oultre* is printed in capitals in the 1605 edition, which clarifies Nostradamus' meaning.

support this interpretation. Perhaps Nostradamus saw several kings called Henri? Until Chyren is satisfactory explained, these quatrains are impenetrable.

Century VI

VI.LXXI

Quand on viendra le grand roy parenter	When they will come to give the last rites to the great king before he has quite given up his soul. He will come who will lament him least, through lions the cross and the crown of the Eagles sold.
Auant qu'il ait du tout l'ame rendue:	
Celuy qui moins le viendra lamenter,	
Par lyons, d'aigles, croix, couronne vendue.	

This general quatrain description could apply to the death of any king not much lamented by his heir. Possibly the last line indicates armorial bearings, but *"lyons"* were also a form of currency, so it seems more likely that the heir sold much of the regalia.

Century VI

VI.LXXII

Par fureur faincte d'esmotion diuine,	Through feigned fury of a divine emotion the wife of the great one will be badly violated. The judges wishing to condemn such a doctrine, the victim is sacrificed to the ignorant people.
Sera la femme du grand fort violee:	
Iuges voulans damner telle doctrine,	
Victime au peuple ignorant imolee.	

Many modern commentators see in this verse a reference to the manner in which Rasputin dominated the wife of the last czar. Although Raputin's sexual prowess was legendary, the word "violates" here should, I feel, be taken metaphorically, although rumors certainly went round the Russian court that he was the czarina's lover. The whole Russian royal family became victims of their vast, ignorant populace when they refused to try to understand the new doctrines of the times. This led to their eventual, tragic deaths.

Century VI

VI.LXXIII

*En cité grande vn moyne &
   artifan,
Pres de la porte logés & aux
   murailles:
Contre Modene fecret, caue
   difant,
Trahis pour faire fouz coleur
   d'efpoufailles.*

In a great city a monk and an artisan are lodged near the gate and the walls. Speaking vainly and secretly against Modena; betrayed for acting under the guise of marriage.

I cannot decipher this quatrain.

Century VI

VI.LXXIIII

*La defchaffee au regne tournera,
Ses ennemis trouués des
   coniurés:
Plus que iamais fon temps
   triomphera,
Trois & feptante à mort trop
   affeurés.*

She who was cast out will return to reign, her enemies found among conspirators. More than ever will her reign be triumphant. At three and seventy death very sure.

Elizabeth I of England was certainly rejected for most of her childhood and then became the victim of conspirators during the reign of her sister, Mary Tudor. England rose to great heights during the Elizabethan period. Elizabeth died in her seventieth year, in 1603. Most commentators insert a comma between *trois & feptante*, thus indicating the first number as the year she died and the second as her age. An interesting conundrum. I leave it to the reader.

Century VI

VI.LXXV

Le grand pilot par Roy fera
mandé,
Laiffer la claffe pour plus haut
lieu attaindre:
Sept ans apres fera contrebandé,
Barbare armée viendra Venife
craindre.

The great pilot will be commissioned by the king to leave the
fleet to attain to higher rank.
Seven years later he will be in
rebellion, Venice will come to
fear the barbarian army.

Gaspard de Coligny was made Henri II's Admiral of the
Fleet, *grand pilot*, in 1552 but resigned the post seven years
later (after the king's death in 1559) to join up with the
Calvinist party. He was one of the principal initiators of the
Huguenot Catholic Wars in France, *fera contrebandé*. These
events occurred at the same time that Venice, line 4, was
attacked by the Sultan Selim II, who took Cyprus from them
in 1570. A good and accurate quatrain.

Century VI

VI.LXXVI

La cité antique d'antenoree[1]
forge,
Plus ne pouuant le tyran
fupporter:
Le manchet[2] fainct au temple
couper gorge,
Les fiens le peuple à mort
viendra bouter.

The ancient city created by Antenor is no longer able to support
the tyrant. A false, one-armed
man in the temple will cut his
throat. The people will come to
put his followers to death.

Padua (*Antenoree*) belonged to Venice which, as I have
mentioned earlier, was governed by an hereditary office of
podestas. But I cannot find any record of a murder committed
in the church there, followed by further killings of followers.

---

[1]*Antenorre*. Antenor was the legendary founder of Padua.
[2]*manchet*. O.F. one-armed.

Century VI

VI.LXXVII

Par la victoire du deçeu fraudulente,
Deux claſſes vne, la reuolte Germaine:
Le chef meurtry & ſon filz dans la tente,
Florence, Imole pourchaſſés dans Romaine.

Through the fraudulent victory of the deceived, two fleets in one, the German revolt. The chief murdered with his son in a tent. Florence and Imola pursued into Romania.

There were numerous revolts during the sixteenth and seventeenth centuries against the Holy Roman Emperor. *Romaine* is most likely to stand for either Romagnia, the Holy Roman Empire, or the Papal States.

Century VI

VI.LXXVIII

Crier victoire du grand Selin croiſſant,
Par les Romains ſera l'Aigle clamé:
Ticcin, Milan, & Gennes n'y conſent,
Puis par eux meſmes Baſil grand reclamé.

To shout aloud the victory of the great crescent moon, the Eagle will be proclaimed by the Romans. Pavia, Milan and Genoa will not agree to it. Then the great Lord is claimed by themselves.

This quatrain is obviously a retroactive one, involving the Ottoman and the Holy Roman empires, whose particular emblems were the crescent moon and the Eagle. The sultan was known in Europe as the Grand Seignior, *Basil*, but not one has been captured by the Roman Empire since Nostradamus' day. The last was the Sultan Jem, captured in the fifteenth century.

Century VI

VI.LXXIX

Pres du Tefin les habitans de Loyre,
Garonne & Saonne, Seine, Tain, & Gironde:
Outre les monts dreſſeront promontoire,
Conflict donné Pau granci, ſubmergé onde.

Near the Ticino the inhabitants of the Loire, Garonne, the Seine, Tain and Gironde. Beyond the mountains they will build a promontory. Conflict engaged. Pau seized, submerged by the wave.

Many commentators accept the word *"Pau"* in line 4 as a shortened version of Napoleon (see also VIII.I). If this is so, the quatrain is a very precise description of an accident which befell Napoleon during the Battle of Lodi, 1796. While the bridge over the Adda was being stormed Napoleon fell into the water, *"ſubmergé onde,"* but was pulled out before he could drown. The places in lines 1 and 2 are areas which suffered from the French campaigns.

Century VI

VI.LXXX

De Fez le regne paruiendra à ceux d'Europe,
Feu leur cité, & lame trenchera:
Le grand d'Aſie terre & mer à grand troupe,
Que bleux, pers,[1] croix, à mort dechaſſera.

From Fez the kingdom will stretch out to those of Europe. The city blazes, the sword will slash. The great man of Asia with a great troop by land and sea, so that the blues, perse, will drive out the cross to death.

Nostradamus says in VI.LIII that the king of Fez will be captured by the Arabs. I think, however, that the rest of this quatrain belongs to a more modern context. Together with the Third Antichrist, "the great man of Asia," we have wars on land and sea and fascinatingly enough Perse is mentioned

---

[1]*pers.* either a shade of royal or dark blue, or Persian.

again, as the man whom Nostradamus believes will succeed the Ayatollah Khomeini. The Persians (Iranians) are not a Christian country, and they will persecute those who are not followers of Islam.

Century VI

VI.LXXXI

Pleurs, crys & plaincts, hurlement effraieur,	*Tears, cries and wailing, howls and terror, an inhuman heart*
Coeur inhumain, cruel, noir, & tranfy:	*both black and cold. Lake Geneva, the Islands, most of the*
Leman, les ifles de Gennes les maieurs,	*people of Genoa. Blood pours, hunger for wheat, mercy to none.*
Sang efpancher, frofaim[1] à nul mercy.	

This may continue the horrors depicted in the last quatrain, with the war spreading through Switzerland, Italy and the Mediterranean. War and injury, famine and terror, all caused by the inhuman beast "both black and cold." I wonder if there is any connection with the hitherto undeciphered Aenobarbe?

Century VI

VI.LXXXII

Par les defers de lieu, libre, & farouche,	*Through the deserts of the free wild place, the nephew of the*
Viendra errer nepueu du grand Pontife:	*Great Pontiff will wander. Killed by seven with a heavy club, by*
Affommé à fept auecques lourde fouche,	*who will afterwards occupy the chalice.*
Par ceux qu'apres occuperont le cyphe.	

Several clues, such as the nephew of the Pope who is killed by people who soon afterwards take part of the Holy Sacrament. But, unfortunately impossible to place.

[1]*frofaim.* a concocted word. Probably from *froment-faim*, a hunger for wheat.

Century VI

VI.LXXXIII

*Celuy qu'aura tant d'honneur
    & caresses,
A son entree de la Gaule
    Belgique:
Vn temps apres sera tant de
    rudesses,
Et sera contre à la fleur tant
    bellique.*

*He will have so much honor and
affection at his entry into Belgian Gaul. A while later he will
act so crudely and will be very
bellicose towards the flower.*

When Charles V abdicated, Philip of Spain was well received
in the Netherlands (*Gaule Belgique*) until his bigotry alienated
the people to such a degree that they rose up in revolt in 1558.
The duc François d'Alençon was invited by the Netherlands
to become their Protector in 1580, but stupidly he attempted
to regain control of Antwerp and lost the loyalty of his
subjects. The flower in line 4 would be the fleur-de-lys of
France led by Henri IV, against whom Philip went to war from
1589 to 1598.

Century VI

VI.LXXXIIII

*Celuy qu'en Sparte Claude[1] ne
    peut regner,
Il fera tant par voye seductiue:
Que au court, long, le fera
    araigner,
Que contre Roy fera sa
    perspectiue.*

*The lame man who could not
rule in Sparta will do much with
his seductive ways. So that, by
the long and short of it he will be
accused of aiming his objectives
against the king.*

Line 1 probably merely refers to the fact that the Spartans
killed all children born imperfect and many girls by leaving
them exposed to the elements. As for famous men in history,
Nostradamus writes in detail of Talleyrand, lame from
childhood, but perhaps this could refer to Lord Byron, who

---

[1]*Claude*. L. *claudus*, lame.

suffered from a clubfoot and worked with the Greek freedom fighters. That would fulfill line 4.

Century VI
VI.LXXXV

La grand cité de Tharſe par
  Gaulois
Sera deſtruite, captifz tous à
  Turban:
Secours par mer du grand
  Portugalois,
Premier d'eſté le iour du ſacre
  Vrban.

The great city of Tarsus will be destroyed by the Gauls, all captured at Turban. Help from the sea from the great Portuguese. The first day of summer, Urban's consecration.

There are two major saints named Urban, whose feasts are celebrated on May 25 and January 23. The former is most likely the one referred to in this context, as summer begins on June 1. There are, incidentally, twelve other minor saints of the same name.

Nostradamus seems to envisage a French army capturing Tarsus in Asia Minor and continuing on to Asia. Portugal was one of the greatest sea powers in Nostradamus' day and he envisages them as allies of the French. A failed quatrain in the main essentials.

Century VI
VI.LXXXVI

Le grand Prelat vn iour apres
  ſon ſonge,
Interpreté au rebours de ſon ſens:
De la Gaſcogne luy ſuruiendra
  vn monge,
Qui fera eſlire le grand Prelat
  de Sens.

One day the great prelate, after his dream is interpreted opposite to its meaning, a monk from Gascony will come to him who will cause the great prelate of Sens to be elected.

Too many prelates and nothing more specific than a misinterpreted dream.

Century VI

VI.LXXXVII

L'election faite dans Frankfort, N'aura nul lieu Milan s'oppoſera: Le ſien plus proche ſemblera ſi grand fort Que outre le Rhyn és mareſchz chaſſera.	The election made in Frankfurt will not be valid. Milan will oppose it. The closest follower will seem so very strong that he will drive him out beyond the Rhine into the marshes.

The election at Frankfurt was probably that of the coronation of Ferdinand as Holy Roman Emperor, which took place in 1558. Philip, who was Ferdinand's rival, had already been given Milan by his uncle, Charles V, before his death in 1542. Philip tries to drive Ferdinand out of Germany in line 4, and into the Netherlands. He was not at all successful in this but continued to intrigue against Ferdinand for the succession until 1562.

Century VI

VI.LXXXVIII

Vn regne grand demourra deſolé, Aupres del Hebro ſe feront aſſemblees: Monts Pyrenees le rendront conſolé, Lors que dans May ſeront terres tremblees.	A great kingdom will remain desolate. Near the Ebro they will be gathered in assemblies. The Pyrenean mountains will console him when in May there will be earth tremors.

The last line is the only one that I can relate to here. Elsewhere Nostradamus refers to a great earthquake that will take place in May, which he tentatively places on the west coast of America during the next decade, certainly some time before the Millennium. The European side of the quatrain is not clear.

Century VI

VI.LXXXIX

*Entre deux cymbes piedz &
  mains eftachés,
De miel face oingt & de laict
  fubftanté:
Guefpes & mouches, fitine[1]
  amour fachés,
Poccilateur faucer, Cyphe
  tempté.*

*Feet and hands bound between
boots, the face anointed with
honey and touched with milk.
Wasps and flies, fatherly love
angered, the cupbearer lies, the
goblet tried.*

The fact that the face of the victim is anointed with milk and
honey indicates that the person referred to was a crowned
king, for this anointment was part of the coronation service.
The wasps and flies may stand for the angry populace. With
hands and feet bound it seems as though this quatrain refers
to Louis XVI on the way to his execution. (See I.LVII.)

Century VI

VI.XC

*L'honniffement puant
  abhominable
Apres le faict fera felicité,
Grand excufé, pour n'eftre
  fauorable,
Qu'à paix Neptune ne fera
  incité.*

*The stinking and abominable
shame, after the deed he will be
congratulated. The great one is
excused for not being favorable,
so that Neptune cannot be tempted towards peace.*

Someone gets away with a deed of such skulduggery that it
is almost incredible. Yet he is unsuspected and congratulated
despite the fact he cannot arrange for a naval peace. He was
presumably in communication with the enemy.

[1]*fitine.* Gk. *phitus*, father.

Century VI

VI.XCI

Du conducteur de la guerre nauale,	Of the leader of the naval war, the red one unbridled, a severe, horrible quarrel. Captive, escaped from the older one in the saddle, when the great Agrippa bears a son.
Rouge effrené, seuere horrible grippe,	
Captif eschappé de l'aisné dans la baste:	
Quant il naistra du grand vn filz Agrippe.	

The naval commanders in Nostradamus' time were the baron de la Garde and M. de la Molé. The rest of the quatrain is obscure unless the "red one" is a Communist leader creating great trouble in more modern times.

Century VI

VI.XCII

Prince de beauté tant venuste,	A prince of such handsome looks intrigues against his person, betrayed to the second rank. The city put to the sword, consumed with a powder that burns. By this, so great a murder, the head of the king is hated.
Au chef menee, le second faict trahy:	
La cité au glaiue de poudre face adufte,	
Par trop grand meurtre le chef du Roy hay.	

Louis XVI was considered to be very handsome as a youth but many intrigues, *menees*, were directed against him, and he was deposed to the "second rank" of a Constitutional monarch. Then he was betrayed by the Revolution. The line *poudre face adufte* has been most cleverly interpreted by James Laver from the latin *fax*, a torch, and *adustus*, burned or consumed by a powder that burns. After his execution on the guillotine the king's head was taken from the wicker basket into which it had fallen, and placed in quicklime. Line 3, *cité au glaiue*, is an excellent description of Revolutionary Paris.

Century VI

VI.XCIII

Prelat auare d'ambition trompé.
Rien ne ſera que trop viendra
cuider:
Ses meſſagiers, & luy bien
attrapé,
Tout au rebours voir, qui le
bois fendroit.

The great prelate deceived by ambition will think nothing is too great (for him). He and his messengers, completely trapped. The man who cuts the woods sees everything in reverse.

I can make nothing of this quatrain.

Century VI

VI.XCIIII

Vn Roy iré ſera aux
ſedifragues,[1]
Quant interdicts ſeront harnois
de guerre:
La poiſon taincte au ſuccre par
les fragues[2]
Par eaux meurtris, mors, diſant
ſerre ſerre.

A king will be angry with the sedifrages when warlike arms are prohibited. The sugar tainted with poison in the strawberries. Murdered by water, death saying close, close.

Those who break the Seat, *ſedifragues*, probably refers to the various Protestant sects who helped break up the unity of the See of Rome.

---

[1]*ſedifragues*. a compound word Nostradamus invented, probably from L. *sedem frangere*, which taken literally means to break a seat.
[2]*fragues*. L. *fraga*, strawberries.

Century VI

VI.XCV

*Par detracteur calumnié à puis
     nay.
Quant iftront faicts enormes &
     martiaux:
La moindre part dubieufe à
     l'aifnay,
Et toft au regne feront faicts
     partiaux.*

*Calumny against the younger
born by the detractor, when enormous, martial deeds will occur.
The least part doubtful for the
elder one. Soon in the kingdom
there will be partisan actions.*

I cannot make anything of this quatrain.

Century VI

VI.XCVI

*Grande cité à foldatz
     abandonnée,
Onques n'y euft mortel tumult fi
     proche,
O quel hideuse calamité
     s'approche,
Fors vne offence n'y fera
     pardonnée.*

*A great city abandoned to the
soldiers, there was never a mortal tumult so close. Oh what
dreadful calamity approaches.
Except for one offense it will not
be forgiven.*

This quatrain is so general that it could apply to the sack of
any city, St. Quentin in 1557, or Paris during the Revolution.
But I believe that line 3 predicts the Millennium. A very
interesting new theory has just been published by the Oxford
astrophysicist Dr. Victor Cube. He suggests that the earth is
bombarded by comets about every one thousand years, and
that the time is now ripe for another comet storm, which
would cause a "nuclear winter." He suggests that an earlier
attack might have been responsible for the Ice Age and have
caused the medieval Church to believe that the Millennium,
Judgment Day, would arrive around A.D. 1000.

Century VI

VI.XCVII

Cinq & quarante degrés ciel
 bruſlera,
Feu approcher de la grand cité
 neufue,
Inſtant grand flamme eſparſe
 ſautera,
Quant on voudra des Normans
 faire preuue.

The sky will burn at forty-five
degrees. Fire approaches the
great New City. Immediately a
huge scattered flame leaps up
when they want to have proof of
the Normans.

New York City lies between 40 and 45 degrees parallel in the USA. It is often referred to by Nostradamus as the *Cité neufue*, which was its contemporary name during Nostradamus' lifetime. It appears that the attack on the city is widespread, *inſtant grand flamme eſparſe ſautera*. It is certainly a futuristic quatrain. Where and how France is involved is unclear—by 1992 it will stand after all for the European Community—but it is also involved in similar quatrains. (See X.XLIX, I.XLI and IX.XLII.)

Century VI

VI.XCVIII

Ruyne aux Volſques[1] de peur ſi
 fort terribles,
Leur grand cité taincte, faict
 peſtilent:
Piller Sol, Lune & violer leurs
 temples:
Et les deux fleuues rougir de
 ſang coulant.

Ruin for the Vocae, so very terrible with fear, their great city
stained by a pestilential deed. To
plunder the Sun and Moon,
violate their temples and redden
the two rivers running with
blood.

The plundered sun and moon stand for gold and silver. The capital city of Languedoc is probably Toulouse. It seems as though a state of general insurrection occurs there. Unlikely to be a successful prediction now.

[1]*Volſques*. People of Languedoc, southern France.

Century VI

VI.XCIX

*L'ennemy docte ſe tournera
    confus,
Grâd camp malade, & de faict
    par embuſches,
Môts Pyrenees & Poenus luy
    ſerôt faicts refus,
Proche du fleuue deſcouurât
    antiques oruches.*

The learned enemy will turn
around confused, the great camp
sick and defeated in the
ambushes. Both the mountains of
the Pyrenees and the Pennines
will be refused to him. Near the
river discovering ancient urns.

I cannot decipher this quatrain.

Century VI

VI.C

*LEGIS CANTIO CONTRA
    INEPTOS CRITICOS.*

*Quos legent hoſce verſus maturè
    cenſunto,
Profanum vulgus & inſcium ne
    attrectato:
Omnesq; Aſtrologi Blenni,[1]
    Barbari procul ſunto,
Qui aliter facit, is ritè, ſacer
    esto.*

INCANTATION OF THE
LAW AGAINST INEPT
CRITICS

May those who read this verse
think upon it deeply. Let the pro-
fane and ignorant herd keep
away. Let all astrologers, idiots
and barbarians stay far off. He
who does otherwise, let him be
priest to the rite.

This quatrain of doggerel verse in medieval Latin gives the
reader a good idea of the type of construction and vocabulary
used by Nostradamus when writing Latin as he would have
done throughout his professional life as doctor and philo-
sopher. The inclusion of astrologers in this verse must mean
those who did not make it a lifetime study, as did Nostradamus. Or perhaps it is just an attempt to bluff the authorities.
Line 4 sounds vaguely like a threat: Let no one study
Nostradamus' work lightly.

[1] *Blenni.* Gk. *Blennos*, simpleton, idiot.

Century VII

VII.I

L'Arc du threſor par Achilles
    deçeu,
Aux procrées[1] ſçeu la
    quadrâgulaire:
Au faict Royal le côment ſera
    ſçeu,
Cors veu pêdu au veu du
    populaire.

The arc of the treasure deceived
by Achilles; the quadrangle
known to the procreators. The
intention will be manifest by a
royal deed. A corpse seen hanging in the sight of the populace.

There are only two well-known Achilles in French history.
The first was Achille de Harlay, Président of the Parlement de
Paris, who contributed to the downfall of Catherine de'
Medicis' favorite, Concini. He was eventually assassinated in
1617. The other was the Marshal of France, Achille Bazaine,
whose incapacity and defeatism led to the fall of France in
1870.

However, I wonder whether this quatrain has magical
overtones? Was Nostradamus trying to raise the spirit of the
Greek hero Achilles through *la quadrâgulaire*, possibly at the
wish of Catherine de' Medicis, who certainly dabbled with the
occult during the first ten years of her marriage before she
conceived her first child. It is believed, incidentally, that the
fault for this infertility lay with the king. He had an operation
in adulthood and Catherine then conceived seven children
who survived childbirth. It is quite possible that the corpse
seen was someone hanged for one of the many capital offenses
that existed at the time, or maybe a hanged man was necessary
to the ritual. I leave this to the reader.

procreés. Other MSS. offer the variant *procès* which would offer the
better reading "in the documents."

Century VII

VII.II

Par Mars ouuert Arles ne donra guerre, *De nuict feront les foldartz eftonnés:* *Noir, blanc à l'inde diffimulés en terre,* *Souz la faincte vmbre traiftres verez & fonnés.*	*Arles opened up by war will not offer resistance, the soldiers will be overcome by night. Black & white concealing indigo on land. Under the false shadow you will see traitors assessed.*

An unintelligible quatrain. What or who are the black, white and indigo?

Century VII

VII.III

Apres de France la victoire nauale, *Les Barchinons, Saillinons,[1] les Phocens,* *Lierre d'or, l'enclume ferré dedans la bafle,* *Ceux de Ptolon[2] au fraud feront confens.*	*After the naval victory of France the people of Barcelona, the Siallinons and those of Marseilles. The robber of gold, the anvil enclosed in the ball. The people of Ptolon will be party to the fraud.*

It is impossible to fix the dating of the French naval battle from the remaining material of the quatrain. The Barchinons may come from Barcelona. Both the Saillinons and Ptolons are unclear.

---

[1] *Saillinons.* Not identified.
[2] *Ptolon.* Either Egypt, the land of Ptolemy or Acre, which was normally known as *Ptolemais.*

Century VII

VII.IIII

Le duc de Langres aſſiegé dedans Dolle, *Accompaigné d'Oſtun & Lyonnois:* *Geneue, Auſpour, ioinct ceux de Mirandole,* *Paſſer les monts contre les Anconnois.*	*The duc de Langres besieged at Dôle, accompanied by people from Autun and Lyons. Geneva, Augsburg allied to those of Mirandola, to cross the mountains against the people of Ancona.*

This complicated quatrain describes the duc de Guise (Langres), together with soldiers from Autun and Lyons, besieged at Dôle during an attack on the Spanish. At the same time armies of the Empires from Geneva, Augsburg and northern Italy will invade the Papal States. Ancona belonged to the Pope.

Century VII

VII.V

Vin ſur la table en ſera reſpandu, *Le tiers n'aura celle qu'il pretendoit:* *Deux fois du noir[1] de Parme deſcendu,* *Perouſe à Pize fera ce qu'il cuidoit.*	*Some of the wine on the table will be spilled, the third will not have that which he claimed. Twice descended from the black one of Parma. Perouse will do to Pisa that which he believed in.*

Century VII

VII.VI

Naples, Palerme, & toute la Secille, *Par main barbare ſera inhabitee,* *Corſicque, Salerne & de Sardeigne l'iſle,* *Faim peſte, guerre fin de maux intemptee.[2]*	*Naples, Palermo and all of Sicily will be uninhabited through barbarian might. Corsica, Salerno and the island of Sardinia; hunger, plague, war, the end of extended evils.*

---

[1]*noir.* The usual anagram for *roi* may be permissible here.
[2]*intemptee.* L. *intentatus,* extended, stretched.

This is probably a retroactive quatrain. It predicts in general terms the invasion of Sicily and southern Italy as well as of Corsica and Sardinia. There were many such raids made by Barbary pirates both before and during the sixteenth century, when Nostradamus wrote the *Propheties*.

Century VII

VII.VII

Sur le combat des grans chevaux legiers,	Upon the struggle of the great light horses it will be claimed
On criera le grand croiſſant confond.	that the great crescent is destroyed. To kill by night, in the
De nuict tuer monts, habits de bergiers,	mountains, dressed in shepherd's clothing, red gulfs in the deep
Abiſmes rouges dans le foſſé profond.	ditch.

The crescent moon was the symbol of the Turks and of Islam. Apparently Nostradamus sees them as suffering a great defeat, probably from a cavalry attack, line 1. The red gulfs are probably rivers of blood resulting from the slaughter. A graphic quatrain, but irritating as it is so unspecific.

Century VII

VII.VIII

Flora fuis, fuis le plus proche Romain,	Florence flee, flee the nearest Roman. At Fiesole will conflict
Au feſulan ſera conflict donné:	be exchanged. Blood shed, the
Sang eſpandu les plus grans prins à main,	greatest ones taken by the hand. Neither temple nor sex will be
Temple ne ſexe ne ſera pardonné.	forgiven.

A failed quatrain. It appears to predict that Florence will suffer a severe attack by Vatican troops. As Fiesole is only a few miles away, it would naturally suffer the same fate.

Century VII

VII.IX

Dame à l'abſence de ſon grand
   capitaine,
Sera priee d'amours du Viceroy,
Faincte promeſſe & malheureuſe
   eſtraine,
Entre les mains du grand
   prince Barroys.

The lady, in the absence of her
great master will be begged for
love by the viceroy. Feigned
promise and misfortune and
love, in the hands of the great
prince of Bar.

France has never had a viceroy, the only comparable offices
being those of the constable of France or the lieutenant
general, an office held by the Guises when Nostradamus
wrote. There is no question that this quatrain could apply to
India, as it is a country ignored by Nostradamus, for whatever
reason.

The title of the duc de Bar was given to the eldest son of
the duc de Lorraine. As the duke was a minor there was no
duc de Bar during that period. It is unlikely that *Dame* refers
to the queen, Catherine de' Medicis, but it may well refer to
Henri II's mistress Diane de Poitiers, who would at this time
be in her late fifties. She never allowed any portraits of her to
be painted showing her after the age of twenty, in order to
preserve her search for youth in her face.

Century VII

VII.X

Par le grand prince limitrophe
   du Mans,
Preux & vaillant chef de grand
   exercite:
Par mer & terre de Gallotz &
   Normans,
Caſpre paſſer Barcelone pillé iſle.

By the great prince bordering Le
Mans, the brave and valiant
leader of the great army. By land
and sea with Bretons and Normans, to pass Gibraltar and
Barcelona to pillage the island.

Le Mans used to be the principal city of Maine in northwest
France; Mayenne, the next in importance, belonged to the
Guise family. During Nostradamus' lifetime Le Mans was held

by Claude, the marquis of Mayenne and duc d'Amale. He
fought at Metz in 1552 and later at Calais, Saint Denis, Dreux
and Montcoeur, but he never invaded Spain or North Africa.
Nostradamus seems to have foreseen a much greater future
for him in the Mediterranean basin than ever occurred, so this
quatrain is, in part, a failure.

Century VII

VII.XI

L'enfant Royal contemnera la
  mere,
Oeil, piedz bleſſés, rude,
  inobeiſſant,
Nouuelle à dame eſtrange &
  bien amere,
Seront tués des ſiens plus de
  cinq cens.

The royal child will scorn his
mother; eye, feet wounded, rude,
disobedient. Strange and very
bitter news to the lady. More
than five hundred of her people
will be killed.

This quatrain seems to refer to the quarrel of a queen with
her son. Since Nostradamus' lifetime there has been only one
notable example of this, between Louis XIII and his mother
Marie de Medicis. Garencières says that more than five
hundred of the queen's supporters were killed in the dispute.
A satisfactory quatrain.

Century VII

VII.XII

Le grand puisné fera fin de la
  guerre,
Aux dieux assemble les excusés:
Cahors, Moissac iront long de
  la serre,
Reffus Lestore, les Agenois
  razés.

The great younger one will make
an end of the war. He assembles
those pardoned before the gods.
Cahors and Moissac will go far
from the prison. A refusal at
Lectoure, the people of Agen
shaved.

The younger brother of a ruling king or the descendant of
a younger brother of the king was known as the Cadet branch.
However this quatrain is unclear. The last line describes what

sounds like retribution, as for example when the French shaved the heads of any person they found collaborating with the Nazis and the Nazis did the same to the Jews in the concentration camps.

Century VII

VII.XIII

De la cité marine & tributaire,	*From the marine tributary city*
La teſte raze prendra la ſatrapie:	*the shaven head will take up the*
Chaſſer ſordide qui puis ſera contṛaire,	*satrapy to chase the sordid man who will then be against him.*
Par quatorze ans tiendra la tyrannie.	*For fourteen years he will hold the tyranny.*

Bonaparte, of the shaven head, will retake Toulon, the marine city, from the English in 1793, from the English military led by Sir Arthur Wellesley, who had made the city a tributary. Napoleon then goes on to overthrow the Directoire *ſordide*, and put an end to the Republic. He did enjoy absolute power (*la tyrannie*) for fourteen years (November, 1799 to April, 1814). Le Pelletier in his commentary believes that the sordid one (*ſordide*) referred to the English but otherwise roughly agrees with this interpretation.

Century VII

VII.XIIII

Faux expoſer viendra topographie,	*He will come to oppose the false topography, the urns of the tombs*
Seront les cruches des monumens ouuertes:	*will be opened. Sect and holy philosophy to thrive; black for*
Palluler ſecte ſaincte philoſophie,	*white, the new for the old.*
Pour blanches, noires, & pour antiques vertes.	

On December 22, 1789, the National Assembly changed the ancient regional districts of France into Départements. Nostradamus feels that the tombs of the French kings, traditionally interred at St. Denis, will be violated and their ashes scattered.

This is, together with the antireligious bias of the quatrain, just a general comment upon the extremes of the Revolution.

Century VII

VII.XV

Deuant cité de l'Infubre[1] contree, *Sept ans fera le fiege deuant mis:* *Le trefgrand Roy y fera fon entree,* *Cité puis libre hors de fes ennemis.*	Before the city of the Insubrian lands the siege will be laid for seven years. A great king enters then the city is free, away from its enemies.

Probably a failed quatrain. Nostradamus seems to predict a very long drawn-out siege of Milan (*Infubre*) which will last for seven years. The liberating king will free Milan from its Spanish masters. This belongs to the seventeenth or eighteenth centuries and is unlikely to be fulfilled now.

Century VII

VII.XVI

Entree profonde par la grand Royne faicte *Rendra le lieu puiffant inacceffible:* *L'armee des troys lyons fera deffaite,* *Faifant dedans cas hideux & terrible.*	The profound entry made by the great queen will make the place powerful and inaccessible. The army of the three lions will be defeated, causing within a thing hideous and terrible.

The great queen, Mary Tudor, held Calais "engraved upon her heart" until it was recaptured for the French by the duc de Guise in 1558. At this period, England was an ally of Spain, due to Mary's marriage to Philip. The three lions are part of the English standard. A comparatively successful quatrain

[1]*Infubre*. L. *Insubria*, the area around Milan

Century VII

VII.XVII

Le prince rare de pitié &
  clemence,
Viendra changer par mort grād
  cognoiſſance:
Par grand repos le regne
  trauaillé,
Lors que le grand toſt ſera
  eſtrillé.

The prince who has little pity or
mercy will come through death to
change (becoming) very know-
ledgeable. The kingdom will be
attended with great tranquility,
when the great one will soon be
passed.

Again, a quatrain I cannot decipher.

Century VII

VII.XVIII

Les aſſiegés couloureront leurs
  paches,
Sept iours apres feront cruelle
  iſſue
Dans repoulſés feu, ſang. Sept
  mis à l'hache
Dame captiue qu'auoit la paix
  tiſſue.

The besieged will color their
pacts, but seven days later they
will make a cruel exit. Thrown
back inside, fire and blood.
Seven put to the axe the lady who
had woven the peace is captive.

This is an obscure quatrain describing a treacherous enemy
who, while besieged, pretends to sue for peace but seven days
later makes a disastrous attempt to escape. Line 4 could well
refer to Nostradamus' period. The Peace of Cambrai, insti-
gated in 1529, was known as the Ladies Charter because it was
negotiated (*tiſſue*) by the mother of François I and the aunt of
Charles V.

Century VII

VII.XIX

Le fort Nicene ne ſera combatu,
Vaincu ſera par rutilant metal
Son faict ſera vn long temps
    debatu,
Aux citadins eſtrange
    eſpouuantal.

The fort at Nice will not engage
in combat, it will be overcome by
shining metal. This deed will be
debated for a long time, strange
and fearful for the citizens.

Nice has been captured twice since Nostradamus wrote the
Prophéties, in 1705 and 1891, both times by the French.

Century VII

VII.XX

Ambaſſadeurs de la Toſcane
    langue,
Auril & May Alpes & mer
    paſſer:
Celuy de veau[1] expoſera
    l'harangue,
Vie Gauloiſe ne venant effacer.

Ambassadors of the Tuscan lan-
guage will cross the Alps and the
sea in April and May. The man
of the calf will deliver an ora-
tion, not coming to wipe out the
French way of life.

The good relations which existed between Napoleon III and
the Pope were spoiled when Cavour arrived in Paris in 1854
to plead the cause of Italian unity. The Congress at Paris took
place during the months Nostradamus predicted, April and
May. The reason for naming Cavour the man of the calf *(celuy
de veau)* is obscure but fascinating. It is a typical Nostradamus
contortion of the facts. Cavour was the envoy of Turin and
Torino means the city of the bull. It was known as *Augusta
Taurinorium* by the Romans, so Cavour is thus the offspring of
the calf.

[1] *de veau.* Some commentators think this should read *de Vaud,* a Swiss
canton; but I quite like my interpretation of Nostradamus' puns in the
second meaning of Cavour.

Century VII

VII.XXI

Par peſtilente inimitié Volſicque,
Diſſimulee chaſſera le tyran:
Au pont de Sorgues ſe fera la
   traffique,
De mettre à mort luy & ſon
   adherant.

By the pestilential enmity of Languedoc the dissimulated tyrant will be driven out. The bargain will be made on the bridge at Sorgues to put to death both him and his follower.

This is probably the bridge at Sorgues, the main town on the river of the same name. It belonged to the Vatican State in 1791. Languedoc is a large province to the west of the Rhône. Otherwise an irritating, vague quatrain.

Century VII

VII.XXII

Les citoyens de Meſopotamie,[1]
Yrés encontre amis de
   Tarraconne,[2]
Ieux, ritz, banquetz, toute gent
   endormie
Vicaire au Roſne, prins cité,
   ceux d'Auſone.[3]

The citizens of Mesopotamia are angry with the friends from Tarraconne. Games, rites, banquets, everyone invited. The vicar at Rhône, the city taken and those of Ausonia.

In this quatrain Nostradamus does not seem to use the word Mesopotamia as modern Iraq and he is probably using the word to describe a European town. The Venassin between the Rhône and the Durance at Avignon makes a great deal of sense in this context. The Vicar (of Rome) was Pope Pius VI, whom Napoleon had captured and imprisoned at Valence in 1799. The second part of line 4 describes how a French army led by General Championnet recaptured Rome and then went on to take Naples in 1799.

[1]*Meſopotamie.* Either modern Iraq, or the Venassin between the Rhône and the Durance at Avignon or Paris between the Seine and Marne.
[2]*Tarraconne.* L. *Tarroca,* Tarragona in Catalonia, Spain, or less likely *Tarraconensis,* the northeastern part of Roman Iberia.
[3]*Auſone.* Southern Italy, probably Naples.

Century VII

VII.XXIII

Le Royal ſceptre sera contrainct
  de prendre,
Ce que ſes predeceſſeurs auoient
  engaigé:
Puis que l'aneau on fera mal
  entendre,
Lors qu'on viendra le palays
  ſaccager.

The royal scepter will be forced
to take that which his predecessor
had pledged. Because they do not
understand about the ring when
they come to sack the palace.

Hugh Allan, at best an unreliable commentator on Nostradamus, wrote categorically in 1943 that the scene of this
pawnbroking of royal jewels would take place in Buckingham
Palace! The ring and the scepter are part of the royal regalia
at most coronations. But otherwise a very frustrating quatrain.

Century VII

VII.XXIIII

L'enſeuely ſortyra du tombeau,
Fera de chaines lier le fort du
  pont:
Empoyſonné auec oeufz de
  Barbeau,
Grand de Lorraine par le
  Marquis du Pont.[1]

He who was buried will come out
of the tomb, he will free the
strong one from the bridge to be
bound with chains. Poisoned
with the roe, or eggs of a barbel,
the great one from Lorraine by
the Marquis du Pont.

The barbel is a freshwater fish found throughout Europe.
What is symbolized here is unclear. The grand one from
Lorraine is probably the duke, Charles III, who was taken
from his family to be reared in the French court. Later the
marquisate of Bar passed to the sons of the House of Lorraine.
Nostradamus predicts that the duc is to be poisoned by the
marquis, one of the younger sons. A failed quatrain.

---

[1]*Marquis du Pont.* The younger son of the House of Lorraine had
the title of Marquis du Pont à Mousson

Century VII

VII.XXV

Par guerre longue tout l'exercite expuiſer,	Through the long war all the army exhausted, so that they do
Que pour ſouldartz ne trouueront pecune:	not find money for the soldiers.
Lieu d'or d'argent, cuir on viendra cuſer,[1]	Instead of gold or silver they will start to coin leather. Gallic brass
Gaulois aerain, ſigne croiſſant de Lune.	and the crescent sign of the moon.

The quatrain refers to the dreadful battles of the First World War which ranged across hundreds of miles, and killed thousands of soldiers each week. Many commentators believe this may refer to campaigns such as Gallipoli. To the east the Allies were fighting on the hills of the Dardanelles and falling before the lethal gunfire of the Turks, *ſigne croiſſant*. I do not understand the reference to payment by leather instead of coinage, but it might refer to barter among the soldiers on the battlefield.

Century VII

VII.XXVI

Fuſtes & galees autour de ſept nauires,	Foists and galleys around seven ships, a mortal war will be let
Sera liuree vne mortelle guerre:	loose. The leader from Madrid
Chef de Madric[2] receura coup de vires,[3]	will receive a wound from two arrows; two escaped and five
Deux eſchapees & cinq menees à terre.	brought to land.

In November, 1555, some privateers attacked a Spanish fleet in the Channel. *Vives* should be read as *virer*, a nautical verb, to attack. The privateers concentrated upon the admiral's ship and succeeded in capturing it, together with four other ships which came to its aid, *cinq menees à terre*. They were towed

[1]*cuſer*. L. *cusare*, O.F. *cudere*, to mint money.
[2]*Madric*. Presumably printer's error for *Madrid*.
[3]*vires*. alternative *vires*, arrows, or *virer*, a nautical word, to attack.

victoriously to Dieppe. An excellent quatrain, but it may be
retroactive due to the date, the same as that of the publication
of the first part of the *Prophéties*.

Century VII

VII.XVII

Au cainct[1] de Vaſt[2] la grand
   caualerie,
Proche à Ferrage empeſchee au
   bagaige:
Prompt à Turin feront tel
   volerie,
Que dans le fort rauiront leur
   hoſtaige.

*At the wall of Vasto the great
cavalry are impeded by the baggage near Ferrara. At Turin
they will speedily commit such
robbery that they will ravish their
hostage in the fort.*

There are nine villages in France named Vast, plus a
monastery near Arras and a harbor near Cherbourg. None of
these seem to help. Alternatively, the quatrain may refer to
Alphonso II, marquis de Vasto, 1502–1544, who was governor
of Milan from 1537 onwards. He retired to Asti in 1554 and
this may stand for Ferrara as it was a duchy in the House of
Este, seized by the Papal States in 1547. An unsatisfactory
quatrain nevertheless, unlikely to be fulfilled in the future.

Century VII

VII.XXVIII

Le capitaine conduira grande
   proye,
Sur la montaigne des ennemis
   plus proche,
Enuironné, par feu fera tel
   voye,
Tous eſchappez or[3] trente mis en
   broche.

*The captain will lead a great
herd on the mountain closest to
the enemy. Surrounded by fire he
forces such a route, all escape
except for thirty put on the spit.*

---

[1] *cainct.* O.F. belt or waist. Possibly used here to mean encircling.
[2] *Vaſt.* uncertain meaning, see commentary.
[3] *or.* misprint for *hors* in other editions, without, except for.

Most commentators understand "put on the spit," *mis en broche*, as meaning that the unlucky victims were run through. However, I think that Nostradamus is describing them as being roasted alive. Apart from that, the quatrain could refer to many possible events either in war or peacetime. I can make nothing further of it.

Century VII

VII.XXIX

Le grand Duc d'Albe ſe viendra rebeller	The great one of Alba will come to rebel, he will betray his great forebears. The great man of Guise will come to vanquish him, led captive, with a monument erected.
A ſes grans peres fera le tradiment:	
Le grand de Guiſe le viendra debeller,	
Captif mené & dreſſé monument.	

At first sight a very clear quatrain, but sadly it is not accurate. The duke of Alba was in charge of all the Spanish forces and the duc de Guise of the French. But de Guise never triumphed over Alba, let alone took him captive. Perhaps Nostradamus foresaw Alba crossing over to the French, which he did from 1555–57, to fight against the Vatican States. Probably wishful thinking on the prophet's part.

Century VII

VII.XXX

Le ſac s'approche, feu, grand ſang eſpandu	The sack approaches, fire and great bloodshed. Po, the great rivers, the enterprise for the clowns. After a long wait from Genoa and Nice, Fussana, Turin; the capture at Savigliano.
Po, grand fleuues, aux bouuiers[1] l'entreprinſe,	
De Gennes, Nice, apres long attendu,	
Fouſſan, Turin, à Sauillan la prinſe.	

---

[1] *bouuiers*. O.F. clowns or cowherds.

Another infuriating quatrain, with lots of names and no real facts. Fossano, Turin and Savigliano were all in Piedmont, but Nice had been lost to the House of Savary. Genoa at this time was an independent state under the Hapsburgs.

Century VII
VII.XXXI

*De Languedoc, & Guienne plus
  de dix,
Mille voudront les Alpes repaſſer:
Grans Allobroges[1] marcher
  contre Brundis
Aquin & Breſſe les viendront
  recaſſer.*

From Languedoc and Guienne more than ten thousand will want to cross the Alps again. The great Savoyards march against Brindisi. Aquino and Bresse will come to drive them back.

The action in this quatrain is unclear. The place names are all so separate. Languedoc and Guienne were in southwest France, Bresse belonged to Savoy until 1601. Brindisi is in southern Italy and along with Aquino, was a vassal of the Two Sicilies. I get very frustrated with quatrains in the Seventh Century, unfinished as it is. Maybe the reason the verses are so obscure is quite simply that Nostradamus had not gone over them properly before his death, and his pupil Chavigny did not have the courage to shape them into more interesting material.

Century VII
VII.XXXII

*Du mont Royal naiſtra d'vne
  caſane,[2]
Qui caue, & compte viendra
  tyranniſer
Dreſſer copie de la marche
  Millane,
Fauene, Florence d'or & gens
  eſpuiſer.*

From the bank of Montereale will be born someone who is both calculating and boring, becoming a tyrant. To raise a force in the Marches of Milan, to drain Faenza and Florence of gold and men.

[1]*Allobroges.* L. the inhabitants of Savoy.
[2]*caſane.* Low L. *casana,* bank.

The Medici family came from the area of Florence called Montereale. Could this be a warning to Catherine concerning her family? Apart from this, one has the usual geographical chaos. Milan belonged to the Hapsburgs, Faenza was part of the Papal States and Florence, as I have said, belonged to the Medicis. Obviously a failed quatrain.

Century VII

VII.XXXIII

Par fraude regne, forces expolier,[1]
La claſſe obſeſſe, paſſages à l'eſpie:
Deux fainctz amys ſe viendront rallier,
Eſueiller hayne de long temps aſſoupie.

The kingdom stripped of its forces by fraud, the fleet blockaded, passages for the spy. Two false friends will come to rally (round), awakening a hatred dormant for a long time.

This is a typical Nostradamus prediction which may have been fulfilled several times since it was written. It is usually interpreted as describing the Fall of France in 1940. Line 3 would apply to the Germans and the Russians and line 4 to the Anglo-French connections. The following quatrain seems to continue this theme.

Century VII

VII.XXXIIII

En grand regret ſera la gent Gauloiſe,
Coeur vain, legier croira temerité:
Pain, ſel, ne vin, eaue: venin ne ceruoiſe,
Plus grand captif, faim, froit, neceſſité.

The French nation will be in great grief, vain and light-hearted they will believe rash things. No bread, salt, wine or water, venom nor ale. The greater one captured. Hunger, cold and want.

This quatrain seems to follow upon VII.XXXIII and is yet a further description of the appalling deprivations suffered by

[1]*expolier.* O.F. plunder, strip, despoil.

the French under German occupation. Bread, salt, wine and water would be considered by Nostradamus as the basics of life. "The greater one captured." I am not certain whom this refers to, certainly not Hitler in this context, although the cold and want (*faim, froit*) continued for some years after the war.

Century VII

VII.XXXV

*Le grande pefche viendra plaindre, plorer
D'auoir efleu, trompés feront en l'aage:
Guiere auec eux ne voudra demourer,
Deçeu fera par ceux de fon langaige.*

The great fish will come to complain and weep for having made his choice, deceived concerning his age. He will hardly want to remain with them, deceived by those of his own tongue.

Henri III, the third son of Catherine de' Medicis and Henri II, was elected king of Poland in the unrestrained manner used at the time, *pefche*, which also implies a lottery. He hated it and on the premature death of his brother Charles IX, he managed to escape from the Polish court and retain his claim to the French throne. This upset the political arrangements of both Poland and France to found new dynasties. Henri III was deceived, *deçeu*, by a fellow Frenchman, Jacques Clément, who also managed to assassinate him. A good, factual quatrain.

Century VII

VII.XXXVI

*Dieu, le ciel tout le diuin verbe à l'vnde,
Porté par rouges fept razes à Bizance:
Contre les oingz trois cens de Trebifconde,
Deux loix mettront, & horreur, puis credence.*

God, the heavens, all the divine words on the waves, carried by seven red-shaven heads to Byzantium. Against the anointed three hundred from Trebizond will make two laws; first horror, the trust.

The seven red heads are almost certainly cardinals of the Roman Catholic Church, who not only wear red robes but red skullcaps. But what are they doing going to Constantinople? Trying to convert the sultan? I can find no record of any incident similar to this so conclude it is a failed quatrain.

Century VII

VII.XXXVII

Dix enuoyés, chef de nef mettre
  à mort,
D'vn aduerty, en claſſe guerre
  ouuerte:
Confuſion chef, l'vn ſe picque &
  mord,
Leryn, ſtecades[1] nefz, cap
  dedans la nerte.[2]

Ten sent to put the captain of the ship to death are warned by one, that there is open revolt in the fleet. Confusion; the leader and the man stab and bite each other at Lerins and Hyères. Ships, prow into the darkness.

This dramatic quatrain heralds the unsuccessful attempted assassination of a naval commander. There is no clue as to whom he might be. The Isles de Lerins are off Cannes and those of Hyères off Toulon. Probably an unsuccessful quatrain.

Century VII

VII.XXXVIII

L'aiſné Royal ſur courſier
  voltigeant,
Picquer viendra, ſi rudement
  courir:
Gueulle, lipee, pied dans l'eſtrein
  pleignant
Trainé, tiré, horriblement
  mourir.

The elder Royal on a frisky horse will spur it so fiercely that it will bolt. Mouth, mouthful, foot complaining in the embrace. Dragged, pulled, to die horribly.

---

[1]ſtecades. L. *Stoechadef.* the Islands of Hyères.
[2]nerte. O.F. black. Possible Gk. *nerthe*, underneath.

The only French prince of the royal line who was killed in a riding accident was Crown Prince Ferdinand in 1842. He was the heir of Louis Philippe and his untimely death caused dynastic problems. A good quatrain.

Century VII

VII.XXXIX

*Le conducteur de l'armée
   Françoise,
Cuidant perdre le principal
   phalange:
Par ſus paire de l'auaigne &
   d'ardoiſe,
Soy parfondra par Gennes gent
   eſtrange.*

The leader of the French army will expect to lose the main phalanx. Upon the pavement of oats and slate the foreign nation will be undermined through Genoa.

I can make nothing of this quatrain apart from the fact that a French leader will lose an important part of his army.

Century VII

VII.XL

*Dedans tonneaux hors oingz
   d'huille & greſſe,
Seront vingt vn deuant le port
   fermés,
Au ſecond guet par mort feront
   proueſſe:
Gaigner les portes & du guet
   aſſommés.*

Within casks anointed outside with oil and grease, twenty-one will be shut before the harbor at the second watch. Through death they will do great deeds to win the gate and be killed by the watch.

It appears that Nostradamus is attempting to describe a seaport being captured rather in the manner of Ali Baba and his Forty Thieves! Apparently they succeed in entering the town but are killed by the guards. A failed quatrain.

Century VII

VII.XLI

Les oz des piedz & des mains
    enſerrés,
Par bruit maiſon long temps
    inhabitee:
Seront par ſonges concauant
    deterrés,
Maiſon ſalubre & ſans bruyt
    habitee.

The bones of the feet and the
hands are locked up. Because of
the noise the house is uninha-
bited for a long time. Digging in
dreams they will be unearthed,
the house healthy and inhabited
without noise.

This is certainly a description of the exorcism of a haunted
house which seems to quieten down when the bones of a victim
are removed. Perhaps line 3 indicates that the source of the
skeleton was discovered in a dream? Exorcism was a ceremony
greatly practiced by the Catholic Church in Europe in
Nostradamus' time and the seventeenth century.

Century VII

VII.XLII

Deux de poiſon ſaiſiz nouueau
    venuz,
Dans la cuiſine du grand
    Prince verſer:
Par le ſouillard tous deux au
    faict congneux,
Prins qui cuidoit de mort l'aiſné
    vexer.

Two newly arrived have seized
the poison to pour it in the
kitchen of the great prince. Both
are caught in the act by the scul-
lion, taken, he who thought to
trouble the elder with death.

This is a specific quatrain but with no facts behind it. Two
conspirators on a prince's kitchen staff try to poison him. They
are caught red-handed by the kitchen boy *le ſouillard*, but as
only one is reported captured, it is possible his accomplice got
away.

Century VII ends abruptly here. Neither Nostradamus nor
his disciple Chavigny give any reason for this. It seems unlikely
that the quatrains were suppressed, more probable that
Nostradamus had not written the full thousand he intended
to do before his death.

Century VIII

VIII.I

PAV, NAY, LORON plus feu
    qu'à ſang ſera.
Laude nager, fuir grand aux
    ſurrez.
Les agaſſas[1] entree refuſera.
Pampon,[2] Durance les tiendra
    enſerrez.

PAY, NAY, LORON will be
more fire than blood. Swim in
praise, the great one to flee the
confluence (of rivers). He will
refuse entry to the magpies.
Pampon and the Durance will
keep them confined.

Although the names in line 1 are all small towns in western
France, Nostradamus does seem to be talking about a person,
not places. The capital letters further indicate their importance; By anagram *PAV NAY LORON* becomes *Napaulon Roy*,
Napoleon the King. The varied spelling of Napoleon's name
with an *au* instead of an *a* was commonplace even in the
nineteenth century and one must also remember Nostradamus' personal and extremely unorthodox orthography. The
agassas, magpie or *Pie*, Pius, would refer to both Pius VI and
VII, who were imprisoned by Napoleon. The confluence of
rivers would then refer to Valence, where the rivers Rhône
and Isère meet and where Pius VI died in 1799. Pius VII was
taken first to Savoa and then on to Fontainbleau in 1872.
Therefore, neither was imprisoned near the Durance. A small
error in such an otherwise accurate quatrain. But on the other
hand, Durance is near Avignon, which belonged to the Papacy
until 1791. Both the Rhône and the Durance meet at the Papal
City.

---

[1]*agaſſas*. A.Pr. *aggasa*, a magpie, also known as *pie*, which is the French
spelling of Pius. A Nostradamus pun.
[2]*Pampon*. Doubtful, possibly Gk. *pamponeros*, depraved?

Century VIII

VIII.II

Condon & Aux & autour de
  Mirande
Le voy du ciel feu qui les
  enuironne.
Sol Mars conioint au Lyon puis
  marmande
Fouldre, grand greſle, mur
  tombe dans Garône.

Condom and Auch and around
Mirande, I see fire from the sky
which encompasses them. The
Sun and Mars conjoint in Leo.
Then at Marmande, lightning,
great hail, a wall falls into the
Garonne.

This is another irritating quatrain with many clues but none
that seem to relate to given fact. It is just possible that line 2
indicates the quatrain is futuristic, but personally I doubt it.
All the towns mentioned are in the Département of Gers in
the southwest, except for Marmande, which is about fifty miles
north. It is not possible to find a specific place where a wall has
fallen along the length of the Garonne.

Century VIII

VIII.III

Au fort chaſteau de Viglanne[1]
  & Reſuiers
Sera ſerré le puiſnay de Nancy:
Dedans Turin ſeront ards[2] les
  premiers,
Lors que de dueil Lyon ſera
  tranſy.

Within the strong castle of Vigilance and Resviers the younger
born of Nancy will be shut up.
In Turin the first ones will be
burned, when Lyons will be
transported with grief.

The names in the first line of this quatrain are difficult to
decipher, but the best combinations are in Italy. There is a
castle built by the Scaligers of Verona at Malescino. There is
also also a monastery founded by Saint Francis in Lake Garda
between San Vigilio and the Riviera. Nancy is the capital of
Lorraine, and the cadet a brother or younger branch of the

[1] *Viglanne.* Probably San Vigilio and the Riviera, but might stand for
Rubberia and Vignola.
[2] *ards.* L. *audere*, to burn.

family, most likely refers to Nicolas, duc de Mercoeur, the father-in-law of Henri III, who did not die until 1577. But despite all this detail, a failed quatrain. The duc was never imprisoned in a castle on Lake Garda. (Turin, line 3, belonged to the French at the time of Nostradamus' writings.)

Century VIII

VIII.IIII

Dedans Monech[1] le coq sera receu,	The Cock will be received into Monaco. The cardinal of France will appear. He will be deceived by the Roman legation. Weakness to the Eagle, strength will be born in the Cock.
Le Cardinal de France apparoistra	
Par Logarion[2] Romain sera deceu	
Foiblesse à l'aigle, & force au coq naistra.	

This was a totally misleading quatrain. If one reads *legation* for *Logarion*, in fact exactly the opposite occurred. The quatrain speaks of the struggle for power in the Mediterranean between the French and the Spanish. Monaco had nominal independence under the Grimaldis but was bound by treaty to help Spain. Nostradamus predicts that this protection refers to Charles, second Cardinal of Lorraine (1524–1547). There were two legates in France, the Vice Regal legate and the Papal Legate, both at Avignon. Nostradamus describes one of these legates deceiving the French, Hapsburg power declining, and that of the French expanding. In fact, this is the opposite of what happened. Monaco became a close ally of France and the French were driven out of Italy in 1559.

---

[1]*Monech. Monaceis,* Monaco.

[2]*Logarion.* Other texts print *legation,* which is a better reading in the context.

Century VIII

VIII.V

Apparoiſtra temple luiſant orné,	*There will appear a shining*
La lampe & cierge à Borne &	*ornate temple, the lamp and the*
Breteuil.	*candle at Borne and Breteuil.*
Pour la lucerne le canton	*For the canton of Lucerne will*
deſtorné,	*be turned aside, when one will*
Quand on verra le grand coq	*see the great cock in his shroud.*
au cercueil.	

Nostradamus predicts that a great French king will die at the same time as the canton of Lucerne will be conquered. This has never happened and is unlikely to happen in the future. A totally failed quatrain.

Century VIII

VIII.VI

Clarté fulgure à Lyon	*Lightning and brightness are*
apparante	*seen shining at Lyon, Malta is*
Luyſant, print Malte ſubit ſera	*taken and will be suddenly*
eſtainte,	*extinguished. Mauris will act*
Sardon,[1] Mauris[2] traitera	*deceitfully, Geneva to London,*
decepuante,	*feigning treason towards the*
Geneue à Londes à coq trahyſon	*cock.*
fainte.	

Malta was an independent state until the French Revolution. The Turks attacked it in 1565. Mauris, possibly Maurice, according to legend was leader of a Theban religion whose adherents were annihilated because they refused to murder Christians. His cult is still strong in Switzerland and Savoy. If Sardon stands for Sardinia, it belonged to the House of Savoy after 1720. Nostradamus indicates that Savoy stands for both regions, which means the quatrain pre-dates 1720. The involvement between Geneva and London probably describes

---

[1]*Sardon.* The most probable interpretation for this is Sardinia.

[2]*Mauris.* St. Maurice, the patron saint of much of the French Alps and Savoy.

Elizabeth I's involvement with Calvin in the Conspiracy of Amboise, 1566.

Century VIII

VIII.VII

*Verceil, Milan donra
    intelligence,
Dedans Tycin[1] sera faite la
    paye.[2]
Courir par Siene eau, sang, feu
    par Florence.
Vnique choir d'hault en bas
    faisant maye.[3]*

Vercelli, Milan will give the news, the wound will be inflicted at Pavia. To run through the waters of the Seine, blood and fire through Florence. The unique one falling from high to low calling for help.

An obscure quatrain. Vercelli and Pavia belonged to the Duchy of Milan and were taken over by the Hapsburgs until the nineteenth century.

Century VIII

VIII.VIII

*Pres de linterne[4] dans de
    tonnes fermez,
Chiuaz[5] fera pour l'aigle la
    menee,
L'esleu casse luy ses gens enfermez,
Dedans Turin rapt espouse
    emmenee.*

Near Focia, enclosed in some barrels Chivasso will plot for the eagle. The elected one driven out, he and his people shut up. Rape within Turin, the bride led away.

An irritating quatrain. The village of Focia occupies the old site of Linternum, but is not likely to be the subject of this verse. Chivasso, a few miles northeast of Turin, was occupied

[1] *Tycin.* L. *Ticinium,* Pavia.
[2] *la paye.* O.F. wound, but possible misprint for the plague.
[3] *maye.* O.F. a kneading-trough. Alternatively a misreading of "*ma 'aie,*" Help me!
[4] *Linterne.* now Focia, near Naples.
[5] *Chiuaz.* Chivasso in Italy.

by the French, but Nostradamus sees it plotting on behalf of the Emperor (Napoleon?). Unclear.

Century VIII

VIII.IX

Pendant que l'aigle & le coq à Sauone	While the eagle is united with the cock at Savona, the Eastern sea and Hungary. The army at Naples, Palerma, the marches of Ancona, Rome and Venice. A great outcry by the barbarian.
Seront vnis Mer Leuant & Ongrie,	
L'armee à Naples, Palerne, Marque d'Ancone	
Rome, Veniſe par Barb'[1] horrible crie.	

At Savona Nostradamus foresees an alliance between the Emperor and the French. Both the Levant and Hungary belonged to the Turks except for the small area retained, and paid for, by the Hapsburgs. Both Naples and Palermo belonged to the Hapsburg Kingdom of the Two Sicilies and Ancona belonged to the Papal States. Nostradamus appears to envisage a Moslem invasion of Italy, possibly just feasible, but it seems unlikely that these remaining Christian forces would align against it. On balance, a quatrain belonging to Europe of the past few centuries, and as such, a failure.

Century VIII

VIII.X

Puanteur grande ſortira de Lauſanne,	A great stench will come from Lausanne but they will not know its origin. They will put out all the people from different places; fire seen in the sky, a great foreign nation defeated.
Qu'on ne ſaura l'origine du fait,	
Lon mettra hors toute la gent loingtaine	
Feu veu au ciel, peuple eſtranger deffait.	

---

[1]*Barb'.* F. shortened form of barbarian, but just possibly refers to the enigmatic Aenobarbe.

The stench from Lausanne is probably Nostradamus'
graphic reference to the Calvinists in general and in particular
to Calvin's second-in-command, de Bèze, who taught in
Lausanne during the second half of the sixteenth century.
Some later commentators refer this quatrain to the meetings
of the early Marxists. Line 4 gives this view some credence.

Century VIII

VIII.XI

Peuple infiny paroiſtra à Vicence	A multitude of people will appear at Vicenza, without
Sans force feu bruſler la Baſilique	force, fire to burn the Basilica.
Pres de Lunage deffait grand de Valence,	Near Lunage the great one of Valenza defeated at the time
Lors que Veniſe par more prendra pique.	when Venice takes up the quarrel through custom.

At the present time the title of Valentinois is held by Prince
Albert of Monaco, son of Prince Rainier and the late Princess
Grace. During Nostradamus' lifetime it belonged first to Diane
de Poitiers, and then to the Grimaldis of Monaco. As to the
place names, Vicenza was in the Republic of Venice, Valenza
belonged to the Hapsburgs, Milan and Valence were in
France. These geopolitical place names make this appear to be
a retroactive quatrain.

Century VIII

VIII.XII

Apparoiſtra aupres de Buffalorre	He will appear near to Buffa-
L'hault & procere entré dedans Milan	lora, the highly born and tall one entered into Milan. The Abbé of
L'abbé de Foix auec ceux de ſaint Morre	Foix with those of Saint-Maur will cause damage dressed up as
Feront la forbe abillez en vilan.	serfs.

Buffalora is a tiny village west of Milan, so small that it is
unlikely Nostradamus would have known of it, unless he

passed through it on his Italian wanderings. The people of St.
Mark are the Benedictines, the connection being that St.
Maurus founded the Order in France. The Abbey at Foix
belonged to the Benedictines. But it is difficult to imagine
quite what Nostradamus envisaged in line 4.

Century VIII

VIII.XIII

*Le croisé frere par amour
    effrenee
Fera par Praytus Bellerophon
    mourir,
Claſſe à mil ans la femme
    forcenee
Beu le breuuage, tous deux
    apres perir.*

*The crusader brother through
impassioned love will cause Bellerophon to die through Proteus.
The fleet for a thousand years.
The maddened woman, the
potion drunk, both of them die.*

This story of poisoning is based on the myth of Bellerophon
and Proteus, king of Argus, whose wife was furious when her
advances to Bellerophon were refused. Queen Anteia persuaded Proteus to send Bellerophon on a mortal mission
which was concealed in a sealed message to Lebates, king of
Lycia. Lebates therefore sent Bellerophon to kill the monster
Chimera, which he succeeded in doing with the help of his
flying horse, Pegasus. Nostradamus perceives the cuckold
husband will be poisoned as well as his wife.

But what relevance this has to the sixteenth century or later
is completely impossible to interpret. I sometimes wonder if
Nostradamus liked to amuse himself when considering the
credulity of the reader. However, this in no way diminishes
the serious, specific aspect of many of his predictions.

Century VIII

VIII.XIIII

*Le grand credit d'or, d'argent
  l'abondance
Fera aueugler par libide
  l'honneur
Sera cogneu d'adultere l'offence,
Qui paruiendra à son grand
  deshonneur.*

*The great credits of gold and
abundance of silver will cause
honor to be blinded by lust. The
offense of the adulterer will
become known, which will occur
to his great dishonor.*

This quatrain appears to indicate a general condemnation
of the great riches which flowed from the Spanish-American
mines into Europe, causing great financial inflation throughout the sixteenth century. Lines 3 and 4 seem to show that
Nostradamus connects monetry lust with sexual lust, a concept
not unknown to the twentieth century!

Century VIII

VIII.XV

*Vers Aquilon grands efforts par
  hommasse
Presque l'Europe & l'vniuers
  vexer,
Les deux eclypses mettra en telle
  chasse,
Et aux Pannons vie & mort
  renforcer.*

*Great exertions toward the North
of a man-woman to vex Europe
and almost all the universe. The
two eclipses will be put into such
a rout that they will reinforce life
or death for the Hungarians.*

This quatrain must certainly tie up with Nostradamus'
predictions concerning the great expansion of the German
Empire. The *hommasse* is interpreted by most commentators as
Germania, and thus the quatrain refers to Nazi Germany.
However, apart from the troubles suffered by the Hungarians,
and the reference to problems in the whole of Europe (line 1),
it remains a rather unsatisfactory quatrain.

Century VIII

VIII.XVI

Au lieu que HIERON feit ſa nef fabriquer,
Si grand deluge ſera & ſi ſubite,
Qu'on n'aura lieu ne terres s'atacquer
L'onde monter Feſulan Olympique.

At the place where HIERON builds his ship, there will be such a great and sudden flood. No one will have a place or land to fall upon. The waters rise to the Olympic Fesulan.

I cannot discover the meaning of the anagram *HIERON*. It does not occur elsewhere in the quatrains. Some commentators believe it to be an anagram of *JASON*, which would fit the atmosphere of the latter part of the quatrain. It is difficult to find any connection between Greece and Fesulan (Fiesole) in central Italy. As to the question of flooding, Fiesole stands only 970 feet above sea level, whereas Mount Olympus rises 9,570 feet above it.

Century VIII

VIII.XVII

Les bien aiſez ſubit ſeront deſmis
Par les trois freres le monde mis en trouble,
Cité marine ſaiſiront ennemis,
Faim, feu, ſang, peſte, & de to' maux le double.

Those at ease will suddenly be cast down, the world put into trouble by three brothers. Their enemies will seize the marine city. Hunger, fire, blood, plague; all evils doubled.

This is a splendid Millennium quatrain. Line 4 gives all the ingredients needed. The mention of the three brothers who will put the world into trouble helps give us a dating. When three brothers are in positions of power during a century, world troubles will start to erupt.

The only well-known three brothers "in power" towards the Millennium are the Kennedys. Tragically, two of them have been assassinated. It seems unlikely that the youngest brother, Edward Kennedy, will now attain any position of power; he is what one might term a "psychological assassinee." During the lifetimes of these three brothers, America will suddenly find itself in trouble. Could the marine city be Hong Kong, due to be handed back to the Chinese in 1997?

Century VIII

VIII.XVIII

De Flora iſſue de ſa mort ſera
  cauſe,
Vn temps deuant par ieuſne &
  vieille bueyre
Par les trois lys luy feront telle
  pauſe,
Par ſon fruit ſauue comme chair
  crue mueyre.

The reasons for her death will be issued from Florence, it will be drunk once by both young and old. Through the three great lilies they will give her a great pause (become thoughtful). Saved through her offspring as raw meat is dampened.

Florence belonged to the de' Medicis family for several centuries, and two of the Medicis daughters married into the royal line, les trois lys, of France: Nostradamus' protector Catherine and later Marie de' Medicis.

Catherine was saved from a possible divorce from her husband, Henri, the dauphin, when after ten barren years she bore him seven children. But the last part of line 4, chair crue mueyre, remains obscure.

Century VIII

VIII.XIX

A ſoubſtenir la grand cappe
  troublee,
Pour l'eſclaircir les rouges
  marcheront,
De mort famille ſera preſque
  accablee.
Les rouges rouges le rouge
  aſſomeront:

To support the great troubled Cappe the reds will march in order to clarify it. A family will almost be overcome by death. The bloody red ones will knock down the red.

Cappe is probably Nostradamus' shortened form of Capet, the name of the French royal line. The French certainly marched against Louis XVI and Marie Antoinette at the time of the Revolution. Republicans marched against them so that the family had to take enforced refuge in the Temple. The royal family was almost destroyed *presque accablee*. The only certain survivor was the king's sister, Elisabeth, and possibly Louis XVII, his eldest son (see V.I.). Then the extremists will guillotine the more moderate revolutionaries, the Girondins. It is possible that Robespierre is also hinted at in the last line.

Century VIII

VIII.XX

Le faux meſſaige par election fainte	*The false message about the rigged election to run through the city, stopping the broken pact. Voices bought, a chapel stained with blood, the empire contracted to another one.*
Courir par vrben, rompue pache arreſte,	
Voix acheptees, de ſang chapelle tainte,	
Et à vn autre l'empire contraicte.	

Possibly a Holy Roman Emperor who uses bribery, *voix acheptees*, to attain his ends. This false election will be followed by a short war which ends when the Pretender is murdered. I think this is a failed quatrain.

Century VIII

VIII.XXI ★

Au port de Agde trois fuſtes entreront	*Three foists will enter the port of Agde carrying the infection and pestilence, not the faith. Passing the bridge they will carry off a million. The bridge is broken by the resistance of the third.*
Portant l'infect non foy & peſtilence	
Paſſant le pont mil milles embleront,	
Et le pont rompre à tierce reſiſtance.	

The enormity of the number of deaths from the plague makes the figures suspect. They are more suitable for the twentieth century. Agde is a seaport.

Century VIII

VIII.XXII

Gorſan, Narbonne, par le ſel
  aduertir
Tucham, la grace Parpignam
  trahye,
La ville rouge n'y vouldra
  conſentir.
Par haulte vol drap gris vie
  faillie.

Coursan, Narbonne through the
salt (marsh?) to warn Tuchan,
the grace of Perpignan betrayed.
The red town will not wish to
consent to it. A high flight, a
gray flag, life ended.

Line 4 is a good example of Nostradamus' convoluted style
when it is hard to get any meaning from the words at all. A
difficult quatrain. Communists have a suprisingly strong hold
in present-day France, particularly outside Paris. But who or
what is Tuchan?

Century VIII

VIII.XXIII

Lettres trouuees de la royne les
  coffres,
Point de ſubſcrit ſans aucun nom
  d'hauteur
Par la police ſeront cachez les
  offres.
Qu'on ne ſcaura qui ſera
  l'amateur.

Letters are found in the queen's
chests. No signature and no
name of the author. The government will conceal the offers, so
that they will not know who the
lover is.

There is no definitive link word that I can pursue in this
quatrain, but if Nostradamus did not meet Mary, Queen of
Scots, wife of Catherine's son, he certainly knew a great deal
about her. She spent most of her childhood years in France
with the Guise family, to whom she was related.

The Casket Letters, as they later became known, were
documents pertaining to the murder of Darnley, Mary, Queen
of Scots' husband, and the events of 1567, a year after
Nostradamus' death. These documents were produced by the
earl of Moreton, in front of commissions of London and York.

The "originals" disappeared after 1584 and their authenticity has always been in dispute.

Century VIII

VIII.XXIIII

Le lieutenant à l'entree de
l'huys,
Affomera le grand de Parpignan,
En fe cuidant fauluer à
Montpertuis.
Sera deceu baftard de Lufignan.

The lieutenant at the door of the house will knock down the great man of Perpignan. Thinking to save himself at Montpertius, the bastard of Lusignan will be deceived.

The Lusignan family died out before Nostradamus' time. It ruled Jerusalem and Cyprus until 1489, and its titles passed to the House of Savoy. One of Nostradamus' patrons was the comte de Tende, governor of Provence, who was the son of the great Bastard of Savoy. If this is so, then Montpertius almost certainly stands for the Perthus Pass in the Pyrenean mountains. Nostradamus must have envisaged Tende or one of his descendants trapping the Spanish around Rousillon. An unlikely quatrain.

Century VIII

VIII.XXV

Coeur de l'amant ouuert
d'amour fertiue
Dans le ruyffeau fera rauyr la
Dame,
Le demy mal contrefera laffiue,
Le pere à deux priuera corps de
l'ame.

The heart of the lover, awakened by furtive love, will ravish the lady in the stream. She will shyly claim to be half injured. The father of each will deprive the body of its soul.

A possible history of incest and rape? The plot may be clear but the references are too general to be of any use.

Century VIII

VIII.XXVI

*De Caron es[1] trouues en
   Barſellonne,
Mys deſcouuers lieu terrouers &
   ruyne,
Le grãd qui tient ne tient
   vouldra Pamplonne.
Par l'abbage de Monferrat[2]
   bruyne.*

*The bones of Cato found in Bar-
celona, placed, discovered, the
site found again and ruined.
The great one who holds, but
does not hold, wants Pamplona.
Drizzle at the Abbey of Montser-
rat.*

None of Cato's famous family died at Barcelona and only
Caius Pacius Cato died in Spain. Technically this is an
unfulfilled quatrain.

Century VIII

VIII.XXVII

*La voye auxelle l'vne ſur l'autre
   fornix[3]
De muy deſer hor mis braue &
   geneſt,
L'eſcript d'empereur le fenix[4]
Veu en celuy ce qu'à nul autre
   n'eſt.*

*The auxiliary way, one arch
upon another. Le Muy deserted
except for the brave one and his
twin. The writing of the emperor
of the phoenix seen by him, but to
no other.*

An impossible quatrain, probably set in Provence. The
aqueduct may be the one that runs from the river Saigne to
Fréjus. A jennet *(geneſt)* is a small, black horse. But who is the
Phoenix Emperor?

---

[1]*es.* alternative reaching *os*, bones. O.F. *ez* means planks or boards.
[2]*Monferrat.* Presumably printer's error for famous Abbey of Mon-
serrat in Catalonia.
[3]*forniz.* A.F. an arch or brothel. I take it in the first meaning.
[4]*fenix.* Phoenix or Phoenecian.

Century VIII

VIII.XXVIII

*Les fimulachres d'or & d'argent
enflez,
Qu'apres le rapt au lac furent
gettez
Au defcouuert eftaincts tous &
troublez.
Au marbre efcript prefcriptz
intergetez.*

*The copies of gold and silver
inflated which after the theft
were thrown into the lake. At
their discovery all is exhausted
and dissipated by the debt. All
scrips and bonds will be wiped
out.*

Could this quatrain possibly describe monetary inflation? In Nostradamus' day only gold, silver and copper were used as coinage. Paper money, *les fimulachres d'or & d'argent enflez*, did not exist. How well this quatrain applies to the twentieth century.

Century VIII

VIII.XXIX ★

*Au quart pillier lon facre[1] à
Saturne.
Par tremblant terre & deluge
fendu
Soubz l'edifice Saturnin trouuee
vrne,
D'or Capion rauy & puis
rendu.*

*At the fourth pillar which they
dedicate to Saturn, split by
earthquake and by blood. Under
Saturn's building an urn is
found. Gold carried off by
Caepio and then restored.*

This is an odd quatrain. Saturn's building presumably means a temple dedicated to him, or possibly the famous church of Saint Saturnin (Sernin) at Toulouse. Caepio was a Roman consul involved in the sacking of Toulouse in 106 B.C. The treasure he found never reached Rome, for which reason Caepio was impeached and expelled from the Senate. Does Nostradamus indicate that he knows where the treasure really ended up?

---

[1]*facre*. O.F., dedicated.

Century VIII

VIII.XXX

*Dedans Tholoze non loing de
  Beluezer
Faiſant vn puys loing, palais
  d'eſpectacle
Treſor trouué vn chacun ira
  vexer,
Et en deux locz tout & pres del
  vaſacle.[1]*

In Toulouse, not far from
Beluzer, making a deep pit, a
palace of spectacle. The treasure
found will vex everyone in two
places, near the Basacle.

Beluzier is as yet unidentified by all of Nostradamus'
commentators. Does this quatrain, again with the theme of
treasure, follow upon VIII.XXIX? It is just possible that these
two quatrains may still be unfulfilled.

Century VIII

VIII.XXXI

*Premier grand fruit le prince
  de Peſquiere
Mais puis viendra bien & cruel
  malin,
Dedans Veniſe perdra ſa gloire
  fiere
Et mys à mal par plus ioyue
  Celin.*

The first great fruit of the prince
of Peschiera; then will come a
cruel and wicked man. In Venice
he will lose his proud glory and
is led into evil by the younger
Selin.

When Mussolin led the Fascists in revolt in Italy the first
prize that fell to him was the prince of Peschiera, Victor
Emmanuel himself, who there performed one of the most
honorable acts of his reign. The prince had gone to the front
after Caporetto, taking command in person, rejecting all
proposals of surrender and determined to fight it out. Their
council of war was also held at Peschiera. The cruel one is
Mussolini, who will lose his glory in Venice and be delivered
to the hands of the younger Selin. Selin normally means

[1]*vaſacle.* Basacle is the name of mill section of Toulouse and also the
castle which protects the main bridge and gate to the city.

crescent or moon. If Nostradamus foresaw some connection between Italy and Islam after the time of Mussolini, he is wrong. But the rest of the quatrain fits nicely.

Century VIII

VIII.XXXII

Garde toy roy Gaulois de ton nepueu *Qui fera tant que ton vnique filz* *Sera meurtry à Venus faifant voeu,* *Accompaigné de nuict que trois & fix.*	*French king, beware of your nephew who will intrigue so much that your only son will be murdered while making his vows to Venus. Accompanied at night by thousand and six.*

An apparently clear quatrain, but I think a failed one. It seems unlikely to belong to the future.

Century VIII

VIII.XXXIII

Le grand naiftra de Veronne & Vincence, *Qui portera vn furnom bien indigne.* *Qui à Venife vouldra faire vengeance,* *Luy mefme prins homme du guet & figne*	*The great one who will be born of Verona and Vicenza carries a very unworthy surname. He who at Venice will wish to take vengeance, himself taken by a man of the watch and sign.*

This quatrain seems to follow, partly at least, from the last. Northern Italy is indicated by the names of Verona and Vicenza. The one born *vn furnom bien indigne* is Mussolini; the word literally means muslin-maker, one of Italy's more lowly professions. The vengeance he desired was against those powers who frustrated his dream of *Mare Nostrum*.

Century VIII

VIII.XXXIIII

Apres victoire du Lyon au Lyon
Sur la montaigne de IVRA
*   Secatombe[1]*
Delues[2] & brodes[3] septieme
*   million*
Lyon, Vlme à Mausol mort &
*   tombe.*

After the victory of the Lion over
the Lion there will be great
slaughter on the mountains of
Jura. Floods, and dark-skinned
people, the seventh million.
Lyons, Ulm, at the mausoleum
death and the tomb.

The Jura mountains run through Franche-Comté. It
belonged to the Hapsburgs until 1674. But the key word
brodes, the dark-skinned people, the people of Africa, brings
this quatrain into the twentieth century. The appalling
flooding throughout Sudan, Bangladesh and Ethiopia during
1988 may well eventually leave a total death roll of seven
million. Concomitant with floods is disease and this too will
decimate the afflicted peoples. Nostradamus, the doctor,
would know that well. The last line is unclear.

Century VIII

VIII.XXXV

Dedans l'entree de Garonne &
*   Bayse*
Et la forest non loing de
*   Damazan*
Du marsaues[4] gelees, puis gresle
*   & bize*
Dordonnois gelle[5] par erreur de
*   mezan.[6]*

At the entrance to Garonne and
Baise, the forest not far from
Damazan. Discoveries of the frozen sea, then hail and north
winds. Frost in the Dardonnais
through the mistake of the
month.

---

[1]*Secatombe*. a misprint for *hecatombe*, a tomb.
[2]*Delues*. possibly from L. *diluvis*, flood, destruction.
[3]*brodes*. O.F. *brode*, black, brown, decadent.
[4]*marsaues*. compound word. O.F. *mar*, sea and O.F. *saue*, discovery
[5]*gelle*. O.F. frost.
[6]*mezan*. L. *mensa*, a month, by metathesis.

I cannot decipher this quatrain. It describes cold and unseasonable weather.

Century VIII

VIII.XXXVI

Sera commis conte oingdre aduché[1]
De Saulne & fainct Aulbin & Bell'oeuure[2]
Pauer de marbre de tours loing efpluché
Non Bleteram refifter & chef d'oeuure.

It will be committed against the anointed bought from the Saulnier, Saint Aubin and Bell'oeuvre. To pave with marble taken from distant towers, not to resist Bleteram and his masterpiece.

Bleteram is yet another of the so-far uncoded Nostradamus words. unless it stands for Bletterans, again in the Franche-Comté belonging to the Hapsburgs until 1674. (See VIII.XX-XIIII.) An enigmatic, difficult quatrain.

Century VIII

VIII.XXXVII

La forterefse aupres de la Tamife
Cherra par lors le Roy dedans ferré,
Aupres du pont fera veu en chemife
Vn deuant mort, puis dans le fort barré.

The fortress near the Thames will fall when the king is locked up inside. He will be seen in his shirt, near the bridge, one facing death, then barred within the fortress.

This is one of Nostradamus' more exciting quatrains and a reasonably exact one too. After his defeat in 1648, Charles I was taken captive to Windsor Castle, overlooking the Thames. He remained there until January 9, 1649. The castle did fall, in a sense, because it came into the hands of the Parliamenta-

---

[1]*aduché.* A.Pr. *aducha,* bought.
[2]*Bell'oeuure.* an enigmatic place name or just literally a "beautiful work."

rians. After his trial, Charles was beheaded, dressed in a white shirt, on January 30, 1649. The nearest bridge would be London Bridge, as Westminster Bridge was not built at that time. This quatrain connects with IX.XLIX.

Century VIII

VIII.XXXVIII

Le Roy de Bloys dans Auignon regner
Vne autre foys le peuple emonopolle,[1]
Dedans' le Roſne par murs fera baigner
Iuſques à cinq le dernier pres de Nolle.[2]

The king of Blois will reign in Avignon; once again the people covered with blood. In the Rhône he will swim near the walls. Up to fire, the last one near Nolle.

I leave this one to the reader. A king of all France will cause war and bloodshed. But I cannot connect this with the last two lines.

Century VIII

VIII.XXXIX

Qu'aura eſté par prince Bizantin,
Sera tollu par prince de Tholoze.
La foy de Foix par le chief Tholentin,
Luy faillira ne refuſant l'eſpouſe.

He who will have been for the Byzantine priest will be taken away by the prince of Toulouse. The faith of Foix through the leader of Tolentino will fail him, not refusing the bride.

The difficulty here is to identify the people in this quatrain. The Byzantine priest may be either a sultan, or a Moslem leader. The prince of Toulouse may be its archbishop, or any number of the hereditary Montmorency family. As Tolentino

---

[1] *emonopolle.* A compound word of Nostradamus' invention. Probably derived from *aimopnoos,* bloodthirsty, or *aimatopotes,* blood-drinker.

[2] *Nolle.* a proper name? Possibly Nola in Italy, but it does not seem to fit the context.

is part of the Papal States, the leader may be the Pope. Foix belonged to the house of Navarre.

Century VIII

VIII.XL

Le fang du Iufte par Taurer la daurade,[1]	The blood of the just for Taur and la Dorade, in order to
Pour fe venger contre les Saturnins[2]	avenge itself against the Saturnins. They will immerse the band
Au nouueau lac plongeront la maynade, [3]	in the new lake. Then they will march against Alba.
Puis marcheront contre les Albanins.[4]	

If one accepts that these two churches stand for Toulouse, the quatrain seems to imply that the inhabitants are fighting both Calvinism as well as a Spanish attack led by the duke of Alba. An unsatisfactory quatrain.

Century VIII

VIII.XLI

Efleu fera Renad ne fonnant mot,	A fox will be elected without
Faifant le faint public viuant pain d'orge[5],	speaking one word, appearing saintly in public. Living on barley bread afterwards he will sud-
Tyrannizer apres tant à vn cop[6],	denly become a tyrant, putting his foot on the throats of the
Mettant à pied des plus grans fus la gorge.	greatest men.

[1] *Taurer la daurade.* Two churches in Toulouse, Notre Dame du Taur and Notre Dame la Daurade?

[2] *Saturnins.* Those of Saturn or of St. Sernin.

[3] *maynade.* A.Pr. *marinada,* a) band of people, b) household, servants

[4] *Albanins.* Probably the troops of the duke of Alba, or just possibly Albanian mercenaries.

[5] *viuant pain d'orge.* This has a secondary meaning, to feather one's nest, very appropriate in this context.

[6] *cop. coup. à un coup,* at a blow.

Napoleon III was known as *le Taciturne* when elected president, and was certainly as cunning as a fox. He fulfills line 3 when he executed his coup d'état in December, 1851, to make way for the Second Empire. He used his power in the way described in lines 3 and 4.

Century VIII

VIII.XLII

Par auarice, par force &
    violence
Viendra vexer les siens chiefz
    d'Orleans,
Pres faint Memire affault &
    refiftance.
Mort dans fa tante diront qu'il
    dort leans.

Through avarice, through force and violence the chief of Orléans will come to vex his supporters. Near St. Memire, assault and resistance. Dead in his tent, they will say he is asleep inside.

If one can read St. Memire as St. Merri—it is otherwise unidentifiable—Louis Philippe d'Orléans will engage in combat around Saint Merri. That Nostradamus reached the title of Orléans is interesting because the founder of the house was the brother of Louis XIII, born long after Nostradamus' death. The cryptic last line may just mean he slept like the dead in his tent after the battle, or possibly something I cannot decipher.

Century VIII

VIII.XLIII

Par le decide[1] de deux chofes
    baftars
Nepueu du fang occupera le
    regne
Dedans lectoyre feront les coups
    de dars
Nepueu par peur pleira
    l'enfeigne.

Through the fall of the two bastard creatures the nephew of the blood will occupy the throne. Within Lectoure there will be blows of lances, the nephew, through fear will fold up his standard.

[1]decide. L. *decidere*, to fall.

Yet again the nephew. The only important nephew in French history appeared over 300 years after Nostradamus' death. He was Louis-Napoleon, son of King Louis of Holland, who was the brother of Napoleon I. The two bastards who fall may be the governments of Louis Philippe and that of the Second Republic. *Lectoyre* may be an anagram of *Le Torcey*, a suburb of Sedan, where, in 1870, Louis-Napoleon was defeated by the Germans and Prussians. He ordered a flag of surrender to be hung on Sedan's church and then on its citadel, *par peur pleira l'enseigne*, after which the emperor formally surrendered to the Germans at Douchery, two miles from Le Torcey.

Century VIII

VIII.XLIIII

Le procrée naturel dogmion,[1]
De sept à neuf du chemin
destorner
A roy de longue & amy aumi
hom,
Doit à Nauarre fort de PAV
prosterner.

The natural offspring of Ogmios will turn off the road between seven and nine. To the king, long friend of the half-man, Navarre must destroy the fort at Pau.

Ogmios turns up in various quatrains but has never been properly identified in other than his classical form. Unclear.

Century VIII

VIII.XLV

La main escharpe & la iambe
bandee,
Longs puis nay de Calais
portera
Au mot du guet la mort sera
tardee,
Puis dans le temple à Pasques
saignera.

With his hand in a sling and his leg bandaged, the younger brother of Calais will reach far. At the word of the watch, death will be delayed. Then he will bleed at Easter in the Temple.

I cannot make anything of this quatrain.

[1]*dogmion.* Ogmios, the Celtic Hercules.

Century VIII

VIII.XLVI

*Pol menſolee mourra trois lieuës
    du roſne,[1]
Fuis les deux prochains taraſc
    deſtrois:
Car Mars fera le plus horrible
    troſne,
De coq & d'aigle de France
    freres trois.*

*Paul the Celibate will die three
leagues from Rome, the two
nearest flee the oppressed monster. When Mars will take up his
horrible throne, the Cock and the
Eagle, France and the three
brothers.*

Pope Paul VI died at his villa exactly three miles from Rome
in 1978. The linking with a pope and three brothers helps
place this quatrain in the second half of this century. Wars will
be raging which Nostradamus seems to feel will become
worldwide, *Car Mars fera le plus horrible trofne.* This appears to
indicate a leading up to the Millennium (see also V.LXXVIII).
Apparently, France, the *coq* will have an important rôle to play.
The Eagle here seems to stand for the USA through the
linkage with the three brothers. (See I.XXVI, II.LCV.)

Century VIII

VIII.XLVII

*Lac Treſmenien portera
    teſmoignage,
Des coniurez ſarez dedans
    Perouſe,
Vn deſpolle contrefera le ſage,
Tuant Tedeſq de ſterne &
    minuſe.*

*Lake Trasimene will bear wit-
ness of the conspirators locked up
in Perugia. A fool will imitate
the wise one, killing the Teutons,
destroying and cutting to pieces.*

I can offer no explanation for this quatrain.

[1]*roſne.* Misspelling of Rome or Rhône.

Century VIII

VIII.XLVIII

*Saturne en Cancer, Iupiter
    auec Mars,
Dedans Feurier Chaldondon[1]
    faluaterre.
Sault Caftallon[2] affailly de trois
    pars,
Pres de Verbiefque[3] conflit
    mortelle guerre.*

Saturn in Cancer, Jupiter with
Mars in February, Chaldondon
Salvatierra. Sierra Morena
besieged on three sides near Verbiesque, war and mortal conflict.

An incomplete astrological dating with two undeciphered
names, Chaldondon and Verbiesque. A very difficult verse.

Century VIII

VIII.XLIX

*Satur. au beuf ioue en l'eau,
    Mars en fleiche,
Six de Feurier mortalité donra,
Ceux de Tardaigne[4] à Bruge fi
    grand breche,
Qu'à Ponterofo[5] chef Barbarin
    mourra.*

Saturn in Taurus, Jupiter in
Aquarius, Mars in Sagittarius.
The sixth of February brings
death. Those of Tardaigne, so
great a breach at Bruges, the
barbarian chief will die at Pon-
teroso.

According to Wöllner this conjunction occurred in 1736 and
will not happen again in the foreseeable future. But McCann
(1942) says that it occurred on February 6, 1971, so Nostradamus seems to have been wrong on both counts.

[1]*Chaldondon?* L. *Chaldons.* soothsayer, otherwise incomprehensible.
[2]*Sault Caftallon.* L. *Saltus Castulonensis,* Sierra Morena.
[3]*Verbiefque,* an unsolved name.
[4]*Tardaigne.* Misspelling of *Sardaingne,* Sardinia.
[5]*Ponterofo.* Unidentified—may mean the red bridge.

Century VIII

VIII.L

La peſtilence l'entour de
  Capadille,
Vn autre faim pres de Sagont
  s'appreſte:
Le cheualier baſtard de bon
  ſenille,
Au grand de Thunes fera
  trancher la teſte.

The plague around Capellades,
another famine is near Sagunto.
The knightly bastard of the good
old man will cause the great one
of Tunis to lose his head.

This quatrain, despite its apparent confusion, is a very
successful hit for Nostradamus. In 1573, Don John of Austria,
the bastard son of the old Charles V, recaptured Tunis for his
half brother, Philip of Spain. Although there is no definite
record of a famine, Spain was suffering from sporadic
outbursts of endemic plague from 1570 to 1574.

Century VIII

VIII.LI

Le Bizantin faiſant oblation,
Apres auoir Cordube à ſoy
  reprinſe:
Son chemin long repos
  pamplation,[1]
Mer paſſant proy par la
  Colongna[2] prinſe.

The Byzantine makes an oblation after having taken back
Córdoba. Long rest on his road,
the vines cut down, at sea the
passing prey captured near Gibraltar.

In this quatrain Nostradamus appears to predict that the
leader of Constantinople will invade Spain near Córdoba.
Córdoba belonged to the Arabs until 1031 and then to the
Moslems until 1236. Line 4 seems to suggest that this Turkish
(?) leader will be caught near the Pillars of Hercules, Gibraltar.
A retroactive quatrain.

---

[1] Pamplation. dubious. Possibly L. pampinatio, to cut vines.
[2] Colongna. Collones d'Hercule, Gibraltar.

Century VIII

VIII.LII

Le roy de Bloys dans Auignon regner,
D'amboise & seme[1] viendra le long de Lyndre
Ongle à Poytiers sainctes aesles ruiner
Deuant Boni.[2]

The king of Blois to reign in Avignon, from Amboise and Seme, the length of the Indre. Claws at Poitiers, holy wings ruined before Boni . . .

Line 1 is identical to the first line of VIII.XXXVIII. The unfinished last line suggests that this is probably another quatrain "rescued" by Chavigny, following upon the unfinished version of Century VII. Alternatively it may have been cut by a censor as heretical, but this seems less likely. Without the final version it is difficult to learn much from this quatrain.

Century VIII

VIII.LIII

Dedans Bolongne vouldra lauer ses fautes,
Il ne pourra au temple du soleil,
Il volera faisant choses si haultes
En hierarchie n'en fut oncq vn pareil.

Within Boulogne he will want to wash away his misdeeds which he cannot (do) at the temple of the Sun. He will fly away doing very great things. In the hierarchy he never had an equal.

Many commentators apply this to Napoleon by reading Bolongne as Boulogne, but there is just a possibility that it may mean Bologna in the Papal States. Tradition held that Westminster Abbey, which Napoleon was unable to enter by right of conquest, was built on the Temple of Apollo, destroyed by an earthquake in A.D. 154. Napoleon flew so high as to think of taking both England and Russia. He had no equal during his lifetime.

---

[1]*seme.?* the Seine. Otherwise not identified.
[2]*Boni* . . . incomplete line.

Century VIII

VIII.LIIII

Soubz la colleur du traicte
  mariage,
Fait magnanime par grand
  Chyren felin,
Quintin, Arras recouurez au
  voyage
D'efpaignolz fait fecond banc
  macelin.

Under the color of the marriage
treaty, a magnanimous act by the
Chyren Selin. St. Quentin and
Arras recovered on the journey.
By the Spanish a second butch-
er's bench is held.

I cannot explain this quatrain nor the mysterious reference
to Chyren Selin.

Century VIII

VIII.LV

Entre deux fleuues fe verra
  enferré,
Tonneaux & caques vnis à
  paffer outre,
Huict pontz rompus chef à tant
  enferré[1]
Enfans parfaictz font iugutez en
  coultre.[2]

He will find himself shut in
between two rivers, casks and
barrels joined to cross beyond.
Eight bridges broken, their chief
run through so many times.
Children's throats slit by the
knife.

I cannot decipher this quatrain.

Century VIII

VIII.LVI

La bande foible le tertre occupera
Ceux du hault lieu feront
  horribles crys,
Le gros troppeau d'eftre coin
  troublera,
Tombe pres D. nebro defcouuers
  les efcris.

The weak band will occupy the
land. Those of high places will
make dreadful cries. The large
herd of the outer corner troubled,
near Edinburgh it falls, discovered by the writings.

[1]enferré. presumably enferré.
[2]coultre. O.F. knife.

D. nebro is taken as meaning Edinburgh through the
phonetic pun "Edinbro." If so, this quatrain describes the
Battle of Dunbar, which took place twenty-five miles east of
the city. Charles II landed in Scotland in 1650. The Highland-
ers, line 1, were more numerous than the Cromwellians, but
their position was weaker. The phrase *estre en coin* is interesting
because before the battle the Scots boasted that they had the
Cromwellians cornered "in a pound." The Cromwellians
routed the Scots on September 3, 1650. Could line 4 be
explained by the fact that Cromwell took possession of all the
papers in the Scottish War Office?

Century VIII

VIII.LVII

De souldat simple paruiendra en
  empire,
De robe courte paruiendra à la
  longue
Vaillant aux armes en eglise ou
  plus pyre,
Vexer les prestres comme l'eau
  fait l'esponge.

From simple soldier he will
attain to Empire, from the short
robe he will grow into the long.
Brave in arms, much worse
towards the Church, he vexes the
priests as water fills a sponge.

This quatrain is an excellent description of Napoleon's
career. From a simple lieutenant he attained to government of
the French Empire. He exchanged his short robe of Consul
for the long robes of Imperial Majesty. But, although brave in
battle, he mishandled the Church and troubled the priests by
the abolition of the clergy. An explicit quatrain.

Century VIII

VIII.LVIII

Regne en querelle aux freres
  diuisé,
Prendre les armes & le nom
  Britannique
Tiltre Anglican sera tard aduisé,
Surprins de nuict mener à l'air
  Gallique.

A kingdom divided by two quar-
reling brothers to take the arms
and the name of Britain. The
Anglican title will be advised to
watch out, surprised by night,
led into the French air.

Since Nostradamus' death there have been no brothers fighting for the English throne with the loser fleeing to France. The nearest this quatrain has come to fulfillment was when James II and his Anglican son-in-law, William of Orange, came to open disagreement in 1668. The Anglican Church may have exerted its influence upon James II. He certainly did flee to France to "take the Gallic air."

Century VIII

VIII.LIX   ★

Par deux fois hault, par deux fois mis à bas	Twice put up and twice cast down the East will also weaken the West. Its adversary, after several battles, chased by sea will fail at time of need.
L'orient auſſi l'occident foyblira	
Son aduerſaire apres pluſieurs combats,	
Par mer chaſſé au beſoing faillira.	

This quatrain seems to describe the geopolitical situation of the twentieth century better than any other. It appears that the man of the East, possibly the Third Antichrist, will make two violent attacks on Western powers, but finally the East will prove the weaker at sea against the West. Certainly a futuristic quatrain.

Century VIII

VII.LX

Premier en Gaule, premier en Romanie,	First in Gaul, first in Romania, over land and sea against the English and Paris. Marvelous deeds by that great violent troop, the wild beast will lose Lorraine.
Par mer & terre aux Angloys & Parys	
Merueilleux faitz par celle grand meſnie	
Violant terax perdra le NORLARIS.	

Napoleon III was the only French leader to lose the Lorraine, but the rest of the quatrain does not fit him very well. James Laver ascribes it to Napoleon I saying that he can be described as the first in France and Rome. Perhaps this is a split quatrain or Nostradamus confused the two men, seeing them as one?

Century VIII

VIII.LXI

Iamais par le decouurement[1] du iour
Ne paruiendra au figne fceptrifere[2]
Que tous fes fieges ne foyent en feiour,
Portant au coq don du TAG[3] amifere.

Never by the revelation of daylight will he attain the mark of the scepter bearer. Until all his sieges are at rest, bringing to the Cock the gift of the armed legion.

The Cock receiving the gift of arms symbolizes France, although it was an obscure symbol until adopted by the Revolutionaries. Most commentators apply this quatrain to Napoleon III. Although I am not happy with this interpretation, I can find none better.

Century VIII

VIII.LXII

Lors qu'on verra expiler[4] le faint temple,
Plus grand du rofne leurs facrez prophaner
Par eux naiftra peftilence fi ample,
Roy fuit iniufte ne fera condamner.

When one sees the holy temple plundered, the greatest of the Rhône profaning their sacred things. Because of them a very great pestilence will appear. The king, unjust, will not condemn them.

A very general quatrain which I cannot relate to anything specific.

[1]*decouurement.* O.F. discovery.
[2]*fceptrifere.* L. scepter-bearing, royal.
[3]*TAG.* variant in other editions, *tagma*, a body of soldiers.
[4]*expiler.* L. *expilare*, to rob, plunder.

Century VIII

VIII.LXIII

Quant l'adultere blessé sans coup aura *Meurdry la femme & le filz par despit,* *Femme assoumee l'enfant estranglera:* *Huit captifz prins, s'estouffer sans respit.*	When the adulterer wounded without a blow will have mur- dered his wife and son out of spite. His wife knocked down he will strangle the child. Eight captives taken, choked beyond help.

Again, too general a quatrain to identify.

Century VIII

VIII.LXIIII

Dedans les Isles les enfans transsportez, *Les deux de sept seront en desespoir,* *Ceux du terrouer[1] en seront supportez,* *Nom pelle[2] prins des ligues fuy l'espoir.*	The infants transported to the islands two out of seven will be in despair. Those of the soil will be supported by it. The name pelle taken, the hope of the leagues fails.

Most twentieth century commentators apply this to modern Britain besieged by the Nazis in the Second World War. But this does not really explain the seven satisfactorily, nor the undeciphered *pelle*.

---

[1]*terrouer.* O.F. soil, land, ground.
[2]*pelle.* This has never been deciphered. Perhaps Garencières got closest with his suggestion of Montpellier.

Century VIII

VIII.LXV

Le vieux fruſtré du principal eſpoir,	The old man disappointed in his main hope will attain to the lead-
Il paruiendra au chef de ſon empire:	ership of his Empire. Twenty months he will hold rule with
Vingt mois tiendra le regne à grand pouuoir,	great force, a cruel tyrant, giv- ing way to one worse.
Tiran, cruel en delaiſſant vn pire.	

The twenty months seem to be the key to this quatrain. If the reader accepts, as I do, that most of Nostradamus' general quatrains refer to France, this may well refer to that country in 1940. In July of that year a rump session of the French Assembly invested Pétain with plenary powers until a new constitution could be formed. After increasing pressure from the Germans to collaborate, he handed over most of his powers to Laval twenty months later, in April 1942.

Century VIII

VIII.LXVI

Quand l'eſcriture D.M.[1] trouuee,	When the inscription D.M. is
Et caue antique à lampe deſcouuerte,	found in the ancient cave, revealed by a lamp. Law, the
Loy, Roy, & Prince Vlpian[2] eſprouuee,	king, and Prince Ulpian tried, the queen and duke in the pavi-
Pauillon Royne & Duc ſous la couuerte.	lion under cover.

Many commentators have suggested ingenious solutions for D.M. but, as I say in the footnote, it is simply the equivalent of "Here lies . . ." on any English tombstone, "In the hands of the Gods." James Laver takes it to mean *du manuscrit*. This probably ties in with the puzzling quatrain of IX.LXXXIV.

[1]D.M. Probably stands for the Latin inscription *Diis Manibus*, which was put on many Roman tombstones.
[2]*Vlpian*. Ulpius is a Roman name.

Century VIII

VIII.LXVII

*PAR. CAR. NERSAF, à ruine
  grand difcorde,
Ne l'vn ne l'autre n'aura
  election,
Nerſaf du peuple aura amour
  & concorde,
Ferrare, Collonne grande
  protection.*

PARIS,   CARCASSONNE,
FRANCE *ruined in great dis-
harmony, neither one nor the
other will be elected. France will
have the love and good will of
the people. Ferrara, Colonna,
great protection.*

PAR. and CAR. probably stand for Paris and Carcassonne but *NERSAF* is not a very good anagram for France. Although Ferrara was joined with the Franco-Papal troops fighting Spain in 1557, Colonna was always firmly pro-Spanish. The key to this quatrain lies in the word *NERSAF*.

Century VIII

VIII.LXVIII

*Vieux Cardinal par le ieuſne
  deceu,
Hors de ſa charge ſe verra
  desarmé,
Arles ne monſtres double ſoit
  aperceu,
Et Liqueduct & le Prince
  embauſmé.*

*The old cardinal is deceived by
the young one, he will find himself disarmed, out of his position.
Do not show, Arles, that the double has been understood. Both
Liqueduct and the prince
embalmed.*

This is an excellent quatrain of which the key word is *Liqueduct*. Cardinal Richelieu was supported by the young Cinq Mars, lost the favor of Louis XIII and had to resign. But at Arles, says the quatrain, he will receive a copy of the treaty with Spain signed by Cinq Mars and the king's brother in 1642. Richelieu tells the king of this treachery. Although very ill, he travels to Paris on a barge, *Liqueduct*, led on the water. The cardinal died at the end of 1642 and the king five months later. As Nostradamus says, both bodies were embalmed.

Century VIII

VIII.LXIX

Aupres du ieune le vieux ange baiſſer,
Et le viendra ſurmonter à la fin:
Dix ans eſgaux au plus vieux rabaiſſer,
De trois deux l'vn l'huitieſme ſeraphin.

Beside the young one the old angel falls and will come to rise above him at the end. Ten years equal to most, the old one falls again, of three, two, one, the eighth seraphim.

This obscure quatrain seems to describe the rivalry of favorites.

Century VIII

VIII.LXX

Il entrera vilain, meſchant, infame
Tyranniſant la Meſopotamie,
Tous amys fait d'adulterine d'ame.
Tertre horrible noir de phiſonomie.

He will enter, wicked, unpleasant, infamous, tyrannizing over Mesopotamia. All friends made by the adulterous woman. The land dreadful and black of aspect.

Mesopotamia is often used to describe Avignon, also between two rivers, at the confluence of the Rhône and the Durance. If this is so, the villain of this obscure quatrain would be the cardinal legate in Avignon, governing as the Pope's deputy.

Century VIII

VIII.LXXI

Croiſtra le nombre ſi grand des aſtronomes
Chaſſez, bannis & liures cenſurez,
L'an mil ſix cens & ſept par ſacre glomes
Que nul aux ſacres ne ſeront aſſeurez.

The number of astrologers will grow so great that they will be driven out, banned, and their books censored, in the year 1607 by sacred assemblies, so that none will be safe from the holy ones.

This dating appears totally successful when reading other commentators who apply it to a Council of Malines of 1607, which was said to have banished astrology. But I can find no record of this council at all. I think this is a case of prophecy fulfilling itself. It was invented to meet the prediction. Therefore, despite the dating, this quatrain is a failure.

Century VIII

VIII.LXXII

Champ Perufin o l'enorme deffaite
Et le conflit tout au pres de Rauenne,
Paffage facre lors qu'on fera la fefte,
Vainqueur vaincu cheval manger la venne.

Oh, what a great defeat on the battlefield of Perugia; the conflict very close to Ravenna. A holy passage when they will celebrate the feast, the conqueror banished to eat horse meat.

This is probably a retrospective quatrain, describing an event which had already occurred when Nostradamus wrote the *Prophéties*. Both Perugia and Ravenna were Papal States and this quatrain describes accurately enough the victory of Gaston de Foix at Ravenna in 1512.

Century VIII

VIII.LXXIII

Soldat Barbare le grand Roy frappera,
Iniuftement non eflongné de mort,
L'auare mere du fait caufe fera
Coniurateur & regne en grand remort.

The king is struck by a barbarian soldier unjustly, not far from death. The greedy ones will be the cause of the deed, conspirator and realm in great remorse.

If used correctly, *barbare* refers to the pirates of Barbary, Algeria, but Nostradamus used it frequently to denote Moslems and others not of the Christian faith. It is otherwise unclear.

Century VIII

VIII.LXXIIII

En terre neufue bien auant Roy entré
Pendant fubges luy viendront faire acueil,
Sa perfidie aura tel recontré
Qu'aux citadins lieu de fefte & recueil.

Far before a king enters into a new land, the subjects will come to bid him welcome. His treachery will have such an effect that to its citizens it is a reception instead of a festival.

The new land, *terre neufue*, is an interesting phrase because it was one of the names for the newly found land of America in Nostradamus' day. If the USA is indicated, this verse indicates that a world leader comes to that country and is given an excellent reception, whereas the whole time the guest is planning treachery.

Could this refer to Gorbachev? Or is it still a futuristic quatrain?

Century VIII

VIII.LXXV

Le pere & filz feront meurdris enfemble
Le prefecteur dedans fon pauillon
La mere à Tours du filz ventre aura enfle.
Caiche verdure de feuilles papillon.

The father and son will be murdered together, the leader within his pavilion. The mother at Tours will have her belly swollen with a son. A verdure chest with little pieces of paper.

The first line of this quatrain is quite definite: A father and son will be murdered together. It cannot apply to France, as no French king and dauphin have been assassinated together. In the case of Louis XVI, there was a space of over two years between the king's death and the presumed death of his young son. Neither was there any pregnant widow at Tours involved with the family. The most important father and son assassination outside France occurred in 1908 when Carlos I and Louis Philippe of Portugal were killed. But the rest of the quatrain still remains unexplained.

Century VIII

VIII.LXXVI

Plus Macelin que roy en Angleterre *Lieu obſcur nay par force aura l'empire:* *Laſche ſans foy, ſans loy ſaignera terre,* *Son temps s'approche ſi pres que ie ſouſpire.*	*More of a butcher than a king in England, born of obscure rank he will gain empire through force. Coward, without faith, without law, he will bleed the land. His time approaches so near that I could sigh.*

Nostradamus' idea of cosmic time was pretty exact when he predicted the advent of Cromwell (1599–1656), thirty years after his own death. Cromwell's description as "more of a butcher than a king" is very apt when one considers the bloodshed of the Civil War. He was a Protestant so Nostradamus regards him, as always, as a heretic. Cromwell came from comparatively humble origins and attained his position through military force, *par force aura l'empire.* The reference to his being a coward *(laſche)* is interesting. Cromwell was so afraid of being assassinated that he was reported to wear an undervest of chain mail.

Century VIII

VIII.LXXVII ★

L'antechriſt trois bien toſt annichilez, *Vingt & ſept ans ſang durera ſa guerre,* *Les heretiques mortz, captifs, exilez,* *Sang corps humain eau rogie greſler terre.*	*The Third Antichrist soon annihilates everything, twenty-seven years of blood his war will last. The unbelievers dead, captive, exiled with blood, human bodies, water and red hail covering the earth.*

Nostradamus envisages three separate Antichrists. The first appears to be Napoleon, the second Hitler and the Third is still to come. Line 1 has an ambiguous reading: It may be intepreted as "the third Antichrist" or the "Antichrist soon annihilates the three." Presumably the three are the Kennedy brothers, two of whom are already dead. Perhaps the third, Edward Kennedy, is a psychological assassinee. With his removal from state politics I now consider that it is unlikely that he is considered as a political person of great depth or importance. Does it make more sense in this context to think that the Third Antichrist is a way of life? I think that Nostradamus believed it to be an actual person.

The war mentioned in the quatrain seems to be one of attrition. After the bombing of Nagaski and Hiroshima large "black raindrops fell, full of dust," as recorded by survivors. So perhaps Nostradamus is not so far out when he speaks of *eau rogie*, the rain of blood. This last war appears to be the worst in this century and there is less than a decade before we can expect it to start. Another Millennium quatrain.

Century VIII

VIII.LXXVIII

Vn Bragamas[1] auec la langue torte
Viendra des dieux le fanctuaire,
Aux heretiques il ouurira la porte
En fufcitant l'eglife militaire.

A soldier of fortune with twisted tongue will come to the sanctuary of the gods. He will open the door for heretics and raise up the Church militant.

This general quatrain could be applied either to France during the Wars of Religion 1542–98, or to Germany during the Thirty Years' War 1618–48.

---

[1] *Bragamas* O.F broadsword or A Pr *Briamanso*, a soldier of fortune

Century VIII

VIII.LXXIX

Qui par fer pere perdra nay de Nonnaire,[1]
De Gorgon fur la fera fang perfetant[2]
En terre eftrange fera fi tout de taire,
Qui bruflera luy mesme & fon entant.[3]

He who loses his father by the sword, born in a nunnery, upon this Gorgon's blood will conceive anew. In a strange land he will do everything to be silent, he who will burn both himself and his child.

The legendary Gorgon was a monster who turned everyone who gazed upon her into stone. Hugh Allen, in his book on Nostradamus (1943) applies this quatrain to himself (page 12). I can make no sense of it.

Century VIII

VIII.LXXX

Des innocens le fang de vefue & vierge.
Tant de maulx faitz par moyen fe grand Roge
Saintz fimulachres trempez en ardant cierge
De frayeur crainte ne verra nul que boge.

The blood of innocents, widow and virgin so many evils committed by the great Red one. Holy images placed over burning candles, terrified by fear more will be seen to move.

The great Red one of line 2 must stand for a revolution, but it is difficult to decide whether it refers to the French or Russian revolution. I am inclined to accept the latter, as Nostradamus describes the French Revolution elsewhere by the "tricolor." Line 1 would therefore refer to the deaths of the czar, czarina, and their children. Line 3 hints vaguely at the influence of the Orthodox Church through Rasputin.

---

[1]*Nonnaire*. Low L. *nonneria*, nunnery.
[2]*perfetant*. L. *(super) fetens*, to conceive while pregnant.
[3]*entant*. Presumably misprint for *enfant*.

Century VIII

VIII.LXXXI

Le neuf empire en defolation,
Sera changé du pole
    aquilonaire.
De la Sicile viendra l'efmotion
Troubler l'emprife à Philip
    tributaire.
	The new empire in desolation will be changed from the Northern Pole. From Sicily will come such trouble that it will bother the enterprise tributary to Philip.

The first two lines of this quatrain sound contemporary by the sheer scope of their context. A ravaged empire moves itself and its civilization southwards. Could this be after the war in the North mentioned in previous quatrains? But the two lines take us back to sixteenth century Europe. Nostradamus seems to see a Hapsburg civil war between Philip and Ferdinand over the division of Charles V's empire. It predicts the uprising against Philip as starting in Sicily.

Century VIII

VIII.LXXXII

Ronge long, fec faifant du bon
    valet,
A la parfin n'aura que fon
    congie,[1]
Poignant poyfon & lettres au
    collet
Sera faifi efchappé en dangie.[2]
	Thin, tall and dry, playing the good valet in the end, will have nothing but his dismissal. Sharp poison and letters in his collar, he will be seized escaping into danger.

Apparently a valet tries to poison his master, is caught and dismissed.

---

[1]*congie*. F. dismissal.
[2]*dangie. dangier*, shortened for rhyme.

Century VIII

VIII.LXXXIII

Le plus grand voile hors du port de Zara, *Pres de Bifance fera fon entreprinfe,* *D'ennemy perte & l'amy ne fera* *Le tiers à deux fera grand pille & prinfe.*	*The largest sail set out of the port of Zara near Byzantium, will carry out its enterprise. There will not be loss of family nor friend; a third will turn on both with great pillage and capture.*

This is another retroactive prophecy describing the atrocities of the Fourth Crusade in 1202. Venice agreed to cross to Egypt with the Crusaders for a large sum of money and half the plunder. The Crusaders could not raise the money so they captured Zara (then in Hungary, now in Yugoslavia). The Pope then excommunicated the whole Crusade, whereupon they sacked Constantinople (Byzantium) and set up Romania, the Roman Empire of the East.

Century VIII

VIII.LXXXIIII

Paterne orra de la Sicile crie, *Tous les aprefts du goulphre de Triefte,* *Qui s'entendra iufque à la trinacrie.[1]* *De tant de voiles fuy, fuy l'horrible pefte.*	*Paterno will hear the cry from Sicily, all the preparations in the Gulf of Trieste. It will be heard as far as Sicily. Flee, oh flee, so many sails, the dreaded pestilence.*

This is probably a continuation of VIII.LXXXI. The Spanish Empire of the Two Sicilies owned Catonia and Paternum, and Trieste belonged to the Hapsburg branch in Venice.

---

[1]*trinacrie.* Trinicia, poetic name for Italy.

Century VIII

VIII.LXXXXV

Entre Bayonne & à ſaint Iean de Lux
Sera poſé de Mars la promottoire
Aux Hanix[1] d'Aquilon Nanar[2] hoſtera lux,
Puis ſuffocqué au lict ſans adiutoire.[3]

Between Bayonne and as far as Saint Jean de Luz will be placed the promontory of Mars. To the Hanix of the North Nanar will remove the light, then suffocate in bed without assistance.

Nostradamus foresees a war or a war zone (Mars) between Bayonne and Saint-Jean-de-Luz in southwest France. The difficulty in interpretation lies in the words *Hanix* and *Nanar*. Another suggestion is that the promontory is Biarritz where Napoleon III, like Mars, the God of War, retired into the arms of various loving women when the north wind ceased to blow. *Hanix* might then come from the Greek, *anscisus*, without force. Napoleon died from the operation for a kidney stone, but his physical condition was weak due to his various debaucheries, and may have made him much frailer than was thought.

Century VIII

VIII.LXXXVI

Par Arnani tholoſer ville franque,
Bande infinie par le mont Adrian,
Paſſe riuiere, Hurin[4] par pont la planque
Bayonne entrer tous Bihoro[5] criant.

Through Emani, Tolosa and Villefranche, an infinite band through the mountains of Adrian. It passes the river, combat over the bridge for a plank. Bayonne will be entered, all crying Bigorre.

[1] *Hanix.?* Gk. *anikatos*, unconquerable. Or L. *Hamaxaeci*, nomads of Northern Europe.
[2] *Nanar.* L. *nonaria*, prostitute?
[3] *adiutoire.* O.F. assistance, aid.
[4] *Hurin.* O.F. dispute, combat
[5] *Bihoro.* *Bigorre*, the battle cry of the Huguenots of Navarre.

The three towns in line 1 and the mountain of Adrian in line 2 are all close together in the southwestern tip of the Spanish Pyrenees. The only river to the north between them and Bayonne is the Bidassoa. As I have said before, *Bigorre* was the battle cry of the Huguenots of Navarre. Originally, Navarre covered the area south of the Pyrenees and north into France. It became a separate state in 1515 and was reunited with France at the accession of Henri de Navarre to the French throne, after Nostradamus' death.

Century VIII

VIII.LXXXVII

Mort conspiree viendra en plein effect,	*A death conspired will come to its full effect, the charge given and*
Charge donnee & voiage de mort,	*the voyage of death. Elected, cre-*
Esleu, crée, receu par siens deffait.	*ated, received; defeated by his followers. With remorse, the*
Sang d'innocence deuant foy par remort.	*innocent blood before him.*

The conspiracy by the French Revolutionaries to rob Louis XVI of both his crown and his life is successfully carried off. The change of his position to constitutional monarch and his flight to Varennes, *the voyage of death,* will be the cause of his death. He will be defeated by his own nation which had earlier elected him. His innocent blood will be a source of remorse to the French.

Century VIII

VIII.LXXXVIII

Dans la Sardeigne vn noble Roy viendra.	*A noble king will come to Sardi-nia who will rule for only three*
Que ne tiendra que trois ans le royaume,	*years in the kingdom. He will join several colors to himself. He*
Plusieurs coulleurs auec soy coniondra,	*himself, after taunts, care spoils slumber.*
Luy mesmes apres soin someil marrit[1] scome.[2]	

[1]*marrit*. O.F. to afflict, spoil.
[2]*scome*. L. *scoma*, scoff, taunt, jeer

When the French Republic took most of his lands, King Charles Emmanuel IV retired to Sardinia where he reigned for only three years, *que trois ans le royaume*. He then abdicated in favor of his brother, Victor Emmanuel I. He then went on to Rome, humiliated and unhappy. He joined the Jesuits and stayed with them until his death in 1819. This was one of the few times in modern history that Sardinia had its own king and not a titular one.

Century VIII

VIII.LXXXIX

Pour ne tumber entre mains de son oncle,
Qui fes enfans par regner trucidez[1],
Orant[2] au peuple mettant pied fur Peloncle[3]
Mort & traifné entre cheuaulx bardez.

In order not to fall into the hands of his uncle who slaughtered his children so that he could reign. Pleading with the people, putting his foot on Peloncle, dead and dragged between armored horses.

The key word to his quatrain is *Peloncle*, which so far remains indecipherable.

Century VIII

VIII.XC

Quand des croifez vn trouué de fens trouble
En lieu du facre verra vn boeuf cornu
Par vierge porc fon lieu lors fera comble,
Par roy plus ordre ne fera fouftenu.

When those of the cross are found, their senses troubled, in place of a sacred thing he will see a horned bull. Through the virgin, the place of the pig will be filled. Order will no longer be maintained by the king.

[1]*trucidez*. L. *trucidare*, to slaughter.
[2]*Orant*. L. *orans*, praying.
[3]*Peloncle*. Doubtful. Possibly Pellonia, the goddess who put enemies to flight?

The men of the cross are either Crusaders or Nazis. The bull may stand for Taurus and the virgin for Virgo, but the rest means very little. An indecipherable quatrain.

Century VIII
VIII.XCI

Frymy[1] les champs des
    Rodanes[2] entrees
Ou les croyſez ſeront preſque vnys,
Les deux braſsieres[3] en piſces
    rencontrees
Et vn grand nombre par deluge
    punis.

Entered among the fields of those of the Rhône where those of the cross are almost united. Two lands meeting in Pisces and a great number punished by the flood.

Yet again, as in the last quatrain, people of the cross. The astrological conjunction here is Pisces with Venus, at a time when the Rhône is in flood.

Century VIII
VIII.XCII

Loin hors du regne mis en
    hazard voiage
Grand oſt duyra pour ſoy
    l'occupera,
Le roy tiendra les ſiens captif
    oſtrage
A ſon retour tout pays pillera.

Far from his kingdom sent on a dangerous journey. He will lead a great army and will hold it for himself. The king will keep his people captive and hostage. He will plunder the whole country on his return.

I had earlier thought that this quatrain was indecipherable, but now believe it may apply to Mao Tse-tung. In the 1930s Chiang Kai-Shek's Nationalist Army had tried to annihilate the Chinese Red Army. But Mao Tse-Tung led his Communist followers on the Long March, an enormous trek through the

---

[1] *Frymy.* misprint for *parmi* in other editions, among.
[2] *Rodanes.* L. *Rhodanus*, the Rhône.
[3] *Braſsieres.* lead strings—possibly standing for Venus, who was bound to Mars by an unbreakable thread forged by Vulcan.

hinterlands of China. Later, he put himself in command of the Red Army and defeated the Nationalist Chinese in 1949. In the 1960s, in the name of the Cultural Revolution, he threw the whole country into disarray, *à son retour tout pays pillera.*

Century VIII

VIII.XCIII

Sept moys sans plus obtiendra prelature
Par son deces grand scisme fera naistre:
Sept moys tiendra vn autre la preture
Pres de Venise paix vnion renaistre.

For seven months, no longer, he will hold the office of prelate. Through his death a great schism will arise. For seven months another acts as prelate near Venice. Peace and union are reborn.

The only popes (*"prelature"*) to live for less than seven months after election have been Sixtus V; Urban VII, who died after two weeks; and Gregory XIV, who died after ten months, all in 1590. An interesting quatrain, but unfortunately there is no record of a schism.

Century VIII

VIII.XCIIII

Deuant le lac ou plus cher fut getté
De sept mois, & son host desconfit
Seront Hyspans par Albannois gastez
Par delay perte en donnant le conflict.

In front of the lake where the dearest one was destroyed for seven months, his army routed. The Spaniards will be devastated by means of Alba. Through delay in giving battle, loss.

Ward applies this quatrain to the English attack on Cadiz by Essex, Howard and Raleigh in June, 1596. The word *cher* in line 1 then becomes treasure or valuables. Their ships were heavy with booty on their return from a seven-month voyage. Cadiz Bay is called a lake by Nostradamus because the root word *Gaddir*, from which Cadiz is derived, means an enclosed

space. During the attack by the English, forty galleons and
thirteen warships were destroyed.

What makes this quatrain so interesting is that Nostradamus
foresaw the war between Spain and England, but when he
wrote the countries were allies because England's queen was
Mary Tudor, wife of King Philip of Spain.

Century VIII

VIII.XCV

Le seducteur sera mis en la fosse,
Et estaché iusques à quelque
temps,
Le clerc vny le chef auec sa
crosse[1]
Pycante droite attraira[2] les
contens.

The seducer will be placed in a
ditch and will be tied up for some
time. The scholar joins the chief
with his cross. The sharp right
(one) will draw the contented
ones.

I have no interpretation for this quatrain.

Century VIII

VIII.XCVI

La synagogue sterile sans nul
fruit
Sera receu entre les infideles
De Babylon la fille du porsuit
Misere & triste luy trenchera les
aisles.

The sterile synagogue without
any fruit will be received by the
infidels. The daughter of the
persecuted one of Babylon. Miserable and sad they will clip her
wings.

This quatrain probably describes the Jews' attitude towards
Moslem countries between 1550 and 1566, which means these
events mostly occurred during Nostradamus' lifetime. After
the wave of persecution suffered by the Jews during this
period in Christian countries, the sultan of Turkey, Suleiman
the Magnificent, offered hospitality to any Jews who settled in
his country, particularly in Constantinople and Salonika. One

[1]*crosse.* O.F. abbey or cross?
[2]*attraira.* O.F. to draw, attract.

such emigré became very powerful. In 1566, the year of Nostradamus' death, Don Joseph Nassi was created duke of Naxos and became the principal adviser to Selim I.

Century VIII

VIII.XCVII

Au fin du VAR changer le pompotans,
Pres du riuage les trois beaux enfans naiſtre.
Ruyne au peuple par aage competans
Regne au pays changer plus voir croiſtre.

At the end of the Var the great powers change. Near the bank three beautiful children are born. Ruin to the people when they are of age. In the country the kingdom is seen to grow and change greatly.

In X.C. *pompotans* stands for England, but probably does not so in this case. The river Var flows into the Mediterranean between Cannes and Nice and was the approximate border of Savoy in Nostradamus' time. The three beautiful children may be a reference to the three Kennedy brothers who bring *ruyne*, scandal, to the USA, linking up with the other quatrains on this subject. Certainly the USA changed its power basis, Korea, withdrawal from Vietnam, etc., during their lifetimes and now its growing influence has made it one of the great world powers. Possibly the quatrain is only partially fulfilled to date?

Century VIII

VIII.XCVIII

Des gens d'egliſe ſang ſera eſpandu,
Comme de l'eau en ſi grande abondance:
Et d'vn long temps ne ſera reſtanché
Ve ve[1] au clerc ruyne & doleance.

Of the churchmen the blood will pour forth as abundantly as water. For a long time it will not be restrained. Woe, woe, ruin and grief for the clergy.

[1]*Ve ve.* L. Vae, alas, woe.

Possibly another quatrain about the persecution of the clergy in France in 1792. The last line does have Jewish linguistic overtones.

Century VIII

VIII.XCIX

Par la puiſſance des trois rois temporelz,
En autre lieu ſera mis le ſaint ſiege:
Où la ſubſtance de l'eſprit corporel,
Sera remys & receu pour vray ſiege.

Through the powers of the temporal kings the sacred seat will be put in another place where the substance of the body and spirit will be restored and received as a true seat.

The only occasion to date since Nostradamus' writing when the Papal See has been moved from the Vatican was when Pope Pius VI was removed by Napoleon to Valence, and died there. But there are hints in Malachy that a pope towards the end of this century will be forced from the Vatican, probably due to the advent of a World War or the coming of the Third Antichrist. Lines 3 and 4 seem to indicate a revival of religious fervor. Possibly a futuristic quatrain?

Century VIII

VIII.C

Pour l'abondance de larme reſpandue
Du hault en bas par le bas au plus hault
Trop grande foy par ieu vie perdue,
De ſoif mourir par habondant deffault.[1]

By the great number of tears shed, from top to bottom and from the bottom to the very top. A life is lost through a game with too much faith. To die of thirst through a great deficiency.

I cannot decipher this quatrain.

[1] The whole of line 4 is difficult to interpret. It probably means drowned, or even to drink oneself to death.

Century IX

IX.I

Dans la maiſon du traducteur de Bourc[1]	In the house of the translator from Bourg letters will be found
Seront les lettres trouuees ſus la table,	on the table. One-eyed, red and white haired will hold the course
Bourgne, roux, blanc, chanu tiendra de cours,	which will change for the new constable.
Qui changera au nouueau conneſtable.	

This is a fascinating quatrain. One of the best-known sixteenth century French scholars was Etienne de la Boétie. If *Bourc* stands for *Boétie*, then the prophecy makes some kind of sense in that the latter had a famous quarrel with the then Constable of France, Anne de Montmorency, over the publication of a book, *La Servitude Volontaire*. Nostradamus seems to foresee that Boétie would have even more trouble with the Constable's successor, Henri de Montmorency. But this did not occur, as Boétie died four years before Anne de Montmorency in 1563. (See also IX.LXXXI.)

Century IX

IX.II

Du hault du mont Auentin voix ouye,	A voice is heard from the top of the Aventine Hill. Go away, go
Vuydez vuydez de tous les deux coſtez,	away, on both sides! The anger will be appeased by the blood of
Du ſang des rouges ſera l'ire aſſomye,[2]	the red ones. From Rimini and Prato, Colonna expelled.
D'Arimin Prato, Columna[3] debotez.[4]	

---

[1]*Bourc.?* Bourg, north of Bordeaux.
[2]*aſſomye.* O.F. to appease.
[3]*Columna.* original spelling of the Colonnas of Rome.
[4]*debotez.* O.F. *debouter*, to expel, drive out.

This is yet another quatrain centred around the feuds of the Vatican States with the great Italian families, like the Colonnas and the Orsinis. In Nostradamus' time, they were allied to the Spanish and thus got deeply involved with the anti-Spanish policies of Pope Paul IV.

Century IX

IX.III

La magna vaqua[1] à Rauenne grand trouble,
Conduictz par quinze enſerrez à Fornaſe
A Rõme naiſtre deux monſtres à teſte double
Sang, feu, deluge, les plus grands à l'eſpaſe.

The magna vaqua near Ravenna in great trouble, led by fifteen shut up at Fornese. At Rome two monsters with double heads are born. Blood, fire, floods the greatest (hanging) in the air.

This quatrain is similar to its predecessor, with the added enigma of the *magna vaqua*, literally, the great cow. It too seems to be involved with the Papal States and the Vatican, together with a hanging and the production of two double-headed monsters. Probably a failed quatrain.

Century IX

IX.IIII

L'an enſuyuant deſcouuertz par deluge,
Deux chefs eſleuz le premier ne tiendra
De fuyr umbre à l'vn d'eux le refuge,
Saccagee caſe[2] qui premier maintiendra.

The following year revealed by a flood two leaders elected, the first will not hold on. For one of them, refuge in fleeing shadows. The victim plundered who maintained the first.

[1]*magna vaqua.* possibly the port Magna Valca between Ravenna and Ferrara, or an unsolved word.
[2]*caſe.* A.Pr. *casa*, the hunt, or victim of a hunt.

Yet another failed quatrain combining a discovery of treasure and vague threats.

Century IX

IX.V

Tiers doit du pied au premier semblera.	The third toe will look like the first one of a new king, of low
A vn nouueau monarque de bas hault	height he will occupy as a tyrant Pisa and Lucca to correct the
Qui Pyſe & Lucques Tyran occupera	fault of his predecessor.
Du precedant corriger le deffault.	

The third estate, established for a second time in 1848, will seem no more than the toe of the first, i.e., very insignificant. Louis Napoleon found it easier to deal with than did Napoleon I. In 1831 Louis Napoleon was involved with Italian revolutionaries and helped to seize the Civita Castellana, which is in Tuscany as are Pisa and Lucca. The fault of Louis Napoleon's predecessor, Napoleon II, was his failure to obtain real power.

Century IX

IX.VI

Par la Guyenne infinité d'Anglois	A great number of English in Guienne will occupy it, calling it
Occuperont par nom d'Anglaquitaine	Anglaquitaine. Of Languedoc, Ispalme, Bordelais which they
Du Languedoc Iſpalme[1] Bourdeloys.	will name after Barboxitaine.
Qu'ilz nommeront apres Barboxitaine.[2]	

[1]*Iſpalme.* unidentified place name.
[2]*Barboxitaine.* Possibly derived from *Barbe-Occitanie*? *Barbe* may refer to the enigmatic Aenobarbe and *Occitanie* was the medieval name for the Mediterranean coast.

The English occupied Guienne, the Languedoc and Bordelais steadily between the twelfth and fifteenth centuries, but
not since Nostradamus' lifetime. Bordelais was one of the
centers of English dominance in southern France. Possibly
Ispalme is a misprint for Lapalme near Narbonne? Barboxitaine seems to stand for "the beard's southwestern France"
and the beard may refer to the strange character which haunts
the quatrains, Aenobarbe, who brings war and tragedy in his
wake (see V.LIX). Not a successful quatrain on the whole.

Century IX

IX.VII

Qui ouurira le monument trouué,	The man who opens the tomb when it is found and who does
Et ne viendra le ferrer promptement.	not shut it immediately, evil will come to him. No one will be able
Mal luy viendra & ne pourra prouué,	to prove it. It might have been better were he a Breton or a Nor-
Si mieux doit estre roy Breton ou Normand.	man king.

Yet another quatrain about the discovery of a tomb. The last
line is suitably enigmatic. Nostradamus' tomb was opened by
drunken soldiers during the Revolution.

Century IX

IX.VIII

Puisnay Roy fait son pere mettre à mort,	The younger son will put his father, the king, to death after
Apres conflit de mort tres inhonefte:	the quarrel, to a death very dishonest. Writings found, sus-
Escrit trouué soubson donra remort,	picion will bring remorse, when the chased wolf lies on the bed-
Quand loup chaffé pofe fus la couchette.	cover.

Although the event of a younger son taking over his father's
throne through murder has happened many times in history

it is hard to find any definite fulfillment of this since Nostradamus' lifetime, nor of the strange details of the last two lines.

Century IX

IX.IX

Quand lampe ardente de feu inextinguible
Sera trouué au temple des Veſtales,
Enfant trouué feu, eau paſſant par trible:[1]
Perir eau Nymes, Tholoſe cheoir les halles.

When the lamp burning with eternal fire will be found in the temple of the Vestals. A child found in the fire, water passing through the sieve. Nîmes to perish in water, the markets will fall in Toulouse.

Nostradamus may have cheated over this verse because in 1557 there was an enormous cloudburst over Nîmes. This was popularly held to be the site of the Temple of Diana, tended by her Vestal Virgins. The water fell to over six feet deep in some places and many antique monuments were discovered. But, against this, nothing of note happened at Toulouse at this time. Probably a failed quatrain. (But see V.VI.)

Century IX

IX.X

Moyne moyneſſe d'enfant mort expoſé,
Mourir par ourſe & rauy par verrier.[2]
Par Fois & Pamyes le camp ſera poſé.
Contre Tholoſe Carcas dreſſer forrier.

The child of a monk and a nun will be exposed to die, killed by a she-bear and carried off by a boar. The army will be camped near Foix and Pamiers. Carcassonne will raise the pillage against Toulouse.

An indecipherable quatrain set in southerwestern France.

[1]*trible.* possibly Fr. *crible,* a sieve.
[2]*verrier.* possibly a word Nostradamus concocted from the Latin *verez,* a boar.

Century IX

IX.XI

Le iuſte à tort à mort lon viendra mettre	They will come to put the just man wrongfully to death. He is killed publicly in their midst. So a great plague will be born in this place that the judges will be forced to flee.
Publiquement & due millieu eſtaint:	
Si grande peſte en ce lieu viendra naiſtre,	
Que les iugeans[1] fouyr ſeront conſtraint.	

This quatrain is generally understood to apply to England and in particular to the unjust (*à tort à mort*) of Charles I, his execution. His death was followed by the Great Plague of London, 1655—56.

Century IX

IX.XII

Le tant d'argent de Diane & Mercure	The great amount of silver of Diana and Mercury, the images will be found in the lake. The sculptor looking for new clay, both he and his followers will be soaked in gold.
Les ſimulachres au lac ſeront trouuez,	
Le figulier cherchant argille neufue	
Luy & les ſiens d'or ſeront abbreuez.	

Another treasure quatrain. Does it relate to VIII.XXVIII and VIII.XXX?

---

[1]*iugeans.* judges, a Nostradamus word.

Century IX

IX.XIII

Les exilez autour de la
  Soulongne
Conduis de nuit pour marcher
  à Lauxois,
Deux de Modene truculent[1] de
  Bologne,
Mys defcouuers par feu de
  Burançoys.

The exiles around Sologne, led
by night to march into Anxas.
Two from Modena for the cruel
one of Bologna; put discovered,
by the fire of the Buzançais.

I cannot find the key word to this quatrain. The place names
have no logical sequence.

Century IX

IX.XIIII

Mys en planure chaulderons
  d'infecteurs,[2]
Vin, miel & huyle, & baftis fur
  forneaulx
Seront plongez fans mal dit mal
  facteurs
Sept, fum extaint au canon des
  borneaux.

The dyers' cauldron put in a flat
place, wine, honey and oil, built
over furnaces. They will be
drowned without saying or doing
an evil thing. Seventh of Borneaux, the snake extinguished at
the cannon.

A typically unintelligible Nostradamus quatrain, of which
there seem to be quite a few in Century IX.

---

[1]truculent. L. truculentus, ferocious, hard, cruel.
[2]infecteurs. L. dyers.

Century IX

IX.XV

Pres de Parpan les rouges detenus,	The red ones detained near Perpignan, those in the middle ruined, led far away. Three cut into pieces and five badly supported for the Lord and Prelate of Burgundy.
Ceux du milieu parfondrez menez loing:	
Trois mis en pieces, & cinq mal fouſtenus,	
Pour le Seigneur & Prelat de Bourgoing.	

Perpignan belonged to Spain until 1659, and red was the Spanish national color. Nostradamus appears to foresee a Franco-Spanish struggle around the Pyrenees. The governor of Burgundy in Nostradamus' time, the duc d'Aumale, died in 1573. The country had four, not five, bishops under him.

Century IX

IX.XVI

De caſtel[1] Franco fortira l'aſſemblee,	From Castille Franco will bring out the assembly. The ambassadors will not agree and cause a schism. The people of Riviera will be in the crowd. The great man will be denied entry to the Gulf.
L'ambaſſadeur non plaiſant fera ſcifme:	
Ceux de Ribiere feront en la meſlee,	
Et au grand goulphre deſnier ont l'entree.	

One of Nostradamus' best quatrains with the names of two principal personages given to us. Rivera was the dictator of Spain, Primo de Rivera, and Franco is Francisco Franco, who helped depose him. Franco was exiled to Morocco but returned triumphantly to Spain when his party came to power. The last line is understood to refer to Franco's exile when he was not able to cross the Mediterranean, *goulphre*, to his native Spain. *Caſtel* should read *Castille* (see III.VIII).

---

[1]*caſtel.* Castille.

Century IX

IX.XVII

Le tiers premier pys que ne feit
  Neron,
Vuidex vaillant que ſang
  humain reſpandre:
R'edifier fera le forneron,
Siecle d'or, mort, nouueau roy
  grand eſclandre.

The third one does firstly worse
than Nero; go, flow, brave
human blood. The furnace will
be rebuilt, a golden century.
Death, a new king and great
scandal.

"The third" in Nostradamus seems always to refer to the Third Estate, whose first effort was its National Convention in Revolutionary France. The prophet refers to it as being worse than Nero's reign, with blood flowing from the guillotines. The guillotine was placed in the Place de la Révolution (now the Place de la Concorde) opposite the Tuileries, where formerly the furnaces for the tile kilns stood. The golden century of the kings (Louis XIV—XVI) is over. Perhaps the great scandal is an indirect reference to the killing of the royal family, treason. (See also III.LIX)

Century IX

IX.XVIII

Le lys Dauffois portera dans
  Nanſy
Iuſques en Flandres electeur de
  l'empire,
Neufue obturee au grand
  Montmorency,
Hors lieux prouez deliure à
  clere peyne.

The lily of the dauphin is taken
as far as Nancy, the Elector of
the Empire as far as Flanders. A
new prison for the great Montmorency, not in the usual place,
delivered up to Clerepeyne.

Louis XIII was the first bearer of the lilies of France and the title of Dauphin since Nostradamus' death. He entered Nancy in September, 1633. The city of Treves had been recovered a year earlier by the Maréchal d'Estrées, who re-established the authority of the Elector. However, in 1633, the Elector was carried off by the Spanish and taken as a prisoner to Brussels.

(Flandres). At the same time in 1632, a revolt was led in southern France by the great Montmorency, who was captured. His family pleaded in vain for his release: instead they obtained for him the doubtful privilege of execution by a private, rather than a public executioner. He was beheaded in the court of the prison, the Hôtel de Ville, which had recently been built, *hors lieux. Deliure à clere peyne* may contain two meanings: It means delivered to clear punishment, but some commentators state that Clerepeyne was the name of the executioner. I have not been able to verify this. It first appears in a commentary by Jaubert in 1656.

Century IX

IX.XIX

Dans le millieu de la foreſt Mayenne,	*In the middle of the Mayenne forest, the Sun in Leo, the light-*
Sol au lyon la fouldre tombera,	*ning will fall. The great bastard*
Le grand baſtard yſſu du gran du Maine,	*born of the great man of Maine, on that day a point will enter the*
Ce iour fougeres pointe en ſang entrera.	*blood of Fougères.*

Mayenne, in northwestern France, has a large forest west of the city. Fougères is about twenty miles further west, the seat of a great family name which died out in the thirteenth century. The title of the Mayennes was used in the fifteenth century by Henri II's mistress, Diane de Poitiers, and also by Henri III while he was duc d'Anjou. No other great families are connected with the house, unfortunately for Nostradamus. As for the dating of the Sun in Leo, it is not specific enough.

Century IX

IX.XX

De nuit viendra par la foreſt de Reines,
Deux pars vaultorte Herne[1] la pierre blanche,
Le moine noir[2] en gris dedans Varennes
Eſleu cap. cauſe tempeſte feu, ſang tranche.

By night will come through the forest of Reines, two partners, by a roundabout way. The queen, the white stone. The monk-king dressed in gray at Varennes. The elected Capet causes tempest, fire and bloody slicing.

This is one of Nostradamus' more remarkable quatrains, describing the flight to Varennes by Louis XVI and Marie Antoinette in 1791. The royal couple, having fled from the Tuileries through a secret door in the queen's apartment, travel through the forest of Reims. This happened, and they also lost their way and chose an extremely bad route, *vaultorte*. The *pierre blanche* probably refers to the affair of the diamond necklace, which finally demolished Marie Antoinette's fragile popularity with the French populace. It may also refer indirectly to the fact that her lady in waiting reported that on capture the queen's hair turned white overnight and that she usually wore white dresses. The king was wearing a simple gray suit when they entered Varennes. It is possible that the word "monk" refers to his impotence earlier in his marriage. He was a Capet, the first elected king of France, and as Nostradamus states, was the cause, the final symptom of a revolution and the shedding of blood. *Tranche* as a verb means to slice, particularly apposite in the context of the guillotine. A really fascinating quatrain with facts and places. See IX.XXXIIII.

---

[1] *Herne*. possible anagram for *Reine*.
[2] *noir*. usual anagram for *roi*, king.

Century IX

IX.XXI

Au temple hault de Bloys ſacre Solonne,	At night, the high temple of Blois at Sacré Solonne. A priest in the
Nuict pont de Loyre, prelat, roy pernicant[1]	Loire bridge a king dying. A messenger, victory for the mar-
Curſeur[2] victoire aux mareſtz de la lone[3]	shes on the water. Destruction for a priestly gift from the whites.
Dou prelature de blancs à bormeant.[4]	

This quatrain is a repetition of Nostradamus' strongly held belief that France would gain a king from Blois. Sacré Solonne is the Church of Saint Solonne, the Cathedral at Blois. Unfortunately, this gets us no further.

Century IX

IX.XXII

Roy & ſa court au lieu de langue halbe,[5]	The king and his court in the place of the clever tongue, in the
Dedans le temple vis à vis du palais	temple facing the palace. In the garden the duke of Mantua and
Dans le iardin Duc de Mantor & d'Albe,	Alba, Alba and Mantua, dag-
Albe & Mantor poignard langue & palais.	ger, tongue and the palace.

The key to this quatrain lies in the identity of Alba and Mantua, which had been joined together in 1536 by Charles V. Their ruler from 1550 to 1587 was Gonzaga, who did suffer an assassination attempt but at Casale, not at Blois. But the famous Château de Blois does not face the Cathedral. An irritating quatrain.

[1]*pernicant*. L. *pernecare*, to kill, or *pernix*, swift
[2]*Curſeur*. O.F. runner or messenger.
[3]*lone*. A.Pr. *lona*, a pool, still water.
[4]*à bormeant*. L. *aboriri*, to miscarry. A.Pr. *abouriment*, destruction.
[5]*halbe*. O.F. *habler*, to talk.

Century IX

IX.XXIII

Puiſnay iouant au freſch deſſouz
la tonne,
Le hault du toict du milieu ſur
la teſte,
Le pere roy au temple ſaint
Solonne,
Sacrifiant ſacrera fum de feſte.

The younger son playing out-
doors under the arbor, the top of
the roof on the middle of his
head. The father king in the
Temple is solemn, sacrificing.
He will consecrate the smoke of
the feast.

The younger son is the second son of Louis XVI and his wife, who was allowed out to play in the Temple Gardens while Louis was imprisoned in a tower, away from the rest of the family, as stated in line 3. The quatrain continues to describe the solemn future of the king, sacrificed to the Revolution on the guillotine.

Century IX

IX.XXIIII

Sur le palais au rochier[1] des
feneſtres
Seront rauis les deux petits
royaux,
Paſſer aurelle[2] Luthece[3] Denis
cloiſtres,
Nonain, mallods[4] aualler verts
noyaulx.

At the palace from the balcony of
the windows, two little royal ones
will be carried off. To pass
Orléans, Paris and the cloisters
of Saint Denis, a nun; the flies
devouring the green pits.

An incomprehensible quatrain.

---

[1] *rochier.* rock. In the context of windows, probably means a balcony.
[2] *aurelle.* L. *Aurelianum*, Orléans.
[3] *Luthece.* L. *Lutecia*, Paris.
[4] *mallods.* O.F. *malots*, flies? *malois*, wicked? or L. *malum*, apple?

Century IX

IX.XXV

Paſſant les pontz venir pres des
roſiers,[1]
Tard arriué pluſtoſt qu'il
cuydera,[2]
Viendront les noues[3] eſpaignolz
à Beſiers,
Qui icelle chaſſe emprinſe[4] caſſera.

Crossing the bridges to come
near the Rosiers, sooner than he
thought he arrived late. The new
Spaniards will come to Beziers,
so that this chase will break the
enterprise.

The interesting points in this quatrain are Nostradamus'
new Spaniards, *noves eſpaignolez*. Béziers was on the Spanish
invasion route to France about fifty miles northeast of the pre-
1659 border. Otherwise, the quatrain remains obscure.

Century IX

IX.XXVI

Nice ſortie ſur nom[5] des letres
aſpres,
La grande cappe[6] fera preſent
non ſien,
Proche de vultry aux murs de
vertes capres
Apres plombin[7] le vent à bon
eſſien.

Departed from the name of Nice
through bitter letters, the great
cappe will present his own thing.
Near Voltai at the wall of the
green columns, after Piombino
the wind in good earnest.

I cannot interpret this quatrain.

[1] *roſiers.* either Rosiers, or rosebushes.
[2] *cuydera.* O.F. to think.
[3] *noues.* O.F. new.
[4] *emprinſe.* O.F. enterprise.
[5] *ſur nom.* Either surname, or "under the name of."
[6] *cappe.* The Pope, cape, O.F. *cape* or *Capet*, then the French royal
line.
[7] *plombin.* Piombino or L. leaden, of lead.

Century IX

IX.XXVII

*De bois la garde vent cloz rond
pont ſera,
Hault le receu frappera le
Daulphin,
Le vieux teccon¹ bois vnis
paſſera,
Paſſant plus oultre du duc le
droit confin.*

The guardian of the forest, the wind will close around the bridge. Received highly he will strike the dauphin. The old craftsmen will pass through the woods in company, going far beyond the known borders of the duke.

It is just possible that this quatrain may be yet another continuing the description of escape of the dauphin, son of Louis XVI, who was reported dead in June, 1795. It implies that the boy is taken out of France, but the method is obscure. (See V.I.)

Century IX

IX.XXVIII

*Voille Symacle² port
Maſſiliolique,³
Dans Venise port marcher aux
Pannons:
Partir du goulfre & ſinus⁴
Illirique
Vaſt⁵ à Socile, Ligurs coups de
canons.*

The allied fleet from the port of Marseilles, in the Venetian harbor to march against Hungary. To leave from the gulf and the bay of Illyria. Devastation in Sicily, for the Ligurians, cannon shot.

Geographically this quatrain covers a lot of ground: Panonia, Hungary, Marseilles, the Gulf of Illyria. But despite all these clues, I cannot decipher it.

¹*teccon.* O.F. A game played with a ball. Possibly from Gk. *tekton*, a craftsman.
²*Symacle.* Gk. *symmachos*, auxiliary, allied with.
³*Maſſiliolique.* L. *Masilioticus*, of Marseilles.
⁴*ſinus.* L. a bay.
⁵*Vaſt.* L. *vastum*, destruction, devastation.

Century IX

IX.XXIX

Lors que celuy qu'à nul ne donne lieu,
Abandonner vouldra lieu prins non prins:
Feu nef par ſaignes, bitument[1] à Charlieu,
Seront Quintin Balez[2] reprins.

When the man will give way to none he will wish to abandon a place taken, yet not taken. A ship on fire through the swamps. Bitumen at Charlieu. Saint Quentin and Calais will be recaptured.

The last line of this quatrain is interesting. The unexpected fall of Calais, so regretted by Mary Tudor, occurred on January 6, 1558, when the duc de Guise recaptured it. Calais was the last bastion of the English in France. After that St. Quentin was given back to the French in the general settlement of 1559.

Century IX

IX.XXX

Au port de POVLA & de ſaint Nicolas,
Perir Normande au goulfre Phanaticque,[3]
Cap.[4] de Biſance raues crier helas,
Secors de Gaddes[5] & du grand Philipique.

At the port of POULA and Saint Nicolas a Normand will punish in the Gulf of Quaerno. Capet cries alas in the streets of Byzantium. Help from Cadiz and the great Philip.

All the places mentioned in this quatrain except Cadiz are in Yugoslavia. If Philip in line 4 was intended to be Philip II, Nostradamus predicted a Franco-Turkish attack on the Hapsburgs in the south, with the Spaniards helping the French. This never took place. A failed quatrain.

[1]*butiment*. O.F. *butimen*, asphalt. pitch.
[2]*Balez*. anagram of Calais?
[3]*Phanaticque*.? L. Sinus Flanaticus, the Gulf of Quaerno.
[4]*Cap*. probably the usual apocope of Capet, the French royal line.
[5]*Gaddes*. L. Gadez, Cadiz.

Century IX

IX.XXXI

*Le tremblement de terre à
  Mortara,[1]
Caſſich[2] ſaint George[3] à demy
  perfondrez,
Paix aſſoupie, la guerre eſueillera,
Dans temple à Paſques abyſmes
  enfondrez.*

*The trembling of the earth at
Martara, the tin island of Saint
George half sunk. Drowsy with
peace, war will arise at Easter.
In the temple abysses opened.*

This is another earthquake quatrain, but it is difficult to
relate it to the British Isles. Earthquakes occur there, but not
of such a dimension that half the land would be destroyed. An
earthquake in Martara would mean a disturbance over 1,000
miles from Britain. But the quatrain should not be totally
dismissed. Geoffrey Goldman, an expert on earthquake, stated
recently that "we are the earthquake generation" and he seems
to foresee that the earthquakes will cover a far larger area than
the so-called earthquake zone. Easter fits comparatively well
with the great earthquake Nostradamus foresees in the west
coast of America in mid-May.

Century IX

IX.XXXII

*De fin porphire profond collon
  trouuee
Deſſoubz la laze[4] eſcriptz
  capitolin:[5]
Os poil retors Romain force
  prouuee,
Claſſe[6] agiter au port de Methelin.*

*A deep column of fine porphyry
is found, inscriptions of the
Capitol under the base; bones,
twisted hair. The Roman
strength tried, the fleet is stirred
at the harbor of Mitylene.*

Yet another difficult quatrain.

[1] *Mortara.* probably misprint for Martara.
[2] *Caſſich.* Gk. *Cassitorides,* the tin islands, a name given to Cornwall and
the Scilly Islands.
[3] *ſaint George.* probably England, as George was adopted as its patron
saint in the fourteenth century.
[4] *laze.* Gk. *laz,* foot or base.
[5] *capitolin.* belonging to the capitol of Rome, i.e., Roman, Latin.
[6] *claſſe.* L. *classus,* fleet.

Century IX

IX.XXXIII

Hercules Roy de Romme & *d'Annemarc,*[1] *De Gaule trois Guion*[2] *furnommé,* *Trembler l'Itale & l'vnde de* *fainct Marc,*[3] *Premier fur tous monarque* *renommé.*	Hercules, king of Rome and of Annemarc. Of Gaul three times the leader will be so called. Italy will tremble and the waters around Saint Mark, the first to be renowned over all kings.

A reference to de Gaulle? For Annemarc see IV.XXVII.

Century IX

IX.XXXIIII

Le part foluz mary fera mittré, *Retour conflict paffera fur le* *thuille:* *Par cinq cens vn trahyr fera* *tiltré,* *Narbon & Saulce par coutaux* *auons d'huille.*	The partner, solitary but married will be mitred; the return, fighting will cross over the Tuileries. By five hundred one traitor will be ennobled. Narbonne and Saulce, we will have oil for knives.

This is again a riveting quatrain following directly upon IX.XX. When Louis XVI and Marie Antoinette were stopped at Varennes they passed the night at the house of a man named Saulce, line 4. The Sauces (modern spelling), have been chandlers and *marchands-épiciers* at Varennes since the sixteenth century, and Nostradamus is able to give us their name! The statement that the king above is mitred (*soulz mary fera mittré*) refers to Louis' return to the Tuileries on June 20, 1792, when the mob invaded the palace and the king was forced to wear the revolutionary cap of liberty, which looks very much like a mitre. It is thought that *coutaux* in line 4 should read as *quartants*, which means oil sold at retail, which was exactly what

---

[1]*Annemarc.*? Hungary and Bohemia, Moravia.
[2]*Guion.* O.F. guide, leader, chief.
[3]*fainct Marc.* Venice, of whom St. Mark is the patron.

the eighteenth century M. Saulce did. In Thiers' *History of France* he comments that when the king and queen returned to the Tuileries for the second time *retour . . . thuille*, the mob murdered five hundred people.

A convincing quatrain. See IX.XX.

Century IX

IX.XXXV

Et Ferdinand blonde ſera
    deſcorte,[1]
Quitter la fleur ſuyere le
    Macedon.[2]
Au grand beſoing defaillira ſa
    routte,
Et marchera contre le
    Myrmidon.[3]

And the fair-haired Ferdinand will disagree, to abandon the flower and follow the Macedonian. In great need his course will fail him and he will march against the Myrmidons.

This could possibly be a quatrain relating to the Second World War, describing the situation of King Ferdinand of Bulgaria.

Century IX

IX.XXXVI

Vn grand Roy prins entre les
    mains d'vn Ioyne,
Non loing de Paſque confuſion
    coup cultre:[4]
Perpet.[5] captifs temps que
    fouldre en la huſne,
Lors que trois freres ſe bleſſeront
    & murtre.

A great king captured by the hands of a young man, not far from Easter. Confusion, a state of the knife. Everlasting captives, times when the lightning is on top, when three brothers will be wounded and murdered.

[1]*deſcorte*. O.F. disagreement, detached.
[2]*Macedon*. The Greeks?
[3]*Myrmidon*. The tribe of Achilles, renowned for their obedience to commands.
[4]*cultre*. L. *coulter*, knife.
[5]*Perpet*. apocope of L. *Perpetulialis*, everlasting.

Here again is the theme of the three brothers, which I have tentatively interpreted as the Kennedys, the three brothers from the *Nouvelle Lande*, America. In this verse Nostradamus indicates that all three brothers will be murdered and this may happen around Easter. Since John F. Kennedy was killed in November, 1963, and his brother Robert Kennedy on June 6, 1968, maybe another assassination is to be expected around Easter (April, May), with possibly a storm thrown in *(fouldre en la huſne)*. But equally, the lightning may refer to a gun on the top of a tall building, which recalls Dallas in 1963. As I have said, I regard Edward Kennedy as possibly a psychological assassinee. This is possibly partly futuristic, but definitely a quatrain of the twentieth century.

Century IX

IX.XXXVII

Pont & molins en Decembre verſez,	*Bridges and mild overturned in December, the Garonne will rise*
En ſi haut lieu montera la Garonne:	*to a very high level. Walls, buildings, Toulouse overthrown,*
Murs, edifices, Tholoſe renuerſez,	*so that none will know his place*
Qu'on ne ſçaura ſon lieu autant matronne.[1]	*before Matronne.*

An unintelligible quatrain. The key word probably lies in *Matronne*.

---

[1]*matronne.* May be a disguised place name?

Century IX

IX.XXXVIII

L'entree de Blaye par Rochelle
& l'Anglois,
Paſſera outre le grand
Aemathien,[1]
Non loing d'Agen attendra le
Gaulois,
Secours Narbonne deceu par
entretien.

The entry at Blaye for la
Rochelle and the English. The
great Macedonia will pass
beyond. Not far from Agen the
Gaul will wait,[2] help from Narbonne misled by a conversation.

Century IX

IX.XXXIX

En Arbiſſel à Veront[3] &
Carcari,
De nuict conduitz pour
Sauonne atrapper,
Le vifz Gaſcon Turbi, & la
Scerry
Derrier mur vieux & neuf
palais gripper.

In Albisola to Veront and Car-
cara led by night to seize
Savona, the swift Gascon, La
Turbie and l'Escarene. To seize
both the old and new palace
behind the wall.

A quatrain with too many place names and nothing upon
which to hang them for an interpretation.

---

[1]*Aemathien.* L. *Emathia,* a poetic name for Macedonia and Thessaly.
[2]Alternative reading, "he will wait for the Frenchman."
[3]*Veront.* Probably not Verona, as all the other places mentioned are
close to Albisola. An unsolved place name?

Century IX

IX.XL

Pres de Quintin dans la foreſt
  bourlis,[1]
Dans l'abbaye ſeront Flamens
  ranches,[2]
Les deux puiſnais de coups my
  eſtourdis
Suitte oppreſſee & garde tous
  aches.

*Near Saint Quentin deceived in
the forest, in the Abbey the Flemish will be cut up. The two
youngest half stunned by blows,
their followers crushed and the
guard all cut to pieces.*

Could this refer to the Battle of Saint Quentin in 1557?
Before the battle, the Spaniards seized the Abbey of Vermon-
dois. But even that information leaves us still unclear as to
what Nostradamus was aiming at.

Century IX

IX.XLI

Le grand Chyren[3] *ſoy ſaiſir*
  d'Auignon,
De Romme letres en miel plein
  d'amertume
Letre ambaſſade partir de
  Chanignon,[4]
Carpentras pris par duc noir
  rouge plume.

*The great Chyren will seize
Avignon, from Rome will come
honeyed letters full of bitterness.
The letter and embassy to leave
from Chanignon. Carpentras
taken by the black duke with a
red feather.*

Nostradamus seems to envisage Henri II as capturing
Avignon, which at that time belonged to the Papacy. Unfortunately Avignon did not come into French hands properly
until 1791, although it was occupied by the French in 1663–
64 and 1768–74. Presumably the letters are dispatches from
an irate Vatican. *Chanignon* is still undeciphered. Carpentras
is near Avignon and part of the papal lands.

[1]*bourlis.* Possible derivative of *boucle*, deceived, or an untraceable
word.
[2]*ranches.* Error for *tranches* in all other editions.
[3]*Chyren.* The usual anagram for Henryc, Henri.
[4]*Chanignon.* An unsolved place or proper name.

Century IX

IX.XLII

De Barſellonne, de Gennes &
    Venise,
De la Secille peſte Monet[1] vnis,
Contra Barbare claſſe prendront
    la viſe,
Barbar, poulſe bien loing iuſqu'à
    Thunis.

From Barcelona, from Genoa
and Venice, from Sicily a pestilence allied with Monaco. They
will take aim against the barbarian fleet. The barbarian driven
back as far as Tunis.

This prediction was well fulfilled in 1571 at the Battle of
Lepanto when the allied fleets of the Papacy, Venice and Spain
crushed the Turks at Lepanto. By 1573, Don John of Austria,
the leader of the expedition, had gone on to recapture Tunis.
Much of the Turkish fleet was composed of ships from their
ally the Algerian Barbary pirates. A successful quatrain.

Century IX

IX.XLIII

Proche à deſcendre l'armee
    Crucigere[2]
Sera guettee par les Iſmaëlites[3]
De tous cottez batus par nef
    Rauiere,[4]
Prompt aſſaillis de dix galeres
    eslites.

Ready to land the army of the
Cross will be watched for by the
Ismaelites. Struck from all side
by the ship Raviere. Quickly
attacked by ten chosen galleys.

I think this is probably a continuation of IX.XLII.

[1] *Monet.* an unusual spelling for *Monech*, Monaco.
[2] *Crucigere.* bearing a cross, a Crusader.
[3] *Iſmaëlites.* biblical name for the Arabs.
[4] *Rauiere.* O.F. impetuosity, or an unidentified place name.

Century IX

IX.XLIIII

Migres migre de Geneſue * treſtous,* *Saturne d'or en fer ſe changera,* *Le contre RAYPOZ[1]* * exterminera tous,* *Auant l'a ruent le ciel ſignes* * fera,*	Leave, leave Geneva everyone. Saturn will change from gold into iron. Those against RAYPOZ will all be extermin- ated. Before the rush the sky will show signs.

Geneva was famous in Nostradamus' time as the Protestant equivalent of the Vatican because Calvin made it his center. Is Nostradamus warning the inhabitants of a Calvinist purge or of an attack by Philip II? Could *RAYPOZ* stand for a traitor? (See footnote.) An intriguing quatrain.

Century IX

IX.XLV

Ne ſera ſoul iamais de demander, *Grand Mendoſus[2] obtiendra ſon* * empire* *Loing de la cour fera* * contremander,* *Pymond, Picard, Paris, Tyrron[3]* * le pire.*	There will never be a single per- son to ask, great Mendosus will attain his empire. Far from the court he will countermand Pied- mont, Picardy and Paris. Tus- cany is the worst.

Mendosus is accepted by most commentators as an anagram for the family of Vendôme, of which the earlier spelling was Vendosme. If this is the case, the quatrain may describe either Henri IV or his father Antoine de Navarre, duc de Vendosme. But despite this excellent lead the rest of the quatrain is very obscure. Piedmont was Italian and belonged to Savoy, Picardy is a Normandy province of France. A disappointing quatrain.

[1] *RAYPOZ.* an unsolved anagram except for one suggestion, Zopyre who betrayed Babylon to Darius.
[2] *Mendoſus.* an anagram for *Vendosme*, the Bourbon branch of the French royal family who won the throne in 1594.
[3] *Tyrron.* probably from the L. *Tyrrheni*, the Etruscans.

Century IX

IX.XLVI

Vuydez, fuyez de Tholofe les
  rouges
Du facrifice faire expiation,
Le chef du mal deffouz l'vmbre
  des courges
Mort eftrangler carne
  omination.[1]

Begone, the red ones, flee from
Toulouse, make expiation to the
sacrifice. The main course of evil
in the shadow of the gourds.
Dead, to strangle the prognosti-
cation of flesh.

Century IX

IX.XLVII

Les foulz fignez d'indigne
  deliurance,
Et de la multe auront contre
  aduis,
Change monarque mis en perille
  pence,[2]
Serrez en caige fe verront vis à
  vis.

The undersigned to an infamous
delivery receiving contrary
advice from the crowds. A
monarch changes, thoughts are
put in danger. Shut in a cage
they will see each other face to
face.

This quatrain could be applied to François II, 1559–1560,
but is is still very vague.

Century IX

IX.XLVIII

La grand cité d'occean
  maritime,
Enuironee de maretz en criftal:
Dans le folftice hyemal[3] & la
  prime,[4]
Sera temptee de vent
  efpouuental.

The great city of the maritime
ocean, surrounded by a swamp
of crystal. In the winter solstice
and the spring (he) will be tried
by a dreadful wind.

[1] *omination*. probably derived from *carne ominato*, prognostic of flesh.
[2] *pence*. This probably comes from F. *penser*, to think, but possibly
from the English, *pence*.
[3] *hyemal*. L. *hiemalus*. (of) winter.
[4] *prime*. O.F. springtime.

This quatrain is interpreted by Allen (1943) as the destruction of Central Park in New York and by Boswell (1941) as the destruction of Tokyo by Russian chemical bombs. The latter was almost correct in his prediction. Nagasaki and Hiroshima were destroyed by atomic (chemical?) bombs in 1945. A curious quatrain.

Century IX

IX.XLIX

Gand & Bruceles marcheront
   contre Enuers
Senat de Londres mettront à
   mort leur roy
Le sel & vin luy seront à
   l'enuers,
Pour eux auoir le regne en
   desarroy.

Ghent and Brussels march against Antwerp. The Parliament of London will put their king to death. The salt and wine will oppose him. Because of them he will have the kingdom in trouble.

Line 2 is the obvious clue to this quatrain, describing the death of Charles I. The king was executed in 1649 by the new-style calendar, in 1648 by the old-style calendar that Nostradamus used, when New Year's Day was on March 25.

Philip IV had made great attempts to reconquer the Netherlands but by 1648 they were anxious to get the Dutch out of the war and ceded several key towns to them. This may indicate that Nostradamus saw lines 1 and 2 as simultaneous. When Philip had achieved this he closed the Scheldt, which ruined Antwerp. It is interesting to note that the quatrain is numbered XL.IX, and Charles was executed in 1649. (See VIII.XXXVII.)

Century IX

IX.L

Mandoſus tost viendra à ſon
hault regne
Mettant arriere vn peu de
Norlaris:
Le rouge blaiſme, le maſle à
l'interregne,
Le ieune crainte & frayeur
Barbaris.

Mendosus will soon come to his
great reign, somewhat putting
aside the Norlaris. The pale red
one, the one in the interregnum,
the frightened young man and
the fear of the Barbaric ones.

As was seen in IX.XLV and X.XVIII, *Mendosus* is an anagram of Vendosme and *Norlaris* an anagram of Lorraine, the home of the Guise family. This quatrain states that Vendosme, Henri IV, will soon come to the throne and relegate the House of Guise to the wings, which indeed happened. The *rouge blaiſme* probably stands for the old cardinal of Bourbon, red in his cardinal's robes and pallid with age. He was actually proclaimed Charles X in 1589, but died the following year. The *maſle* may stand for the duc de Mayenne, who was lieutenant general during the interregnum. The young man *(le ieune crainte)* would then be the duc de Guise and *Barbaris* stands for Philip II of Spain, who claimed the throne of France through his daughter Isabella, his wife having been a sister of Henri II of France. A satisfactory quatrain.

Century IX

IX.LI

Contre les rouges ſectes ſe
banderont,
Feu, eau, fer, corde par paix ſe
minera,[1]
Au point mourir ceux qui
machineront,
Fors vn que monde ſur tout
ruynera.

Against the red ones sects will
unite. Fire, water, iron, the rope,
will weaken through peace.
Those who plot are at point of
dying except one who above all
will ruin the world.

[1] *minera*. O.F. *miner*, to ruin, destroy.

This quatrain must have a twentieth century interpretation. The Reds fit here as Communist countries in a modern politico-social setting. The conditions described in lines 1 and 2 existed between the two World Wars with Fascism, Communism, Nazism and line 2 obviously refers to the *Cordon Sanitaire*. Line 3 describes Western statesmen, mostly appeasers like Chamberlain and Pétain. Their exception is Hitler, in line 4, who attempted to rule the world.

Century IX

IX.LII

La paix s'approche d'vn costé, & la guerre	Peace approaches from one side. Never was the pursuit of war so
Oncques ne feut la pourſuitte ſi grande,	great. Men and women moan, innocent blood on the land and
Plaindre hõme, fẽme, ſang innocent par terre	this will be throughout the whole of France.
Et ce ſera de France à toute bande.	

On April 13, 1559, the king of France declared in the Peace of Cateau-Cambrésis that he would stop fighting the Spanish and would turn his attention to liquidating heretics in France. The declared peace between France and Spain sparked the Civil War between the Catholics and Huguenots, a time of bloodshed for all France, which indeed happened. A good general quatrain.

Century IX

IX.LIII

Le Neron ieune dans les trois cheminees	In three chimneys the young Nero will throw out to burn the
Fera de paiges vifz pour ardoir[1] getter,[2]	living pages. He is happy who will be far from such happen-
Heureux qui loing ſera de telz menees,	ings. Three of his family will ambush him to death.
Trois de ſon ſang le feront mort guetter.	

[1] *ardoir.* O.F. to burn.
[2] *getter.* O.F. for jeter, to throw.

Rafael Sabatini, the well-known novelist, wrote in one of his historical novels of a young man being thrown into a fireplace. Otherwise I can offer no clue.

Century IX

IX.LIIII

Arriuera au port de Corſibonne,
Pres de Rauenne qui pillera la dame,
En mer profonde legat de la Vlisbonne
Souz roc cachez rauiront ſeptante ames.

There will arrive at Porto Corsini near Ravenna, one of whom will plunder the lady. The legate in Lisbon in the deep sea. Hidden under the rock they will carry off seventy souls.

Perhaps the Dome stands for the Catholic Church to be plundered at Porto Corsini, which is eight miles north of Ravenna.

Century IX

IX.LV

L'horrible guerre qu'en l'occident s'apreſte
L'an enſuiuant viendra la peſtilence,
Si fort horrible que ieune, vieulx, ne beſte,
Sang, feu, Mercure, Mars, Iupiter en France.

The dreadful war which is prepared in the West, the following year the pestilence will come, so very dreadful that young nor old nor animal (will survive). Blood, fire, Mercury, Mars, Jupiter in France.

This quatrain is generally applied to the First World War, which was followed by the dreadful influenza epidemic of 1917–18 governed by the conjunction of Mercury, Mars and Jupiter always one indicating disaster. However it may equally well apply to AIDS, the plague of the last decades of this century. Nostradamus' mention of animals is interesting. One theory of the origin of AIDS holds that the disease mutated from the Green Monkey of Africa to human beings. Certainly Africa is the source of the AIDS epidemic. This is also a good

Millennium quatrain with the prime ingredients of disease, war and fire. Possibly a quatrain that has not yet been completely fulfilled.

Century IX

IX.LVI

*Camp pres de Noudam paſſera
    Gouſſan ville,
Et à Maiotes[1] laiſſera ſon
    enſeigne,
Conuertira en instant plus de
    mille,
Cherchant les deux remettre en
    chaine & legne.[2]*

The army near Noudan will pass Goussainville and will leave its scar at Maiotes. In an instant more than a thousand will be converted, looking for the two who will put back chain and wood.

A difficult quatrain. Both Noudan and Goussainville are to the west of Paris, but Maiotes is unsolved and I am unclear as to the exact meaning of *legne* in line 4.

Century IX

IX.LVII

*Au lieu de DRVX[3] vn Roy
    repoſera,
Et cherchera loy changeant
    d'Anatheme,
Pendant le ciel ſi tres fort
    tonnera,
Portee neufue Roy tuera
    ſoymeſme.*

In the place of DRVX a king will rest and look for a law to change Anathema. While the sky thunders so loudly the king will kill himself at the new gate.

The clue to this unsolved quatrain must be *DRVX*.

---

[1] *Maiotes*. a place name, Mantes? or possibly Gk. *memaotes*, soliders.
[2] *legne*. A.Pr. *legna*, firewood.
[3] *DRVX*. possibly an anagram for Dreux?

Century IX

IX.LVIII

Au coſté gauche à l'endroit de Vitry
Seront guettez les trois rouges de France,
Tous aſſoumez rouge, noir non murdry,
Par les Bretons remis en aſſeurance.

To the left side of the place of Vitry the three red ones of France will be watched. All those killed are red, the black not murdered. Reassured in safety by the Bretons.

The red ones of France are probably Revolutionaries, all of whom are killed with their followers. Like the following quatrain this is practically unintelligible.

Century IX

IX.LIX

A la Ferté prendra la Vidame
Nicol tenu rouge qu'auoit produit la vie.
La grand Loyſe naiſtra que fera clame.[1]
Donnant Bourgongne à Bretons par enuie.

At the Ferté Vidame he will take Nicol the red, who had produced life. To the great Louis who acts secretly one will be born, who gives Burgundy to the Bretons through envy.

A quatrain about a mythological illegitimate child born to someone called Louis who has some connection with Burgundy and the Bretons.

---

[1]*clame*. L. *clam*. secretly.

Century IX

IX.LX

*Conflict Barbar en la Cornere
     noire.
Sang efpandu trembler la
     d'Almatie,
Grand Ifmaël[1] mettra fon
     promontoire,
Ranes[2] trembler fecours Lufitanie.*

*In a black headdress the Barba-
rian fights, blood shed, Dalmatia
trembles. The great Ismaël will
wake his promontory. Frogs
tremble under aid from Portugal.*

I can make nothing of this quatrain except for the rising
power of the Arab countries during these last decades.

Century IX

IX.LXI

*La pille faite à la cofte marine,
La cita noua & parenz amenez
Plufieurs de Malte par le fait
     de Meffine,
Eftroit ferrez feront mal
     guerdonnez.*

*The plunder taken on the sea
coast, in the new city and relations brought forward. Several
of Malta will be closely shut up,
through the deeds of Messina,
poorly rewarded.*

I am unable to decipher this quatrain.

Century IX

IX.LXII

*Au grand de Cheramon agora
Seront croifez par ranc tous
     attachez,
Le pertinax[3] Oppi,[4] &
     Mandragora,[5]
Raugon[6] d'Octobre le tiers feront
     lafchez.*

*To the great one of Cheramon
agora will all the crosses by rank
be attached. The long lasting
Opium and Mandrake, the
Raugon will be released on
October the third.*

[1]*Ifmaël.* the Arab nation.
[2]*Ranes.* L. *rama,* a frog.
[3]*pertinax.* L. long-lasting.
[4]*Oppi.* Gk. opium.
[5]*Mandragora.* Gk. mandrake.
[6]*Raugon.* An unsolved place name?

This is a very odd quatrain. Cheramon Agora was actually the name of a town in Asia Minor, believed to be present-day Usak. Both opium and the mandrake root had mysterious virtues and were used in occult practices. But what this has to do with a town in Asia Minor, I cannot tell.

Century IX

IX.LXIII

Plainctes & pleurs crys & grands vrlemens
Pres de Narbon à Bayonne & en Foix
O quel horrible calamitz changemens,
Auant que Mars reuolu quelques foys.

Complaints and tears, cries and great howls, near Narbonne, Bayonne and in Foix. Oh, what dreadful calamities and changes, before Mars has revolved a few times.

Each revolution of the planet Mars lasts 687 days. The only definite fact one can glean from this quatrain is that a calamity will occur, probably war *(Mars)* after a certain number of revolutions. But there is no date to start the time factor so the quatrain remains obscure.

Century IX

IX.LXIIII

L'Aemathion[1] paſſer montz Pyrennees,
En Mars Narbon ne fera reſiſtance,
Par mer & terre fera ſi grand menee.
Cap.[2] n'ayant terre ſeure pour demeurance.

The Aemathian will cross the Pyrenees in March. Narbonne will not make any resistance. He will carry on a very great intrigue by land and sea. Cap having no land in which to stay safely.

[1]*Aemathion.* either Macedonian or from Thessaly.
[2]*Cap.* Capet, Nostradamus' usual abbreviation of the French royal line.

For line 1 see IX.XXXVIII. *Cap.* is Nostradamus' usual shortening of the Capet name, the French royal line. But on occasions he has used *Cappe* to mean cape and even the Pope. Probably a failed quatrain about sixteenth century politics.

Century IX

IX.LXV

Dedans le coing de luna viendra rendre,
Ou sera prins & mys en terre estrange,
Les fruitz immeurs seront à grand esclandre
Grand vitupere à l'vn grande louange.

He will be taken to the corner of Luna where he will be placed on foreign land. The unripe fruit will be the subject of great scandal. Great blame, to the others great praise.

If Luna is to be understood as the moon, this quatrain is surprisingly good. The Americans landed on the moon led by Neil Armstrong in 1969. The "unripe fruit which causes great scandal" is the tragic explosion of the Space Shuttle Challenger in 1986. The great praise goes to the others, the Russians, who have satisfactorily installed their space station, the MIR, which is in continual use.

Century IX

IX.LXVI

Paix, vnion sera & changement,
Estatz, offices bas hault, & hault bien bas,
Dresser voiage le fruict premier torment,
Guerre cesser, ciuil proces debatz.

There will be peace, union and change, estates and offices low (become) high, those high very low. To prepare for a journey torments the first child. War to cease, legal processes debates.

This quatrain could apply to any postwar period because of the inevitable changes that follow war, both for the victors and the vanquished.

Century IX

IX.LXVII

Du hault des montz à l'entour
  de Lizer
Port à la roche Valen. cent
  assemblez
De chasteau neuf pierre late en
  donzere,
Contre le crest Romans foy
  assemblez.

From the top of the mountains
around Isère a hundred assembled at the gate to the Vatican
rock. From Châteauneuf, Pier-
relatte in Danzère. Against the
Crest, Romans assembled in
faith.

This quatrain implies religious troubles especially in line 4,
with those of Rome assembled against the Moslem *crest*,
crescent. Almost certainly a failed quatrain.

Century IX

IX.LXVIII

Du mont Aymar[1] sera noble
  obscurcie,
Le mal viendra au ioinct de
  sonne & rosne
Dans bois caichez soldatz iour de
  Lucie,[2]
Qui ne fut onc vn si horrible
  throsne.

The noble of Mont Aymar will
become obscure the evil will come
at the junction of the Saône and
the Rhône. Soldiers hidden in
the woods on (Saint) Lucy's day,
there was never so horrible a
throne.

This last line is horribly reminiscent of another quatrain
where Nostradamus describes war "on its dreadful throne,"
VIII.XLVI. This one probably describes the sack of Lyons,
between the junction of the rivers, in 1793. It was done by
soldiers of the Revolutionary forces and there was great
bloodshed. The key word, *mont Aymar*, is still undeciphered.

[1] *Mont Aymar.* Montélimar? or "by the mountains of slaughter."
[2] *Lucie.* St. Lucy's day, December 13.

Century IX

IX.LXIX

Sur le mont de Bailly & la Bresle
Seront caichez de Grenoble les fiers,
Oultre Lyon, Vien. eulx si grande gresle,
Langoult[1] en terre n'en restera vn tiers.

On the mountain of Sain Bel and l'Arbesle the proud people of Grenoble will be hidden. Beyond Lyons at Vienne there will be such great hail. Locusts on the land, not a third of it will remain.

A quatrain with lots of place names and a swarm of locusts but I cannot interpret it.

Century IX

IX.LXX

Harnois trenchant dans les flambeaux cachez
Dedans Lyon le iour Sacrement,[2]
Ceux de Vienne seront trestous hachez
Par les cantons Latins Mascon ne ment.

Sharp armor hidden in the torches at Lyons on the day of the sacrament. All those of Vienne will be cut to pieces by the Latin cantons. Mâcon does not lie.

Century IX

IX.LXXI

Aux lieux sacrez animaux veu à trixe,[3]
Auec celuy qui n'osera le iour:
A Carcassonne pour disgrace propice,
Sera posé pour plus ample seiour.

Animals with hair seen at the holy places with one who does not dare (to face) the day. Carcassonne is suitable for the disgrace and will be left for a longer stay.

A complicated quatrain without any apparent meaning.

[1] *Langoult.* O.F. *langouste,* a locust, not crayfish, as in modern French.
[2] *Sacrement.* Understood as Corpus Christi, the first Thursday after Trinity Sunday.
[3] *trixe.* Gk. *thrix,* hair or wool. Perhaps sheep in this context?

Century IX

IX.LXXII

Encor feront les faincts temples pollus,
Et expillez par Senat Tholoffain,
Saturne deux trois cicles reuollus,
Dans Auril, May, gens de nouueau leuain.

Again the holy temples will be polluted and plundered by the Senate of Toulouse. Saturn having completed two or three cycles in April and May, there will be people of a new leaven.

A cycle of Saturn lasts for 29.5 years. Presumably these "two or three" cycles follow the sack of Toulouse. Nostradamus appears to fear that the Calvinists will take over and despoil the churches. It is also possible that line 3 may mean two times three cycles of Saturn, i.e., six, which would total 177 years, a figure also mentioned by Nostradamus in his preface.

Century IX

IX.LXXIII

Dans Fois entrez Roy ceiulee Turbao,
Et regnera moins reuolu Saturne,
Roy Turban blanc Bizance coeur ban,
Sol, Mars, Mercure pres la hurne.

The king enters Foix wearing a blue turban, he will reign for less than a revolution of Saturn. The king with the white turban, his heart banished to Byzantium, Sun, Mars and Mercury near Aquarius.

This quatrain, because of the turbans, apparently describes a Moslem or Eastern invasion. Foix is understood to belong to a blue-turbaned man who rules for less than one cycle of Saturn, 29.5 years. In other quatrains the Ayatollah, the man of the white turban, is described as being followed by the "man in blue, perse." McCann (1942) dates this quatrain as February 18, 1981, but I think it is still unfulfilled. The Perse may be the precursor of the Antichrist or the Antichrist himself.

Century IX

IX.LXXIIII

*Dans la cité de Fertſod[1]
    homicide,
Fait & fait multe beuf arant
    ne macter,[2]
Retour encores aux honneurs
    d'Artemide,
Et à Vulcan corps morts
    ſepulturer.[3]*

In the homicidal city of Fertsod
again and again many oxen
plow, not sacrificed. Again a
return to the honors of Artemis.
To Vulcan the corpses of the
dead for burial.

Fertfod is obviously the clue to this quatrain but unfortunately it has not been deciphered as yet.

Century IX

IX.LXXV

*Del l'Ambraxie & du pays de
    Thrace,
Peuple par mer mal & ſecours
    Gaulois,
Perpetuelle en Prouence la
    trace,
Auec veſtiges de leur couſtume &
    loix.*

From Arta and the country of
Thrace, people ill by sea, help
from the Gauls. In Provence
their perpetual trace, remnants
of their customs and law.

This quatrain appears to describe the Greeks returning to
ask aid from southern France, and particularly Provence, of
which their early colonial settlers were particularly fond.

---

[1]*Fertfod*. La Ferté? Sodom?
[2]*macter*. L. *mactare*, to slaughter.
[3]*ſepulturer*. O.F. *sepultrer*, to bury.

Century IX

IX.LXXVI

Auec le noir[1] Rapax &
   ſanguinaire,
Yſſu du peaultre[2] de l'inhumain
   Neron,
Emmy[3] deux fleuues main
   gauche militaire,
Sera murtry par Ioyne
   chaulueron.[4]

With the rapacious and bloody
king, sprung from the pallet of
the inhuman Nero. Between two
rivers, the military on the left, he
will be murdered by à bald young
man.

I cannot interpret this quatrain.

Century IX

IX.LXXVII

Le regne prins le Roy conuiera,
La dame prinſe à mort iurez à
   ſort,
La vie à Royne fils on deſniera,
Et la pellix[5] au fort de la
   conſort.

The kingdom taken, the king will
plot, the lady taken to death by
those sworn by lot. They will
refuse life to the queen's son and
the mistress suffers the same fate
as the wife.

For once a good, clear quatrain describing the fates of Marie
Antoinette and Mme. du Barry. After the royal family's
imprisonment, Louis XVI was executed in January, 1793. He
was condemned by the Convention who elected their powers
to itself. However, the queen, who was not executed until the
following October, was judged by a newly created revolutionary tribunal with a jury elected by lot. This was an institution
unknown to the France of Nostradamus' day. The third line
tells of the fate of their son Louis XVII; his kingdom was
denied to him. The last line is the most interesting of all. While
the queen was imprisoned in the Conciergerie the mistress of
Louis XV, Mme. du Barry, was held in the prison of Sainte-
Pélagie. An impressive quatrain.

[1] *noir.* usual anagram for *roi.*
[2] *peaultre.* pallet, brothel, rudder (Laver).
[3] *Emmy.* O.F. in between.
[4] *chaulueron.* Diminutive of *chauve,* bald.
[5] *pellix.* L. *pelex,* concubine.

Century IX

IX.LXXVIII

*La dame Greque de beauté
    laydique,[1]
Heureuſe faicte de procs
    innumerable,
Hors tranſlatee au regne
    Hiſpanique,
Captiue prinſe mourir mort
    miſerable.*

*The Greek woman of the beauty
of Lais is made happy by innumerable suitors. Transferred out to
the Spanish kingdom she is captured, taken to die a wretched
death.*

Several modern commentators interpret the lady as Demo-
cracy, which originated in Greece and which started to die out
in Europe beginning with the Spanish Civil War, 1936.

Century IX

IX.LXXIX

*Le chef de claſſe par fraude
    ſtratageme,
Fera timides ſortir de leurs
    galleres,
Sortis murtris chef renieur de
    creſme,
Puis par l'embusche luy
    rendront les ſaleres.*

*The leader of the fleet through
deceitful trickery will make the
scared come out of their galleys.
Having come out, murdered, the
leader to renounce the holy oil.
Then through an ambush they
give him his just deserts.*

The holy oil in line 3 smacks of the oil used in the coronation
of kings, but otherwise this is completely obscure.

---

[1]*laydique. Lais* was the most beautiful woman in Corinth, but possibly
this is derived from the opposite meaning, *laid*, ugly.

Century IX

IX.LXXX

Le Duc voudra les ſiens exterminer,
Enuoyera les plus forts lieux eſtranges,
Par tyrannie Pize & Luc ruiner,
Puis les Barbares ſans vin feront vendanges.

The duke wants to kill his followers. He will send the strongest to the most alien places. Through tyranny he ruins both Pisa and Lucca then the Barbarians will harvest grapes without wine.

I cannot decipher this quatrain.

Century IX

IX.LXXXI

Le Roy ruſé entendra ſes embuſches
De trois quartiers ennemis aſſaillir,
Vn nombre eſtrange larmes de coqueluches[1]
Viendra Lemprin[2] du traducteur faillir.

The crafty king will understand his ambushes, from three sides the enemies threaten. A large amount of strange tears from the hooded ones. The splendor of the translator will fail.

Could the translator of line 4 be the same as the one in IX.I who also gets into trouble with Church and State?

---

[1]*coqueluches.* hooded men, probably monks.
[2]*Lemprin.* Gk. *lampros,* splendor.

Century IX

IX.LXXXII

Par le deluge & peſtilence forte
La cité grande de long temps
  aſſiegee,
La ſentinelle & garde de main
  morte,
Subite prinſe, mais de nul
  oultragee.

By the flood and the great plague
the great city is besieged for a
long time. The sentry and guard
killed by hand, suddenly captured but none wronged.

Yet another vague, generalized quatrain. A great city,
troubled by floods and the plague, is besieged and vanquished.
Probably a failed quatrain.

Century IX

IX.LXXXIII

Sol vingt de taurus ſi fort terre
  trembler,
Le grand theatre rempli
  ruinera,
L'air, ciel & terre obſcurcir &
  troubler,
Lors l'infidelle Dieu & ſainctz
  voguera.

The sun in twenty degrees of
Taurus there will be a great
earthquake. The great theater,
full, will be ruined. Darkness
and trouble in the air, sky and
land when they call upon the
faithless God and the Saints.

This quatrain is a typical description of an earthquake.
Nostradamus gives the day but not the year of its happening.
Sol vingt de Taurus means twenty days after the sun moves into
Taurus, giving us either I May by the old Julian calendar, or
May 21 by the present one. This seems to link with the general
quatrains of doom around the Millennium. Even God appears
to have failed mankind. See quatrains I.LXXXVII and
X.XLIX for other general disasters of this type and period.

Century IX

IX.LXXXIIII

Roy exposé parfaira L'hecatombe,
Apres auoir trouué son origine,
Torrent ouurir de marbre &
plomb la tombe
D'vn grand Romain d'enseigne
Medusine.

The king exposed will complete the slaughter once he has found his origin. A torrent to open the tomb of marble and lead, of a great Roman with the Medusine motto.

The key to this quatrain lies in the word *Medusine*. If it is an anagram of *Deus in Me*, this would indicate that the tomb uncovered accidentally in a flood is the real tomb of St. Peter, as that was his device. This would mean that the one uncovered some years ago is not that of St. Peter, but of another early pope.

Century IX

IX.LXXXV

Passer Guienne, Languedoc & le
Rosne,
D'Agen tenens de Marmande &
la Roole,
D'ouurir par foy par roy¹
Phocé² tiēdra son trosne
Conflit aupres saint Pol de
Mauseole.³

To pass Guienne, Languedoc and the Rhône from Agen, holding Marmande and La Réole. To open the wall through the king. Marseilles will hold its throne. A battle near St. Pol-de-Mausole.

Apart from the fact that Nostradamus knew Agen, Marseilles and St. Pol-de-Mausole, there is no cohesive factor in this quatrain.

---

¹*par roy.* possibly O.F. *parroi*, wall?
²*Phocé.* Marseilles.
³St. Pol-de-Mausole. A convent, then an asylum where Van Gogh once stayed, outside St. Rémy-de-Provence.

Century IX

IX.LXXXVI

*Du bourg Lareyne paruiẽdront
  droit à Chartres
Et feront pres du pont Authoni
  panſe,[1]
Sept pour la paix cautelleux
  comme martres
Feront entree d'armee à Paris
  clauſe.*

*From Bourg-la-Reine they will
go directly to Chartres, they will
pause near the Pont d'Anthony.
Seven for peace, as crafty as
martens, they will enter a closed
Paris with weapons.*

The "seven for peace," the seven allied nations who joined
against Napoleon and entered Paris on July 3, 1815, were
Austria, England, Prussia, Portugal, Sweden, Spain and
Russia. The city was stripped of its troops when the French
army was evacuated to Chartres, taking up positions on their
way to the Loire, passing through Bourg-la-Reine and the
Pont d'Anthony, under which they are reputed to have
camped. A good quatrain.

Century IX

IX.LXXXVII

*Par la foreſt du Touphon[2]
  eſſartee,
Par hermitaige ſera poſé le
  temple,
Le duc d'Eſtampes par ſa ruſe
  inuentee,
Du mont Lehori prelat donra
  exemple.*

*In the cleared forest of Touphon
the temple will be placed near the
Hermitage. The duc d'Etampes,
through the ruse he invented,
will give an example to the priest
of Mont Lehori.*

The clue to this quatrain probably lies in line 3. Three
mistresses of French kings held the title d'Estampes. First
Anne de Pisselieu, then Diane de Poitiers and later Henri IV's
mistress, Gabrielle d'Estrées. But I cannot decipher *mont Lehori*
in line 4.

[1]*panſe.* misprint for *pauſe*, to rhyme with line 4.
[2]*Touphon.* doubtful. Possibly Gk. *tophion*, a plaster quarry, or F.
touffe, a clump.

Century IX

IX.LXXXVIII

Calais, Arras ſecours à
  Theroanne,
Paix & ſemblant ſimulera
  leſcoutte,[1]
Soulde[2] d'Alabrox[3] deſcendre
  par Roāne
Deſtornay peuple qui deffera la
  routte.[4]

Calais and Arras, help to
Thérouanne, the spy will simu-
late peace and semblance. The
soldiers of Savoy go down by
Roanne. Those who would stop
the rout are turned away.

This quatrain must refer to incidents before 1558, when
Calais fell to the French. Both Arras and Thérouanne
belonged to Spain. When Calais fell, Philip II, husband of the
English queen, lost all rights to Calais. On February 5, 1556,
the Treaty of Vaucelles was declared between France and
Spain. Therefore, this quatrain was probably written between
the truce and the Spanish attack of 1557. Savoy *(Alabrox)* was
almost completely occupied by the French during this period,
so it is possible that a garrison of soldiers was sent there after
St. Quentin. The borders of Savoy were only thirty-five miles
from Roanne.

Century IX

IX.LXXXIX

Sept ans ſera Philip. fortune
  proſpere,
Rabaiſſera des Arabes l'effaict,
Puis ſon mydi[5] perplex rebors
  affaire
Ieuſne ognyon[6] abyſmera ſon fort.

Fortune will favor Philip for
seven years, he will cut down
again the exactions of the Arabs.
Men in the middle of a perplex-
ing, contrary affair, young
Ogmios will destroy his strong-
hold.

[1]*leſcoutte*. O.F spy, scout.
[2]*Soulde*. O.F. pay or mercenaries.
[3]*Alabrox*. classical inhabitants of Savoy.
[4]*routte*. either O.F. *route*, a rout, or *route*, a road?
[5]*ſon mydi*. either in middle age, or to the South?
[6]*ognyon*. The Celtic Hercules.

The first seven years of Louis Philippe's reign, 1830–38, were extremely fortunate. He managed to subdue the Arabs (*Rabaiſſera des Arabes l'effaict*) and to consolidate the French occupation of Algeria. In the middle of his reign, 1838–40, he will be troubled by the Eastern question and the result shames both him and France. Finally, in 1848, the French dethrone him and keep him under guard.

Century IX

IX.XC

Vn capitaine de la grand Germanie	*A captain of Greater Germany will come to deliver false help.*
Se viendra rendre par ſimulé ſecours	*King of Kings. To support Hungary, his war will cause great shedding of blood.*
Vn Roy des roys ayde de Pannonie,[1]	
Que ſa reuolte fera de ſang grand cours.	

The Greater Germany sounds uncannily like the *Grossdeutschland* of Hitler's Germany, the Third Reich. The second line of the quatrain is excellent. Hitler annexed Poland under the pretext of help, as Nostradamus says in I.XLV. For a time Hitler was almost all-powerful in Europe, Russia and Asia, truly a king of kings, lord of all he surveyed. He also captured Hungary, line 3, and the war he started killed about fourteen million people among the soldiers of both sides and according to some estimates as many again among the civilian population and the concentration camps.

---

[1]*Pannonie*. Panonia, classical Hungary.

Century IX

IX.XCI

L'horrible peſte Perynte[1] & *Nicopolle,[2]* *Le Cherſonnez[3] tiendra &* *Marceloyne,[4]* *La Theſſalie vaſtera l'Amphipolle,[5]* *Mal incogneu & le refus* *d'Anthoine.*	*The dreadful plague at Perinthus and Nicopolis will take the Peninsula and Macedonia. It will lay waste Thessaly and Amphibolis, an unknown evil, refused by Anthony.*

We have a plethora of place names ranging throughout Greece and parts of Turkey but there seems no linking factor save that of plague. Anthony may stand for Antoine de Navarre, father of Henri IV, but the whole quatrain seems unlikely.

Century IX

IX.XCII ★

Le Roy vouldra dans cité *neufue entrer* *Par ennemys expugner[6] lon* *viendra* *Captif libere faulx dire &* *perpetrer,* *Roy dehors eſtre, loin d'ennemys tiendra.*	*The king will want to enter the new city, they will come to subdue it through its enemies. A captive, falsely faced to speak and act. The king to be outside he will stay far from the enemy.*

The *cité neufue* may refer to New York (as in VI.XCVII) being actually attacked during a war. This has not happened to date, so this quatrain must be regarded as futuristic and probably a Millennium quatrain as well. See X.XLIX where

[1]*Perynte.* Modern Eski Eregli.
[2]*Nicopolle.* Modern Preveza.
[3]*Cherſonnez.* Either the Gallipoli Peninsula (Chersonese) or the Peloponnesus.
[4]*Marceloyne.* probable error for Macedoine.
[5]*Amphipolle.* near modern Salonika.
[6]*expugner.* L. *expugnare*, to storm, subdue, violate.

Nostradamus sees New York as being attacked through its water supply. The king outside *(Roy dehors eſtre)* may refer to the President of the United States and other essential staff, holed up in a secret underground bunker away from the city, from which they will continue to direct the war.

Century IX

IX.XCIII

Les ennemis du fort bien eſlongnez,	*The enemies are very far from the strong man, the bastion is*
Par chariots conduict le baſtion,	*brought by wagons. Above, the*
Par ſur les murs de Bourges eſgrongnez,	*crumbled walls of Bourges, when Hercules strikes the Mace-*
Quand Hercules battra l'Haemathion.[1]	*donian.*

This quatrain describes Aemathion, who in this context can stand for Louis XIV, pushing back his enemies and conse-quently enlarging the borders of France. Bastions of earth were constructed at the fortification by Vauban. It was during his time that Bourges fell into ruin. The final line refers to a labor worthy of Hercules, the construction of the lengthy Languedoc Canal. It was started in 1666 and finished in 1681 at the cost, at that time, of 34,000,000 francs and it was the wonder of the age. This new route freed the French from dependency on the western area of the Mediterranean and became the French equivalent of the Pillars of Hercules, Gibraltar.

[1]*Haemathion.* As Aemathion, Macedonian, or from Thessaly.

Century IX

IX.XCIIII

Foibles galleres feront vnies enfemble,
Ennemis faux le plus fort en rampart:
Faible affaillies Vratiflaue tremble,
Lubecq & Myfne tiendront barbare part.

Weak galleys will be joined together, the false enemy is strongest on the ramparts. Bratislava trembles, the weak attacked. Lübeck and Meissen will take the Barbarian's side.

An incomprehensible quatrain, probably a failed one.

Century IX

IX.XCV

Le nouueau faict[1] conduyra l'exercite,[2]
Proche apamé[3] iufques au pres du riuage,
Tendant fecour de Milannoile[4] eflite,
Duc yeux priué à Milan fer de cage.

The new fact will lead the army almost cut off as far as the river bank, holding out for help from the Milanese elite. The duc loses his eyes in an iron cage in Milan.

Milan belonged to the Hapsburgs until 1859. A lot of commentators take the last line as referring to Mussolini, but his public hanging was somewhat different from losing his eyes in an iron cage. Probably a failed quatrain.

[1] *faict.* a fact, or the newly elected one.
[2] *exercite.* L. *exercitus*, army.
[3] *apamé.* Gk. *apamao*, to cut off.
[4] *Milannoile.* probably Milanese.

Century IX

IX.XCVI

Dans cité entrer exercit[1] desniee,
Duc entrera par persuasion,
Aux foibles portes clam[2] armee
amenee,
Mettront feu, mort de sang
effusion.

The army denied entry to the city,
the duke will enter through per-
suasion. Secretly the army led to
the weak gates. They put it to
fire, death and the flowing of
blood.

I cannot interpret this quatrain.

Century IX

IX.XCVII

De mer copies en trois parts
diuisees,
A la seconde les viures
failleront,
Desesperez cherchant champs
Helisees,
Premiers en breche entrez
victoire auront.

The forces at sea divided into
three parts, the second one will
run out of supplies. In despair,
looking for the Elysian Fields,
the first entering the breach will
have victory.

In this quatrain we have two battles, one naval and one on
land. The Elysian Fields were the Greek version of heaven,
probably standing for the goal the army was attempting to
reach. But I cannot grasp any solid facts from this quatrain.

Century IX

IX.XCVIII

Les afftigez par faute d'vn seul
taint,
Contremenant[3] à partie opposite,
Aux Lygonnois mandera que
contraint
Seront de rendre le grand chef
de Molite.[4]

Those afflicted through the fault
of a single infected one, the
transgressor will be in the oppo-
site party. He will send to the
Lyonnais and compel them to
give themselves up to the great
leader of Molite.

[1]*exercit*. L. *exercitus*, army.
[2]*clam*. L. secretly.
[3]*Contremenant*. error for *contrevenant*.
[4]*Molite*? either *Melita*, Malta, or Gk. *molos*, war.

I cannot interpret this quatrain.

Century IX

IX.XCIX

Vent Aquilon fera partir le siege,
Par murs geter cendres, chauls,
* & pousiere,*
Par pluye apres qui leur fera
* bien piege,[1]*
Dernier secours encontre leur
* frontiere.*

The North wind will cause the siege to be raised, to throw the cinders over the walls, lime and dust. Afterwards, through rain which does them much harm, the last help is met at their frontier.

Most commentators take this quatrain as describing Napoleon's retreat from Moscow, the north *(Aquilon)*. He finds help only at the frontiers of his empire, having lost so many men due to the appalling weather they encountered on the expedition.

Century IX

IX.C

Naualle pugne[2] nuit sera
* superee,[3]*
Le feu aux naues[4] à l'Occident
* ruine:*
Rubriche neufue la grand nef
* coloree,*
Ire à vaincu, & victoire en bruine.

A naval battle will be overcome at night. Fire in the ruined strips of the West. A new coding, the great ship colored with anger to the vanquished. Victory in a mist.

This quatrain may well describe Pearl Harbor, which was attacked very early one morning in 1941 by Japanese planes which bombed the American fleet. The great tankers were set on fire to the ruin of America, the West, line 2. Does the new coding, *rubriche neufue*, mean the formula for this new type of warmongering attack, which finally brings anger to a defeated Japan and hazy glimpses of victory to a stunned America? The *coloree* of the ships is probably camouflage. A good quatrain.

[1]*piege*. A. Pr. *piegi*, worse, harmful.
[2]*pugne*. L. *pugna*, battle.
[3]*superee*. L. *superatus*, overcome.
[4]*naues*. L., ships.

Century X

X.I

L'ennemy l'ennemy foy promiſe
Ne ſe tiendra, les captifs
  retenus:
Prins preme[1] mort & le reste
  en chemiſe,
Damné le reſte pour eſtre
  souſtenus.

To the enemy the enemy faith promised will not be kept, the captives retained. One is taken near to death the remainder in their shirts, the rest damned for being supporters.

This quatrain is usually read nowadays as a general quatrain about the Vichy régime, when the Germans failed to make collaboration a two-way proposition to the French people.

Century X

X.II

Voille gallere voil de nef
  cachera,
La grande claſſe[2] viendra ſortir
  la moindre
Dix naues[3] proches le torneront
  poulſer,
Grande vaincue vnie à ſoy
  ioindre.

The ship's sail will hide the sailing galley, the great fleet will drive out the lesser one. Nearby ten ships will turn to drive it back, the great one conquered, to join united in faith.

There may possibly be a connection between this quatrain and IX.C. It describes a naval battle in which ships are either camouflaged or hidden by a smoke screen. The great one who is conquered may be the USA, which joins the Allies after the attack on Pearl Harbor 1941. Alternatively, it could apply to one of the many actions which took place in the Mediterranean from 1940 to 1943.

[1]*preme.* O.F. close, near.
[2]*claſſe.* L. *classus,* fleet.
[3]*naues.* L. *navus,* ship.

Century X

X.III

En apres cinq troupeau ne mettra hors vn Fuytif pour Penelon l'afchera, Faulx murmurer fecours venir par lors, Le chef le fiege lors habandonnera.	After the fifth will not put out a flock, a fugitive will be turned loose for Penelon. To murmur falsely, then to come in aid, then the chief will abandon the siege.

The key word to this quatrain is *Penelon*, which has not been deciphered. It may possibly be an anagram for *Polone*, Poland.

Century X

X.IIII

Sus la minuict conducteur de l'armee Se fauluera, fubit efuanouy, Sept ans apres la fame non blafmee, A fon retour ne dira oncq ouy.	At midnight the leader of the army will run away, suddenly disappeared. Seven years later, his reputation unblemished to his return "yes" will not once be said.

After his defeat at the Battle of Worcester 1651, Charles II fled to France through Scotland, in disguise. His usurper, Cromwell, actually ruled for seven years, and Charles was restored in 1660. Nostradamus' last line is ambiguous. Not all the English welcomed the return of the Stuart monarchy. It is a general quatrain but fits these events quite simply.

Century X

X.V

Albi & Caftres feront nouuelle ligue, Neuf Arriens Lisbon & Portugues, Carcas, Tholoffe confumeront leur brigue Quand chief neuf monftre de Lauragues.	Albi and Castres will make a new alliance, new Arians, Lisbon and the Portuguese. Carcassonne, Toulouse will join their intrigue when a new chief is the monster from the Lauragues.

The new Arians are the interesting subject here. Certainly
Hitler used Portugal and the Portuguese as a Fifth Column
during the Second World War. But it is more likely that
Nostradamus referred to the Albigensian Crusade, 1208–13.

Century X

X.VI

Sardon[1] Nemans ſi hault
   desborderont,
Qu'on cuidera[2] Deucalion
   renaiſtre,
Dans le colloſſe la plus part
   fuyront,
Veſta ſepulchre feu eſtaint
   apparoiſtre.

*The Gardon will flood. Nîmes so
high that they will think Duca-
lion has been reborn. In the col-
ossus the greater part will flee,
Vesta's fire appears extinguished
in the tomb.*

According to Jaubert a storm broke out at Nîmes in 1557,
which lasted from 5 A.M. to 9 P.M. and caused the local river
Gardon to flood. Apparently many antiquities were revealed
when the waters withdrew. Exactly the same thing happened
October 3, 1988, when a cloudburst flooded Nîmes in several
hours, 8 A.M. TO 2 P.M., to a height of 2 meters of water. Shall
we find further Roman remains when the floods and mud
withdraw?

Century X

X.VII

Le grand conflit qu'on appreſte
   à Nancy.
L'aemathien dira tout ie
   ſoubmetz,
L'iſle Britanne par vin, ſel
   enſolcy,
Hem. mi deux Phi. long temps
   ne tiĕdra Metz.

*The great fight that they prepare
at Nancy; Amathien will say, I
subjugate all. The British Isles
in trouble through wine and salt.
Hem. mir, Philip two. Metz will
not hold out for long.*

[1] *Sardon.* probable error for Gardon.
[2] *cuidera.* O.F. to think, believe.

The reference to wine and salt, taxes, the gabelle, are linked by this quatrain in some way with England (see IX.XLIX). But I am not happy with the various suggestions made by commentators to date. It seems more probable that *deux Phi* refers to Philip II, an ever-present personality in Nostradamus' *Prophéties*, who will attack French-occupied Lorraine. Metz was finally ceded to France in 1648 but had been under its control from 1552, so Nostradamus is simply stating a known, contemporary fact. Nancy was handed back to its duke in 1661 having been occupied for twenty-seven years.

Century X

X.VIII

Index & poulſe parfondera[1] le front
De Senegalia le Conte à ſon filz propre
La Myrnarmee[2] par pluſieurs de prinfront
Trois dans ſept iours bleſſes mors.

With index finger and thumb he will wet the forehead, the count of Senegalia to his own son. Through several, Venus in short order, three are wounded to death in seven days.

On June 15, 1856, the prince imperial, son of Napoleon III, was baptized *(index & poulſe parfondera).* His godfather was Pope Pius IX, who was the son of Count Mastia Ferretti of Senegallia. Venus may be interpreted as the Empress Eugénie, but line 4 remains unexplained.

Century X

X.IX

★

De Caſtillon figuieres iour de brune,
De feme infame naiſtra ſouuerain prince
Surnon de chauſſes perhume luy poſthume,
Onc Roy ne feut ſi pire en ſa prouince.

In the Castle of Figueras on a misty day a sovereign prince will be borne of an unworthy woman. The surname of Chausses on the ground will make him posthumous. Never was so bad a king in his province.

[1] *parfondera*. L. *parfundere*, to sprinkle, moisten.
[2] *Myrnarmee*. L. *Mimnermia*, a surname of Venus.

See X.XI also for another reference to posthumous child. Loomis suggests that this verse describes one of Nostradamus' Antichrists.

Century X

X.X

Tafche de murdre enormes
   adulteres,
Grand ennemy de tout le genre
   humain
Que fera pire qu'ayeulx, oncles,
   ne peres
En fer, feu, eau, fanguin &
   inhumain.

Stained with murder and enormous adulteries, great enemy of
all mankind he will be worse
than his ancestor, uncles and
fathers. In steel, fire and water,
bloody and inhuman.

The epithet *grand ennemy de tout le genre humain* was applied to Napoleon by the Venetian ambassador, Morenigo. So perhaps the rest of the generalities also apply to him.

Century X

X.XI

Dessoubz Ionchere du dangereux
   paffage
Fera paffer le pofthume fa bande,
Les monts Pyrens paffer hors fon
   bagaige
De Parpignam courira duc à
   tende.

In the dangerous passage underneath Junquera, the posthumous
man will make his men cross. To
cross the Pyrenean mountains
without his baggage the duke
will hasten to Perpignan from
Tende.

This quatrain may be related to X.IX through the connection of the posthumous child. Otherwise I cannot place it.

Century X

X.XII

*Esleu en Pape, d'esleu sera
  mocqué,
Subit soudain esmeu prompt &
  timide,
Par trop bon doulx à mourir
  prouocqué,
Crainte estainte la nuit de sa
  mort guide.*

*Elected as pope he will be mocked
when elected, suddenly and
unexpectedly moved, prompt and
timid. Caused to die through too
much goodness and kindness he
will fear for the guide killed on
the night of his death.*

This quatrain is applied by most commentators to Cardinal
Santa Severina, who was elected as Pope Gregory XIV in 1591,
but who died two months later, his election having been
declared illegal. But his successor, Innocent IX, also died
within two months of taking office.

Century X

X.XIII

*Soulz la pasture d'animaux
  ruminant
Par eux conduicts au ventre
  herbipolique[1]
Soldatz caichez les armes bruit
  menant,
Non loing temptez de cite
  Antipolique.*

*Beneath the food of ruminating
animals; led by them into the
center of their feeding place. Soldiers hidden, their weapons
being noisy, tried not far from
the city of Antibes.*

---

[1]*herbipolique*.? the marketplace?

Century X

X.XIIII

Vrnel Vaucile[1] sans conseil de soy mesmes
Hardit timide par crainte prins vaincu,
Accompaigné de plusieurs putains blesmes
A Barcellonne aux chartreux conuaincu.

Vrnel Vaucile without a plan of his own, bold, timid for fear of being taken and captured. Accompanied by several pale whores converted in the Carthusian convent at Barcelona.

The interpretation here depends upon *Vrnel Vaucile* in line 1. It does not seem to have any connection with the monastery at St. Urgel. The Carthusian convent at Barcelona is that of Mont Allegro.

Century X

X.XV

Pere duc vieux d'ans & de soif chargé,
Au iour extreme filz desniant les guiere[2]
Dedans le puis vif mort viendra plongé,
Senat au fil[3] la mort longue & legiere.

The duke, father, old in years and troubled with thirst, on the last day his son denying him the jug. Into the well, plunged alive, he will die. The Senate to the son, a death long and light.

A son is hanged for denying his thirsty father water to drink and then puts him down the well! The worst type of Nostradamus' writing because it is open to ridicule.

[1]*Vrnel Vaucile. Llanos de Urgel*, Plain of Urgel?
[2]*les guiere.* F. *d'aiguiere*, jug.
[3]*fil.* probably *filz*, son.

Century X

X.XVI

*Heureux au regne de France,
    heureux de vie
Ignorant ſang mort fureur &
    rapine,
Par non flateurs ſeras mys en
    enuie,
Roy deſrobé trop de foy en
    cuiſne.*

Happy in the kingdom of
France, happy in life, ignorant
of blood, death anger and rage.
By a flattering name he will be
envied, a king robbed, too much
faith in the kitchen.

When he is happily established on the French throne, Louis
XVIII will not die a violent death but lives happily. Because
of this he was given the nickname "*le Désiré*," "the flattering
name" (line 3). His guilt lies in the fact that he does not
sufficiently occupy himself with the public good. He was also
a renowned glutton, line 4.

Century X

X.XVII

*La royne Ergaſte[1] voiant ſa fille
    bleſme,
Par vn regret dans l'eſtomach
    encloz,
Crys lamentables ſeront lors
    d'Angoleſme,
Et au germain mariage fort
    clos.*

The captive queen, seeing her
daughter pale because of the
unhappiness locked up in her
stomach. Lamentable cries will
come from Angoulême and the
marriage to the cousin greatly
impeded.

The *royne Ergaſte* is a queen confined to manual labor in a
penitentiary. Marie Antoinette was compelled to sew her own
clothes when imprisoned in the Temple. Perhaps this is not
the general impression of manual labor, but it certainly was
painful to the queen. *Ergaſte* also means captive, which Marie
Antoinette certainly was. She saw her daughter, Madame
Royale, pale with suffering. Madame Royale was betrothed to

---

[1]*Ergaſte, Ergastulus,* penitentiary.

the duc d'Angoulême in 1787, and married him in 1799. But
she remained childless (*l'eſtomach encloz*), probably due to the
troubles experienced with her family when enclosed in the
Temple.

Century X

X.XVIII

Le ranc Lorrain fera place à Vendoſme,	The house of Lorraine will make way for Vendôme, the high put
Le hault mys bas & le bas mys en hault,	low and the low exalted. The son
Le filz d'Hamon[1] ſera eſleu dans Rome,	of Hamon will be elected in Rome, and the two great ones
Et les deux grands ſeront mys en deffault.	will be put at a loss.

This is a very successful prediction for Nostradamus. Henri
IV, duc de Vendôme, will eclipse the house of Lorraine, and
Henri IV, earlier known as "*le petit Béarnais*," will be elevated
to the high rank of king of France. This son of Hamon, the
heretic, will be accepted as king by Rome. The two great ones
who lose are the two Pretenders, the duc de Guise and the duc
de Mayenne.

Century X

X.XIX

Iour que ſera par royne ſaluee,	The day she will be saluted as
Le iour apres le ſalut, la priere,	queen, the prayer the day after
Le compte fait raiſon & valbuee,	the blessing. The account is right and valid, once humble there
Par auant humble oncques ne feut ſi fiere.	was never so proud a woman.

It is suggested that this quatrain applies to Elizabeth I of
England when she succeeded her sister, the childless Mary
Tudor.

---

[1]*Hamon.? Mamon*, wealth, in some editions.

Century X

X.XX

Tous les amys qu'auront tenu
    party,
Pour rude en lettres mys mort
    & ſaccagé,
Biens publiez par fixe grand
    neanty,[1]
Onc Romain peuple ne feut
    tant outragé.

All of the friends who have
belonged to the party, put to
death and looked for the uncouth
letters. The public possessions,
the great one annihlated by six.
Never were the Roman people so
wronged.

This quatrain made little sense in Nostradamus' day, but
applies quite accurately to post-Fascist Italy. The drastic
remedy makes it appear more modern.

Century X

X.XXI

Par le deſpit du Roy ſouſtenant
    moindre,
Sera meurdry luy preſentant les
    bagues,
Le pere au filz voulant nobleſſe
    poindre
Fait comme à Perſe iadis feirent
    les Magues.

Through the king's spite in supporting the lesser one, he will be
murdered presenting the jewels
to him. The father wishing to
impress his son with nobility did
what the Magi used to do in Persia.

I can offer no explanation of this complicated quatrain.

[1]*neanty.* O.F. *néantir,* to annihilate.

Century X

X.XXII

Pour ne vouloir confentir au
  diuorce,
Qui puis apres fera cogneu
  indigne,
Le roy des Ifles fera chaffé par
  force
Mis à fon lieu que de roy
  n'aura figne.

For not wanting to consent to the
divorce which then afterwards
will be recognized as unworthy,
the king of the islands will be
forced to flee, and one put in his
place who has no sign of kingship.

This and quatrain X.LX describe the abdication of Edward
VIII in 1936. The king's act was not popular among the
British people, who had little love for the already twice-
divorced Mrs. Simpson. Edward was therefore forced to leave
the court and England because of Mrs. Simpson's unsuitable
social position (*cogneu indigne*). Finally, George VI, who was
not in line for the kingship, is forced to accede to the British
throne.

Century X

X.XXIII

Au peuple ingrat faictes les
  remonftrances,
Par lors l'armee fe faifira
  d'Antibe,
Dans l'arc Monech feront les
  doleances,
Et à Freius l'vn l'autre prendra
  ribe.

Remonstrances are made to the
ungrateful people, then the army
will seize Antibes. In the arch of
Monaco the complaints will
occur, and at Fréjus the shore
will be taken by one from the
other.

When Louis XVIII issued a proclamation urging fidelity to
his new régime, the only place that remained loyal to
Napoleon was Antibes. Both Louis and Napoleon used Fréjus,
the former to embark for England, the latter when leaving for
Elba.

Century X

X.XXIIII

Le captif prince aux Italles
vaincu
Paſſera Gennes par mer iuſqu'à
Marſeille,
Par grand effort des forens[1]
ſuruaincu
Sauf coup de feu barril liqueur
d'abeille.

The captive prince conquered in
Italy will cross from Genoa to
Marseilles by sea. By a great
effort the foreigners will be overcome except for a gunshot, a bar-
rel of bee's honey.

This quatrain appears to be linked with IV.XXVI, in which
Napoleon's emblem of the bee also appears. Napoleon, a
closely guarded prisoner on Elba, escapes by sea in March and
lands at Cannes, on the south coast of France, as is Marseilles.
He is overcome again at Waterloo, where he seeks death in
vain. The bees of his emblem will spill all their sweetness.

Century X

X.XXV

Par Nebro ouurir de Briſanne[2]
paſſage,
Bien eſlongnez el tago fara
mueſtra,
Dans Pelligouxe[3] ſera commis
l'outrage
De la grand dame aſſiſe sur
l'orchestra.

Through the Ebro will be opened
a passage to Brisanne, far away
the Tago will make a demonstra-
tion. The outrage committed in
Pelligouxe, of the great lady sitting in the orchestra.

I find it difficult to interpret this quatrain.

---

[1]*forens.* O.F. foreigner, stranger.
[2]*Briſanne.* Unsolved place name.
[3]*Pelligouxe.* Unsolved place name.

Century X

X.XXVI

Le *fucceffeur vengera fon beau
    frere,*
*Occuper regne fouz vmbre de
    vengeance,*
*Occis oftacle fon fang mort
    vitupere,*
*Long temps Bretaigne tiendra
    auec la France.*

*The successor will avenge his
handsome brother and occupy
the realm under the shadow of
vengeance. He is killed, the
obstacle of the blameworthy
dead, his blood. For a long time
Britain will hold with France.*

This quatrain appears to predict the assassination of Robert
Kennedy, following upon that of his brother the president,
John F. Kennedy. It is interesting to see that Nostradamus
foresees two brothers killed within a short period of time.
Robert Kennedy's stand in the name of his brother leads to his
death. One wonders what may happen to the third brother,
Edward Kennedy. The last line seems to imply that once de
Gaulle is dead Britain's relationship with France and the
Common Market is a successful one. (See I.XXVI, VIII.XLVI,
VIII.LXXVII.)

Century X

X.XXVII

*Par le cinquieme & vn grand
    Hercules
Viendront le temple ouurir de
    main bellique,
Vn Clement, Iule & Afcans
    recules,
Lefpe, clef, aigle n'eurent onc fi
    grand picque.*

*Through the fifth and a great
Hercules, they will come to open
the temple with the hand of war.
One, Clement, Julius and
Ascans put back, the sword, the
key. The eagle never once felt so
great a dislike.*

Century X

X.XXVIII

Second & tiers qui font prime
  musicque
Sera par Roy en honneur
  sublimee,
Par grasse & maigre presque
  demy eticque
Raport de Venus faulx randra
deprimee.

The second and third make first-
class music. They will be sub-
limely honored by the king.
Through fat and thin, even half
emaciated, to be made debased by
the false report of Venus.

Century X

X.XXIX

De Pol MANSOL dans cauerne
  caprine
Caché & prins extrait hors par
  la barbe,
Captif mené comme beste mastine
Par Begourdans amenee pres de
  Tarbe.

In the great cave of St. Pol-de-
Mausole, hidden and seized,
pulled out by the beard, the captive led like an animal, a mastiff, brought near to Tarbes by
the people of Bigorre.

As mentioned elsewhere St. Pol-de-Mausole is situated just
outside Nostradamus' birthplace in St. Rémy-de-Provence.
The quatrain describes a captive who is taken to Bigorre in
Navarre.

Century X

X.XXX

Nepueu & sang du sainct
  nouueau venu,
Par le surnom soustient arcs &
  couuert
Seront chassez mis à mort chassez
  nu,
En rouge & noir conuertiront
leur vert.

Nephew and of the blood of the
newly created saint, through his
surname he will sustain the
arches and the roof. They will be
driven out naked and chased to
their deaths, their queen will be
converted to red from black.

I cannot decipher this quatrain.

Century X

X.XXXI

Le ſaint empire viendra en Germanie,	The Holy Empire will come to Germany, the Arabs will find
Iſmaelites[1] trouueront lieux ouuerts.	open places. The asses will also want Carmania, the supporters
Anes vouldront auſſi la Carmanie,	completely covered with earth.
Les ſouſtenens de terre tous couuerts.	

Hogue interprets the first line of this quatrain as "The Russians will enter Afghanistan." I cannot follow his train of thought. To me, this quatrain appears to relate to the Holy Roman Empire and its trouble with the Turks and the Arabs. Carmania is a province in Persia, now Iran, situated at the entrance to the Persian Gulf.

Century X

X.XXXII

Le grand empire chacun an deuoir eſtre	The empire each year should become great. One will come to
Vn ſur les autres le viendra obtenir,	hold (power) over all the others. But his kingdom and life will
Mais peu de temps ſera ſon regne & eſtre,	last a short time. In two years he will be able to maintain himself
Deux ans aux naues ſe pourra ſouſtenir.	in his ships.

Yet another quatrain I cannot decipher.

---

[1] *Iſmaelites.* Not Jews, but Arabs who claim descent from Ishmael, the son of Abraham.

Century X

X.XXXIII

La faction cruelle à robbe longue, *Viendra cacher fouz les pointus poignars* *Saifir Florence le duc & lieu diphlongue[1]* *Sa defcouuerte par immeurs & flangnards.[2]*	The cruel party, wearing long robes will hide sharp daggers beneath. The duke to seize Florence and the place of two words. Its discovery through young ones and flatterers.

The first two lines are reminiscent of the assassination of Julius Caesar in Rome at the Ides of March. But the capture of Florence obviously places the quatrain in the sixteenth or seventeenth century.

Century X

X.XXXIIII

Gauloys qu'empire par guerre occupera *Par son beau frere mineur fera trahy,* *Par cheval rude voltigeant traynera,* *Du fait le frere long temps fera hay.*	The Gaul who gains his empire through war will be betrayed by his younger brother in law. He will be dragged by an untrained nervous horse. For the act the brother will be hated for a long time.

This quatrain describes very aptly the situation of the king of Naples, Joachim Murat, who married Napoleon's younger sister, Caroline. Murat first betrayed Napoleon in 1814, but joined up with him again in 1815. He was also a renowned cavalry leader and had a severe accident falling from his horse. Apparently, according to Robb (1942) this quatrain converted the eminent professors Jacques Barzun and Professor Siceloff of Columbia University because of its accuracy. They were reputed to say that the chances of the quatrain being fulfilled were "about zero". This comment could probably refer to many of Nostradamus' quatrains.

[1] *diphlongue.* Error for *diphtongue,* double word.
[2] *flangnards.* Pr. flatterer, wheedler.

Century X

X.XXXV

Puyſnay royal flagrand d'ardant libide,	The younger son of a king, flagrant with burning lust to enjoy his first cousin. Women's attire in the temple of Diana, who will be murdered by the unknown man from Marne.
Pour ſe iouyr de couſine germaine,	
Habit de femme au temple d'Arthemide:	
Allant murdry par incognu du Marne.	

The last line of this quatrain suggests that a duc, the younger son of a king, probably the duc de Maine or Mayenne, will be involved in a royal scandal. But, unfortunately, although a possible situation, it does not tie in with anything specific. Probably a failed quatrain.

Century X

X.XXXVI

Apres le Roy du ſoucq guerres parlant,	After the king (of the stump?) speaks of wars, the United Island will despise him. For several years the good one gnaws and pillages. Through tyranny on the island its values change.
L'iſle Harmotique[1] le tiendra à meſpris,	
Quelques ans bons rongeant vn & pillant	
Par tyrannie à l'iſle changeant pris.	

The United Islands are probably the British Isles, bringing the date of the quatrain to 1604 or later. Line 3 may describe privateers of the late sixteenth and seventeenth centuries such as Drake, Hawkins and Raleigh. But *du foucq* in line 1 defies interpretation and I do not see its relevance to James, so that this may be a failed quatrain.

---

[1]*Harmotique.* Dubious. Possibly from Gk. *armoskitos*, joined together, united.

Century X

X.XXXVII

Laſſemblee grande pres du lac de
*   Borget,*
Se ralieront pres de
*   Montmelian,*
Marchans plus oultre penſifz
*   feront proget*
Chambry, Moriane combat ſainct
*   Iulian.*

The great crowd near the lake of
Le Bourget will rally near to
Montmelian. Going further
ahead, the thoughtful ones draw
up a plan. Chambery, St. Julien
de Maurienne, fight.

Yet another incomprehensible quatrain.

Century X

X.XXXVIII

Amour alegre non loing poſe le
*   ſiege,*
Au ſainct barbar ſeront les
*   garniſons,*
Vrſins Hadrie pour Gaulois
*   feront plaige,*
Pour peur rendus de l'armee
*   aux Griſons.*[1]

"Light of love" will not hold the
siege for long, all the garrisons
will be for the converted barba-
rian. The Ursins and Adria give
security for the French, for fear
of the army being handed over to
the Grisons.

The normal nickname for Henri IV of France among his contemporaries was *"vert galant,"* perpetually gallant, which is very close to Nostradamus' *Amour alegre*, light of love. During the siege of Paris in 1590, Henri was not able to hold the garrisons for more than four months because of the advance of the duc de Parma from Flanders. Nostradamus described the occupants of the garrisons as devoted to barbarous things, by which he means they are clerical revolutionaries. Henri himself also changed his religion to obtain the French throne: "Paris is worth a mass." The connection with Switzerland, other than Protestantism, is unclear.

---

[1] *Griſons.* people of southeast Switzerland.

Century X

X.XXXIX

Premier fils vefue malheureux mariage,
Sans nuls enfans deux Ifles en difcord,
Auant dixhuict incompetant eage,
De l'autre pres plus bas fera l'accord.

The first son, a widow, an unfortunate marriage without any children. Two islands thrown into discord. Before eighteen years of age, a minor. Of the other even younger will be the betrothal.

This is an excellent quatrain and appears to have been understood by Nostradamus' contemporaries at the French court. It describes the fate of François II and his child bride, Mary, Queen of Scots. François II, the eldest son of the widowed Catherine de' Medicis, married Mary Stuart. Their short marriage was childless. Mary's return to Scotland caused discord between Scotland and England. François was still not quite eighteen years old when he died (seventeen years, ten months, fifteen days). His younger brother, who became Charles IX, was betrothed to Elizabeth of Austria when he was only eleven years old. An accurate quatrain.

Century X

X.XL

Le ieune nay au regne Britannique,
Qu'aura le pere mourant recommandé,
Iceluy mort LONOLE[1] donra topique,
Et à fon fils le regne demandé.

The young one born to the kingdom of Britain, which his dying father has commended to him. Once he is dead, London will disagree with him and the kingdom will be demanded back from his son.

[1]LONOLE. probably error for *Londres*, London.

This quatrain continues upon X.XXII, the abdication of Edward VIII in 1936. He is the true heir to the throne of Britain, left to him by his dying father. But he causes scandal (*topique*) in London by his behavior with Mrs. Simpson. Public hostility towards her earlier divorces caused the king to abdicate, the kingdom taken back from him by popular opinion, and given to his brother.

Century X

X.XLI

En la frontiere de Cauſſade &
  Charlus,
Non guieres loing du fonds de
  la vallee,
De ville Franche muſicque à ſon
  de luths,
Enuironnez combouls[1] & grand
  myttee.[2]
	On the boundary of Caussade
	and Caylus, not very far from
	the depths of the valley. Music
	from Villefranche to the sound of
	lutes, surrounded by cymbals
	and many stringed instruments.

Since all the places mentioned here are small villages within fifty miles of Agen, where Nostradamus once lived, could he be describing a local festival?

Century X

X.XLII

Le regne humain d'Anglique
  geniture,
Fera ſon regne paix vnion tenir,
Captiue guerre demy de ſa
  cloſture,
Long temps la paix leur fera
  maintenir.
	The human reign of English
	offspring will cause the kingdom
	to be united in peace. Half cap-
	tured in his enclosure in the war.
	For a long time peace will be
	maintained by them.

---

[1]*combouls.* Gk. *kumbalou,* cymbal.
[2]*myttee.* dubious. Possibly Gk. *mitos,* stringed instrument?

This is a general but very apt quatrain which describes
Britain and the Pax Britannica of the nineteenth century, or
the long peace England enjoyed under Walpole and the early
Georges.

Century X

X.XLIII

Le trop bon temps trop de bonté royalle:	Too much of the good times and too much royal bounty, made and quickly undone by sudden negligence. He will lightly believe his loyal wife false, who benevolently is put to death.
Fais & deffais prompt subit negligence,	
Legier croira faux d'espouse loyalle,	
Luy mis à mort par sa beneuolence.	

Both Louis XVI and his loyal wife Marie Antoinette were
put to death by the Revolutionaries. Louis irritated his advisers
because he did not apply himself properly to affairs of state.
He displayed great weakness and irresolution of character, as
seen in the case of the diamond necklace when he was quite
prepared to believe the queen was involved. All of these
characteristics, plus a basic benevolence, left him defenseless
before the Revolutionaries.

Century X

X.XLIIII

Par lors qu'vn Roy sera contre les siens,	When a king is against his people a native of Blois will subdue the league. Mammel, Cordoba and the Dalmatians. Of the seven then a shadow to the king, new money and dead ghosts.
Natif de Bloys subiuguera Ligures:	
Mammel,[1] Cordube & les Dalmatiens,	
Des sept puis l'ōbre à Roy estrennes[2] & lemures.[3]	

[1] *Mammel.* if place name perhaps Mamel in the Baltic. O.F. *mamelle*, breast.

[2] *estrennes.* Handsel, New Year money.

[3] *lemures.* L. *lemures*, ghosts.

Quatrain VIII.XXXVIII discusses a king who will come from Blois. It probably refers to Henri III of France, who subjugates the League, line 2. He was descended from the comte de Blois and is elsewhere called *le grand du Blois* by Nostradamus. The seven in line 4 are the children of Catherine de' Medicis and Henri II, who are but shades of their parents.

Century X

X.XLV

Lombre du regne de Nauarre non vray,
Fera la vie de fort[1] illegitime:
La veu promis incertain de Cambray,[2]
Roy Orleans donra mur legitime.

The shadow of the kingdom of Navarre is not true, it will make the life of a strong man illegal. The uncertain promise of Cambrai, the king at Orléans will make a lawful boundary.

Henri de Navarre, Henri IV, initially had only the shadow of a kingdom because he had to storm Paris by force. He led an irregular life and kept many mistresses including the wife of a governor of Cambrai to whom in return Henri granted hereditary possession of the town, line 3. Cambrai may also have a retrospective meaning of the Peace of Cambrai of 1529. Orléans may stand for either the town or the family.

Century X

X.XLVI

Vie fort mort de L'OR vilaine indigne,
Sera de Saxe non nouueau electeur:
De Brunfuic mandra d'amour figne,
Faux le rendant au peuple feducteur.

Because of the gold, the life, fate and death of an unworthy, sordid man. He will not become the new Elector of Saxony. From Brunswick he will send for a sign of love, the false seducer giving it to the people.

[1]*fort*. Presumed misprint for *fort*.
[2]*Cambray*. The peace of Cambrai, 1529, at which the French gave up their claims to Flanders.

In this quatrain, set in Germany, Nostradamus states that Saxony will not have a new Elector. Maurice of Saxony did not enter the war against Charles V until 1552 and the Duchy of Brunswick played no significant role during the sixteenth century. Quite an accurate quatrain but partially, at least, retrospective.

Century X

X.XLVII

De Bourze ville à la dame Guyrlande,
L'on mettra¹ ſus par la trahiſon faicte,
Le grand prelat de Leon par Formande,²
Faux pellerins & rauiſſeurs defaicte.

In the town of Burgos, at the lady of the Garland, they will deliver the verdict on the treason committed. The great prelate of Leon through Formade, undone by false pilgrims and thieves.

The secret of this quatrain lies with the "Lady of the Garland."

Century X

X.XLVIII

Du plus profond de l'Eſpaigne enſeigne,
Sortant du bout & des fins de l'Europe,
Troubles paſſant aupres du pont de Laigne,
Sera deffaicte par bandes ſa grand troppe.

Banners from the furthest corners of Spain, coming out from the ends and borders of Europe. Trouble passing near the bridge at Laigne, its great army will be routed by bands (of men).

The first line of this quatrain contains a good description of the Spanish Civil War, with the increasing involvement of the Germans and Italians. Nostradamus sees this trouble develop-

---

¹*mettra.* literally, impose a verdict.
²*Formande.*? Formentera in the Balearics?

ing towards the Second World War, which raged throughout Europe. Laignes is a town forty miles northwest of Dijon, which was occupied by the Germans. Nostradamus also foresees this occupying force being routed, which it was, by the Allied Forces in 1944–45. A good general quatrain.

Century X

X.XLIX

Iardin du monde au pres de cité neufue,	The garden of the World near the New City, in the road of the hollow mountains. It will be seized and plunged in the tank, forced to drink water poisoned with sulphur.
Dans le chemin des montaignes cauees,	
Sera ſaiſi & plongé dans la Cuue,	
Beuuant par force eaux ſoulfre enuenimees.	

This extraordinary quatrain talks of a city, New York, being poisoned through its water supply, an idea more suited to James Bond than to Nostradamus. The *cité neufue* is New York. The *Iardin du monde* is possibly a way of describing it as a world center. The second line is interesting. Could the "road of hollow mountains" be the nearest Nostradamus could get towards describing a street lined with skyscrapers? The tank is unclear. It could well mean a reservoir which becomes poisoned by sulphuric acid. This is not as unlikely as one might think. A similar thing happened in Britain in summer 1988 when a load of chemicals was wrongly dumped into a water system. (See IX.XCII, I.LXXXVII.)

Century X

X.L

La Meuſe au iour terre de Luxembourg,	By day the Meuse in the land of Luxembourg will find Saturn and three in Aquarius. Mountain and plain, town city and borough. A flood in Lorraine betrayed by the great urn.
Deſcouurira Saturne & trois en lurne,	
Montaigne & pleine, ville, cité & bourg,	
Lorrain deluge trahiſon par grand hurne.	

Insufficient material for dating, this quatrain describes an enormous flood.

Century X

X.LI

Des lieux plus bas du pays de Lorraine, *Seront des baſſes Allemaignes vnis,* *Par ceux du ſiege Picards, Normans, du Maiſne,* *Et aux cantons ce ſeront reunis.*	Some of the lowest places in the country of Lorraine will be united with the Lower Germany. Through the people of the seats of Picardy, Normandy and Maine, they will be reunited with the cantons.

In 1871, Lorraine and the regions to the south, *plus bas*, such as Alsace, were united with Lower Germany, with the consent of those defeated in the Siege of Paris in 1871. All the areas mentioned suffered German occupation. Lorraine was not returned to France until 1919. Quite a comprehensive quatrain.

Century X

X.LII

Au lieu où LAYE & Scelde ſe marient, *Seront les nopces de long temps maniees,* *Au lieu d'Anuers où la crappe[1] charient,[2]* *Ieune vieilleſſe conforte intaminee.*	At the place where the Laye and the Scheldt join, a long time earlier, the marriage will be arranged. At the place in Antwerp where the chaff is carried, a young, undefiled wife and old age.

An obscure marriage which takes place between a very young girl and her old suitor. The rest makes no sense. Probably a failed quatrain. The Laye and the Scheldt rivers join up at Ghent.

---

[1]*crappe*. O.F. chaff (of wheat)
[2]*charient*. O.F. to carry, cast about.

Century X

X.LIII

Les trois pellices de loing
　s'entrebatron,
La pus grand moindre
　demeurera à l'escoute:
Le grand Selin n'en sera plus
　patron,
Le nommera feu pelte blanche
　routte.

Three prostitutes will quarrel for
a long time. The greatest will
remain to hear the least. The
great Selin will no longer be her
patron. She will call him fire,
shield, a white rout.

If Selin refers as usual to Henri II, this quatrain would
describe his many royal mistresses, Diane de Poitiers' rivals,
such as Gabrielle d'Estrées. White may refer to Diana, as she
normally wore only this color and her château on the Loire,
Annecet, was decorated entirely in black and white.

Century X

X.LIIII

Nee en ce monde par concubine
　fertiue,
A deux hault mise par les tristes
　nouuelles,
Entre ennemis sera prinse
　captiue,
Et amené à Malings &
　Bruxelles.

Born into this world of a furtive
concubine, to two raised high by
the bad news. She will be taken
captive among enemies and
brought to Malines and Brussels.

I cannot decipher this quatrain.

Century X

X.LV

Les malheureuses nopces
　celebreront,
En grande ioye, mais la fin
　malheureuse:
Mary & mere nore
　desdaigneront,
Le Phybe mort, & nore plus
　piteuse.

The unfortunate marriage will
be celebrated with great joy, but
the end is unhappy. The mother
will despise the daughter-in-law,
Mary. The Apollo dead and the
daughter-in-law more pitiable.

The word *"Mary"* is, as can be seen, spelled with a *y* in the original text, which makes Mary, Queen of Scots an obvious target for this quatrain. Mary's wedding to François II was not the happiest. Her mother-in-law, Catherine de' Medicis, caused great trouble with England by insisting that the English standard be linked with Mary's Scottish one, a symbol which Elizabeth I did not take lightly. The feeling of dislike between the two women was reciprocal. Mary used to refer to Catherine as "the merchant's daughter." *Phybe* may stand for François II, Mary's husband in that first syllable, *Phye, phi* stands for *F.* and the *be* for *beta*, the second letter of the Greek alphabet, thus F.II, François II. The young couple married in 1558 but by 1560 the young Apollo, François, the great hunter, was dead and Mary left in the perilous coils of the Scottish situation. A very good, convoluted quatrain.

Century X

X.LVI

Prelat royal ſon baiſſant trop tiré,
Grand fleux de ſang ſortira par
* sa bouche,*
Le regne Anglicque par regne
* reſpiré,*
Long temps mort vif en Tunys
* comme ſouche.*

The royal priest bowing too low, a great flow of blood will come out of his mouth. The Anglican reign, the breathing realm, for a long time dead as a stump of wood, living in Tunis.

I cannot decipher this quatrain.

Century X

X.LVII

Le ſubleué ne cognoiſtra ſon
* ſceptre,*
Les enfans ieunes des plus
* grands honnira:*
Oncques ne fut vn plus ord[1]
* cruel eſtre,*
Pour leurs eſpouſes à mort noir[2]
* bannira.*

The uplifted one will not know his scepter, he will disgrace the young children of the great ones. There was never so filthy or cruel a person. As for their wives, the king will banish them to death.

[1] *ord.* O.F. filth.
[2] *noir.* usual anagram for roi, king.

Century X

X.LVIII

Au temps du dueil que le felin monarque,	*At a time of mourning the feline monarch will make war with the*
Guerroyera le ieune Aemathien:	*young Aemathien. France will*
Gaule branſler perecliter la barque,	*shake, the barque will be in danger. Marseilles to be tried, a talk*
Tenter Phoſſens[1] au Ponant[2] entretien.	*in the West.*

Aemathien, the child of dawn and therefore the sun, refers here to Louis XIV, who adopted the sun as his device and was also called the Sun King. While there is a time of mourning for Louis XIII, the wily Philip of Spain will go to war against the new king. France is deeply shaken by the War of the Fronde, and the Barque of the Papacy is threatened by the new development of Jansenism.

Phoſſens is Marseilles, which Louis XIV entered by breaching its walls in 1660. A year earlier he had been to Ponant, in the west of France, and it was on the island of Bidussoa that he concluded the Peace of the Pyrenees and his marriage to the Infanta Maria Theresa. The island is still called *"Isle de la Conférence."*

Century X

X.LIX

Dedans Lyons vingt cinq d'vne alaine,	*In Lyons, twenty-five of the same breath. Five citizens, Germans,*
Cinq citoyens Germains, Breſſans, Latins,	*Bressans, Latins; under a noble they will lead a long trail and*
Par deſſous noble conduiront longue traine,	*are discovered by the barking of the mastiffs.*
Et deſcouuers par abbois de maſtins.	

---

[1] *Phoſſens*. people of Phocea, Marseilles.
[2] *Ponant*. read Occident.

Century X

X.LX

*Ie pleure Niſſe, Mannego, Pize,
  Gennes,
Sauone, Sienne, Capue,
  Modene, Malte:
Le deſſus ſang & glaiue par
  eſtrennes,
Feu, trembler terre, eau,
  malheureuſe nolte.[1]*

I weep for Nice, Monaco, Pisa,
Genoa, Savona, Siena, Capua,
Modena and Malta. The blood
and sword above for a gift, fire,
the earth will tremble. Water an
unhappy reluctance.

This quatrain appears to describe an earthquake which
involves not only southern France, Nice, but Monaco and a
great deal of Italy, including Malta. If this were to happen it
would be an earthquake of calamitous effect. There are usual
additions of fire and fighting, but in this case it is followed by
a flood. Possibly a future quatrain, or maybe a Millennium one
for the end of this century.

Century X

X.LXI

*Betta,[2] Vienne, Emorre,[3]
  Sacarbance,[4]
Voudront liurer aux Barbares
  Pannone:
Par picque & feu, enorme
  violance,
Les coniurez deſcouuers par
  matrone.*

Betta, Vienna, Emort, Sopron.
They will want to deliver Hungary to the barbarians. Great
violence through pikes and fire,
the conspirators discovered by a
matron.

This quatrain appears to be linked with the two following
ones, X.LXII and LXIII, but they all remain obscure.

[1]*nolte.* probably from L. *noluntas*, unwillingness?
[2]*Betta,* possibly *Baetis*, the Guadalquivir River?
[3]*Emorre.* uncertain place name.
[4]*Sacarbance.* L. *Scarbantia*, modern Sopron.

Century X

X.LXII

Pres de Sorbin pour aſſaillir
    Ongrie,
L'herault de Bude les viendra
    aduertir:
Chef Bizantin, Sallon de
    Sclauonie,
A loy d'Arabes les viendra
    conuertir.

Near Sorbia, in order to assail the hungry, the herald of Brudes will come to warn them. The Byzantine chief, Salona of Slavonia, will come to convert them to Arabian law.

Century X

X.LXIII

Cydron,[1] Raguſe,[2] la cité au
    sainct Hieron,[3]
Reuerdira le medicant ſecours,
Mort fils de Roy par mort de
    deux heron,[4]
L'Arabe Ongrie feront vn meſme
    cours.

Cydonia, Ragussa, the city holy to Hieron, the healing help will make it green again. The king's son dead because of the death of two heroes, Arabia and Hungary will take the same step.

Century X

X.LXIIII

Pleure Milan, pleure Luques,
    Florance,
Que ton grand Duc ſur le char
    montera,
Changer le ſiege pres de Veniſe
    s'aduance,
Lors que Colomne[5] à Rome
    changera.

Weep Milan, weep Lucca and Florence, when your great duke climbs into the chariot. To change the seat it advances close to Venice, when at Rome the Colonnas will change.

[1] *Cydron.* Cydonia, now modern Canea.
[2] *Raguſe.* now Denmark
[3] *Hieron.* a dubious personal name?
[4] *heron.* a false rhyme for heroes.
[5] *Colomne.* Colonna, a great Roman family.

This is a general quatrain about the situation in Italy during the nineteenth century. When the Grand Duke left Italy, Austria abandoned the province of Venetia to Napoleon III, who, in turn, gave it to Victor Emmanuel. Florence became Italy's new capital city until the seat of all Italian government was moved to Rome. It was from then onwards that the temporal powers to the Papacy declined. A good quatrain.

Century X

X.LXV

O vaſte Romme ta ruyne
s'approche,
Non de tes murs de ton ſang &
ſuſtance:
L'aspre par lettres fera ſi
horrible coche,
Fer poinctu mis à tous iuſques
au manche.

O great Rome, your ruin approaches, not of your walls but of your blood and substance. The harsh one in letters will make so horrid a notch, pointed steel wounding, all up in the sleeve.

This quatrain probably refers to the attempt made to assassinate Pope John Paul II. Not the well-publicized attempt in Rome by Ali Agça, supposedly of the Bulgarian Secret Service, but another less public event which occurred when he was touring the world. One of the priests in his entourage attempted to stab the Pope with a cut-down sword or knife which he had hidden up his sleeve. Nostradamus issues several warnings to John Paul II, whose papal reign he sees as being troubled not only by violence, but by *la peste*, the plague of AIDS.

Century X

X.LXVI

Le chef de Londres par regne
l'Americh,
L'iſle d'Eſcoſſe tempiera par gellee:
Roy Reb auront vn ſi faux
antechriſt,
Que les mettra treſtous dans la
meſlee.

The London premier through American power will burden the island of Scotland with a cold thing. Reb the King will have so dreadful an Antichrist who will bring them all into trouble.

An interesting quatrain, definitely belonging to the twentieth century. During the Prime Ministership of Harold Macmillan, Scotland was certainly burdened by a "cold thing," the Polaris submarine. In this new age of the INF Treaty things will be drastically changed. It would be helpful if one could decipher *Roy Reb*, as it is during his time of power that the Third Antichrist will appear and there will be trouble in Britain and America. (See II.V.)

Century X

X.LXVII ★

Le tremblement ſi fort au mois de May,
Saturne, Caper, Iupiter, Mercure au beuf:
Venus auſſi Cancer, Mars, en Nonnay,[1]
Tombera greſſe lors plus groſſe qu'vn euf.

A very great troubling in the month of May, Saturn in Capricorn, Jupiter and Mercury in Taurus. Venus also in Cancer, Mars in Virgo, then hail will fall greater than an egg.

This conjunction of planets is very rare, but Nostradamus predicts it in the month of May, together with extraordinary weather, in this case a fall of hail. Nostradamus seems to foresee an increase in earthquakes world-wide, starting in the 1980s. There are numerous quatrains referring to these quakes, and to one in particular on the west coast of America which will be so severe it will be recorded by seismographs as far away as New York. (See I.LXXXVII.) In other quatrains, such as this one, he places the quake in May at the end of the eighth decade. It is extraordinary that Nostradamus should be so aware of an event which will occur in a country which had scarcely been discovered in his time. The earthquake ties up with other major world disasters such as flood and famine. The three planets, Neptune, Mars and Uranus, all bad news, move into their malign aspects on May 8, 1989 our calendar. Neptune is the God of earthquakes.

---

[1]*Nonnay.* Virgo. *Nonnay, nonne,* stands for a nun, a virgin.

530   *Erika Cheetham*

Century X

X.LXVIII

L'armee de mer deuant cité tiendra.
Puis partira ſans faire longue alee,
Citoyens grande proye en terre prendra,
Retourner claſſe reprendre grand emblee.[1]

The army of the sea will stand before the city, then depart, without making a long passage. A great prey of citizens will be taken on land. The fleet returns to seize, great robbery.

I cannot decipher this quatrain.

Century X

X.LXIX

Le fait luyſant de neuf vieux eſleué
Seront ſi grand par midi aquilon,
De ſa ſeur propre grande alles[2] leué.
Fuyant murdry au buyſſon d'ambellon.[3]

The shining deed of the new old one exalted will be so great in the south and north. Raised by his own sister, great crowds arise. When fleeing, is murdered in the bushes at Ambellon.

The clue to this unsolved quatrain lies in the word *Ambellon*.

Century X

X.LXX

L'oeil par obiect fera telle excroiſſance,
Tant & ardante que tumbera la neige,
Champ arrouſé viendra en deſcroiſſance,
Que le primat ſuccumbera à Rege.

Because of an object the eye will swell so much, burning so greatly that the snows will fall. The watered fields will start to shrink when the Primate dies at Reggio.

[1] *emblee*. O.F. robbery, thieving.
[2] *alles*. O.F. trip, speed, crowd
[3] *ambellon*. Dubious, village of Ambal?

A failed quatrain in that no pope has died at Reggio and it seems unlikely that this will happen before the end of the century. However, I suppose it must always be borne in mind.

Century X

X.LXXI

La terre & l'air gelleront si grand eau, *Lors qu'on viendra pour ieudi venerer,* *Ce qui sera iamais ne feut si beau,* *Des quatre pars le viendront honnorer.*	*The earth and air will freeze so much water when they come to worship on Thursdays. He who will come will never be as fair as the few partners who come to honor him.*

An interesting quatrain. To date we have the Christians who worship on a Sunday, the Jews on Saturday and the Moslems, Friday. So perhaps this relates to the quatrain which talks of *jeudi pour sa feste* and may be the day of the Third Antichrist. (See quatrain X.XCV.)

Century X

X.LXXII

L'an mil neuf cens nonante neuf sept mois *Du ciel viendra vn grand Roy deffraieur* *Resusciter le grand Roy d'Angolmois.*[1] *Auant apres Mars regner par bon heur.*	*In the year 1999, and seven months from the sky will come the great King of Terror. He will bring to life the great king of the Mongols. Before and after war reigns happily.*

In this gloomy prediction of the coming of the Third Antichrist in July, 1999, Nostradamus seems to foresee the coming of the Millennium. He was greatly influenced towards

---

[1] *Angolmois.* Anagram of the O.F. *Mongolois.*

this opinion by contemporary thought. This quatrain indicates that it will be preceded by the coming of the Third Antichrist from the East, "the king of the Mongols," before the Final Coming of the Great King of Terror. It is interesting to note that Nostradamus foresees war both before and after his coming. He therefore does not envisage an instant End of the World. (See IV.L, X.LXXIV, X.LXXV.)

Century X

X.LXXIII

Le temps prefent auecques le paffé
Sera iugé par grand Iouialifte,
Le monde tard luy fera laffé,
Et defloial par le clergé iuriste.

The present time together with the past will be judged by the great man of Jupiter. Too late will the world be tired of him, disloyal through the oath taking clergy.

Century X

X.LXXIIII

Au reuolu du grand nombre
*   feptiefme*
Apparoiftra au temps Ieux
*   d'Hacatombe,*
Non efloigné du grand eage
*   milliefme,*
Que les entres fortiront de leur
*   tombe.*

The year of the great Seventh number accomplished; it will appear at the time of the games of slaughter. Not far from the age of the great Millennium when the dead will come out of their graves.

Seven is always an important number for numerologists, it signifies many things. Nostradamus predicts that at the time of the seventh number (does this mean at the end of the seventies?) war will break out on an immense scale. In a sense this has been true, with localized wars breaking out all over the world. The date of the final war will be not far from the Millennium (see X.LXXII). The last line is purely horrific. Does Nostradamus have a vision of the second judgment?

Century X

X.LXXV ★

Tant attendu ne reuiendra iamais	Long awaited it will never return in Europe, he will appear in Asia. One of the league issued from the great Hermes, he will grow above all the other powers in the Orient.
Dedans l'Europe, en Aſie apparoiſtra	
Vn de la ligue yſſu du grand Hermes,	
Et ſur tous roys des orientz croiſtra.	

This seems to be a continuation of quatrain X.LXXII where Nostradamus talks about the King of the Mongols bringing war to the world. It may also refer to the last quatrain, X.LXXIV, and the war of the seventh number. But Nostradamus sees this Third Antichrist as rising "above all powers in the Orient." At the present time it seems that he will probably surface in China.

Century X

X.LXXVI

Le grand ſenat diſcernera la pompe,	The great Senate will see the parade for one who afterwards will be driven out, vanquished. His adherents will be there at the sound of a trumpet, their possessions for sale, the enemies driven out.
A l'vn qu'apres ſera vaincu chaſſé,	
Ses adherans feront à ſon de trompe,	
Biens publiez ennemys deſchaſſez.	

Unfortunately no definite setting is given for these events.

Century X

X.LXXVII

Trente adherans de l'ordre des
    quyretres[1]
Bannys leurs biens donnez ſes
    aduerſaires,
Tous leurs bienfais ſeront pour
    deſmerites
Claſſe eſpargie deliurez aux
    corſaires. ·

Thirty members of the order of
Quirites banished, their belong-
ings given to their bold adversaries. All their good actions will
be taken as wrong; the fleet scattered, delivered up to the Corsairs.

This quatrain is usually applies to post-Fascist Italy in 1945.
The Corsairs are then understood to be the Russians, who
received a large part of the Italian navy. General, but
satisfactory.

Century X

X.LXXVIII

Subite ioye en ſubite triſteſſe
Sera à Romme aux graces
    embraſſees
Dueil, cris, pleurs, larm. ſang
    excellant lieſſe
Contraires bandes ſurprinſes &
    trouſſees.

Sudden joy into sudden sadness
will be at Rome for the graces
embraced. Mourning, cries,
tears, weeping, blood, great
rejoicing. Contrary bands surprised and trussed up.

Century X

X.LXXIX

Les vieux chemins ſeront tous
    embelys,
Lon paſſera à Memphis
    ſomentrée,[2]
Le grand Mercure d'Hercules
    fleur de lys
Faiſant trembler terre, mer &
    contree.

The old roads will all be
improved, they will go (somewhere) similar to Memphis. The
great Mercury of Hercules'
fleur-de-lys will cause land, sea
and country to tremble.

[1]*quyretres.* a) L. Roman citizens, b) Low L. renowned warriors.
[2]*ſomentrée.* Gk. *symmetros*, like, dissembling.

The key words of Memphis and the great Mercury of Hercules are the basis of this quatrain but I cannot decipher it.

Century X

X.LXXX

Au regne grand du grand regne regnant,	In the kingdom of the great one, reigning with a powerful rule by force of arms, he will cause to be opened the great gates of brass. The king and the duke allied, the port demolished, the ship at the bottom. A severe day.
Par force d'armes les grands portes d'arain	
Fera ouurir le roy & duc ioignant,	
Port demoly nef à fons iour ferain.	

A difficult quatrain because it has no proper names on which to base an interpretation. Kings and dukes are frequent in the *Prophéties* and something more specific is needed. A failed quatrain?

Century X

X.LXXXI ★

Mys trefor temple citadins Hefperiques	Treasure is placed in a temple by Western citizens, withdrawn therein to a secret place. The temple to open by hungry bonds, recaptured, ravished, a terrible prey in the midst.
Dans iceluy retiré en fecret lieu,	
Le temple ouurir les liens fameliques.	
Reprens rauys proye horrible au milieu.	

During the sixteenth century gold poured into Spain from her possessions in the New World. Can one take Nostradamus literally in this case, that a great amount of treasure is hidden in some Spanish cathedral? It must be remembered that most Spanish cathedrals were adorned with riches from the New World. But problems arise with line 3, *liens fameliques.* It has been suggested that this is an imaginative description of economic crisis in the United States—the other meaning of *Hesperique.* Is this to be followed by a road on Fort Knox, the greatest gold hoard in the world? Perhaps it just means a great run on gold, as is happening at the moment.

Century X

X.LXXXII

Cris, pleurs, larmes viendront
   auec coteaux
Semblant fouyr donront dernier
   aſſault
Lentour parques planter profons
   plateaux,
Vifs repoulſez & meurdrys de
   prinſault.[1]

With the knives will come cries, tears and weeping. Seeming to flee they will make a final assault. Around, sparingly, they will set up high platforms, the living pushed back and murdered instantly.

A régime that throws people to their deaths from high platforms?

Century X

X.LXXXIII

De batailler ne ſera donné ſigne,
Du parc ſeront contraint de ſortir
   hors,
De Gand lentour ſera cogneu
   l'enſigne,
Qui fera mettre de tous les ſiens
   à mors.

The signal will not be given to fight, they will be obliged to go out of the park. The banner around Ghent will be recognized. He who will put all his followers to death.

Century X

X.LXXXIIII

La naturelle à ſi hault non bas
Le tard retour fera martis
   contens,
Le Recloing[2] ne ſera ſans debarz
En empliant & perdant tout ſon
   temps.

The illegitimate girl so high, not low, the late return will content the grieved ones. The Reconciled one will not be without disputes, by employing and wasting all her time.

[1]*prinſault.* O.F. first, at once, immediately.
[2]*Recloing.* Dubious? Possible derived from L. *recolligo*, to regain, be reconciled.

Many commentators regard line 1 as describing Elizabeth Tudor, Elizabeth I, whom Pope Paul IV declared to be a bastard through the illegality of Anne Boleyn's marriage to Henri VIII.

Century X

X.LXXXV

Le vieil tribung au point de la trehemide	*The old tribune on the point of trembling will be pressed not to*
Sera preffee captif ne defliurer,	*give up the captive. The old, not*
Le veuil non veuil le mal parlant timide	*old, speaking timidly of the evil; to free his friends in a lawful*
Pàr legitime à fes amys liurer.	*manner.*

This quatrain has been suggested as applying to France between 1940 and 1943, when Maréchal Pétain negotiated with the Germans about prisoners of war who were being used as slave labor.

Century X

X.LXXXVI

Comme vn gryphon viendra le roy d'Europe	*The king of Europe will come like a griffon, accompanied by*
Accompaigné de ceux d'Aquilon,	*those of the North. He will lead a*
De rouges & blancz conduira grand troppe	*great troop of red and white. They will march against the king*
Et yront contre le roy de Babilon.[1]	*of Babylon.*

The king of Europe may be understood as standing for the allied forces who marched against Napoleon, king of Egypt, in 1815, before he was made First Consul. The red and white uniforms of the great army are the tunics of the English and Austrian forces. The English may well be described as from the North in this context, as also Russia.

---

[1] *Babilon.* In medieval texts the king of Babylon is usually interpreted as the king of Egypt.

Century X

X.LXXXVII

Grand roy viendra prendre port
*   pres de Niſſe*
Le grand empire de la mort ſi
*   enfera*
Aux Antipolles poſera ſon geniſſe,
Par mer la Pille tout eſuanoira.

A great king will come to anchor
near Nice, the death of the great
Empire is thus accomplished. He
will place his heifer in Antibes,
plunder at sea, all will vanish.

It would be interesting to be able to decipher exactly what
Nostradamus meant by *geniſſe*, the heifer of line 3.

Century X

X.LXXXVIII

Piedz & Cheual à la ſeconde
*   veille*
Feront entree vaſtient tout par
*   la mer,*
Dedans le poil entrera de
*   Marſeille,*
Pleurs, crys, & ſang, onc nul
*   temps ſi amer.*

Foot and horse at the second
watch they will make an entry
laying waste all at sea. He will
enter the port of Marseilles.
Tears, cries, blood, never a time
so bitter.

Yet another quatrain of grief and lamentation.

Century X

X.LXXXIX

De brique en marbre ſeront les
*   murs reduits*
Sept & cinquante annees
*   pacifiques,*
Ioie aux humains renoué
*   Laqueduict,*
Santé, grandz fruict ioye &
*   temps melifique.*

The walls will change from brick
to marble, seventy-five peaceful
years. Joy to human kind, the
aqueduct reopened. Health,
abundant fruit, joy and melli-
fluous times.

Perhaps this quatrain is one that describes the peaceful
world that Nostradamus envisages after the Millennium?

Century X

X.XC

Cent foys mourra le tyran
   inhumain.
Mys à son lieu scauant &
   debonnaire,
Tout le senat sera dessoubz sa
   main,
Faché sera par malin themeraire.

A hundred times the inhuman tyrant will die and a wise and carefree man put in his place. He will have the whole senate in his hands, he will be troubled by a wretched scoundrel.

Napoleon died "a hundred deaths" through his enforced captivity on St. Helena. In his place Louis XVIII is elected, known popularly as "*le debonnaire*," as in the text. Both Parliament and the Senate profess allegiance to their new king down to the last man (*le senat sera dessoubz sa main*). The trouble in line 4 was the assassination of the duc de Berry, who had been in line for the throne through his father, Charles X.

Century X

X.XCI

Clergé Romain l'an mil six cens
   & neuf,
Au chef de l'an feras election
D'vn gris & noir de la
   Compagne yssu,
Qui onc ne feut si maling.

In the year 1609, the Roman clergy at the night of the year will have an election. One of the gray and black come forth from Campania. Never was there one so wicked as he.

An almost successful quatrain, foiled by circumstances. Pope Paul V reigned from 1605 to 1621. He fell seriously ill in 1609, whether induced or not is not certain. However, according to contemporary reports there was a lot of intriguing going on in both the French and Roman courts, in the hope of his opportune death. Paul V recovered and whomever the French had hoped to put in the Vatican did not succeed.

Century X

X.XCII

Deuant le pere l'enfant ſera tué:
Le pere apres entre cordes de
    ionc,
Geneuois peuple ſera eſuertué,
Giſant le chief au milieu comme
    vn tronc.

In front of the father the child will be killed, the father afterwards, between ropes of rushes. The people of Geneva will be exercised, the chief lying in their midst like a trunk.

I cannot interpret this quatrain.

Century X

X.XCIII

La barque neufue receura les
    voyages,
Là & aupres transfereront l'empire,
Beaucaire, Arles retiendront les
    hoſtages,
Pres deux colomnes trouuees de
    porphire.

The new Barque will go on voyages, far and near they will transfer the Empire. Beaucaire and Arles will retain the hostages, near where two columns of porphyry are found.

The Papacy (*la barque neufue*) will move from the Vatican according to this quatrain. Both Beaucaire and Arles are near the Rhône river which borders on Valence where Pope Pius VI was held in captivity. There has long been a legend that the Papacy will leave Rome at the time of the Millennium.

Century X

X.XCIIII

De Nîſmes, d'Arles, & Vienne
    contemner,
N'obey tout à l'edict Heſpericque:[1]
Aux labouriez[2] pour le grand
    condamner,
Six eſchappez en habit ſeraphicque.[3]

Scorn fron Nîmes, Arles and Vienne, not to obey all the Western edict. In order that the great may condemn the tormented, six escape in Franciscan garb.

[1] *Heſpericque.* Western, American?
[2] *labouriez.* O.F. *labourier*, to torment.
[3] *ſeraphicque.* The true name of the Franciscans is the Order of Seraphim.

Possibly a failed quatrain.

Century X

X.XCV

Dans les Efpaignes viendra Roy trefpuiffant,
Par mer & terre fubiugant or midy,
Ce mal fera rabaiffant le croiffant,
Baiffer les aefles a ceux du vendredy.[1]

Into Spain will come a very powerful king, he will subjugate the south by land and sea. This evil will cause a lowering of the crescent again, a lowering of the wings by the people of Friday.

The nearest this quatrain appears to be fulfilled is when Philip II of Spain, who persecuted the Moors, *ceux de vendredy*, made several futile expeditions to North Africa and became involved in the Battle of Lepanto 1571. (See also X.LXXI.)

Century X

X.XCVI

Religion du nom des mers vaincra,
Contre la fecte fils Adaluncatif,[2]
Secte obftinee deploree craindra,
Des deux bleffez par Aleph & Aleph.[3]

The religion called by the seas will overcome, against the seat of the son Adaluncatif. The stubborn lamentable sect the two men wounded by Alpha and Alpha.

This quatrain should be easy to decipher but is not. The anagram *Adaluncatif* is unsolved, as are the two *Alephs* or *Alphas* in the last line.

---

[1] *vendredy*. The Moslems celebrate their Sabbath on a Friday.

[2] *Adaluncatif*. Unsolved name, possibly containing the word Caliph in the anagram?

[3] *Aleph & Aleph. Aleph*, A in Hebrew, *Alif* in Arabic, *Alpha* in Greek.

Century X

X.XCVII

*Triremes pleines tout aage
        captif,
Temps bon à mal, le doux pour
        amertume:
Proye à Barbares trop toſt ſeront
        haſtifs,
Cupid de veoir plaindre au
        vent la plume.*

*Triremes full of captives of all
ages, good times for bad, sweet
ones for the bitter. Hasty, they
will be too quickly prey for the
Barbarians, anxious to see the
plume (of smoke) wail in the
wind.*

Again, probably a retroactive quatrain because of the use of
the word "*triremes*."

Century X

X.XCVIII

*La ſplendeur claire à pucelle
        ioyeuſe,
Ne luyra plus long temps ſera
        ſans ſel:
Auec marchans,[1] ruffiens loups
        odieuſe,
Tous peſle meſle monſtre vniuerſel.*

*For the joyful maiden the bright
splendor will shine no more, for
a long time she will lack salt.
With merchants, bullies, odious
wolves. All confusion, the universal monster.*

Line 2 indicates a time of anarchy when the empire of the
"joyful maiden" will no longer have enough control even to
collect taxes (from *la gabelle*, the French tax on salt contemporary in France in Nostradamus' time). The Third Republic in
France was typified as Marianne. If she is the *pucelle ioyeuse*,
this quatrain may well refer to France between 1940 and 1944.
Salt has a secondary meaning of wisdom. Perhaps France
lacked this in some of her actions during the Occupation? The
confusion and beasts would then refer to the Nazis.

---

[1]*marchans.* May mean mercenaries rather than merchants in this
context.

Century X

X.XCIX

La fin le loup, le lyon, beuf, &
l'afne,
Timide dama[1] feront auec
maftins,
Plus ne cherra à eux la douce
manne,
Plus vigilance & cuftode aux
maftins.

The end of the wolf, the lion, ox
and ass, the timid deer will be
among the mastiffs. No longer
will the sweet manna fall upon
them. More vigilance and
guarding of the mastiffs.

Does this quatrain indicate the end of the good time
Nostradamus predicts after the Millennium, "when the ox
shall lie down with the wolf," and bad times return, demanding guards and vigilance?

Century X

X.C

Le grand empire fera par
Angleterre,
Le pempotam[2] des ans plus de
trois cens:
Grandes copies[3] paffer par mer
& terre,
Les Lufitains[4] n'en feront pas
contens.

A great Empire will be for Eng-
land the all-powerful for more
than three hundred years. Great
forces cross by land and sea. The
Portuguese will not be pleased.

In this powerful quatrain with which Nostradamus ends his
Prophéties, he foresees a great future for Britain which will last
for over three hundred years. Most commentators take this as
starting with the reign of Elizabeth I and ending with that of
Victoria. The forces of line 3 may mean both the First and
Second World Wars, as by the end of those Britain had been
stripped of most of her colonies and the rest were soon to claim
independence of one kind or another. But what do the
Portuguese, line 4, have to do with these matters? A good,
ambiguous quatrain with which to end the Nostradamus legend.

[1]*dama*. L. a deer.
[2]*pempotam*. from Gk. *pan*, all, and L. *potens*, powerful, all-powerful.
[3]*copies*. L. *copia*, troops.
[4]*Lufitains*. Classical name for the Portuguese.

INDEX